Chaucer and the Energy of Creation

Geoffrey Chaucer, ca. 1490. Courtesy of the Library,
University of California, Los Angeles.

Chaucer and the Energy of Creation

The Design and the Organization of the *Canterbury Tales*

Edward I. Condren

University Press of Florida

Gainesville · Tallahassee · Tampa · Boca Raton
Pensacola · Orlando · Miami · Jacksonville

04 03 02 01 00 99 6 5 4 3 2 1

Portions of chapters 5, 10, 12, and 13, reproduced here by permission, appeared in an earlier form in the following journals: *Papers on Language and Literature* 21 (1985): 233–257, copyright by the Board of Trustees, Southern Illinois University; *Criticism* 26 (1984): 99–114, copyright by Wayne State University Press; *The Chaucer Review* 21 (1989): 192–218, copyright by Pennsylvania State University Press; *Viator* 4 (1973): 177–205, copyright by the Regents of the University of California.

LIBRARY OF CONGRESS CATALOGING-IN-PUBLICATION DATA
Condren, Edward I.
Chaucer and the energy of creation: the design and the organization
of the Canterbury tales / Edward I. Condren.
p. cm.
Includes bibliographical references and index.
ISBN 0-8130-1679-7 (cloth: alk. paper)
1. Chaucer, Geoffrey, d. 1400. Canterbury tales. 2. Christian pilgrims and pilgrimages in literature. 3. Tales, Medieval—History and criticism. 4. Chaucer, Geoffrey, d. 1400—Technique. 5. Storytelling in literature. 6. Rhetoric, Medieval. I. Title.
PR1874/C63 1999
821'.1—dc21 99-18810

The University Press of Florida is the scholarly publishing agency for the State University System of Florida, comprising Florida A & M University, Florida Atlantic University, Florida International University, Florida State University, University of Central Florida, University of Florida, University of North Florida, University of South Florida, and University of West Florida.

University Press of Florida
15 Northwest 15th Street
Gainesville, FL 32611
http://www.upf.com

For Gail
wisest and dearest

Contents

Acknowledgments

Intellectual debts are a pleasure to honor. Years ago, fresh from a boisterous career in another profession, I had the rare good fortune to work at Cornell with Robert E. Kaske, whose evident love for his field made me want to follow. Father Shook, Kenneth Kee, Norman Garmonsway, John Leyerle, and the great traditions of both the Pontifical Institute of Mediaeval Studies and the Medieval Centre in the Graduate School at the University of Toronto gave me a sense of the shape and the appeal of the medieval world, which has never ceased to delight me. To my close friends at UCLA—Chuck Berst, Dick Lanham, Andy Kelly, Florence Ridley, and the late Will Matthews—I am extremely grateful for many years of patient encouragement and warm collegiality. Humanism at its best.

Although the present book owes its deepest debt to the pleasure I constantly take in Chaucer, it also bears the stamp of several generations of scholars and critics whose own writings richly celebrate his poetry. These intellectual forebears are gratefully cited within. Dolores Frese and Laura Howes, who read the manuscript for the press, contributed enormously to matters of balance, emphasis, strategy, and tone. I am grateful to both. Then too, many years of satisfying discourse with eager, bright students— silent collaborators in the chapters that follow—have made this book much less outlandish than it might otherwise have been. But my deepest debt, of course, is to my wife and family, who often reminded me of the discipline that separates getting it right from getting it written.

The Energy of Creation

What could be more medieval than the *Canterbury Tales*. A whole pan-
orama of fourteenth-century village and city life arrayed before us: the three
estates, both sexes, all ages, several degrees of wealth, all in harmonious
progress toward Canterbury, confirming the orderliness that the nineteenth
century found so appealing. Actually, the *Canterbury Tales* works against
the medieval grain. Some of the great monuments of Middle English literature begin with images of disorder—the wandering soul of *Piers Plowman*,
the self-pitying dreamer in *Pearl*, the grumbling complainers of the *Second
Shepherd's Play* who ironically leave their flock unattended,[1] the opening
scenes of *Sir Gawain and the Green Knight* where the hearty appear weak
and the headless strong—only to unveil in due time a well-ordered universe. The *Canterbury Tales*, perhaps the greatest monument of all, develops very differently. A group of men and women assemble for the purpose
of setting out on a pilgrimage, as faithful fourteenth-century Christians often did, accompanied by an ingenuous reporter whose scrupulous account
unfolds as thriftily as the journey itself. All this orderly progress soon yields
to bawdy fabliaux rebutting a lofty romance, and to an unfinished tale that
had barely begun. Later we see wives ruling husbands, religion made a
business, and—despite the promising beginning—an incomplete pilgrimage and an unfinished storytelling contest.

This scant deference to traditional notions of order has led some to
conclude that, as "a form of praxis, a working upon the world in order to
transform it," the poem holds up to skeptical view the systems and institutions that give rise to these traditions.[2] In actual fact, however, the
poem's relationship to the fourteenth century is far less definitive than
may be supposed. On the one hand, Chaucer often shows the institutional
practices of the surrounding culture compromising the values they were
originally designed to uphold. On the other, he seems to respect these
institutions, however flawed their practices. Thus the poem keeps its read-

ers off balance by seeming to remain off balance itself. For the *Canterbury Tales*'s later apparent departure from images of orderliness does not simply reverse the typical movement of Middle English literature, following the same path but now in the opposite direction, from order to chaos. Rather, the poem offers at every turn a view of reality different from public belief and tradition, without endorsing or condemning either the publicly accepted values of the day or the unconventional ones it places next to them. We might state the point in one sentence: To view Chaucer as a reformer by definition, by assuming that every language act is also a social act, is to overlook his evident love affair with the world he creates— a world he neither condemns, endorses, burdens with ideology, nor seeks to improve, but a world he shows as a dynamic, human, endlessly fascinating entity unto itself.

Nor does the *Canterbury Tales* force its audience to choose one view of reality over another, as if every argument had but two sides, with one or the other (who knows which?) representing the truth and its rival patently wrong. It establishes instead an important principle found at all levels of nature: that elusive reality shuttles precariously between opposing forces whose very opposition brings that reality into being. As everyone knows, there are as many diametrical oppositions in the *Canterbury Tales* as in every philosopher from Abelard through Boethius and beyond.[3] The Clerk's understanding of marriage disagrees completely with the Wife of Bath's. The Nun's Priest's delightful fable of a rooster and a fox would win no applause from the Parson who condemns "fables and swich wrecchednesse" (X.34). Pertelote's theory of the physiological origin of dreams opposes Chauntecleer's belief that they come from God. Justinus's advice to January directly contradicts Placebo's.

Less often noted, the frame that opens and closes the poem presents two opposing halves, not only where its opening lines celebrating a new beginning of the natural world point to its closing lines, which prepare human beings for death, but also in the catalogue of pilgrims that follows the opening and the catalogue of sins that precedes the closing. The tales, too, divide evenly into two thematic halves. The twelve tales in the first five fragments seem driven by some desire to enhance the physical circumstances of life; the twelve tales in the second five concern the attempt to reshape the world for the purpose of gaining access to a higher order. The first half explores various kinds of management; the second, various kinds of creation. It matters little that the "enhanced physical life" in the first half and the "higher order" in the second are often fallaciously defined and doubtfully achieved, as for example the Wife of Bath's campaign for marital sovereignty in the first half and the Canon's Yeoman's fascination with converting lead into gold in the second. The desire itself is more important to the poem's overall design than the objective sought. Though the pilgrims and the characters they create in their tales may fall short of their own ideals in both halves of the poem, they do so for different reasons: a failure to balance competing forces of human nature in the first half, an inability to coordinate substance and form in the second.

One of the poem's subtler oppositions, highly instructive for understanding Chaucer's method, contrasts the Host and the Narrator. Harry Bailly and Chaucer-the-Pilgrim are complete opposites—the one gregarious, intolerant of values other than his own, yet unable to understand even his own; the other demure, fully able to understand the standards of others, though unable to discriminate among them, yet holding no criteria of his own. Because each of these two pilgrims represents an extreme example of a certain type, neither is a fully believable character, although touches of both reside in everyone. Similarly, no one would seriously argue, outside of literature, either that the Wife of Bath's campaign for female sovereignty or that Griselda's unconditional subservience to her husband holds promise for a harmonious marriage or an ideal society, although one or the other strategy may be effective in a given situation. On the contrary, both of these pairs—the Host and the Narrator as well as the Wife of Bath and Griselda—define the limits of the spectrum within which may be found the poet himself in the first instance and a promising philosophy of marriage in the second. The same is true of the whole litany of opposing pairs with which Chaucer criticism has long been familiar.

These oppositions, apparently mutually exclusive, have been mentioned here neither to solve the dilemmas nor to survey the discussion but to suggest instead a frequent pattern in nature: that any dynamic entity in the presence of appropriate stimuli often responds as if it were indecisively shuttling back and forth between extremes. To take one example, Chaucer's Knight is a spectacular man of action, an efficient overachiever in the field, yet putty in the presence of pageantry. In turn, his two young heroes, Palamon and Arcite, are bland captives, inactive and ineffective, until they see Emelye. To take a very different example, the Pardoner commands a brilliant range of subtle rhetorical skills. Yet, facing "wel nyne and twenty" (I.24) potential critics, he amateurishly advances a transparent self-image while foolishly blaspheming their religion. Critics, too, follow suit. Having flirted with Chaucerian enticement stronger than we can resist, as the enticer himself must have known we would, we claim imaginatively that the Merchant is leaving town to escape debt, that

Alisoun of Bath has set her cap for the Clerk, that the Miller and the Reeve have known each other for years. In time our more rigorous critical selves return to acknowledge the absence of hard evidence. That these and other antitheses continue to resist reconciliation may only reflect a modern habit of bipolar critical thought. Like an anatomist with only two tables, the mind continually dichotomizes all things in order to grasp what they are. But the poem comfortably embraces both views; for in the *Canterbury Tales* opposite positions do not vie with each other for the right to be called true, but rather set the boundaries of interpolation for finding truth.[4] Thus, unlike much fourteenth-century literature, the poem insists we treat it as a subject rather than as a fixed object. What seems to be called for, then, is a critical methodology sensitive to process and receptive to the possibility that this very process not only reveals the poem's meaning but may actually be that meaning.

Despite this dynamic nature, the long debate on the question of unity has sought to fix the poem in its critical place. But by failing to pin the poem down, the debate exemplifies the very point about dynamism and incompatible extremes that the poem sets out to explore. On whether the poem is unified or a collection of largely unrelated pieces, Donald Howard presents a forceful case for progressively complex levels of order: civil, domestic, and private.[5] Indeed, the well-attested medieval belief in the unity of all things creates an *a priori* presumption of unity in the *Canterbury Tales*.[6] On the other hand, Derek Pearsall argues that the poem must be assessed on what is there, not on what we think would have been there.[7] His claim that the poem is both unfinished and incomplete[8] shifts the discussion from whether the poem has a unified organization to whether Chaucer had finished working on it. His point is hard to deny, in view of the well-known fact that for many years Chaucer had been teaching himself to write, beginning (so the theory goes) as a translator of Latin and French works, then becoming an adapter, and finally emerging as a fully original English poet. By the time he came to assemble the *Canterbury Tales* he must, therefore, have had a whole trunk full of old manuscripts from which to draw. The prior existence—if they did exist—of so many items that were later included in "the tales of Caunterbury" (X.1086) gives enormous *a priori* probability to the theory of disparate pieces.

The fascinating discussion of whether Chaucer had finished his poem—even if only in design—may in fact lie outside the critical enterprise. Yes, a critic must indeed work with what an author has actually written, not with assumptions about intention or completion. But notice that I say "critical enterprise" where others would argue that questions of the poem's completeness belong properly to the "editorial enterprise." As with most Chaucerian subjects, however, the friendly struggle between editor and critic cannot be fully resolved. Nevertheless, one of the metaphors E. Talbot Donaldson uses in discussing an editor's main task hints that editors of Chaucer may face problems more complicated than might be supposed: "In the event that no MS gives a satisfactory reading, the editor cudgels his brains to see if he can find in the preserved readings clues to—one might say ruins of—the original reading."[9] The remark implies that Chaucer's text is somehow analogous to the buildings of a medieval monastery, complete at its original creation, increasingly corrupt over the course of time. With many an author the metaphor may be apt, since corruption often begins after a work leaves its author's hands to circulate among scribes, editors, and collectors. But in the case of Chaucer corruption may belong to earlier stages too. We have abundant evidence that he continually reworked his poetry to improve its artistry, or in other words to remove corruption from the aesthetic idea he was working toward. Hence to examine the preserved readings for ruins of the original might lead us, not to the magnificent edifice where late the sweet birds sang, but to material more like rubble than what now survives.

I exaggerate, of course. No one would seriously suggest wrenching from Alisoun the Arthurian tale she now tells in order to return to her the tale now told by the Shipman, which an earlier conception may have assigned to her. Criticism and textual scholarship stand in agreement here. More often a compromise must be struck between the editor's and the critic's realms. Accordingly, the pages that follow must compromise by quoting from what the majority of scholars agree is the best available text of the *Canterbury Tales*, the Ellesmere manuscript.[10] Without a doubt this text is defective, as any man-made thing is doomed to defect. Indeed, Hengwrt, "undoubtedly the earliest manuscript," is gaining adherents, despite lacking several important tales and presenting the remainder in an incomprehensible order.[11] We must work with something, however, and the something with which we work must be as complete a text as possible, yet cannot be a construct of our own. But we must also be open to the possibility that the *Canterbury Tales*, like every living being, is leading to a completeness and unity that can only be inferred from the teeming, apparent *discordia* of its present state. For we shall see that in several of the completed tales, as well as in some fragments and blocks of material where the sequence of tales has long been settled by textual studies, a carefully designed pattern arranged by Chaucer himself gives meaning to the whole poem, and coincidentally confirms the Ellesmere ordering of the poem's largest fragments.

The references above to Howard and Pearsall were not meant to imply that they are the only critics to speak on opposite sides of the debate on completeness and unity, or on any other Chaucerian debate, for that matter. I called upon these well-respected champions of rival camps—Palamon and Arcite in the critical lists—to illustrate the process of thought by which complex issues are often reduced to two opposing positions. For *all* dynamic things, not only critical positions, oscillate between extremes—the planets fluctuate in orbit, tides ebb and flow, lungs expand and contract, and cycles of fallow and fertile, hunger and fulfillment, youth and age, light and dark, constantly recur. While these fluctuations have always existed, only in the present century has science come to understand that this same phenomenon applies to all dynamic structures. From the study of thermodynamics we have learned that all such entities, when subjected to an external force, eventually pursue one of only three tendencies, newly canonized with old names: entropy, cybernetics, and synergy. A brief summary, suited to humanists' ears, may help us understand what this fourteenth-century man of science seems to have observed on his own, since it is the contention of this study that Chaucer understood these principles and used them to organize his terrestrial pilgrimage. There is nothing new under the sun, only new corn "out of olde feldes" (*PF,* 22).

Since the mid-nineteenth century science has accepted nature's tendency toward disorder.[12] Though energy can never be lost, it is usable only when segregated in an orderly fashion, as in a boiler or a cascading waterfall, where energy has a very slight tendency toward disorder. But if valves are opened, if the stream is undirected, permitting energy to scatter in a disorderly fashion, the tendency toward disorder would be high. If permitted, a low tendency toward disorder will always increase, whereas a spontaneous tendency in the opposite direction has never been observed. All nature would become increasingly disorderly, were it not for the paradoxical tendency called cybernetics, a process of applying correctives to reach self-governance.[13] As in political systems where general elections both reject and select, so all systems heal themselves in the same way. Lightning keeps forests healthy by burning undergrowth, organisms maintain vigor through biochemical processes that both stifle and promote. And so it is in all nature, a constant alternation from order to disorder and back to order again, perhaps on different terms.[14]

We may call the third tendency transcendence, though it is known among scientists as "synergy," the process by which things in nature, under certain conditions, elevate themselves to a more complex order than they had belonged to earlier.[15] Phase transitions (as the completion of this process is called) are still only imperfectly understood by science because their molecular behavior produces unpredictable responses to stimuli. Examples include the lacework patterns of snowflakes and ice crystals and the hexagonal columns in boiling water, where hot water rises in the center of the column and colder water falls down the sides.[16] The manipulation of heat in metals produces similar phenomena. When a magnet is subjected to heat its molecular rearrangement makes the magnet lose its power. When it is cooled, magnetism returns. At very low temperatures certain metals suddenly assume an orderly molecular structure that offers no electrical resistance, allowing "superconductivity." Similarly, when the electrical current passing through a neon light reaches a certain intensity, its random light waves suddenly produce a single laser wave of enormous strength.[17]

It is important for an understanding of this entire process to distinguish between the stimulus that leads to a phase transition and the pattern that defines the completed transition. Similar to the hermeneutic circle of analysis and synthesis in literary criticism, the stimulus belongs to the microcosm, and the wider parameter of order at the other end of the transition to the macrocosm. Though molecules may react to the stimulus in a predictable way, it is by no means clear why they would impose on themselves the particular behavior that defines the transition. This is not to suggest a reductionist theory of matter.[18] Rather, a circular relationship joins microcosmic conditions and macrocosmic order. The behavior of individual parts signals that these parts are entering a phase transition, but it is the independent law of that transition that actually constrains the parts to behave in such a way, indeed in a manner alien to their nature. H. H. Pattee has observed, in speaking of the most fascinating phase transition known, "The central problem of the origin of life [is to determine] when aggregations of matter obeying only elementary physical laws first began to constrain individual molecules to a functional, collective behavior."[19]

Though Chaucer knew nothing of the interesting processes just noted, he was certainly aware of the most fascinating phase transition known: the origin of life. For life, too, has the same three tendencies. Disease is disorder, an organism's healing process produces stability, and the occurrence of new life is transcendence. Of course, the more complex the creature, the more complex the process. For systems not involving deliberate activity, an organism maintains its ideal balance automatically, as with its autonomic nervous system and pH balance (literally "potential of Hydrogen"; in practice the balance of alkali and acid). But at conscious levels creatures gain only a vague intimation of an ideal condition, while they have a much clearer sense of privation when the ideal is missing. If the discomfort is of a simple order, like hunger, the corrective is self-evident, and the overcorrection all too frequent. At subtler levels the notion of how to rectify an imbalance may vary from creature to creature and often be wrong. Insecurity over the faithfulness of a spouse, certainly a "perturbation" of an intimated ideal, may make one man "tempte his wyf" (IV.452), while another keeps a "hond on hire alway" (IV.2091). The false corrections prompted by one imbalance merely beget another.

Human beings, subject to nature's patterns in their behavioral as well as their physical lives, face a more complex dynamism than lesser forms of creation, since their free will exerts some control over the energy that "Zephirus" and "smale foweles" only appear to command in the metaphors of poetry. The three tendencies that humanity displays put the future constantly in doubt. A person may: (a) pursue a progressively disorganized existence, leading to chaos; (b) survive the pressures exerted from opposing directions to achieve a fluctuating stability in the midst of commotion; or (c) strike out in a new direction to reach something loftier than mere stability, to create a more complex, more satisfying order of existence. Certainly Chaucer's pilgrims are on their way to Canterbury because of an intimation of the benefits of pilgrimage. Yet many of their later self-portrayals imply that, as a group, their confused understanding of these benefits fluctuates between extremes, a triumphant procession with the 144,000 male virgins of Revelation at one extreme (Pr.T., VII.579–85), mere relief from unwanted suffering at the other (the old man in the Pard.T., VI.720–38). That pilgrims en route to St. Thomas's shrine would think only of fleshly comfort, instead of the Godhead with whom St. Thomas communes, suggests a kind of chaos, a failure to realize the spiritual possibilities available to man. Not that the potentially religious dimension of the Canterbury trip is canceled by the physical impulses that may have led to it. On the contrary, physical and religious pressures acting in concert can lift one to a higher, more complex form of order than is offered by either the physical or the religious alone—in short, to spiritual communion.

The pattern we have been discussing appears through no coincidence, for it seems to have provided Dante with guiding motifs for the three canticles of his Commedia, one of the strongest influences on Chaucer's development.[20] That the Inferno, Purgatorio, and Paradiso were in Chaucer's mind at the time he turned his attention to the Canterbury Tales seems obvious from the prayer he makes at the end of *Troilus and Criseyde* to "sende [him] myght to make in som comedye" (*T&C,* V.1788) and from the many allusions to Dante throughout the pilgrimage. Chaucer perhaps thought of himself as analogous to Dante. Not only does his *House of Fame* guide him through the upper spheres, as Dante was guided through the cosmos in the *Commedia,* but when Chaucer's golden-eagle guide (cf. Dante's dream of a golden eagle in *Purg.,* IX.13–29) addresses him by name "Geffrey" (*HF,* 729), the passage parallels *Purgatorio,* XXX.55ff., where the newly arrived guide, Beatrice, addresses Dante by name. Of course, every reader instinctively recognizes that Chaucer is a very different poet from Dante, despite his thinking of himself and his predecessor in the same breath, as it were. Piero Boitani convincingly demonstrates this difference by showing that the adjustments Chaucer makes to Dante's expression, in passages where he is clearly following him, indicate that Chaucer is not on a "journey . . . such as Dante's . . . presented as if made in the flesh and culminating with a vision of God," but that he "is and will remain secular."[21]

Although Hell and Heaven are occasionally mentioned in Chaucer's tales, he takes us neither to the one nor to the other, preferring instead to confine his poem to the verifiable world he knows and to the problems human nature brings. However, it is by no means misleading to keep the *Commedia*'s triptych structure in mind, provided we collapse Dante's vertical hierarchy, whose "subject . . . in the literal sense only, is the state of souls after death, pure and simple," to Chaucer's horizontal display of life on earth before death.[22] If Dante visits the damned and the saved in order to guide the suffering, Chaucer pictures humanity struggling somewhere between failure and success. At best a precarious equilibrium prevails.

Despite the very different planes on which Dante and Chaucer pursue their respective journeys, the former cosmic and the latter terrestrial, they nevertheless base their tripartite divisions on the same principles. *Inferno* for Dante is defined by a variety of disorders, not merely a privation of the order found later in *Paradiso,* but an active, disrupting disorder. In *Inferno*'s famous mixed metaphor of Cantos I and V, where the sun is silent and all light is mute, Dante overlooks the dark that might have been assumed from light's failure to shine, while preferring to emphasize the much more complex failure to greet man's rational faculty.[23] A horrifying place entirely bereft of truth comes before our eyes, for the damned on the fifth circle cannot speak with words but only gurgle in their throats. Kenneth Atchity (1969) calls this "the prime expression of chaotic human nature; for language is the prime technique reason has contrived to maintain order" (p. 31). By the time we reach the pit of Hell where horrible giants ascend like towers crowning a walled city, we learn that the evil thought of one of them, Nimrod, caused the confusion of many languages in the world. He understands no language other than his own, and no one understands his (*Inf.*, XXXI.76–81). In *Purgatorio,* on the other hand, active disorder no longer reigns, despite the confusion everywhere. The characters one finds there, Richard Neuse notes, "are not yet fixed—as those in the other two canticles appear to be—but in transition, like actual, living persons" (1991, p. 5). Virgil even calls new arrivals, including himself and Dante, "pilgrims" (*Purg.*, II.63), because Purgatory is, as Charles Singleton says, "a 'Christian' place, as Hell is not. Here in Purgatory as nowhere else the essential condition of the Christian pilgrim can be reflected; for here even the souls are wayfarers" (1954, p. 23). Nearing the end of *Purgatorio,* when Beatrice takes over the role of guide, a new kind of synaesthetic image begins to take shape, the antithesis of the images of disorder in *Inferno.* She conflates speech and vision. Where the opening canticle imparted the notion of a mute sun, stressing loss of a faculty, here Dante has Beatrice combine two senses in one image: the light of her speech will dazzle him, she warns (*Purg.*, XXXIII.73–78). It is premature, however, for the pilgrim fails to understand her words, hears them but cannot "see" them.

It is in *Paradiso* that a transcendent order is revealed, unlike anything seen earlier. Undeveloped faculties that had earlier limited Dante, especially with respect to light, now reach a highly acute state. True, the mute sun of *Inferno* seemed not to produce an audible sound, but we doubt that such a sound, if it had been heard, could have been understood. Like Nimrod, whose disordered capacities convert all language into unintelligible noise, the dwellers in *Inferno* cannot benefit from sound. In *Paradiso,* however, Dante has no limit. After a momentary blinding, a new power gives him the ability to look directly into brilliant light. In Canto XXX of *Paradiso* dazzling images that conflate sight, sound, and fragrance—living light (49), sparkling river (64–66), intoxicating odors (67), smiling flora (77), eyelids that drink from a flowing stream and eyes that expand the stream to a wide sea (88–90)—testify to Dante's new order of being, fit to be in the presence of the Beatific Vision.[24]

By claiming that Chaucer based his design for the *Canterbury Tales* on the same principles that influenced Dante, I do not wish to imply that Chaucer received his idea from Dante, though he may have. It is more likely that Dante and Chaucer were both inspired by the pattern of dynamics common to every closed system, found in biology and behavior no less than in human thought. The terms used by modern science—entropy, cybernetics, and synergy—are the same as the cyclic patterns found under different triads in many other contexts: chaos, stability, and transcendence are general terms applicable to many systems. William Anderson has even found that these three tendencies in Dante's canticles parallel the three *gunas* of Indian philosophy.[25]

The following study of the tales and fragments of Chaucer's masterpiece implies something of the circular reasoning we have been discussing. The joy of experiencing life is certainly as much a presence as the disequilibrium, discomfort, and unwanted states that detract from it. Whether the particular macrocosmic pattern proposed here constrains the microcosmic elements in the poem to behave as they do may be less certain. But perhaps certainty lies beyond critical grasp. Auguste Rodin once described his art as the freeing of a sculpture from the material surrounding it. Having recognized from the beginning the finished sculpture trapped within, Rodin removes what does not belong to the order he already perceives, since every creation—from life to evolution to laser light to art and beyond—is but the realization of what has been latent from the beginning. Though we might think a phase transition occurred in this instance when Rodin worked his clay into "Walking Man," the shaping of the medium may have nothing to do with it, neither for Rodin whose transition occurred at the original conception of the work, nor for us who are brought to a threshold of transition when we come upon it and find what we could never have conceived in the raw material from which it was made. Some viewers may think Rodin cut away too much in producing his headless sculpture, as others reading *Canterbury Tales* think it unfinished and incomplete. Every great work of art is both an accomplished phase transition in its own right and an invitation to others to experience a phase transition of their own. Whether readers see the macrocosm described here, or see some other, or see none at all, is as unique and private a creation as the poem itself.

The Organization of the *Canterbury Tales*

Long before Chaucer turned to the *Canterbury Tales,* while his dream visions were still exploring the nature of his poetic calling, he apparently gave extended thought, in the allegorical fable he called "the book of Seint Valentynes day of the Parlement of Briddes" (X.1086), to the three natural responses described in the previous chapter. We might briefly consider the *Parlement* for the light it sheds on this design. For the two patterns which govern the *Canterbury Tales,* its series of oppositions and the responses they cause, also drive the *Parlement of Foules.*

The *Parlement*'s most immediate design places dynamic activity in direct conceptual and stylistic opposition to static display. Representing the former are the narrator, the exchange between the narrator and Africanus, and especially the assemblage of birds in the second half of the poem. Opposed to this dynamic half of the poem, though covering precisely the same subject, are the *Somnium Scipionis* and the dual-captioned garden with its statuesque images. Now both of these approaches convey in the *Parlement* a wide spectrum of activity associated with the "mating game."[1] But they do so in different ways, both of which are embraced by the goddess presiding over the second half of the poem. For "nature" has two meanings in the *Parlement.* One is called Natura, or Dame Nature, or Lady Nature, or a host of other names meant to conjure a figure—more statue than lady—like the one of whom Alanus de Insulis writes in *De planctu Naturae.* She lives (or better, may be found) like a Scotist's abstraction, in works of literature where she subsumes all those activities and phenomena associated with the extended, living world. With this "nature" the present book has little to do. The other "nature" is the totality of all those activities themselves, taken individually or collectively in all their vitality. It is a nature that ultimately reifies Ockham's view that there is no such thing as "love," only people who perform various loving acts.[2]

Whereas the figures in the garden are headings, mere reminders of human characteristics, the parliament of birds shows us the very characteristics themselves. The former comprise an intellectual category inviting readers to create their own images from a wide variety of possible manifestations; the other is a flesh-and-blood example. To readers familiar with Ovid, the figure of Priapus, for example, might suggest everything from "love and fertility at its most natural" to "brutally excessive male dominance."[3] But to those who witness the parliament and hear the gaggle of lower class birds shouting, "Com of! . . . Whan shal youre cursede pletynge have an ende?" (*PF,* 494–95), frustration and urgency are a palpable, unmistakable reality. Chaucer's natural preference for the urgency of felt life over the learned abstraction may easily be seen by comparing his treatment of Lady Nature with her counterpart in the *De planctu Naturae.* By reducing Alanus's 451-line description of her "aray and face" to a mere two-line reference (*PF,* 316–17), and by describing real birds cackling angrily at each other, instead of embroidered birds that only move with the folds of Lady Nature's garments, Chaucer keeps Alanus's influence, if not his name, as far from his *Parlement* as possible.[4] It is the energy of this vital, unpredictable, exasperating, and exhausting "nature," as it appears in the *Canterbury Tales,* that the present study proposes to discuss.

If the tension between a passive display of abstractions and a living enactment of emotions provides the energizing engine in *Parlement of Foules,* the responses of the birds in the second half of *Parlement* represent the possible choices every dynamic entity faces when stimulated: either chaos, stability, or transcendence. (a) *Chaos:* When the lesser birds sense a "batayle" among the tercels, while descending to bickering, ridicule, and name calling among themselves, the meeting lurches toward a melee of feathers and smoke. At length Nature herself shouts "Pes," adding that despite all this advice they are no nearer a solution. (b) *Stability:* The three royal tercels are not in the least interested in choosing a mate. They wish merely to strike poses, to celebrate their virtues, and to maintain their honored positions: "non loveth hire so wel as I" (*PF,* 435); "I love hire as wel as ye, / And lenger have served hire" (*PF,* 452–53); "I am hire treweste man . . . and faynest wolde hire ese" (*PF,* 479–80). That the formel asks respite for a year, in effect rejecting all three suitors, produces no anguish in the tercelets, who will gladly return next year to make yet other protests of magnificence, which may again fail to win a mate. (c) *Transcendence:* Finally, when the business of choosing mates is amicably concluded (except for the tercelets, one suspects), all the birds assemble for a collaborative expression of harmony that could not possibly have been predicted in the chaos of a few minutes earlier. They sing a roundel in joyous gratitude for the completion of their parliament and in anticipation of the mating season about to begin, a more complex and satisfying expression than anyone has yet made in the poem, and a more telling demonstration of love than anything in the Garden of Love.

No literary strategy, however canonized by its time, nor dynamic pattern, however universal, can ever be more than a preface to a literary work, a suggestion of one possible approach among many that the work may be asking its readers to follow. Let us turn, then, to the *Canterbury Tales*, with the reminder that acceptance of the patterns discussed thus far must await "the awful business of facing [the] poem directly."[5] Moreover, the *Canterbury Tales* marks so great a departure, in both kind and quality, from other writings of its time that the only reliable instruction on how it is to be read must come from the poem itself, for nothing "should be permitted to replace an interpretation of the poem arising from the poem." As it happens, the most useful tutorial for the poem is also the poem's most famous sentence, its opening eighteen lines where Chaucer applies the apparently contradictory principles of opposition and synthesis to accomplish gently what the opening of Genesis accomplishes thunderously. Before our very eyes he creates the earth and everything on it:

> Whan that Aprill with his shoures soote
> The droghte of March hath perced to the roote,
> And bathed every veyne in swich licour
> Of which vertu engendred is the flour; 4
> Whan Zephirus eek with his sweete breeth
> Inspired hath in every holt and heeth
> The tendre croppes, and the yonge sonne
> Hath in the Ram his half cours yronne, 8
> And smale foweles maken melodye,
> That slepen al the nyght with open ye
> (So Priketh hem Nature in hir corages),
> Thanne longen folk to goon on pilgrimages, 12
> And palmeres for to seken straunge strondes,
> To ferne halwes, kowthe in sondry londes;
> And specially from every shires ende
> Of Engelond to Caunterbury they wende, 16
> The hooly blisful martir for to seke,
> That hem hath holpen whan that they were seeke.

The ease of this lyric opening so bedazzles the ear and the eye that we may miss a yet-more-dazzling movement occurring as if incidentally.

Earth, air, fire, and water play subordinate roles both semantically and syntactically, as the sweet showers of April and the equally sweet breath of the west wind freshen a mere temporal clause, while the progress of the sun and March's drought only remotely imply fire and earth. Yet, according to medieval science, these are the four basic elements of which all things are made, two pairs of opposites. Neither of the properties of fire— that is, hot and dry—may be found in cold, moist water. Cold, dry earth opposes hot, moist air. In short, all things result from an uncertain combination of opposites.[6]

That these lines implicitly mark the process of creation is evident in the gentle ascent they make up what Theseus will call the "faire cheyne of love" (I.2988). Add four elements in the right mix and plant life appears in the "flour" of line 4 and again in the "tendre croppes" of line 7. Yet life does not just happen when the right elements enrich the poetic tureen, unless they are stirred by the right metaphors. In lines 2–4 images of penetration and insemination underscore the masculine principle implied etymologically by "vertu" (<L.*vir*, man) and physiologically by "engendered," a verb of simple begetting. Lines 5 and 6 make the same point, although their ethereal metaphor of the west wind's gentle breath calls up the loftier "inspired" (<L.*inspirare*, to breathe [spirit] into). Having acquired simple corporeal existence by line 4, plant life receives an essence two lines later. In addition, Chaucer's version of creation incorporates the two contradictory accounts of Creation in the opening chapters of Genesis: (1) that God's positive, external acts of division, culminating with His dividing man into male and female, individually created all things (Genesis 1:1–2:4a); (2) that God's inspiration, beginning with His breathing a soul into the slime that then became man, set in motion a process of internal activity that brought all things into existence (Genesis 2:4b– 3:24). We may even add that by realizing the events of creation within lines of poetry Chaucer also includes Scripture's final account found in John 1:1: "In the beginning was the Word." Taking his initial impulse from the texture of language, and letting spirit be breathed into matter, Chaucer then permits everything else to evolve from the interaction of opposites.[7]

At just this point an interesting paradox develops. While the metaphors that had turned from physical "engendering" to metaphysical "inspiring" now turn back again to the corporeal activity of the eighth line, where the young sun runs his course half way into the sign of the Ram, the created universe continues to ascend. Like a clock's pendulum, whose swing from one extreme to the opposite provides the energy to measure time's continuous advance, each change of direction in nature's energy lifts the poem to the next link in creation's chain. The eighth line's return to physical activity seems to beget the small fowls of line 9, who are nevertheless associated with melody, an aesthetic dimension more sophisticated than any kind of order yet mentioned. These same birds are next identified in the tenth line with explicit physical activity, a swing away from melody, prompting in turn the next higher level of creation, the human level of line 12.

A subtle shift in tense here effects an equally subtle transition from particular to universal. Since the present perfect tense appears four times in the first three clauses—"hath perced" (2), "[hath] bathed" (3), "Inspired hath" (6), and "Hath . . . yronne" (8)—we anticipate the same tense when another parallel clause begins in line 9. But the actual verb "maken" throws us off. It cannot be the past participle, which normally appears "maked." Nevertheless, "maken" suggests a slant-form past participle, while actually expressing the present tense, thus effecting a gentle transition to the unambiguous grammatical present of the next two lines and preparing us for the universal present-tense main verb of the whole eighteen-line sentence: people long to go on pilgrimages.

Ah, but do they? Do they long for the pilgrimage, or for the mere going? For it is just at this point that the whole, carefully controlled ascent tumbles. While wonderful images of harmony characterize most of nature, a jarring image of disharmony characterizes human nature.[8] The lines move quite logically through successively higher levels of creation—from simple matter to plant life, from plant life to animal life, and from animal life to human life. Words like "pilgrimages," "ferne halwes," and especially "the hooly blisful martir" prepare for a still higher level. Yet that ascent dramatically breaks off at the very moment when the poem anticipates communion with the saints and angels. Our expectation that these pilgrims are traveling to Canterbury for pious purposes suddenly shatters in the face of an opposing purpose, the desire to draw upon St. Thomas's power to cure bodily ill. Brought by the poem to the very threshold of spiritual perception, a threshold that other creatures could neither recognize nor cross, the pilgrims retreat to a concern they share with lesser creatures, a preoccupation with physical well-being. In the whole of these opening lines, then, only Man leaves doubt whether God's creation is actually advancing, or merely swinging back and forth.

Softly folded into this wonderful opening sentence, as if in symphonic overture, lies the structural pattern of the entire *Canterbury Tales,* the dynamic principle by which nature expresses itself in pairs of opposite extremes whose interaction brings reality into existence. This principle—

one of the most fundamental patterns in nature, a constant shifting back and forth between opposite extremes, from "shoures soote" to the "droghte of March," from the warm daylight of the "yonge sonne" to the cold nighttime of birds sleeping "with open ye"—provides the poem with its source of energy. Like the unvarying waves of a sine curve, which alternate between positive and negative values, Chaucer's lines appear to retreat from one kind of excess until they reach another in the opposite direction. Although these alternations normally make possible nature's miraculous stability, the energy they produce occasionally leads away from stability, either toward an increasingly disorganized state or toward a newer, more complex order of existence. The imaginative image of the "yonge sonne," conceived as both the celestial sun penetrating the house of the Ram early in its annual course and as some king's princely son flanked by "tendre croppes" on one side and small melody-makers on the other, emphasizes the stability of the yearly cycle and the universality of romance. But at the same time the ominous word "seeke" (I.18) which ends the first sentence, alludes to a larger disorganization which ends life. Yet the fructifying combination of April's showers and the west wind, as well as the implied fruitfulness associated with romance, allude to the possibility of new life springing into existence.

Oppositions may be viewed in two ways: first, as the friction that provides the energy in all dynamic activity, and second, as the extreme limits that enclose some entity in equilibrium. If the opening lines of *Canterbury Tales* call greater attention to the former of these, we might look at a different part of the poem to see a demonstration of the latter, a method of showing underlying similarities in every pair of opposites and differences in every pair of similitudes. The self-contained, "finished" unit known as Fragment VII follows a symmetrical ring structure:[9]

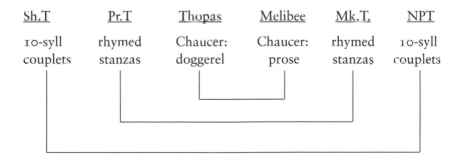

Sh.T	Pr.T	Thopas	Melibee	Mk.T.	NPT
10-syll couplets	rhymed stanzas	Chaucer: doggerel	Chaucer: prose	rhymed stanzas	10-syll couplets

Figure 1

The two tales on the innermost ring, while obviously linked through their assignment to Chaucer-the-Pilgrim, also form a logical pair because "they are not . . . 'literature' at all," in contrast to the other tales in the fragment.[10] The *Tale of Sir Thopas* does "noght elles but despendest tyme" (VII.931), the Narrator says,[11] and the *Melibee*, offering no poetry at all, flogs its prose interminably. The two tales in the next ring, the *Prioress's Tale* and the *Monk's Tale*, are both written in rhyming stanzas, while the outermost ring, holding the *Shipman's Tale* and the *Nun's Priest's Tale*, contains decasyllabic couplets. To proceed from the first to the last of these tales in Fragment VII, is to make a formal round-trip into Chaucer's literary past. After leaving the *Shipman's Tale*, written in the metric form which occupied his last years, we pass through the *Prioress's Tale*'s rime royal, the favored form of a decade earlier when he produced *Troilus and Criseyde* and *Parlement of Foules*, and finally reach his inchoate beginnings. *Thopas* and *Melibee* lie before us like grotesque exaggerations of literature's two elements, substance so completely sacrificed to form that only "rym dogerel" (VII.925) remains (*Thopas*), and form so completely sacrificed to substance that it befits a treatise rather than literature (*Melibee*).[12] By the end of *Sir Thopas* Chaucer has even used poetic form to imply the complete disappearance of poetry. As J. A. Burrow pointed out in the brilliantly titled essay "*Sir Thopas*: An Agony in Three Fits," the tale was undoubtedly intended by Chaucer to be divided into three sections, with the second halving the length of the first, and the third halving that of the second. If Harry Bailly had not interrupted the tale it would have proceeded through an interminable series of fitts of endlessly decreasing length.[13] Thus, at the center of the fragment, we have before us an image of the poetic void at the beginning of Chaucer's career. Whereas the first half of this tour regresses and dismantles, the second advances and rebuilds, taking us first through the Monk's self-taught lesson in the matter of tragedy, which recalls both the metric form of Chaucer's middle years and the genre of *Troilus and Criseyde*, and concluding in the magnificent *Nun's Priest's Tale*, which returns to his final meter, coordinates matter and form with splendid irony, and is widely praised as one of his finest tales.

Cyclic patterns are never perfectly circular; the tales in Fragment VII do not simply cover the same ground twice. The two tales that open the fragment, the Shipman's and the Prioress's, are completely self-absorbed, concentrating almost entirely on details of plot and style, while the closing two, the Monk's and the Nun's Priest's, have a wider context embracing both the events of their stories as well as a detached commentary on those events. In the seventh fragment, then, what appears to be a symmetrical pattern of oppositions from one perspective becomes a cyclical pattern implying balance and equilibrium from another. Central to the concept of equilibrium, the material between these oppositions seems to have been generated by them. Though Fragment VII's closing tales (MkT and NPT) mirror the form of its opening tales (ShT and PrT), while opposing them in substance, this combination of similarity and opposition encourages us to consider literature's need to keep form and substance in balance, the very subject which Chaucer-the-Pilgrim's two intervening tales implicitly demonstrate.

To place these interesting microcosmic details into the macrocosmic plan that determines their shape, I propose to begin by joining Manly and Rickert in accepting Robert L. Campbell's conclusion that fifty-seven manuscripts have enough of the *Canterbury Tales* to provide useful information about the larger poem.[14] These manuscripts testify to the poem's survival in ten separate fragments of various lengths, as all the leading editions of the poem note. This analysis can only be approximate, of course, since it counts complete sentences in the two prose tales, *Melibee* and *Parson's Tale,* as equivalent to lines of poetry.

If it is true that the clearest indication Chaucer was organizing the whole of his poem when he left it "unfinished" is to be found in the structural patterns he did finish,[15] Figure 2 clearly shows that the first and

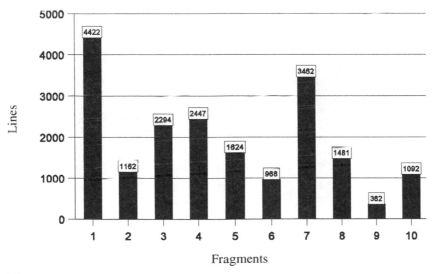

Figure 2

seventh fragments, being much larger than the others, may partially reveal this organization. However, Fragments III, IV, and V provide further evidence, for they too are "an obviously intended, poetically explicated sequence."[16] Considered thus, that is, as a single block of material, if not a single fragment, the lines from the beginning of the Wife's *Prologue* to the end of the *Franklin's Tale* constitute, with Fragments I and VII, a highly suggestive hint of the poem's organization. These three major sections, averaging almost 5,000 lines each, contain respectively five, seven, and six tales/sections, while the remaining four groups (taking IX and X as a single group, since the first line of X refers to the just-completed *Manciple's Tale* of IX) average about 1,300 lines each and contain one, two, two, and two tales, with the last adding the brief ten-sentence *Retracciouns*. The arrangement now looks very different from Figure 2. Figure 3 shows that 14,249 lines of a total of 19,314—almost 74 percent—are found in only three sections. Since there can be no doubt that Chaucer invested more organizational energy in these three major sections than in the four smaller ones, his larger design may well be found in the relation these major sections bear to each other.[17]

The chapters that follow argue that the three large sections of the *Canterbury Tales* correspond to the three conditions of nature described in chapter 1. Not, however, as Dante shows them in *Inferno* and *Paradiso*— "eternally fixed in their places," as Charles S. Singleton says (1965, p.

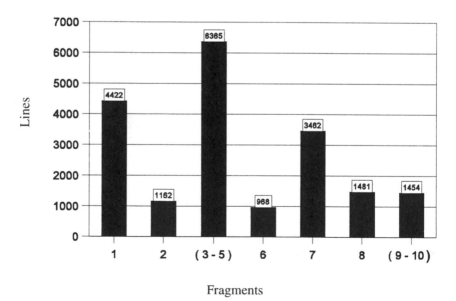

Figure 3

113)—but as he shows them in *Purgatorio,* pilgrims *in via,* analogous to what nature shows everywhere, tendencies leading toward stability, chaos, or transcendence. The first section (Fragment I), extending from the *General Prologue* to the end of the *Cook's Tale,* represents a tendency toward disorder. The almost perfectly organized and balanced social order in the *General Prologue* and the *Knight's Tale* becomes progressively disorganized in the remaining tales of Fragment I, culminating in the chaotic, joyless world of the *Cook's Tale,* whose complete social disorder, corresponding to the *Inferno*'s ontological disorder, suddenly disintegrates into nothingness. The second section (Fragments III, IV, and V), a tightly organized group of seven tales extending from the Wife of Bath's first words to the end of the *Franklin's Tale,* presents a boisterous world at truce rather than at peace, whose appearance resembles Dante's *Purgatorio* in the confusing inter-changes and cross-purposes of its inhabitants, but which also implies, as Dante does not, a formula for achieving a stable society. And the third section (Fragment VII), from the *Shipman's Tale* through the *Nun's Priest's Tale,* demonstrates a process of rearrangement, a magical transition to a new state of being, more complex, more highly organized than what had gone before. Dante shows this state as a completed moral judgment, a sal-vation already attained in *Paradiso,* while Chaucer shows it as the applica-tion of aesthetic standards. In Chaucer's Fragment VII the realms of nature and language fuse in transcendence, both as a phenomenon to be under-stood and as a realization in the lines of poetry.

To this third section a small proviso must be added, before the parallel-ism with the other two is fully recognized. Whereas the first section is governed by the nearly overwhelming *Knight's Tale,* with an organization from which the remainder of the fragment increasingly descends, and whereas the second section has its general subject announced by the pow-erful performance of the Wife of Bath, which very nearly dominates all else, the third section seems to lack a corresponding major tale to set the tone and subject for its group of six. Though it is true the Knight and the Wife of Bath dominate their respective sections, they do so not only be-cause of the length of their performances, but also because of the effect they have in setting the thematic concerns touched off in the tales that follow theirs. If we look for the one pilgrim who has the same effect on the tales of Fragment VII, and who is most often thought parallel to the Wife, and thus likely to parallel her in setting the themes that follow, we cannot find a better candidate than the Pardoner, whose tale, not coinci-dentally, immediately precedes the six tales of Fragment VII.[18] His earlier interruption of the Wife's Prologue has already placed him in her context, while his constant effort to create a world of appearances makes him one of her sect. And his own Prologue, like hers in attracting greater attention than the tale that follows it, closely echoes several important motifs that she had first introduced. Thus, the *Pardoner's Prologue and Tale* serves for the third section of the *Canterbury Tales* (Fragment VII) a function similar to what the *Knight's Tale* provides for the first (Fragment I) and the Wife's performance provides for the second (Fragments III, IV, and V).

PART I

3

The First Fragment

While there may be some justice for viewing the tales of the First Fragment as an assortment of love triangles, as is often done, "triangle" ill-suits everything except the idealistic attraction of Palamon and Arcite for the courtly Emelye in ancient Athens, and "love" never reappears after this first display. For the scene shifts to rural Oxford, where an ardent scholar's seduction of a carpenter's young wife—crudely climaxed at the hands of a rejected fop—shares center stage with the duping of the gullible carpenter. We next move to a Canterbury locale for the sexual ingenuity of a pair of boudoir athletes, clerks in northern accents, who do not so much want to resolve a rivalry in love—two women are ready to hand—as to retaliate for a stolen sack of grain. And the final tale in the fragment ends after fifty-eight lines describing negligence, intemperance, carousing, and a married woman who has turned sex into a business. No, the fragment cannot be said to focus on love triangles. With barnyard ingenuity on the rise and ethical standards on the wane, whatever romance might be implied is entirely overshadowed.[1]

This increasing degradation—certainly intended by Chaucer—parallels another pattern: the displacement of main characters. As the fragment progresses and its socio-moral substrata progressively descend, dislocations become more pronounced. All the pilgrims introduced in the *General Prologue* are, literally speaking, away from home, yet their separations are apparently temporary. Like their modern counterparts who take two-week trips to historic destinations, returning more enriched by calories than by learning, we assume that these pilgrims too will return to permanent homes that may never have been out of their thoughts. The *Knight's Tale*, told by a pilgrim whose own domestic arrangements are unclear (he may have a home somewhere, although the impedimenta with which he travels hint of a home on the open road), gives the motif a deeper texture in the dislocation of Palamon and Arcite. Perhaps not unlike the earlier removal of Ipolita and Emelye, these young cousins are imprisoned in Athens against their will, their homeland still in mind (I.1283, 1355). As events develop, Athens becomes their new home, a land associated with noble conduct, a place where their own nobility seems to belong.

By the time we reach the *Miller's Tale*, dislocation brings greater complexity. Since Nicholas only boards in John's home to attend school nearby, this semi-permanent residence is once removed from what must be a permanent home elsewhere. His conduct, like what one often sees among those living away from home, is risqué, inconsiderate, exploitive, and selfish. Though he temporarily usurps the bed and wife of another, raising the dislocation ante considerably, nothing in the tale suggests his conduct is to be thought seriously heinous, certainly not worse than a scalded *towte* can remedy.

As the *Reeve's Tale* sinks to a lower level, dislocation increases. Here the principal characters also live away at college, where they might be assumed to live as playfully, selfishly, and exploitatively a risqué life as Nicholas does. But in the course of the tale they spend the night at the home of a crooked miller whose ethics they adopt, perhaps only long enough to prove the truth of a proverb: "gif a man in a point be agreved, . . . in another he sal be releved" (I.4181–82). Thus when they occupy beds and women to whom they are not entitled they are already twice-removed from their permanent homes. The *Cook's Tale* has another twice-removed living arrangement, though here Perkyn Revelour freely leaves his second home, where he has been an unsatisfactory apprentice, deliberately chooses a third, apparently permanent home ("he sente his bed and his array" [I.4418]), and settles in among depressingly sleazy companions whose life will shortly be his own.

Fragment I may not be quite the *Inferno* in Inglissh (to adapt Lydgate), for despite abundant venality, the dynamism of its felt life still remains earthly, salvageable, whereas Dante's lost souls suffer in a permanently fixed abyss. Yet its direction reminds us of Dante. Like the steady descent through *Inferno's* successively deeper levels of disorder, among souls permanently fixed in a place remote from their intended home, Chaucer's First Fragment, descending through five levels of increasing disorder, reaches a nadir where its denizens dwell in permanent, joyless self-indulgence. Its orderly beginning and its lofty first tale are left behind, as subsequent tale-tellers lead the way toward abominable disorder. Given enough time, the fragment's present direction might have called for a concluding tale with characters fixed in an utterly abandoned eternity. A completed *Cook's Tale* might have done just that, especially since the tales preceding the Cook's drive inexorably toward a conclusion shaped unwittingly by the characters within. The *Knight's Tale* seems predestined to grant Palamon, Arcite, and Emelye exactly what they ask for; the exaggerated character traits of Nicholas, Absolon, and John in the *Miller's Tale* determine their inescapable desserts; and the miller in the *Reeve's Tale* similarly earns his just recompense. It is likely that the *Cook's Tale* too would devise for its characters inescapable rewards equal to their shameless pursuits. On the other hand, the *Cook's Tale*'s present, perhaps intentionally incomplete form may better suit a poem about life on earth, where men and women given to throwing dice, drinking, and swiving suddenly vanish.

In view of the thematic significance of the *Cook's Tale*'s sudden termination, the numerical composition of the four tales of this fragment may also have been deliberate. That Chaucer was sympathetic to poem length as an aesthetic ingredient is evident in several places: the *Parlement of Foules* has exactly a hundred stanzas; the *Wife of Bath's Tale,* from the end of the grammatical sentence where the king gives the convicted knight to the ladies (III.898), has 366 lines remaining, corresponding to the knight's allowance of a year and a day to complete his quest; and the three fitts in the *Tale of Sir Thopas* are successively halved (see chapter 14). Here in Fragment I, Chaucer may again have been experimenting with number composition.[2] If we consider the Knight's performance to begin when he first speaks (I.853), rather than when Chaucer's editors show a large break six lines later, the four parts of the *Knight's Tale* have line counts which seem to fulfill a deliberate plan: 502, 526, 602, and 626. The recurrence of 2 and 26 in the units and tens columns does not seem coincidental. Nor does the equality between means and extremes: the sum of parts 1 and 4 is 1,128 lines; similarly the sum of parts 2 and 3 is 1,128. Of more significance, 1,128 is almost exactly the number of lines in the three remaining tales of Fragment I. The *Miller's Tale* (668 lines), the *Reeve's Tale* (404), and the *Cook's Tale* (58) total 1,130 lines, two lines longer than half the *Knight's Tale*. It may have occurred to Chaucer to use mathematical proportion to underscore the several disintegrations in the First Fragment. The line totals of the *Knight's Tale* are in obvious harmony. Those of the remainder of the fragment, though halving the opening tale, show nothing but random disorganization. If this design is not coincidental, it suggests that the *Cook's Tale* was never intended to be longer than what now survives and that the dramatic interplay between tales was probably composed after the tales themselves were completed.

The Imperfect Knight and His Perfect Tale

Opinions of the highest-ranking pilgrim in the *Canterbury Tales* are not as settled now as they were a couple of generations ago, when criticism used to agree with the Narrator that the first tale-teller was "a verray, parfit gentil knyght" (I.72). Never mind that any agreement with the Narrator— who says elsewhere you shall not find "A bettre felawe" (I.648) than the Summoner, who calls the Shipman "a good felawe" (I.395), the Merchant a "worthy man" (I.279), and the Pardoner "a noble ecclesiaste" (I.708)— should be cause for concern. The Knight was praised for fighting well in Christian rather than secular wars, for avoiding ostentatious dress, for making a pilgrimage of thanksgiving rather than of petition, for setting a fine example for his son the Squire, and so forth. Recently, however, there have been doubts. What were first called the doomed ideals of knighthood, then the obsolescent ideals of Chaucer's own Knight, received scathing denouncement by Terry Jones, who saw in the Knight a cold-blooded professional killer.[1]

Though Jones's judgment may be excessive, the opposite view—that the Knight should be taken as a paragon of chivalry—may be just as unlikely. After all, should anyone be called "parfit," a word Chaucer uses only three times to describe people, once for the Knight and twice for a physician, all potentially ambivalent uses?[2] And is the phrase "parfit knyght" tautological or oxymoronic? Perhaps the survivors of Lithuania and Russia, where the Knight coincidentally helped raze the towns while fighting invaders from central Asia,[3] might claim "parfit knyght" really means "perfect villain." And "gentil" seems an unlikely qualifier for "knyght," implying more complexity than a man of broil and battle is likely to possess. In view of his ten separately named campaigns, his eighteen single combats (I.61, 63), and his present entourage, which includes son, servant, and horses, there may be some truth to the theory that Chaucer's leading pilgrim is a Knight-Mercenary, perhaps traveling here with "al his meynee." If true, then what many take as a pilgrimage of thanksgiving, on the slim evidence that "he was late ycome from his viage" (I.77), may in fact be his only home between campaigns. Though nothing proves he is not a landed knight, there is even less reason to think that he is. We simply do not know.

Some slight support for the opinion that the Knight belongs somewhere between the Narrator's and Jones's views, or rather embodies a little of both, comes from the few mild limitations we can infer. The thrilling fondness for chivalry he assumes in his contemporaries (I.1252–58) suggests he rides anachronistically from a former age, uneasily in his own. His frequent self-admonitions to refrain from digressing (I.885, 985, 1000, 1201)—what Marshall Leicester calls his "awareness of the need to discipline his imagination" (1990, p. 225)—confirm a tenuous contact with his immediate audience. Another possible limitation may be faintly seen in his fustian tunic, stained with what must be rust from his mailcoat (I.75–76). Though this detail helps create a becoming image of humility, two other references to rust in the *General Prologue* give it a potentially ambiguous significance. The Reeve's rusty blade (I.618), perhaps connoting latent powers waning from disuse, and the Parson's proverb, "if gold ruste, what shal iren do" (I.500), suggest that the stained mailshirt may slightly undercut the Knight. So often in the field, he may have little need for, nor even possess another garment.

But these are minor qualifications in keeping with the ambivalent portraits of many another pilgrim. This much is clear: the impression the Knight makes on the pilgrimage as a man of peace, in stopping the fight between the Host and the Pardoner and in gently rebuking the Monk for telling stories of one-sided heaviness, differs greatly from the man of war he must actually be on campaign. To gain further insight into the Knight's character and dedication we can only turn to the tale he tells. Here, however, one must proceed with caution. For the well-established practice of interpreting the psyches of certain pilgrims on the evidence of their tales does not traditionally extend to the Knight, who provides fewer personal details than some other pilgrims do and, in any case, was probably created after the tale he would tell was in nearly final form.

No Chaucerian characters destined for major roles make less auspicious entrances than the "Nat fully quyke, ne fully dede" (I.1015) Palamon and Arcite, who nonetheless hold center stage in the *Knight's Tale* from the moment pillagers find them lying side by side in a heap of fallen warriors. Chaucer himself encourages this attention at the conclusion of Book I (if we may look ahead for a moment) when, in a *demande d'amour* whose literary antecedents reach as far back as the unsolvable puzzles of Andreas Capellanus, he has his Knight ask who has the worse situation: the still imprisoned Palamon who can daily see his beloved, or the newly freed Arcite who sees her not at all (I.1347–54). Of course, the Knight's question cannot be answered. The two young men are indistinguishable; both are still imprisoned at that point in the tale, Palamon literally and Arcite metaphorically (I.1224), and neither has a better chance of access to Emelye.

Though indistinguishable, critical discussion has nevertheless attempted to differentiate them, with most readers seeing greater virtue in Palamon, on the assumption that his ultimate possession of Emelye must confirm the justice that an orderly tale like the Knight's would naturally uphold.[4] A few support Arcite on the ground that the tale's genre elevates him to heroic stature.[5] Both lines of reasoning overlook three important considerations. First, justice, as understood by nearly everyone in the *Knight's Tale,* depends entirely on point of view. The queens and duchesses who interrupt Theseus's homecoming imply that Creon's injustice toward them is the greater because of their lofty rank (I.919–26, 954–56). From Palamon's point of view, justice in love should rest on a principle of "first come, first served," since he is the first to spot Emelye in the garden below his prison cell (I.1146). From Arcite's it should depend on the probability of putting love into earthly practice, because he was the first to declare his wish to possess Emelye the woman (I.1155–59).

If these illogical, arbitrary arguments sound familiar, it is no wonder. Chaucer satirized them, as well as the young knights' willingness to abandon them for an equally arbitrary judgment in the lists, when he assigned them to the three tercels in the *Parlement of Foules,* who clack irrelevantly that justice depends, respectively, on the rank of the lover, on the length of his loving service, and on the quality of his love, and who are just as quick as Palamon and Arcite to say "Al redy!" (*PF,* 540) at the suggestion of combat.[6] Second, each petitioner in the *Knight's Tale* assumes that his (or her) arguments will be vindicated, and justice restored, when a desired object has been granted. Failure to receive the object would demonstrate injustice. Yet the Boethian underpinnings of the tale make abundantly clear, as we shall see, that all such objects are transitory goods that have nothing whatever to do with justice. The point applies equally to critical discussions of a character's worth. To assume either that Palamon's final possession of Emelye demonstrates his greater worth, or that Arcite's elevation to tragic stature demonstrates his, is to ignore the same Boethian truth that Palamon and Arcite ignore during much of the *Knight's Tale:*

that to receive the arbitrary gifts of Fortune, whether the winning of a woman or celebration in song, demonstrates nothing—either in the Athenian lists or in the critical arena. (Would those who believe Palamon is proved worthier by gaining the girl use the same argument to prove that Diomede is worthier than Troilus because he ends up with Criseyde?) Third, these attempts to find differences between Palamon and Arcite in order to justify the tale's conclusion proceed from the tacit assumption that Chaucer would rather idealize the world than describe it, that he would rather have fortune turn out in his tale as enlightened people would want it to turn out in the world than show fortune turning out as it usually does. However, our experience with Chaucer elsewhere has shown him less a didactic poet than one of profound mimetic insight. Had he structured the *Knight's Tale* as an image of how the humane prosper and the venal do not, or how the world would look if it were governed by the values of modern criticism, he might have sacrificed that insight to "falsen [his] mateere" (I.3175).

The false premises on which these arguments rest are, nevertheless, quite beside the point, for not a shred of evidence separates one knight from the other. Even the most familiar argument said to distinguish the two, and cited by everyone since Arcite first noted it, fails to stand up. In contrast to Arcite's earthy practicality, so the argument goes, Palamon has a more highly developed sense of spiritual value. He refers to Emelye with a metaphysical conceit, calling her "Venus" (I.1102) and addressing a prayer to her as if she had divine power (I.1104–7), while Arcite argues that Emelye the woman is not yet spoken for and may thus be claimed by himself. Despite Arcite's rhetorical agility, his argument is unpersuasive. Palamon at first unmistakably identifies Emelye as a lady in line I.1098, only later alluding to her divinity in a weak subjunctive clause (I.1101) and a fulsome prayer (I.1102–11). Moreover, Arcite surely knows that Palamon spoke hyperbolically in calling Emelye Venus, for Palamon immediately objects when Arcite tries to take his words literally. The argument, then, has nothing to do with the way each knight views Emelye, but at most with the different ways they express themselves on this one subject.

Another alleged difference suggests that Arcite views the world fatalistically, while Palamon does not. It is certainly true that Arcite comforts his cousin in prison, before their rivalry develops, with a speech about the inevitability of fortune (I.1081–91). And after their argument gains momentum it is still Arcite who acknowledges the inevitability of love (I.1169), resigning himself, with unwitting prescience, to Juno's and

Mars's will that he follow his Theban kinsman to a death "That shapen was . . . erst than my sherte" (I.1566). Despite the convincing ring of such fatalistic protests, this same Arcite argues elsewhere, in a complicated speech (I.1255–67) drawn from Boethius, that fate may not be inexorable. Images of a wealthy man slain by his intimates and a drunken man losing his way imply that one's fortune is something distinct from himself toward which he moves willy-nilly. But the speech does not focus on the inevitability of a particular fate, as if there were one path for each man on earth that must be followed regardless of that man's desires. Rather, Arcite concentrates on the variety of courses open to man and the strong possibility that he will choose an undesirable one, as does the drunken man in his simile. Now this emphasis suggests man's inability to draw a connection between a particular path and its peculiar destination. Were he capable of doing so—if he had the wit in one of the images, the sobriety in the other—he would surely avoid the path leading to his murder or to the wrong house and choose the better road. In turn, this capability implies that the crucial factor does indeed reside within man—the less his wit the more he is a victim of fate; the greater his wit the more he is able to control it. Arcite, it seems, believes both in fate's power over man and in man's power over fate.

More important, Palamon displays an identical ambivalence, arguing first that destiny lies beyond his control,

> "And if so be my destynee be shapen
> By eterne word to dyen in prisoun,
> Of oure lynage have som compassioun,
> That is so lowe ybroght by tirannye . . . .
>   "What governance is in this prescience,
> That giltelees tormenteth innocence?" (I.1108–11, 1313–14)

and later that his cousin has the very "wisdom and manhede" to take charge of his own destiny:

> "Allas," quod he, "Arcita, cosyn myn,
> Of al oure strif, God woot, the fruyt is thyn.
> Thow walkest now in Thebes at thy large,
> And of my wo thow yevest litel charge.
> Thou mayst, syn thou hast wisdom and manhede,
> Assemblen alle the folk of oure kynrede,
> And make a werre so sharp on this citee
> That by som aventure or some tretee

Thow mayst have hire to lady and to wyf
For whom that I moste nedes lese my lyf." (I.1281–90)

Every apparent difference between Palamon and Arcite vanishes in a similar way. Though each young knight affects an attitude opposite his cousin's, both behave identically. The most celebrated difference between the two, represented by their respective patron deities—Venus for Palamon, Mars for Arcite—guides neither cousin in practice. Palamon imagines his newly freed Martian cousin will return directly to Thebes to raise an army against Athens (I.1285–90), whereas the opposite actually occurs. Arcite changes his name to Philostrate (I.1428), the love-stricken, and labors for years at Theseus's court. Surprisingly it is Palamon, the presumed acolyte of love, who later intends to raise an army (I.1480–84). Patron deities notwithstanding, the two knights are absolutely interchangeable as lovers and as warriors.[7]

Other unusual details reveal the obvious care Chaucer has taken to make Palamon and Arcite as nearly alike as possible. The two young men are cousins of the royal house of Thebes, yet bear identical coats of arms. This detail would have been thought impossible in the Middle Ages, when the sons of two sisters would have been considered from distinct branches of the royal family and thus not "in oon armes" (I.1012).[8] After being taken together to Athens and placed in the same prison cell, they eventually fall in love with the same lady at the same moment. Identical metaphors describe them: both are called wild boars (I.1658, 1699) and lions (I.1598, 1656); both are likened to hunted animals, as well as to those who hunt them (I.1637–43). In single combat neither gains advantage over the other as they fight ankle-deep in their commingled blood (I.1660). And as lovers neither claims Emelye's favor, if we can judge from the lady's indifference to the knights (I.1809–10) and from her desire to remain a maiden rather than marry (I.2304–6). Hence, the *Knight's Tale* offers strong indications that in some sense Palamon and Arcite are to be understood as not merely similar, but actually identical.

To understand the point of this deliberate interchangeability calls for a glance at a cornerstone of medieval thought, Boethius's *Consolation of Philosophy*, which Chaucer translated at about the time he is assumed to have completed an earlier version of the *Knight's Tale*.[9] Written some time during its author's two-year imprisonment before being put to death, the *Consolation* represents an imagined conversation between a persona of the author (signified in the present discussion by quotation marks around the author's name, "Boethius") and an apparition whom he calls Lady

Philosophy. Jean de Meun, an earlier translator of the same work, explains in his own preface that "Boeces establist et represente soi [i.e., the character I am calling "Boethius"] en partie de homme troublé et tourmenté et demené par passions sensibles et establist [Lady Philosophy] en partie de homme ellevé et ensuivant les biens entendibles."[10] As the continuing debate alternates between complaint and consolation, it implies that all human beings simultaneously embrace the passionate responses of the body and the dispassionate thoughts of the mind and that the ideal condition of man is a harmony of the two, with each faculty reinforcing and constraining the other. One does not need an extended familiarity with medieval allegory to recognize that this entire two-part conversation reflects the author's vacillation between competing values. Although Boethian wisdom is often taken to be the words of Lady Philosophy alone, properly speaking it should be understood as a balance between the sensible and intelligible goods that the two halves of this conversation comprise. If the *Consolation*'s theme bears any relationship to the *Knight's Tale,* the young cousins Palamon and Arcite stand firmly on the side of "Boethius," as identical allegorical representations of the quest for sensible goods. Their complaints are as valid—and limited—as the complaints of the suffering "Boethius."

Matching this use of Boethius's thematic material, Chaucer's tale also follows the *Consolation*'s structural design in which competing viewpoints oppose each other dramatically. The *Knight's Tale*'s literal story describes a rivalry between two young knights and how that rivalry is absorbed into Theseus's sense of order. This immediate story, the material of countless romances, presents Palamon and Arcite as individual adversaries oblivious to anyone's position but their own—capricious, mercurial, frustrated rivals, who reach for any argument, however absurd, as long as it appears to justify their aims.[11] Chaucer complicates this central story by shaping it into a twofold allegory. The first develops these young rivals as a single entity, Palamon/Arcite, passing through the cycle of harmony, disharmony, and back to harmony again. The second represents the three ages of man: Youth, Maturity, and *Elde.*[12]

As to the allegorical meaning of the two young Theban cousins, we have already noted Chaucer's care in treating them as virtually identical in the beginning of the tale. But immediately after they both fall in love and argue over who has the greater right to the object of that love, that is, within twenty lines of passion's arousal (i.e., by line I.1206), the tale physically separates them from each other. Chaucer departs significantly from Boccaccio here, for in the *Teseida* Palamone and Arcita remain together to lament their mutual love for the same unattainable lady. We can readily see the reason for Chaucer's different handling. Since passion may be understood as internal disunity caused by the disparity between what one has and what one desires, this separation of Palamon from Arcite allegorically represents the disintegrating effect untempered Passion produces in man. The young knights become separated from each other, if not distinguishable, only when their newly aroused passion moves them to "surrender their reason to their appetites," as Dante says of the carnal sinners he meets in the second circle.[13] This first allegorical design, then, initially shows the young knights in harmony and balance, then turns that condition into an internally divided state of turmoil, not to be unified again until much later in the tale, when the literal death of one of the rivals signifies the end of internal strife, after Passion will have been tempered with dispassionate Reason. The second allegorical dimension, unparalleled in the *Consolation,* adapts the tale to a "parliament of three ages": Palamon and Arcite, taken together, represent Youth; the grandfatherly Egeus represents the opposite extreme, *Elde;* and Theseus represents Maturity, a position chronologically midway between Youth and Age on one hand—he is literally Egeus's son—and behaviorally between Passion and Dispassion on the other, as he struggles to keep his actions and reactions in harmony with both.[14]

Both of these allegories emphasize the cyclic forces that make humanity part of the natural order. The sequence of harmony, disharmony, and back to harmony again, as well as the wavering between passion and dispassion, echo nature's fundamental movement, the alternate tensing and relaxing in successively opposite directions that energizes all life. However, the *Knight's Tale* gives less attention to the struggle between passion and dispassion, although effectively representing that struggle in Theseus' decision-making, than to the tension between man's actions and his largely futile effort to explain those actions as something different from, more important than, mere illustrations of nature. It is therefore ironic that critical arguments favoring either Palamon or Arcite as more deserving of Emelye's hand demonstrate the tale's very point. For readers are nowhere more human, nowhere more like Chaucer's own characters, than when struggling to see in the *Knight's Tale* a world informed and controlled by the intellectual constructs of man.

The presence of a double allegory—on top of a love that lasts for several years without the lady's awareness and destroys a noble kinship to boot—may seem to contradict the assertion, made above, that Chaucer does not falsify his material. It is not Chaucer's lack of skill, however, that makes us suspect he departs from verisimilitude, but our own inexperience with mixed genres. When a single tale creates expectations of a literal story, as well as the apparently contradictory expectations of allegory, compromises must be made.[15] A case in point is the perfect interchangeability of Palamon and Arcite, whose falling in love with the same lady at exactly the same time, though required by allegory, makes "a somewhat distant claim to credibility" (Kolve 1984, p. 90). One may add the tale's conclusion to the list of improbabilities, which at least one critic admits seems "arbitrary and unpredictable" and to which Richard Neuse called attention twenty years earlier: "Why should Chaucer have set this elaborate astrological machinery in motion to 'determine' precisely what the protagonists freely choose for themselves?"[16]

The critical assumption that free choice and determinism cannot coexist fails to recognize that the two differ from each other only in the breadth of an observer's vision. The narrower the view, the freer and more realistic the choice appears to be; the wider the view, the more determined and allegorical. It is precisely to satisfy both of these apparently contradictory demands that Chaucer designed not only the conclusion but the entire tale as well, in as realistic a story as the two side-by-side genres of allegory and romance will permit. To see how he accomplishes this in the *Knight's Tale* calls for a reassessment of some fundamental matters.

In his very stimulating *Chaucer and the Imagery of Narrative*, V. A. Kolve remarks that the orderly world that Theseus tries to establish throughout the poem "is created by means of an appalling disorder." The wood must be destroyed to make the lists, animals dislodged from their "reste and pees" (p. 131). As creatures of feeling, quick to empathize and thus intolerant of destruction, we feel uneasy at much of what occurs in the *Knight's Tale*. But as rational beings we reconcile ourselves to that destruction by assuming that civilized life represents a higher form of order, indeed creation's highest form: "The wild wood is transformed—by art and ceremony and rule of law—as Theseus seeks to translate human aggression, sexuality, and (finally) sorrow into forms that will allow civilized life to continue" (Kolve, p. 131). And yet, we have good reason to ask, with the Wife of Bath in another context, "Who peyntede the leon?" (III.692). For the main issue in the *Knight's Tale* is not order from an exclusively rational perspective, but the constant presence of two kinds of order, the order of nature that controls life everywhere, no matter what Theseus or anyone else may wish to do about it, and the order of intellect in which man continually seeks refuge in his attempts to understand the events of his life.

It is an old story how man wraps the realities of his life, usually those he shares with animals, in dignified ceremonies to make himself more presentable. He cloaks violence in knighthood, coupling in courtship, a carnivorous nature in the ceremony of the hunt. One of Theseus's commands causes lists to be created in order to elevate what might otherwise be a male battle for sexual supremacy (a thoroughly natural phenomenon) to something noble. The "art and ceremony and rule of law" with which Theseus transforms the story amount to a kind of rhetoric, as Donaldson puts it in discussing the *Nun's Priest's Tale,* man's attempt to deny that he is nature's hostage, to conceal from himself his fundamental similarity with the animal world.[17] For this reason a prison setting, both for the young men who are literally in a cell and for the young woman whose garden is a kind of prison, is entirely appropriate.[18] Helpless at their youthful age to avoid the mating game to which the cycle of nature constrains both sexes, Emelye and her two admirers are compelled to take part, as elsewhere Troilus and Criseyde are compelled by the same nature to take part in the same cycle, and in the same way. Being men, Palamon, Arcite, and Troilus are struck suddenly by Love and helpless thereafter to think of anything else. Being women, Emelye and Criseyde respond to Love more slowly, preferring to remain unmarried, yet finally offer no resistance to the natural cycle that they too must follow. The *Knight's Tale* affirms humanity's dependence on one of nature's strongest impulses, while also demonstrating a reluctance to accept that impulse as a mere fact of nature.

The tale makes us see death in a similar way. Neither appalling nor disorderly from nature's perspective, but one of the most orderly events in life, death is foreordained in fact, if not in time or manner, by the coming into existence of each living thing. Arcite's death at the end of the tale and the destruction of a grove at its center are as necessary as the passionate impulses of both cousins at its beginning. The former two are needed to sustain the life of the world, the latter the life of individuals and their species. Man's reluctance to accept his own inclusion in nature's cycle reaches full force in the lament over the death of Arcite, as if it were an affront by Fortune, in contrast to his silent approval of the grove's destruction because that death serves man.

Nowhere is the tale more rhetorical, nowhere more transparent in dignifying the ordinary, than in its attempt to lay all man's impulses on the charge of a star. While it is true that cosmic forces "seem to determine not only the general outcome of the tournament and the brute fact of Arcite's downfall but the hour of his accident, the area of his injury, and the manner and day of his death" (Schweitzer, p. 20), here too a double perspective is called for, because the celestial machinery itself has ambivalent meaning. Centuries of poets before and since Chaucer have accounted for the universal impulses of man's animal nature—his passions, his fears, even his death—by attributing them to celestial determinism. A behavior pattern is observed first, its explanation invented later; the event begets the star. However, once that tradition is firmly in place, a poet can begin with an abstract representation of some impulse (love, let us say), expressed in a convenient concrete symbol (the celestial body named Venus), and then proceed to a specific human situation exemplifying that impulse; the star begets the event. In the *Knight's Tale* Chaucer shows us both the particular situation of two knights in love with one woman and the universal situation of human beings, including their sexual impulses, as part of nature. Thus, in the same events he depicts the free choices of individuals in life as well as the determined actions of human beings in nature. And the question of whether he may perhaps falsify the former in order to accommodate the latter need not arise, because the tale's actual subject is neither the one nor the other but man's attempt to absorb both in the orderly structures of his own thought.

Especially in its metaphors does the tale represent the simultaneous existence of free choice and determinism. Let us look closely at the lines describing Arcite roaming through a grove outside Athens on that May morning when Fortune or Destiny would bring the two Theban cousins together for the first time in several years. Arcite, disguised as Philostrate, has already had a long career at the Athenian court, first as a hewer and drawer, then as a page, and most recently as a squire, for all of which his sole motivation has been love for Emelye:

> Whan that Arcite hadde romed al his fille,
> And songen al the roundel lustily,
> Into a studie he fil sodeynly,
> As doon thise loveres in hir queynte geres,
> Now in the crope, now doun in the breres,
> Now up, now doun, as boket in a welle.
> Right as the Friday, soothly for to telle,
> Now it shyneth, now it reyneth faste,
> Right so kan geery Venus overcaste
> The hertes of hir folk; right as hir day
> Is gereful, right so chaungeth she array.
> Selde is the Friday al the wowke ylike. (I.1528–39)

The first few of these lines suggest an Arcite of changeable mood. Lustily he sings a roundel to the May morning, and then falls immediately into a melancholy mood. The remainder of the passage intensifies the idea of rapid and extreme change—notwithstanding the Knight's (perhaps unintended) sexual iconography, as "queynte geres," high and low foliage, and the up-and-down action of a bucket going in and out of a well leave little doubt about the preoccupations of lovers. A subtle shift in the cause of these alternating extremes of conduct, from internal to external, conveys an idea of the simultaneity of free choice and determinism. Arcite himself is responsible for his change from gaiety to melancholy at the beginning of the passage. But by its end—shifting so gently that we scarcely notice—Venus has caused the change. The passage, however, has two movements. It implies progress through a week, which seldom ends as it began, and the progress of lovers. Though Friday seems to do its own shining and raining in lines I.1534–35, by line I.1538 the rapidly alternating sunshine and rain are credited to "geery Venus" who changes her array. Similarly the cause influencing lovers shifts from internal to external. The typical lovers of line 1531 control their own activities, as tree-climbers control their own climbing. But buckets in a well must await the raising and lowering by someone controlling the bucket. Again it is Venus who "overcaste / The hertes of hir folk" to sustain the notion of lovers' sudden changes. Arcite is indeed the lover who changes his moods, but he is simultaneously the helpless recipient of what is done to him. As both the star in charge of a day and the goddess in charge of lovers, Venus joins the passage's two movements.

What these metaphors imply in the first part of this scene becomes explicit as the scene unfolds. Concealed in the brush nearby lies the recently escaped Palamon, who, on overhearing Arcite's melancholic complaint, rushes from hiding, discloses his identity, and challenges his cousin. Palamon's appeal to a sense of order, conveyed in expressions like "'false traytour . . . to my conseil sworn . . . And hast byjaped heere duc Theseus, / And falsly chaunged hast thy name . . .'" (I.1580–86), provokes a counter challenge from Arcite embodying an internal contradiction between general determinism and particular freedom similar to what was just observed in words about the weather, love, and lovers:

"By God that sit above,
Nere it that thou art sik and wood for love,
And eek that thow no wepne hast in this place,
Thou sholdest nevere out of this grove pace,
That thou ne sholdest dyen of myn hond.

For I defye the seurete and the bond
Which that thou seist that I have maad to thee.
What! Verray fool, thynk wel that love is free,
And I wol love hire maugree al thy myght!" (I.1599–1607)

Because chivalry constrains him in a general way, Arcite cannot slay an unarmed and distraught man. He brings food, clothing, bedding, and weapons to Palamon so that his cousin might rest comfortably and engage in battle the next day as an equal. And yet, despite Arcite's adherence to the ethical standard that controls his life in general, he uses that very ethic to advance the paradoxical belief that in a particular situation "love is free," unfettered by the constraining rules of orderliness. Arcite apparently believes that external laws determine man's general inclinations, while the man himself is free to choose his particular conduct.

Although the *Knight's Tale* depicts a pattern of antitheses, with passion at one extreme and dispassion at the opposite, it does not represent the latter, that is, Lady Philosophy's position, with the same clarity or depth as it represents the former in the hot-blooded, rival-locked cousins. One reason is that the plan to show both extremes, Passion as well as Dispassion, as equally insufficient when used as exclusive guides for man presents a difficult problem in iconography. If the depiction of silly frustrated lovers has a long, witty tradition, the depiction of Dispassion or Reason as an equally ludicrous figure does not. Indeed to ridicule dispassion would run counter to many long-cherished scholastic traditions. In any case, many of Lady Philosophy's arguments are already scattered throughout the tale to point out the flawed stance of silly, frustrated lovers like Palamon and Arcite.[19]

Two successive soliloquies near the end of Book I, one by each of the two rivals, reveal Chaucer's technique of letting his own characters draw upon Lady Philosophy's arguments for purposes she never intended. In the first of these (I.1223–74) Arcite laments his false freedom shortly after being released from prison. Formerly convinced that freedom from prison would provide total happiness, he now believes happiness depends on the sight of Emelye: "blisse [comes from] / Oonly the sighte of hire whom that I serve" (I.1230–31); pain comes from her absence. Exploiting the metaphor of the beatific vision, he argues that his new freedom has placed him "Noght in purgatorie, but in helle" (I.1226), whereas his cousin dwells in "paradys" (I.1237). Abandoning metaphysical for earthly metaphors, in order paradoxically to switch subjects from passion to philosophy, he now laments the things Man mistakenly seeks in hope of finding happiness—wealth, which often makes him prey to others, freedom from prison, though he might then be slain at home—and finally compares his quest for that bliss with the wayward path of a drunk. The correct path, he now insists, would be imprisonment, for it would bring him the sight of Emelye.

The same metaphor of a drunk and a similar list—riches, honors, power, glory, delight—occur in the *Consolation* (III.Pr.ii.86–88, 118–19), where Lady Philosophy grants that each of these has a certain limited value. But her point differs so greatly from Arcite's that it measures the difference between their respective values. In Lady Philosophy's metaphor the inebriate's home represents the permanent good of a tranquil mind, while the false direction taken by the tippler suggests the transitory goods man wrongly believes will make him completely happy. Arcite's sharply different usage implies that the drunk's correct address represents the sight of Emelye—in fact one of the transitory goods in Lady Philosophy's list— while the false paths to that home represent the fruitless ways to achieve that sight. Thus, despite Arcite's indebtedness to Lady Philosophy's words, he completely misses her point, taking "Boethius's" position instead. He misses his own point too, that nothing of "erthe, water, fir, ne eir" (I.1246) can offer complete happiness.

Within seven lines the scene shifts to a soliloquy by the other cousin, Palamon (I.1303–21), who is now noticeably less metaphysical than either Arcite was above or he himself was when he first saw Emelye and was reminded of Venus. Here, still locked in a literal prison, Palamon too belongs firmly on the side of "Boethius," claiming injustice because his own point of view has not been served. He speciously argues that he deserves at least as much pleasure on earth as a beast enjoys, because Man is superior to a beast. But he neglects to mention the crucial faculty that man possesses and a beast does not, his rational faculty—his immortal soul, to continue the theological terminology. Indeed, if man tries "for Goddes sake, to letten of his wille" (I.1317), as Palamon says he does, he may enjoy rewards to which beasts are not entitled. By failing to acknowledge the basis on which man is superior to a beast, and by wailing that his sole ambition is to acquire no more than may be gained by any "sheep that rouketh in the folde" (I.1308), he implies he deserves no better reward than a beast's. The same analogy occurs in Boethius, where Lady Philosophy argues that a beast knows only how to seek pleasure, implying that if man, too, seeks only pleasure he reduces himself to a beast's level. As Arcite does above, here Palamon echoes Lady Philosophy's words, but misses her point:

And yif thilke delices mowen maken folk blisful, thanne by the same cause moten thise beestis ben clepid blisful, of whiche beestis al the entencioun hasteth to fulfille here bodily jolyte. (*Boece*, III.Pr.vii.12–16)

Much later in the tale the influence of Lady Philosophy's words can still be seen, no longer providing insight into young knights driven by passion, but now advancing the notion that the workings of the world are under celestial dominance. On the eve of their formal battle in the lists, when Palamon and Arcite make prayerful appeals to their patron deities, Venus and Mars respectively, each knight receives a promise of success. Mars's assurance that Arcite will be the victor implies he will win Emelye as a prize; but Venus promises Emelye to Palamon. Hence, an argument develops in the heavens between Venus and Mars, reflecting the rivalry between Palamon and Arcite and ultimately calling for a resolution by Saturn (I.2453–78). The suffering implicit in all of Saturn's activities has led some to think he represents a principle of disorder,[20] and consequently that the tale testifies to Fortune's chaotic plan to let evil triumph over good. On the contrary, possession of Emelye is, at best, an apparent good, not a moral absolute; failure to win her cannot be evil. More to the point, the apparent disorder which some find death to be is one of the most orderly phenomena in nature. Saturn knows this well. He nevertheless appears malevolent to those who feel his sting most sharply because they confuse ill-fortune with moral evil. And the judicious distribution of ill-fortune happens to be Saturn's only responsibility. But the ill-fortune he dispenses here to bring about the death of Arcite, though called horrific by many, ultimately achieves the profoundest orderliness in the whole tale, the fulfillment of everyone's wish.

Lady Philosophy also points out the necessity of pain and suffering to produce balance. While admitting that ill-fortune is considered "confusioun" by those who must suffer it (*Boece*, IV.Pr.vi.237), she argues that every unpleasant thing implies its opposite:

Certes it is leveful to the hevene to maken clere dayes, and after that to coveren tho same dayes with dirke nyghtes. The yeer hath eek leve to apparaylen the visage of the erthe, now with floures, and now with fruyt, and to confownden hem somtyme with reynes and with coldes. The see hath eek his ryght to ben somtyme calm and blaundysschyng with smothe watir, and somtyme to ben horrible with wawes and with tempestes. (*Boece*, II.Pr.ii.37–46)

Fortune, too, must ebb and flow:

Thow hast bytaken thiself to the governaunce of Fortune and forthi it byhoveth the to ben obeisaunt to the maneris of thi lady. Enforcestow the to aresten or withholden the swyftnesse and the sweighe of hir turnynge wheel? O thow fool of alle mortel foolis! Yif Fortune bygan to duelle stable, she cessede thanne to ben Fortune. (*Boece,* II.Pr.i.107–15)

Let us now return to the point raised earlier, regarding the difficulty in creating an icon for Dispassion. In the *Consolation,* the character "Boethius" appears inferior to Lady Philosophy because the philosophic complaint that he says causes him the greatest suffering carries less conviction than his complaint about his very real physical suffering. Lady Philosophy's distance from the petty concerns of man thus gives her a loftier pose. However, her indifference arises not from the pettiness of man's interests, but from her own inability to empathize with any physical desire at all. For this reason Lady Philosophy's consolation remains as insufficient in its way as "Boethius's" petulant yearning does in another. In the *Knight's Tale,* too, anguish grows from a gathering crescendo of ill-fortune: women suffer from the injustice of a conqueror; two knights are imprisoned, then become sufferers in love; friendship turns to enmity; and perhaps the sharpest ill-fortune, Arcite dies, the more poignantly by following close upon what appeared to be ultimate good fortune. In response to this last named misfortune a symbolic figure of Dispassion does arise. Differing from those who passionately denounce this most unfortunate death, and corresponding to Lady Philosophy more closely than does anyone else in the tale, Theseus's old father Egeus recites lines that include one of the most oft-quoted sentiments in all of Chaucer:

"Right as ther dyed nevere man," quod he,
"That he ne lyvede in erthe in some degree,
Right so ther lyvede never man," he seyde,
"In al this world, that som tyme he ne deyde.
This world nys but a thurghfare ful of wo,
And we been pilgrymes, passynge to and fro.
Deeth is an ende of every worldly soore." (I.2843–49)

It is not difficult to understand why Chaucer assigned this speech to Egeus, in contrast to *Il Philostrato* where Theseus himself delivers a corresponding speech. At an age two generations senior to Palamon and Arcite, and thus perfectly tailored to one of Chaucer's patterns, an allegory of three ages, Egeus is also better suited to recite the dispassionate philosophy called for in the other pattern. But the speech just quoted is more than dispassionate; it is fatuous, as unlikely to console Arcite's mourners in either ancient Athens or medieval England as to brighten faces at a modern funeral. Attempting to put in perspective this saddest of ill-fortunes, the death of Arcite, as if he were trumping Fortune's highest card with the accumulated wisdom of the ages, Egeus instead merely offers a bathetic platitude that errs as much on one side of a balanced human ideal as the lovesick moans of the young knight-cousins miss it on the other. The simplicity of *Elde*'s philosophy matches the simplicity of Youth's passion.

The constantly changing face of Nature—her waxing and waning, the infinite variety that contributes to her unity—escapes the charge of caprice because her moods may be mathematically predicted and readily perceived. Flux maintains the world in a delicate balance: The "accordaunce . . . of thynges is bounde with love, that governeth erthe and see, and hath also comandement to the hevene" (*Boece*, II.Met.viii, 13–16). The fortunes of human life, by contrast, continually seem capricious, or unjust, because man thinks he deserves unrelieved good fortune. Since the vicissitudes of human existence follow no easily recognized pattern, man forgets that he too must obey a law of harmony, that his only practical strategy is to maintain a balance between sensible and intelligible goods. Whereas the *Consolation* does not represent such a law dramatically, only implying such a balance in the coexistence of "Boethius" and Lady Philosophy, the *Knight's Tale* does, assigning the role to Theseus who represents man's dynamic struggle to achieve balance between passionate action and dispassionate reason.

Early in the tale a casual description of Theseus's banner has more significance than we might think: A "rede statue of Mars . . . shyneth in his white baner large" (I.975–76). These two colors are later featured individually in the banners of Palamon and Arcite. As noted earlier, Arcite may not be as Martian as he thinks, nor Palamon as Venusian, but the red banner of the former (I.2583) and the white banner of the latter (I.2586) stand dramatically separated from each other as these rivals in love prepare for the lists. Surely the evenly balanced red and white of Theseus's banner suggests that the Duke represents an integration of the two young knights and, by implication, of the love and war to which their patron deities are dedicated.

More than banners make this integration clear. Theseus's very entrance in the tale demonstrates that his passions embrace both love and war. His first appearance shows him returning from a triumphant campaign among the Scythians, for he was "in his tyme swich a conquerour / That gretter was ther noon under the sonne" (I.862–63). The spoils of that war include Ypolita, "The faire, hardy queene of Scithia" (I.882), whom Theseus wed immediately after the victory. In other words, explicit evidence within the first twenty-five lines of the tale shows Theseus as both a warrior and a lover, roles whose close juxtaposition suggests a greater underlying similarity than difference. Elsewhere in the tale further evidence points to the continued presence of both passions: Creon feels the sting of Theseus's brief punitive exercise at Thebes; Palamon and Arcite experience his swift decisiveness both at their initial capture and later when discovered at large in a grove. Through it all Theseus understands the significance of young love, even remarking that he too was once a lover, "For in my tyme a servant was I oon" (I.1814).

Throughout the tale we actually see Theseus's rational faculty laboring to control this passion, as "he learns to look at things no longer as they reflect only his own interests, but to look into them also as they reflect the interests of others" (Roney 1990, p. 113). As a result, passion and reason work together, producing responses that are both appropriate to Athens's ruler and suited to each situation at hand.[21] An early instance occurs during his triumphant victory march homeward to Athens, when the rejoicing and the pageantry at the homecoming of the conquering Duke with his new bride are so great that Chaucer's Knight wants to tell us all about it. Picture Theseus's dilemma. Having "come almoost unto the toun, / In al his wele and in his mooste pride" (I.894–95), he longs for his hero's welcome. But he also recognizes the just pleas of a company of aggrieved ladies whose slain husbands' bodies are currently being desecrated by Creon in distant Thebes. Despite his annoyance that these ladies "Perturben so my feste with criynge" (I.906), he recognizes his greater obligation to the mourning ladies and proceeds directly to Thebes (966–74). Notice, too, in the Knight's storytelling a small demonstration of reason triumphing over desire, when the Knight refrains from detailing the pageantry he would rather describe because he knows the weak oxen pulling his pointel must plow on.

The same pattern repeats itself in all of Theseus's actions—an intemperately stated position followed by a compassionate retraction. He sentences Palamon and Arcite "to dwellen in prisoun / Perpetuelly—he nolde no raunsoun" (I.1023–24), but later releases Arcite at the request of his friend Perotheus. That this release was not granted lightly seems evident from its terms: Arcite, found anywhere at large in Theseus's lands, would be instantly executed. And yet even this resolve does not last when, some years later, Theseus discovers the two cousins fighting in a grove outside

Athens.[22] With Palamon a recent escapee and Arcite in violation of his parole, Theseus has every right to dispatch both on the spot. Palamon himself reminds the Duke that they merit death, and even requests it, as long as both cousins receive the same fate. Accordingly, Theseus decrees death (I.1747), but shortly thereafter gives way to the pleas of the ladies in his company to spare the knight-cousins. Chaucer's Knight provides the best gloss on Theseus's change of mind:

> And though he first for ire quook and sterte,
> He hath considered shortly, in a clause,
> The trespas of hem bothe, and eek the cause,
> And although that his ire hir gilt accused,
> Yet in his resoun he hem bothe excused . . . (I.1762–66)

Under the influence of consideration (I.1763), reason (I.1766), and thought (I.1767), ire melts into compassion (I.1770); a self-interested passion becomes a reasonable concern for others. The linguistic tableau at lines I.1765–66 shows ire (passion) and reason (dispassion) opposing each other in two antithetical clauses, as they would contend with each other in Theseus's mind.

Unlike the earlier release of Arcite, which showed Theseus's generosity, this change of mind is prompted by the softly spoken thought that a position tenaciously and unreasonably held befits beasts more than men:

> "Fy
> Upon a lord that wol have no mercy,
> But been a leon, bothe in word and dede,
> To hem that been in repentaunce and drede,
> As wel as to a proud despitous man
> That wol mayntene that he first bigan.
> That lord hath litel of discrecioun,
> That in swich cas kan no divisioun
> But weyeth pride and humblesse after oon." (I.1773–81)

Here the first few lines do not actually refer to Theseus but describe what he would be if he were unwilling to yield. However, the term "leon" had just been used to describe both Palamon (I.1656) and Arcite (I.1598), and thus carries much significance as a description of those entirely under the control of passion. Hence, we can see Theseus's deliberative process here struggling to rise above the merely passionate levels on which Palamon and Arcite still remain.

By changing the rules of the tournament Theseus gives yet another instance of his ability to temper passion with reason. He had originally decided to let the lists determine which of the two cousins would either "Sleen his contrarie, or out of lystes dryve" (I.1859). At the opening of the lists, however, a herald announces a modification of the rules: though strength will still determine the victor, there shall be no bloodshed. Like lines I.1773–81, quoted above, these words too describe a method of making decisions based on intellective processes, especially discretion:

> "The lord hath of his heigh discrecioun
> Considered that it were destruccioun
> To gentil blood to fighten in the gyse
> Of mortal bataille now in this emprise.
> Wherfore, to shapen that they shal nat dye,
> He wol his firste purpos modifye." (I.2537–42)

The new rules have an immediate effect on the people who recognize in them the benevolence of an ideal ruler: "God save swich a lord, that is so good / He wilneth no destruccion of blood!" (I.2563–64).

Thus far we have seen Theseus judiciously blending passion with reason over relatively easy matters primarily involving the interests of others. Later in the tale, however, Theseus's own passions are greatly moved by the death of Arcite for whom he has developed much affection. Egeus alone is able to retrieve him from sorrow. Not, however, with his speech at I.2843–49 (quoted above, where it was called "fatuous"); nor even by turning him to the "bisy cure" of attending to Arcite's funeral. Rather, he performs for Theseus a service similar to the one Theseus performed for the knight-cousins when they were debilitated by passion for Emelye. He places Arcite's death in the philosophic perspective that leads Theseus to his "Prime Moevere" speech with its double emphasis, one on the transience of all things—the oak and the stone, man and woman, king and page—the other on the hopeful belief "That speces of thynges and progressiouns / Shullen enduren by successiouns (I.3013–14). He adds to Theseus's fatalism something more helpful than the bleak injunction "To maken vertu of necessitee" (I.3042). The waning of an oak implies the waxing of its offspring; the wasted stone testifies to the activity that has worn it down. No species enjoys absolute stability, but endures through succession (I.3013–14). Each member of a group inevitably and necessarily comes to an end, in order that its successor may take its rightful place and ensure the permanence of the species. Accordingly, Theseus turns immediately from a rationalized acceptance of life's limit to the joyful business of succession. The former may help us understand the loss of life; but only the latter can effectively turn us from grief.

This chain of reasoning offered by Theseus differs enormously from the strict position taken by Egeus and derived ultimately from Lady Philosophy. Egeus remains dispassionate, almost clinical as he explains that "Deeth is an ende of every worldly soore" (I.2849). We are told that his words were intended to give the people a means of comforting themselves—as if grief could ever be assuaged through philosophic understanding. But he has nothing further to offer. Theseus, however, combines the best features of philosophic *Elde* and passionate Youth. His rational faculty permits him, with his father's help, to understand human mortality, while his acquaintance with passion enables him to effect the more practical and joyous note on which the tale ends. That the two faculties simultaneously complement each other demonstrates the ideal of human orderliness that Theseus represents. The succession to which Theseus's words call attention has had to await the slow maturation of Palamon and Arcite, a process whose completion signals the successful conclusion of Chaucer's two allegorical designs as well as the resolution of the romantic rivalry.

Much earlier in the tale passionate speeches by Palamon and Arcite made it seem that the former loved Emelye as a goddess, the latter loved her as a woman. As we saw, that difference was stylistic rather than real. Nevertheless, their stated positions define the full spectrum of human love, ethereal at one extreme, physical at the other. There is no reason to suppose that Palamon loses his spiritual attraction for Emelye as the tale progresses, but he clearly acquires the complementary impulse first expressed by Arcite. His prayer to Venus ignores victory and renown by asking simply to "have fully possessioun / Of Emelye, and dye in thy servyse" (I.2242–43). The physical inclinations implicit in the word "possessioun" and the spiritual allusion in the phrase "thy [that is, Venus's] servyse" reveal a deeper recognition of his dual nature than he displayed earlier.

The evidence of Arcite's character growth is equally persuasive. Before he became a rival in love, he offered formulaic wisdom about the nature of the world and specifically about man's fortune in it. After that rivalry develops, however, we hear not the least indication of his willingness to place passion in perspective. His awareness of a dimension beyond the physical vanishes. Later, however, following his victory in the lists, when his death is imminent, Arcite makes a more eloquent and profound statement, far more suggestive of abstract powers, than anything we have yet heard from him. That final speech confirms his passion for Emelye as well as the wisdom to recognize virtue beyond the limited sphere of his own good fortune. His words to Emelye praising Palamon (I.2783–96) end his rivalry with his cousin and demonstrate a wisdom not seen in him earlier. Moreover, they answer his own dying lament, still echoing painfully in our ears, "What is this world? What asketh men to have? / Now with his love, now in his colde grave / Allone, withouten any compaignye" (I.2777–79). Frustrated in life as an only partly developed man, Arcite achieves by its end the full integration of his faculties. If life is then a struggle to find that integration, death here symbolizes the end of the struggle—the death of what estranges man from himself.

Confirming this view of Arcite's death, the tale's description of his last moments notes that although "The vital strengthe is lost and al ago. / Oonly the intellect" (I.2802–3) remains active. That the intellect "dwelled in his herte" (I.2804) presents a striking image of passion and reason operating harmoniously at last, and recalls an earlier description of Theseus who thought in his heart (I.1772) and melted ire into compassion by combining reason and sentiment (I.1760–84). On the threshold of death Arcite finally achieves the balance for which Theseus alone has stood as an ideal.

With internal strife thus abated, the newly integrated Palamon/Arcite may advance to maturity. Though only Palamon still lives literally, he symbolically carries with him Arcite's identity as well, since Arcite's very act of describing Palamon's virtues in lines I.2783–97 demonstrates that the words fit himself too. In time Palamon will be joined in marriage to Emelye, whom Arcite had earlier called "wyf" (I.2775). If the symbolic means by which Youth advances to Maturity is the death of internal strife, a wedding ceremony well suits that literal advance. Theseus's campaign against the Amazons had concluded in a wedding, though the actual ceremony took place offstage. Now, many years later, the same pattern repeats itself. Serving not as a climax to this tale but as the beginning of some other, and thus diminished in comparison with everything else that transpires, as Theseus's wedding was earlier, the wedding of Palamon and Emelye shows that man himself will endure, despite the pitiable loss of Arcite. As the strife between formerly hostile nations concluded in a truce, so the internal strife of Youth governed by passion subsides in a wedding ceremony, symbolizing the rational social structure that endorses and directs that passion.

Good and bad fortune throughout the *Knight's Tale* has meant no more than the constant dynamism of all creation. All things come into existence, have their day, and subside; but the greatest wonder of it all—the only "thyng that parfit is and stable" (I.3009)—is the inevitable coming into existence of a new thing as each old passes away. Lady Philosophy had stressed that each good fortune implied an ill. But the principle works two ways: every ill-fortune, every waning, every death, implies the creation of a new being which is none other than the rebirth of all nature. The wedding of Palamon and Emelye, bringing "parfit joye, lastynge everemo" (I.3072), reaffirms the world's immortal pattern of beginnings, and brings to appropriate conclusion the Knight's perception of the world.

At length we return to the Knight who has crafted this long tale of the nature of man. Though very few personal details have accompanied the Knight's performance, apart from those which merely fill in his career, readers nevertheless feel they understand his ethical values, and hugely approve of them. The superficial similarities between himself, the ranking pilgrim, and Duke Theseus, the ranking personage in his tale, encourage us to believe that traits of character we observe in the Duke may also be attributed to the Knight. His occasional intervention to prevent a quarrel, or restore order when one has broken out, echoes Theseus's function in restoring justice in Thebes, in halting the combat between Palamon and Arcite, and in supervising the orderly resolution of their lovers' dispute. Not least, the Knight's brief lecture to the Monk about the one-sided heaviness of *de casibus* tragedies (VII.2767–79) could have taken its model from Theseus's speech on the "faire cheyne of love" (I.2988), which acknowledges the heaviness of death, but counters with an affirmation of life.

And yet our sense of the ethical standard-bearer fails to match our sense of the man. We have no idea what makes him laugh, whether he "snybbeth" his son as the Franklin does or entices him as the Wife of Bath says hawks are caught. Though he seems less in need of Becket's intercession than most of the other pilgrims, his journey to Canterbury—no less than the tale he tells on the way—reflects a life of formulaic responses. Perhaps the only certain way to get a rise from him is to threaten some unpleasantness. Consider one crucial difference between him and the character he seems most to resemble. Theseus frequently struggles with himself to keep from passionate excess, to maintain balance between his initial impulses and the more reasonable responses he makes upon reflection. The Knight never struggles. His balance is perfect, and for this reason somewhat lifeless. There is something unsettling in his tale of the balanced ideal of passion and reason. However insightfully he notes one or another influence on man, he nonetheless falsifies the whole by implying we can examine these influences one at a time. Intending to schematize the human condition, he anatomizes it fatally. One telling instance of this formulaic tendency, among many, may be inferred from his professed inability to describe Palamon's suffering in prison:

> Who koude ryme in Englyssh proprely
> His martirdom? For sothe it am nat I;
> Therfore I passe as lightly as I may. (I.1459–61)

These words lament more than failed metrics, since 3,000 lines amply demonstrate that he could summon up a few more rhymes. They reveal rather a failure of emotion. The Knight has no difficulty recognizing the fact of imprisonment or even the fact of grief. It is the specific nature of grief, its degree of suffering, its mental anguish that he cannot imagine. How sharply different is Duke Theseus, who later grieves genuinely and deeply for Arcite. The Knight may well believe that his perspective on his own life approaches the ideal set by his character Theseus, for he takes pains to suggest that his austerity, his peacemaking role, his very presence on a pilgrimage of thanksgiving, and the tale he tells during it, testify to a balanced life of action and introspection. But the studied nature of these traits and the excessively schematic representations in his tale convince us he more closely resembles Egeus than either Theseus or the young cousins. He has perhaps divided his life into compartments, disciplining even his active life of combat into a procession of dispassionate formulas. The Knight's performance, then, wanders closer to treatise than to literature. His profound understanding of the forces that influence human life emerges more clearly than his sensitive representation of the men and women who live it. Despite his tale's thorough integration of man's conflicting impulses, the Knight himself appears to lack the dynamism and spontaneity that give life its greatest appeal.

The Miller, the Reeve, the Cook

It may be doubted that the "noble storie" just completed would win a popularity contest in any age, especially since it is ideally suited to the "gentils," as Harry Bailly says with strained praise. His enthusiastic remark, "the game is wel bigonne" (I.3117), may have more aspiration than truth. He now has an urgent need for a pilgrim who can satisfy two requirements: he or she must be high enough on the "lered" or social scale to follow next after a knight, yet be likely to tell a tale the "lewed" can enjoy. His gaze naturally falls upon "a lord ful fat and in good poynt" (I.200), the Monk, better known for pricking after the hare than wearing a penitential shirt of hair. The Narrator, too, might have made the same choice, given the chance, for he seemed to endorse the Monk's rejection of a strict monastic rule for the active life of a huntsman (I.173–89).

The Miller will have none of this. Perhaps a good thing, too, for the tale he insists upon telling turns out to be a great deal livelier than the *de casibus* lessons later told by the Monk. The *Knight's Tale* needs a powerful corrective, the Miller implies with his coy use of the word "noble" (I.3126) to describe the rustic tale he intends to tell. He apparently believes that love triangles pine away for years of idealized frustration only in fanciful literature, never in life, and that two hundred knights jousting in lists a mile around to represent passionate desire may well enrich the same literature, but could never portray real people who much prefer the direct pleasures of felt life, like the frontal thrust of his leading man in line I.3276.

It has long been recognized that the corrective he insists upon applying achieves an unconscious irony by re-creating, in a vastly different setting to be sure, precisely the same tale the Knight has just finished telling.[1] Not only because the *Miller's Tale* features two young men who pursue Alisoun as ardently as Palamon and Arcite pursue Emelye, but because, like the *Knight's Tale,* it creates characters who think they control their lives, when in fact their supposed control follows a time-immemorial script crafted by nature and their own excesses, as "each one receives a punishment of his own making" (Woods 1994, p. 172). When Nicholas shouts "Help! Water! Water!" (I.3815) to cool his burning bum, an image of the Flood flashes before our eyes and we sense again, as we did in the previous tale on learning that Arcite was thrown from his horse, the presence of an unfathomable force effecting an event "That shapen was . . . erst than my shertc" (I.1566), as Palamon presciently said. It is Absolon's prissiness, as much as Alisoun's mischief, that makes her shove her sunny side out the shot window to give the parish clerk an unsavory rebuke; the opinion that John is "wood" (I.3833, 3846, 3848) must be credited as much to his own colossal stupidity as to clerkish skill; and Nicholas's inordinate pleasure in his own ingenuity "scalded [his] towte" (I.3853) as much as Absolon's hot poker did. That this remake of the *Knight's Tale* alters only its inconsequential details, not its philosophic import, scarcely dawns upon its teller, for a new interest catches his eye, the Reeve, with whom he has an exchange that nearly dominates the critical dialogue.

The tightly constructed pair of tales told by the Miller and the Reeve almost always force critics to discuss whether these two ribalds knew each other before they meet on the pilgrimage to Canterbury. Several of the Reeve's characteristics, especially that he once was a carpenter (I.3861), show up in the *Miller's Tale,* angering the Reeve and making many a critic suspect that the tale exploits an actual incident from the Reeve's marriage. Others, like Robert M. Jordan, complain that such critics "exercise . . . imaginative ingenuity comparable to the writer's creative effort," while still others insist the pilgrims live only in the text and to imagine for them any dimension beyond the scant evidence of the *Canterbury Tales* is absurd.[2]

As with human beings in life, Chaucer's characters do not react to other characters as much as to their reputations. No matter that reliable reports may be lacking; a reputation may easily be created—by observing, extrapolating, and speculating. The Narrator's remark that the Pardoner must be either a gelding or a mare (I.691) creates a reputation that arises from the smooth face and high voice he can see and hear, not from certain private knowledge. The Wife's assumption that no clerk can speak well of women (III.706) rests on her observations of her bookish fellow pilgrim and her speculation that he must be like her scholarly fifth husband. Often individuals labor to stanch their reputations, disliking either their exaggeration or their accuracy. The Monk's decision to produce serious literature attempts to rebut the Host's patronizing comments about the gentle pasture where Whatsizname walks (VII.1928–33). The Host's sudden show of bravado, "I am perilous with knyf in honde" (VII.1919), tries to erase the suspicion that he may be the coward milksop his wife claims he is, better suited to a spinning wheel than a knife (VII.1897–1916). Something of this sort may lie behind the exchange between the Miller and the Reeve, for they behave toward each other as modern critics behave toward them, shaping their remarks on the basis of a suspected, rather than a known, past.

The Miller scores the first hit:

> "I wol telle a legende and a lyf
> Bothe of a carpenter and of his wyf,
> How that a clerk hath set the wrightes cappe." (I.3141–43)

An outrageous beginning. To a medieval audience the cliché, "a legende and a lyf," announces a religious text (*legend*) and an illustrative saint's life (*lyf*) as unambiguously as the phrase "once upon a time" announces a children's story to modern listeners. Anticipating a homily, few would miss the reference in the next line, "a carpenter and . . . his wyf." Everyone in the Middle Ages had heard this particular story a hundred times, and often seen Nativity plays enacted at festival time in town squares throughout England. Hence, the last of the three lines just quoted seems to promise a shocking story of Saint Joseph, a carpenter, cuckolded by the traditional perpetrator of bawdy shenanigans in *fabliaux*, a clerk.

Little wonder the three lines together meet with a sudden, rude volley. The objection, however, does not make the point we expect it to make. Instead of scolding the Miller for an anticipated blasphemy, the Reeve aims at a lesser offense, the injuring of any man and the defaming of any woman. This off-center parry, not some off-the-text information, exposes him to the second hit, the Miller's playful admonition not to take things personally. Its argument is mockingly simplistic. Since the major premise of his imagined syllogism, "no unmarried man is a cuckold," is true by definition rather than by logic, we cannot convert its double negative into a universal positive, "Every married man is a cuckold" (cf. I.3151–66). We learn nothing about either cuckoldry or married men. Nevertheless, the effectiveness of this teasing attack—magnified by presuming for this former carpenter a slow intelligence similar to the dull wit of the carpenter in the upcoming tale—may be measured by how long the Reeve simmers in silence without losing any of his desire to strike back.

The salvo which must await the conclusion of the *Miller's Tale* is again wide of the mark. Its beginning, fairly bubbling with animosity,

"So theek," quod he, "ful wel koude I thee quite
With bleryng of a proud milleres ye,
If that me liste speke of ribaudye . . ." (I.3864–66)

congeals to a bitterly sour exposure of personality. In short, the Reeve does take offense at the *Miller's Tale*—his personality precludes any other reaction. Most important, the Miller's certainty that the Reeve would act just as he does must have inspired the baiting attack in the first place.

This series of reactions, a process of drawing inferences about a character and on that basis predicting the character's future actions, insofar as it depends on one character's ability to visualize another's point of view, provides a revealing glimpse into the dynamism of the First Fragment. Chaucer seems to have placed several themes in a coordinated relationship with each other: awareness of the points of view of others, order, joy, and clearly defined spaces. We notice, as we proceed through the opening four tales, that as each successive teller's awareness of viewpoints other than his own decreases, his tale's respect for order, as reflected in its observance of discrete spaces and regard for the boundaries between them, similarly decreases.[3] There is also a marked decrease in the joy each successive tale contains.

The Knight's awareness of others' interests rests on abundant textual evidence. "He nevere yet no vileynye ne sayde / In al his lyf unto no maner wight" (I.70–71), the Narrator tells us. His admonition following the *Pardoner's Tale*, "Namoore of this, for it is right ynough!" (VI.962), reprimands the pilgrims for laughing at the Host and the Pardoner, as much as it rebukes these antagonists for arguing. His sincere invitation to both combatants to make peace and restore good cheer confers on them more dignity than they may deserve. His firm interruption of the Monk in the next fragment (VII.2767), after the tragedy of Croesus makes relief from heavy-handed moralizing seem ever more unlikely, takes particular care first to acknowledge the effectiveness of the Monk's *de casibus* tragedies before it chides him for ignoring the upward movement of Fortune's wheel.

This obvious ability to understand and empathize with others parallels the Knight's disposition to create a tale with clearly defined enclosures, in particular the prison cell, the garden, and the lists. He uses the first of these for the orderly representation of passion's imprisonment of Palamon and Arcite, the second to show Emelye's restriction to a defined genre and specific role within that genre, and the last, under the purview of three distinct oratories, to represent Youth's orderly ascent to maturity, when its unbridled passions play themselves out by following a law of nature as much as a decree of Theseus. Even Arcite's release from prison respects boundaries, since it occurs through a lawful order of Duke Theseus. Similarly the small threat Emelye makes to the orderliness expected of her, saying she prefers "to ben a mayden al [her] lyf" (I.2305), yields shortly to the tale's lawful, orderly design; she observes the limits of her garden, as it were:[4]

> "if my destynee be shapen so
> That I shal nedes have oon of hem two,
> As sende me hym that moost desireth me." (I.2323–25)

The tale's lone instance of a violated enclosure is Palamon's escape from prison, made necessary because Arcite's prior release means that Palamon too must be free, else no confrontation can occur. These details make clear a connection between the philosophic orderliness of the *Tale,* as discussed in the previous chapter, and its respect for spatial order, for real estate clearly marked off by walls, fences, forests, grandstands, and so forth.

The Miller is less deferential than the Knight, less solicitous of others. Yet he shows some awareness of how others might think or feel, if we can judge from the skillful way he toys with the Reeve. In this respect he shares characteristics with the majority of humanity, chiefly in pursuit of his own interests but capable of understanding another's. He may therefore be more complex than either the Knight, who is more altruistic than the average, or the Reeve, who is less so. The cuckolded Carpenter John of his tale may be monumentally stupid, ignorant of Cato's warnings about old men marrying young wives (I.3227–28), but he cares about the well-being of others. For example, he immediately comes to Nicholas's aid—with what rustic aid he knows (cf. I.3468ff.)—when he hears of his boarder's trancelike condition. And later, when he learns of an impending flood greater even than Noe's, John thinks first of his wife, "Allas, my wyf! / And shal she drenche? Allas, myn Alisoun!" (I.3522–23). The same combination of ambivalent attitudes marks the conduct of Absolon who may be foppish, artful, too studied to lead a normal life, but whose wholesome affection for Alisoun even her husband finds inoffensive.

For the most extended example of simultaneous self-interest and alter-awareness in the *Miller's Tale,* we must look to the *hende* clerk, who boards with the carpenter and his young wife. The consummate artificer whose skill outdoes everyone while undoing himself, Nicholas is to boudoir what Falstaff is to tavern. From his first sudden grope (I.3276) to "the revel and the melodye; . . . [the] bisynesse of myrthe and of solas" (I.3652–54) with Alisoun in the carpenter's bed, he seems single-mindedly bent on carnal pleasure. Nevertheless, his apparent preoccupation with flesh should not make us miss the enjoyment he derives from intellectual activity, especially (perhaps exclusively) when manipulating others. His ability to understand how people will behave determines his strategy for success, in one instance after a mere three lines, in another after a trance, a miracle play, a revelation, and some carpentry. In fact, it is this considerable ability, lapsing only in a final hubristic stretch, that discloses the chief object of Nicholas's love, himself in both his sensual and intellectual dimensions.

A witty indication of Nicholas's delight in his own person takes suggestive form in Chaucer's playful use of the psaltery—a stringed instrument plied with the hand—on which he has the Miller's young student perform a nightly melody. I do not mean to imply that Nicholas's psaltery is not a musical instrument. But readers who see it as only a musical instrument should pay closer attention. Of course, there is no indication that it is more than a musical instrument in the opening lines where it is described as occupying a prominent place in Nicholas's room (I.3213). Yet later, after the young man has forced his attentions on Alisoun, after she has agreed, provided they wait for a suitable time, and after Nicholas has rubbed her thoroughly about her loins, he then races to his room where he "pleyeth faste, and maketh melodie" (I.3306). To argue that we are to imagine a young man sublimating natural inclinations in literal music, applying his *hende* hand only to holy hymns, is to rob Chaucer of his greatest talent, the understanding of human nature.[5]

Other details suggest that Nicholas's self-satisfaction is not only onanistic, but derives from his ability to adopt the perspectives of other characters in the tale. His elaborate plan to remove John from the scene of his intended embrace with Alisoun, for example, affords him intellectual pleasure in imagining John's mental processes, so to speak, as John hears again the Mystery Play of Noe, believes he will be a second Noe, and that the dramaturgical enmity between Noe and his wife represented in that play will naturally attend this reenactment of the Great Flood. Though wonderfully creative through most of the tale, Nicholas's imagination falls short near its end, when Absolon surprises him by foregoing a second nocturnal kiss at the shot window for a vengeful lesson aimed at the buttocks.

Commensurate with the ambivalent sensitivity of his characters, the Miller is less than meticulous about his tale's spatial separations. Areas are clearly marked off, but often transgressed. The three tubs suspended from the roof to "save" the carpenter, his wife, and Nicholas are abandoned by two of them within twelve lines of being occupied. Earlier, when John was attempting to offer aid, he broke into Nicholas's room by ordering the door knocked down, a foreshadowing of the breaches to occur in his own room. Though the bedroom he shares with his wife ought to symbolize the sacrosanct nature of their marriage, it is penetrated first by Absolon's serenade (I.3352–69), and later by the clerk Nicholas who usurps the husband's place (I.3651). Its privacy is penetrated again by the activities at the shot window, whose very shape suggests the locus of violation to Alisoun's person. Never mind the most insulting penetration of all, which triggers the tale's climax.

The Reeve takes us farther down this road. The physical details and metaphors describing him in the *General Prologue*—his calfless legs, rusty blade, secrecy, and the shrewd, probably crooked way he pursues his own needs (I.587–622)—imply a man who seldom interacts with others. He rides to the rear of the other pilgrims (I.622), perhaps to keep an eye on them, lest they do to him what he probably does too readily to his employer. The sum of all these images, underscored later in his self-pitying *apologia* (I.3864–98), is an unforthcoming man limited to his own perspective. He thinks of himself, rather than St. Joseph, on hearing the word "carpenter," not only because the extended world was normally assumed to show us ourselves, as Kolve reminds us, but because the Reeve has no reference outside himself.[6]

Compared with the Miller's fun-loving romp where everyone tries to snatch a little pleasure, the *Reeve's Tale* has the barest hint of joy, a mere shadow of sensitivity, and then only when predicting the behavior of a loose stallion. And its demarcation between one space and another, one person and another, almost fades from sight. The Reeve's incomplete socialization makes him construct a tale where defined activities are usurped, where enclosures neither keep in nor keep out, indeed where all order recedes ever farther from view. Hardly a discrete space or boundary remains that has not been transgressed, unbound, or ignored. The manciple's job of bringing grain to the mill is temporarily assumed by two students whose northern dialect and innocence of the crafty world of the mill mark them as entirely out of place. They are no match for the experienced thief of a miller who believes "he hadde litherly biset his whyle / But if he koude two students bigyle" (to adapt one of Nicholas's self-assurances):

> "They wene that no man may hem bigyle,
> But by my thrift, yet shal I blere hir ye,
> For al the sleighte in hir philosophye. . . .
> 'The gretteste clerkes been noght wisest men.'" (I.4048–54)

Within a short time the students' "ybounde" (I.4060) stallion is set loose to trespass in a field reserved for mares. Half a bushel of their "sakked and ybounde" (I.4070) grain is liberated. The resolution of the tale comes about when the miller ignores the parallel between loose stallions and loose students, an odd inconsistency for one who routinely breaches boundaries. Impressed by his own cleverness, and certain the clerks cannot enter his domain with mere classroom skills, he fatuously enters theirs with a little anti-intellectual irony whose spatial metaphor underscores the disorder soon to occur:

> "Myn hous is streit, but ye han lerned art;
> Ye konne by argumentes make a place
> A myle brood of twenty foot of space.
> Lat se now if this place may suffise,
> Or make it rowm with speche, as is youre gise." (I.4122–26)

As his earlier promise to "blere hir ye" predicted success with grain, this taunt, describing what he thinks is a preposterous impossibility, ironically predicts the clerks' success with his daughter and his wife, achieved with "lerned art" and "speche." Think of the transgressions in the scene. First, Aleyn invades Malyn's bed and Malyn herself, without much resistance. Then the infant's cradle is appropriated, inducing the miller's wife to enter John's bed, and John to enter the wife. Aleyn's boastful recounting of the night's triumph, "I have thries in this shorte nyght / Swyved the milleres doghter bolt upright" (I.4265–66), now enters the wrong ear, causing the miller to reveal that he values Malyn for the wrong reason—not as a daughter but as a piece of goods—and setting off a brawl in which the wife, with the help of the Cross of Bromeholm, lays a staff upon the wrong head. The great fun that the climax provides as literature obscures an appalling social disarray in the whole tale, a mean-spirited tour-de-force of revenge: the miller's against the students' learning, Aleyn's against the miller's thievery, John's against Aleyn's sexual success, the wife's against what she assumes is the clerks' fistfight.

One transgression in the bedroom, however, produces the tale's lone encouraging moment. It occurs shortly after Aleyn, preparing to leave Malyn's bed, whispers a few sweet words into her ear. The context must first be understood before the full force of the scene can be appreciated. Aleyn did not enter Malyn's bed for the sheer pleasure of possessing her, but mainly to use her as a weapon of revenge for the miller's theft. Never admired for herself—she does not actually appear until the tale's end— Malyn is a quintessential one-night stand for Aleyn, a "wenche" (I.4178), an anecdote not even worth saving for an evening's merriment at Soler Hall, but for broadcasting to the first available ear. Despite these evident facts, Aleyn speaks to Malyn as if she were a courtly lady, worthy of a

troubadour's love song, a traditional *aube* found in countless courtly romances (Kaske 1959, pp. 295–310):

> "Fare weel, Malyne, sweete wight!
> The day is come; I may no lenger byde;
> But everemo, wher so I go or ryde,
> I is thyn awen clerk, swa have I seel!" (I.4236–39)

To all but Malyn these words are the transparent drivel a young man
suspects girls like to hear in such situations. But then, a magical transformation occurs. This thickly grown, pug-nosed, broad-buttocked (cf.
I.3973–75) chattel of her father recasts herself as the courtly lady Aleyn
pretended she was. Not only does she borrow terms from courtly literature, "deere lemman . . . goode lemman" (I.4240, 4247) and commend
him to God's keeping, but she actually rises to courtly conduct. She tells
him where her father has hidden the stolen grain. It is uncertain whether
Malyn here expresses gratitude for a night of loving attention, or responds
to the effect of an elevated poetic genre. This much is certain: Malyn's act
is the only noble gesture in an otherwise banal, niggardly, vengeful—albeit witty—tale.

We know nothing of the Cook as a person, save his abilities with food
and ale and his unfortunate "mormal" (I.386). We do suspect that he
misses the point of Solomon's advice, quoted as the Reeve completes his
tale, "'Ne bryng nat every man into thyn hous'" (I.4331). Although the
motto seems sympathetic to the miller, undone by letting two men spend
the night in his house, the whole speech applauds the miller's comeuppance. Whose side is he on, we wonder, the miller's or the clerks'? Very
likely he takes no side but his own. As one in an allied profession, about
which he promises a tale, he would appreciate the motto's sympathy for
innkeepers. Yet as one who enjoyed the tale (cf. I.4325–27), he takes pleasure in twitting the Host by endorsing the poetic justice it dishes out to an
innkeeper.

His tale obviously shows less respect for rules and place than the Reeve's,
as the Reeve's shows less than the Miller's, and the Miller's less than the
Knight's. If the *Miller's Tale* emphasizes the invasion of spaces, and the
Reeve's Tale shifts its emphasis to the invasion of property and people, the
Cook's Tale makes "invasion" a superfluous word. No invasion is necessary because no boundary exists. Perkyn Revelour apparently cares nothing about his apprenticeship, leaping "Out of the shoppe" (I.4378) as often
as he does. The twenty-three lines that describe him (I.4365–88) include
seven images of sudden movement, a hopping, leaping, dancing, dice-cast-
ing instability that invites as a simile the quick darting movements of a

goldfinch in the thicket. His master, too, seems to disregard the rules of apprenticeship, since he grants his charge written permission to leave, though the lad is far from adequate. Most appalling of all, the wife of the equally debauched companion with whom Perkyn intends to live reverses her life's compartments. The shop that ought to produce her income remains open only for the sake of appearances, while her sexual life, which ought to be the private activity of her marriage, produces her income.

The several elements one can find to applaud in the characters or action of the *Miller's Tale* and *Reeve's Tale* find no counterpart in the *Cook's Tale*. Following the exemplary, if humorless, *Knight's Tale*, the spontaneous naturalism of Alisoun, stands in sharp contrast to Absolon, whose anticipation is too naïvely eager, whose reaction to rejection is too outraged, to earn anything like scorn. Even the ingenuity of Nicholas wins him admirers. And we take some small satisfaction from the resourcefulness of Aleyn and John, from the comeuppance dealt their host, and especially from the momentary elevation of Malyn. But the Cook's brief performance contains not a single element to redeem either its characters or its action.

We are left at the end of Fragment I where Dante leaves us at the end of *Inferno*, with an image of two kinds of treason, spiritual and social. The final glimpse Dante gives of Hell shows Judas Iscariot, Brutus, and Cassius, best known in modern times as betrayers of their patrons. Taken together, however, they represent the undermining of the dual aspect of human existence that Dante emphasizes throughout the *Commedia*: the spiritual and the social, or Church and Empire in Dante's terminology. Judas's patron established the spiritual foundation of the medieval world; the patron of Brutus and Cassius, Caesar, laid the secular foundation of the Empire. Chaucer's First Fragment leads progressively to the same conclusion. Perkyn Revelour and by implication all others in the First Fragment whose thieving actions are of his sort destroy the social orderliness on which the most numerous and fundamental third estate, the working class, was based. Though his conduct is primarily secular in nature, his disregard for the conditions of his apprenticeship and for the service he owes his master carry spiritual implications as well. The wife's conduct is primarily offensive in a spiritual way, but has social overtones too. The shop she keeps for the sake of appearances compromises social order, while the more important breach of her own marital fidelity and the temptation that her sexual availability presents to others have powerful spiritual consequences.

❦

The *Man of Law's Tale*

To resurrect a world that vanished at the fifty-eighth line of the *Cook's Tale* (i.e., I.4422) the *Canterbury Tales* needs a new beginning. It is obvious that Chaucer intended the *Man of Law's Tale* to be this new beginning, for it contains passages closely paralleling the poem's concluding tale. Like a matched pair of bookends embracing everything that stands between them, the *Man of Law's Tale* and the *Parson's Tale* use nearly identical images of the sun as a universal, immutable indicator of the time of day, the exciting dynamic of a beginning and the inexorable movement bringing the cycle to an end, while also including closely similar images that undermine this permanence by calling attention to the cessation of time and the end of days, that is, to death.

"Degrees . . . fyve and fourty" (II.12) in the Introduction to the *Man of Law's Tale* anticipates the precisely measured "Degreës nyne and twenty" (X.4) in the *Parson's Prologue*. The former, an image of morning, alludes to an equilateral triangle, an absolute formula used here for measuring the sun's height, yet includes as one of the triangle's legs an insubstantial shadow, suggesting that all things are transitory:

> [He] saugh wel that the shadwe of every tree
> Was as in lengthe the same quantitee
> That was the body erect that caused it.
> And therfore by the shadwe he took his wit
> That Phebus, which that shoon so clere and brighte,
> Degrees was fyve and fourty clombe on highte. (II.7–12)

The latter, an image of late afternoon, relies on the same universal geometry to mark the sun's elevation, though its reference to the twenty-nine degrees through which it will swiftly set—hardly a coincidental reference to the twenty-nine pilgrims who began the pilgrimage (cf. I.24)—conveys an inescapable feeling of impermanence. This image too includes a shadow, now of the pilgrim author rather than of trees, to remind us that he and his fellow pilgrims—indeed all who are *nel mezzo del cammin di nostra vita* (*Inf.*, I.1)—are but shades in waiting:

> The sonne fro the south lyne was descended
> So lowe that he nas nat, to my sighte,
> Degreës nyne and twenty as in highte. . . .
> My shadwe was at thilke tyme, as there
> Of swiche feet as my lengthe parted were
> In sixe feet equal of proporcioun. (X.2–9)

An equally obvious parallel between the Second Fragment and the Tenth occurs in their prominent references to literature, where, again, the former lists Chaucer's works from the beginning of his career, while the latter views the entire career from a perspective close to its end. The idea of qualitative distinctions, which makes the Man of Law separate a "thrifty tale" (II.46) from a "wikke ensample" (II.78), moves the Parson to eschew fables and rum-ram-rufs—indeed, all fictions—in favor of "Moralitee and vertuous mateere" (X.38) and causes the pilgrim Narrator to be grateful for having written some works and repentant for writing others. Several levels of Chaucerian irony prevent us from inferring the critical principles on which these three pilgrims judge some works to have reached the permanent status of art and others to be ephemeral. But neither the quality of specific works nor the method by which they are judged concerns us at present; what interests us here is the principle of quality stressed at the outset of this new beginning and again at the close of the entire poem. With all human action, including literature, inherent merit matters.

While the concept of immutability—of both geometry in the extended world and aesthetics in the intuitive—reintroduces a principle not heard since the *Knight's Tale*'s disquisition on the permanence of Nature's cycles, the idea of impermanence sustains a theme that gained increased prominence as the First Fragment progressed. When the Reeve was indulging himself in a spate of dyspeptic metaphors to lament his advancing age, he twice referred to the "tappe of lyf" that Death draws until "almoost al empty is the tonne" (I.3892–94), emphasizing the wasting away of a life that ebbs with each drip. The metaphor reappears in the Host's words to the Man of Law, intended by him to call attention to wasted time. But the effect is entirely different:

> "Lordynges, the tyme wasteth nyght and day,
> And steleth from us, what pryvely slepynge,
> And what thurgh necligence in oure wakynge,

As dooth the streem that turneth nevere agayn,
Descendynge fro the montaigne into playn." (II.20–24)

The figure certainly stresses irreversibility, but its effect hardly emphasizes a wasted life. Here the mountain stream that trickles to the plain carries the imagination to what the fruitful plain will produce from its refreshed soil. Even the witty variation on irreversibility, the loss of "Malkynes maydenhede" (II.30), points forward to the new life that a loss of virginity often implies, as well as casting a knowing glance backward at the *Reeve's Tale* where, not three hundred lines earlier, a girl with the similar name Malin lost her maidenhood.[1] Instability may be as great a certainty in the beginning of Fragment II as it was by the end of Fragment I, but the force of the earlier appearance led to nothingness, here it leads to a new beginning.[2]

The *Man of Law's Tale* of a woman whose seemingly interminable wandering in a rudderless boat strains verisimilitude by lasting more than eight years (cf. II.499, 902) proves too strong for even a modern audience to resist reading symbolically, especially since the Tale follows the entropic Fragment I, where characters and tale tellers increasingly lose their social and moral bearings. In the previous chapter we saw that the living/ spatial arrangements of central characters grow less stable as Fragment I progresses. These circumstances, of no great significance in themselves, collectively focus attention on the more important ethical instability that has been increasing in significance from the *General Prologue* to the *Cook's Tale*. By the end of the First Fragment, then, there has been a growing sense that the main characters of these tales are approaching a condition of spatial, ethical, and moral aimlessness for which a rudderless boat is an ideal symbol. Hence the *Man of Law's Tale*, like an overture to a symphony or a banner carrying an emblematic heading, prepares us to understand the approaching parade of pilgrims who have somehow lost their way, have become distracted by transitory concerns they think more important than the lasting ones by which they should be living their lives. True it is that Custance is exiled from her rightful place by impious forces eager to destroy her, rather than by her own doing. Yet at the same time she represents perfectly those who, while on earth, journey as exiles from their rightful heavenly home. The real referents of this journey, for which the *Man of Law's Tale* serves as a kind of proem, are the pilgrims who will shortly tell their own tales.

This is not to suggest that Custance joins a long line of other medieval wanderers, like Long Will in *Piers Plowman*, Gawain in *Sir Gawain and the Green Knight*, Red Crosse Knight in the pseudo-medieval *Faerie*

Queene, and many others. The usual wanderer in medieval literature is in dire need of Christian Truth—often without realizing it—which eventually comes as a result of the wanderer's surviving arduous challenges during some quest. Despite the public profession of faith and the glorious reputation of Sir Gawain—to take the most obvious example from those just noted—his adventure with the Green Knight reveals a shaky interior, more deeply involved with form than faith at the beginning of the poem, more devoted to a green girdle than to God's Providence at its end. Custance is a reverse image of the typical wanderer—indeed, perhaps not a wanderer at all. The certainty of her unblemished spiritual commitment to Christ at the outset of her series of ordeals clashes paradoxically with her precarious physical circumstances. Whereas Gawain's lapse of faith exposes him to grave spiritual danger, for which physical anxiety is but a symbol, Custance's unwavering commitment to Christ protects her from spiritual danger, symbolized again by her physical safety.

Again like *Sir Gawain and the Green Knight,* the tale of Custance pursues a second genre, inviting us to meditate on the relationship between the two, that is, between the literal story of a woman cast in a rudderless boat and an allegory of how displaced persons might find rudder and sail in their own lives. Double genres are not unknown in Chaucer, as is clear in chapter 4's discussion of the *Knight's Tale* where the story of Palamon and Arcite is both an allegory and a romance. Or in medieval literature in general. Indeed, the technique Chaucer (and perhaps Trivet before him) uses in the *Man of Law's Tale* conceptually parallels the technique in a more familiar example, the Old English poem *Beowulf.* Both works explore the relationship between well-known, highly significant events from the past and an individual life woven into these events. The Old English work accurately recreates the Germanic past as it was understood from scops' renditions of heroic lays, and doubtless from verbal accounts passed down from generation to generation, yet places among these stories the life of Beowulf whose historicity is highly doubtful. Beowulf's involvement in these events—participating in some, listening to others sung by scops or alluded to by the voice of the poem—gives coherence to what would otherwise have seemed a randomly recollected Germanic past. So too the *Man of Law's Tale* refers to historical figures approximately contemporaneous with each other—Tiberius, Alla, and Maurice—who might otherwise seem unrelated. The Custance whom we find among these people and whose presence highlights and unifies specific aspects of their careers may well have been thought equally historical, as some believe.[3]

Nevertheless, we may assume that Nicholas Trivet, "one of the most

learned and sophisticated men of the fourteenth century," and certainly
Chaucer who used Trivet as his source, must have doubted the historical
accuracy of Custance's thrice being set in a rudderless boat to drift for
more than eight years—three years to get from Syria to Northumbria,
more than five from Northumbria to a location where a senator sailing
from Syria to Rome might intercept her. Never mind what others may
have thought, Trivet and Chaucer surely knew that, like the *Beowulf* poet,
they were placing a fictionalized woman and the even greater fiction of
her journey in an accurately recorded history. The difference between the
two works (among many other differences, of course) lies in the way we
would describe the history being represented. In *Beowulf* we see the history of constant bloodshed, of broken truces, and failed attempts to avoid
war among various Germanic tribes; in Chaucer's *Tale* we see a loosely
dramatized history of the spread of Christianity.[4]

That the *Tale* describes allegorically the method by which the homeward path may be found is perhaps less apparent than its suitability as an
emblem for all those who are wanderers still. On its surface the story
makes plain that Custance needs rescuing. She has been cast adrift, a prey
to the perilous winds and storms of lengthy voyages, because enemies
wish to destroy her. Yet, beyond a single reference to her sorrow, "After
hir deeth ful often may she wayte" (II.467), it never dwells on her hard-
ships at sea, nor shows her in grave danger. Certainly the voyage made
her a "wery womman ful of care," praying "The lyf out of hir body for to
twynne" (II.514–17), but we are not given this description until after she
lands in Northumbria (II.508). Indeed, five stanzas explain how she was
kept safe on her first voyage (II.470–504), while three others offer an
identical explanation for her survival on her second (II.827–33, 932–45):

> "In [Crist] triste I, and in his mooder deere,
> That is to me my seyl and eek my steere." (II.832–33)

On the other hand, wherever Custance travels in the Tale, conversion to
Christianity follows, for the ports at which she arrives are deeply involved
in the historical spread of Christianity. From a medieval Christian point of
view, if any saving occurs it is not the rescuing of Custance, whose faith has
been ever steadfast, but the salvation of the lands where Custance comes
ashore. Allegorically the lands she arrives at are saved, while the *gesta* aspect of the Tale preserves the story in which she herself is saved.

To emphasize a connection between Custance's arrival and the advent
of Christianity, Chaucer describes Custance's reception in Northumbria
with a line he would use again:

She was so diligent, withouten slouthe,
To serve and plesen everich in that place
That alle hir loven that looken in hir face. (II.530–32)

This same image occurs later in the *Clerk's Tale* when Griselda's arrival
suggests the joy of heaven, said to be at its greatest because of the constant presence of the face of God. Custance evokes from Chaucer fewer
scriptural allusions to the Christian God than Griselda does (see chapter
10), yet this powerful image suggests that he may have held her in the
same light in which he viewed Griselda, for it has no parallel in either
Trivet or Gower, yet is almost identical to the line describing Christlike
Griselda:

[She] koude so the peples herte embrace,
That ech hire lovede that looked on hir face. (IV.412–13)

The effect of Custance's presence receives added strength from the image of a lamb that Chaucer uses three times in the *Man of Law's Tale,*
twice unambiguously referring to Christ, "O cleere, o welful auter, hooly
croys, / Reed of the Lambes blood ful of pitee, . . . The Kyng of Hevene
with his woundes newe, / The white Lamb, that hurt was with a spere"
(II.451–59), and finally as an image of Custance[5]:

For as the lomb toward his deeth is broght,
So stant this innocent bifore the kyng. (II.617–18)

Here Chaucer again anticipates the parallel between Griselda and Christ:

Grisildis moot al suffre and al consente,
And as a lamb she sitteth meke and stille,
And leet this crueel sergeant doon his wille. (IV.537–39)

It is possible that Trivet, too, intended to stress conversion as a motif in
his telling of Custance's story. His sources follow several of the folk stories of young women persecuted by incestuous fathers, implying a motive
of ordinary lust—a self-referential desire that anyone can understand,
though deplore. Trivet alters this detail to have Custance persecuted by
evil mothers-in-law, perhaps because he wished to imply an objection to
the new faith Custance brought with her, requiring first the Syrians and
then the Northumbrians to abandon their old customs. Whatever Trivet
intended, Chaucer makes the point explicit, giving Alla's mother only one
motive for her horrible plot against Custance: "Hir thoughte a despit that
he sholde take / So strange a creature unto his make" (II.699–700), where
"strange" can only be understood as a reference to Custance's alien cul-

ture, including her Christianity, echoing the motive of the Sultan's mother some years earlier in Syria:

> The mooder of the Sowdan, welle of vices,
> Espied hath hir sones pleyn entente,
> How he wol lete his olde sacrifices. (II.323–25)

Further comparison of the three extant fourteenth-century versions of Custance's story suggests that Chaucer wanted to make conversion to Christianity the central motif of the *Man of Law's Tale*. All three texts include a scene in which Custance is one day walking by the sea with Hermengyld, newly converted by the recently arrived Custance. The party comes upon a blind man, one of only three other Christians living in Northumbria, the rest having fled to Wales. The blind man begs Hermengyld to restore his eyesight. Naturally fearful that her husband will learn of her Christianity and put her to death, she nonetheless yields to Custance's entreaties to "wirche / The wyl of Crist, as doghter of his chirche" (II.566–67). Chaucer's text keeps the miracle off-stage, as it were, by not explicitly saying the man was cured. It stresses, instead, the impact this encounter has on Hermengyld's husband, the constable, who converts to Christianity in the next stanza, though keeping this fact quiet for "many a wyntres space" (II.577). Chaucer obviously cares less about the miraculous curing of a blind man than about the subsequent conversion of the constable, a subtle shift of emphasis from both Trivet and Gower where the actual restoration of the blind man's sight is as important as the conversion:

> *Trivet:* E Hermigild, deuaunt Elda e sa mene qe lui suy, de bone fei e ferme fist sur lez eus de lui ennueugles la seinte crois e lui dist en sa laungge Sessone: "Bisene man, in Iesu name in rode ysclawe, haue thi sith." E si meintenaunt fu allumine, e regardoit bien e clerement. (Bryan and Dempster 1941, p. 170)
>
> *Gower:* Vpon his word hire herte afflihte
> Thenkende what was best to done,
> Bot natheles sche herde his bone
> And seide, "In trust of Cristes lawe
> Which don was on the crois and slawe,
> Thou bysne man, behold and se."
> With that to God vpon his kne
> Thonkende he tok his sihte anon,
> Whereof thei merueile euerychon . . . (*Conf. Aman.*, II.766–74)

Immediately following this scene Trivet shifts the subject to politics. First noting that most of the Christians of the day lived in Wales (a point Chaucer sensibly places before the miracle, to account for Hermengyld's concern for her husband's possible anger), Trivet then recounts that Hermengyld and her husband Elda went to Wales to be baptized, nodding in a most politic way to the Welsh Bishop Lucius, whom he later calls upon to marry Alla and Custance. Gower too emphasizes something other than Elda's acceptance of the Christian faith, namely the constable's eagerness to please the unmarried king by telling him of Custance. He also includes the identification of Bishop Lucius, though saving this historical detail for the wedding in Wales, after which he then transitions to the next evil plot against Custance. Chaucer alone leaves miracles and politics out of his story in favor of the effect that Custance and Hermengyld have on the constable, who converts to Christianity immediately.

The foregoing has attempted to point out that the *Man of Law's Tale* gets the *Canterbury Tales* going again by forging a link between the wasted world to which the First Fragment descends and the hopeful world that commences with the great collection of tales from the Wife of Bath's opening words to the end of the *Franklin's Tale*. With the possible exception of the Clerk, all of the seven pilgrims who will tell tales in this section of the poem—what I have been calling Part II—have lost their way, become wanderers not only to Canterbury but in their lives and perhaps because of this loss find themselves on Canterbury's road. Whether they will also recover their bearings, find rudder and sail, in the manner suggested by Custance's example remains to be seen.

PART II

7

爨

Stability and the Language of Agreements

It has been almost a century since George Lyman Kittredge set in place one of the most enduring canons of Chaucerian scholarship, that the tales extending from the Wife of Bath's to the Franklin's, that is, Fragments III, IV, and V, constitute "a whole act of [Chaucer's] Human Comedy," which has ever after been known by Eleanor Prescott Hammond's irresistible title "the Marriage Group."[1] Of the two parts of Kittredge's claim, that these tales constitute a group, and that the group is unified by the discussion of marriage, we might first inquire briefly into the manuscript evidence for the former, since Kittredge could not have known the great Manly-Rickert study of the manuscripts of the *Canterbury Tales*. In particular, what evidence is there among the extant manuscripts that each of these three fragments was intended by Chaucer to be a group by itself? And what may be said about the order in which he wanted these fragments, or these seven tales, to be arranged?

The fifty-seven manuscripts mentioned in chapter 2 as having enough of the *Canterbury Tales* to provide clues to the order Chaucer intended leave no doubt that he wanted Fragment III (WB, Fr, Su) to be a unit unto itself, since only eight manuscripts differ from Ellesmere and of these only one, Holkham, follows a different order.[2] The manuscript evidence that Fragment IV (Cl, Me) similarly constitutes an authorial unit, though less strong, is nonetheless still convincing. Nine manuscripts include perfect examples of Ellesmere's Fragment IV, nine more have variant links, and two more reverse the order of the two tales. Thus, in twenty of the fifty-seven manuscripts these two tales are contiguous. In another twenty-six manuscripts all the material intervening between the Clerk and the Merchant belongs to what we have been calling "the marriage group." Thus it is reasonable to conclude that Chaucer thought of the *Clerk's Tale* and the *Merchant's Tale* as related to each other, and virtually certain (forty-six manuscripts) he intended them to reside somewhere among the other five tales in Fragments III and V. The same may be said for the tales in Fragment V (Sq, Fk). Sixteen manuscripts follow the Ellesmere order, another reverses the order (Fk, Sq), and twenty-six more have these two tales surrounding one or more tales from Fragments III or IV, with no tale from outside this group intervening.

But now, let us make a daring assertion. Unless there is near certainty regarding the order of tales in a particular fragment (as there seems to be with WB, Fr, and Su in Fragment III), the appearance of two tales in the same fragment need not compel a conclusion that Chaucer always intended them to be contiguous in the larger poem. Apart from the sequence of tales in Fragment III, the order in which the remaining four tales are to appear cannot be determined purely on the evidence of the manuscripts. There are two rival orders for this section of the *Canterbury Tales,* which we may call the Non-Ellesmere order and the Ellesmere order. Despite scholarly preference for manuscripts of the Ellesmere type, eighteen manuscripts arrange these tales according to the ring structure of the Non-Ellesmere type (Figure 4), with four others showing a closer approximation of the Non-Ellesmere type than of the Ellesmere type.[3]

Sq., Me., │ WB., Fr., Su. │ Cl., Fk.

Non-Ellesmere Order — 18 MSS

Figure 4

The outer ring (Sq, Fk) holds the two tales that open in idyllic settings, are influenced by magic, and focus centrally on spoken falsehoods. The intermediate ring (Me, Cl) includes the two tales describing more-or-less arranged marriages that later develop serious difficulties, where subterfuge governs both stories, a false spouse threatens both marriages (Damian in *Merchant's Tale* and a presumed second wife in *Clerk's Tale*), and a reconciliation finally occurs. At the heart of the Non-Ellesmere order is the intact Fragment III.

Figure 5 displays the Ellesmere order, supported by eleven manuscripts that seem to be based on the temporal sequence of the Canterbury pilgrimage.[4]

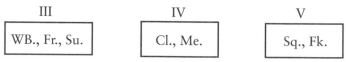

III	IV	V
WB., Fr., Su.	Cl., Me.	Sq., Fk.

Ellesmere Order — 11 MSS

Figure 5

Since the Clerk and the Merchant both refer to the Wife of Bath (IV.1170, IV.1685), we must assume that on their fictional pilgrimage they tell their tales after she tells hers. The evidence that Fragment V should follow Fragment IV rests on a similar assumption. Chaucer's decision not to identify the speaker who opens the Fifth Fragment, though the context clearly implies that speaker must be the Host, suggests that the speaker had already been mentioned by name, in other words was in mid-speech, as several manuscripts indicate by showing no editorial break between IV.2440 and V.1. If true, then only Fragment IV can possibly precede Fragment V, for it alone concludes with the Host speaking (see IV.2419–40).[5] Moreover, as Ralph Hanna III says, "The division into two fragments, done by Victorian students of tale order, is simply misleading" (Larry D. Benson 1987, p. 1128).

That the extant manuscripts provide persuasive arguments for both the Non-Ellesmere and the Ellesmere arrangements, though giving more weight to the former, should not be looked upon as evidence of scribal or editorial ruin (to use Donaldson's metaphor again), enticing the modern scholar to reconstruct the *author's* final intention. On the contrary, it should encourage us to accept that Chaucer was considering both arrangements and to imagine the questions he was trying to solve as he deliberated over the two. Although neither of these designs necessarily precludes the other, they emphasize different things. A linear design is analytic and experiential; a spatial design is synthetic and ontological. Linear designs emphasize causal relationships and the passage of time as the post-lapsarian world experiences it. Spatial designs represent a distanced, timeless stance, as if one viewed the whole from afar and saw at once the connections among all its parts. Items presented in a linear sequence can represent thought in the process of occurring, as one idea gives rise to another, while spatial designs, especially ring structures, emphasize the completeness, the separability of a philosophical idea whose complexity is only grasped with difficulty.

While it is theoretically possible, though enormously demanding, for an author to represent his material as linear experience, say in a temporal sequence like the Canterbury pilgrimage, yet also present the subject in all its intricacy, there is no evidence in the surviving manuscripts that Chaucer attempted such a combination for the first half of the *Canterbury Tales*. The rival orders for the seven tales we have been discussing point *either* to the strongly developed Ellesmere pattern where each of the six tales following the Wife of Bath's picks up some thread she has left dangling, but suggests nothing about the ontology of its chief subject, *or* to the prominent ring structure of the Non-Ellesmere type where some organic unity is suggested but no concession is made to an unfolding scene.

The revisions Chaucer made to the ends of the *Clerk's Tale* and the *Squire's Tale* shed light on which design he turned to and are also instructive in suggesting why he did so. The original lines IV.1212a–g at the end of the *Clerk's Tale* do not anticipate the next tale, and are therefore a perfectly suitable conclusion for tales arranged in a circular pattern where continuity from one tale to the next is not a requirement. Then too, the abrupt cessation of the *Squire's Tale* and the absence of a Squire-Franklin link (the link we now have is, after all, missing from twenty-two manuscripts) would tend to imply an arrangement according to ring structure. On the other hand, the links that all editors now believe represent Chaucer's final intention make obvious the connections between the preceding and following tales. Lines IV.1213–44 exposing the Merchant's transparent self-concern also identify Griselda by name (IV.1224), echo the "wepe . . . and waille" (IV.1212) of the Clerk's conclusion, and make a ludicrous disclaimer regarding the tale about to be told. Similarly, the lines between the Squire's abruptly concluded tale and the Franklin's pedantic opening lubricate the transition from one view of romance to another, from one set of assumptions about literature to another. It is obvious, therefore, that Chaucer changed his strategy for the first half of the poem. As he revised his material he apparently decided to reject ring structure in favor of a purely chronological sequence.

Here we might recall an observation made at the outset of this book, that the pilgrims who tell tales in the first half of the poem concentrate on rearranging the world as each tale-teller thinks the world might best be ordered, while the second half includes various longings for an order of perfection not normally found in the extended world. In keeping with this pattern of oppositions, the chronological sequences by which life must be lived on earth are better suited to the first half of the poem, while the spatial structures that reflect philosophical and/or aesthetic order seem more appropriate to the second half.

Let us now turn to Kittredge's second point, with which I must disagree: that these tales are unified by the subject of marriage. To be sure, it is unseemly for a modern critic to argue against Kittredge. What does it matter that only four of these seven tales focus squarely on marital relations, and that many other tales elsewhere in the Canterbury group have as much, or more, to do with the same subject, when the whole field of Chaucer studies has so benefited from the discussion which that most footnoted of all Chaucerians first introduced?

Among the many attempts to develop Kittredge's thesis one of the most insightful is a comparison of the Wife and the Friar by Penn R. Szittya.

Referring to "the two fictional levels in which the Chaucerian world operates, the world of the frame and the world of the tales themselves," Szittya notes that "relations among the pilgrims are dramatic while relations among the tales tend to be thematic" (1975, p. 386). He chooses the latter for special attention, rather than focus on the frame and its dramatic relationships, which would have drawn him into the usual discussion of the Friar's attempt to requite the Summoner. The result gives us what is perhaps the first long look at the Friar's thematic relationship to the Wife. The strong parallels Szittya finds in language, structure, and characterization prompt him to pose a key question:

> If the Wife's, Friar's, and Summoner's tales are seen as an interlocking series of responses to each other, does this mean that the two clerics' squabble is not . . . an interruption of the Marriage Group at all, but in fact part of it? (p. 392)

Even before considering Szittya's specific arguments, one is inclined to answer an emphatic "Yes!" It is highly unlikely that Chaucer would have arranged these tales—indeed all seven tales from the Wife's to the Franklin's—into a single group, as almost all the manuscript evidence suggests he did, without giving attention to their thematic unity. But intuition cannot guide us to the unity of this section; we must base our arguments on the text. Provided we resist the twentieth-century title "Marriage Group" and the consequent implication that the tales that do not concern the problems of marriage (FrT, SuT, and SqT) are conceptually different from the performance of the Wife, which is awash in them, Kittredge's proposal that Fragments III, IV, and V should be considered a unit unto itself still provides the best approach to the text.

The prologues and tales in this group that unquestionably concern marriage—those of the Wife of Bath, the Clerk, the Merchant, and the Franklin—parallel each other in an interesting way. All four include a serious threat to the intimacy that marriage exclusively reserves to spouses. Nothing unique yet, since real or imagined adultery lurks in the whole of literary history. Here, however, marital fidelity parallels linguistic fidelity. The question of whether someone has remained faithful to his or her marriage arises at the same time as the question of which truth is being accurately reflected in a given speech: objective reality, or the speaker's attempt to manipulate a listener. Let us note a few examples. The Wife of Bath, the first pilgrim in this group to exploit language as a tool for concealment, appears especially eager to establish an ambivalent sexual reputation, suggesting on the one hand that she was a frequent adulteress (cf. I.467, III.243–45, III.397–99) and on the other that she has remained technically chaste throughout her whole life (cf. III.447–49, 484–88). She leaves even the Narrator in some doubt about her premarital experience:

Housbondes at chirche dore she hadde fyve,
Withouten oother compaignye in youthe. (I.460–61)[6]

Whether the pilgrim Chaucer refers here to a youthful innocent or a young wanton is beside the point, when Alisoun's own voice speaks ambivalently enough, not only on the matter of extramarital activity, but on every other subject as well. In the *Clerk's Tale,* too, Walter's literal announcement of a second marriage (IV. 954) masks his ploy to test yet again Griselda's vow of obedience. That this "second wife" is in fact Griselda's long-lost daughter reveals not only Walter's falsehood in announcing a new marriage but also his earlier falsehood in insinuating the deaths of Griselda's children. In the *Merchant's Tale,* the young wife May, caught trysting in a tree, claims that her mere "struggle with a man" (IV.2374) was designed to restore her husband's eyesight. It scarcely matters whether January accepts this false explanation or merely pretends to do so. Both possibilities underscore the disparity between speech and intention. The motif shows itself with equal clarity in the *Franklin's Tale,* where Dorigen's actual promise to become Aurelius's love, if he removes the rocks threatening her husband's return, not only plays at obvious make-believe (V.988) but means precisely the opposite, that she will never become his love because her marriage to Arveragus is as solid as the rocks on Brittany's coast.

The skeptical reader might well object that a large difference separates a husband's claim of a forthcoming marriage, which in fact will never take place (*Clerk's Tale*), from a woman's ingenious explanation on being caught by her husband in the arms of another man (*Merchant's Tale*). Agreed. But this difference demonstrates all the more strongly that the common motif in these four tales is not only marriage, but also the relationship between language and meaning, especially when that language bears on a prior promise.[7]

Once we understand this unifying theme, we need no longer exclude from the group the *Friar's* and *Summoner's Tales* with the irrelevant dismissal that they merely provide a humorous interlude in the continuing debate about marriage. For these two tales point out that the Wife's performance should be viewed in a much larger context than marriage. They serve as glosses—footnotes clarifying the central point of the Wife of Bath's performance—by continually emphasizing the hazards of using language as a tool for deception. Similarly, the *Squire's Tale,* usually excluded from the discussion, makes the same point, since false language is its most sustained theme. In the tale within that tale a peregrine falcon explains to Canacee that her tercelet lover, who "swoor he yaf his herte to me" (V.542), broke that pledge of eternal love. Lacking Canacee's mirror, the falcon could not recognize that her lover's devotion, which faded in the presence of "newefangelnesse" (V.610), would be different from his pledge:

> "sodeynly he loved this kyte so
> That al his love is clene fro me ago,
> And hath his trouthe falsed in this wyse." (V.625–27)

There is little wonder that scholarship has given less attention to this larger genus than to the narrower subject, for marriage is often thought to be society's most intriguing social institution. And yet, whatever else may be said of it—that it is a sacred institution, that it legitimizes one of the strongest human impulses, and so forth—it has its origin in a verbal agreement between two parties. In essence marriage is a contract, a subset of language. All contracts, including marriage, are subject to doubt as to whether both parties understand the language of their agreement in the same way and whether that language accurately reflects the intention of each. But unlike other contracts, whose language by itself creates enforceable terms, marriage depends on the understanding that the spoken words that create it and the unspoken intention of the parties entering it not disagree in any way. In the Christian era equivocation could well mean that no marriage exists.[8] Four of these tales certainly make us wonder whether all the characters within understand their marriage contracts in the same way. But *all* of these tales force attention on the larger genus, the entire range of human agreements. In order to emphasize this larger subject, Chaucer shapes the *Friar's* and *Summoner's Tales* into a kind of essay on equivocation, which both unmasks the Wife of Bath's preceding hour on stage, her *tour de force* of linguistic deception, and unifies the entire group of seven tales. To Szittya's question, then, we shall offer a qualified "Yes." The *Friar's* and *Summoner's Tales* do respond to the Wife's performance, not in the sense that they add new or contradictory ideas to her wide range of subjects, but in the sense that they highlight a serious flaw in her character by focusing on the essence of her performance, the relation between literal language and intention.

Kittredge's missed emphasis notwithstanding, he was absolutely correct that the tales of Fragments III, IV, and V—all of them—are very tightly organized. Figure 6 shows how these seven tales, newly arranged around the larger topic of whether language and meaning agree or disagree, divide into two opposing methods for improving the social order:

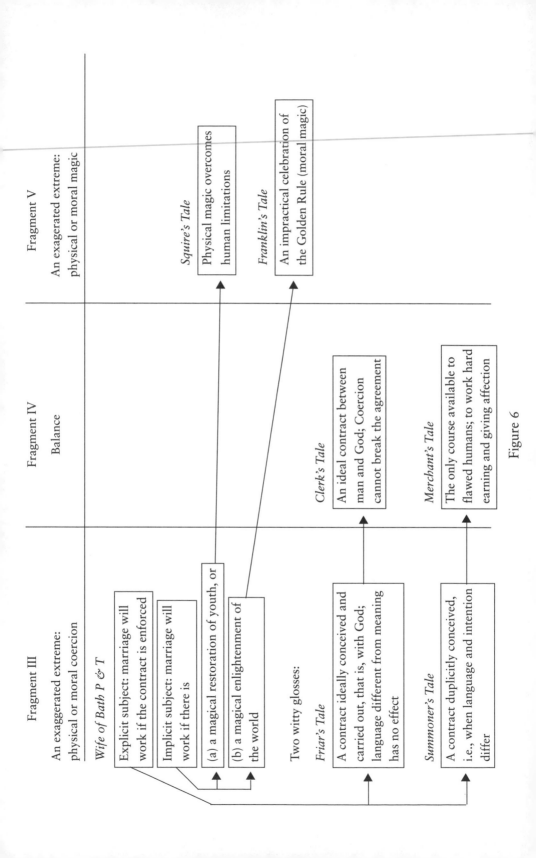

Fragment III

An exaggerated extreme:
physical or moral coercion

Wife of Bath P & T

Explicit subject: marriage will
work if the contract is enforced

Implicit subject: marriage will
work if there is

(a) a magical restoration of youth, or

(b) a magical enlightenment of
the world

Two witty glosses:

Friar's Tale

A contract ideally conceived and
carried out, that is, with God;
language different from meaning
has no effect

Summoner's Tale

A contract duplicitly conceived,
i.e., when language and intention
differ

Fragment IV

Balance

Clerk's Tale

An ideal contract between
man and God; Coercion
cannot break the agreement

Merchant's Tale

The only course available to
flawed humans; to work hard
earning and giving affection

Fragment V

An exaggerated extreme:
physical or moral magic

Squire's Tale

Physical magic overcomes
human limitations

Franklin's Tale

An impractical celebration of
the Golden Rule (moral magic)

Figure 6

either by enforcing the literal language of agreements, or by invoking magic.

The *Friar's Tale* and *Summoner's Tale* wittily gloss the strategy of enforcement as well as touch off the two tales of Fragment IV, with the *Friar's Tale* giving rise to the *Clerk's Tale* and the *Summoner's Tale* touching off the *Merchant's Tale*. Both the *Friar's Tale* in Fragment III and the tale which it inspires in Fragment IV, the *Clerk's Tale*, show the implications of the contract between God and individual human beings by showing what happens when one party to an agreement honors the literal meaning of words, while the other does not. In the *Friar's Tale* the contract is ironically honored by the devil who virtually represents God by articulating His covenant with humanity; in the *Clerk's Tale* the contract is honored by Griselda, a nearly allegorical representation of Christ. Similarly, the *Summoner's Tale* and its companion, the *Merchant's Tale*, develop the same point, a practical description of what happens when neither party to an agreement honors the literal meaning of his words. Finally, the two tales of Fragment V develop the second suggestion, that magic may be the last resort for a disintegrating society. The *Squire's Tale* celebrates the physical magic of a golden ring whose power protects against verbal deception, while the *Franklin's Tale* extols the ethical magic of the Golden Rule where social order is maintained when each party to an agreement wishes not to be outdone in *gentillesse*.

❄

Two Weavers from Bath

Somewhere between London and Canterbury a voice, loud from anguish yet clear from hope, shatters the air to announce one of the greatest characters in all of English literature:

"Experience, though noon auctoritee
Were in this world, is right ynogh for me
To speke of wo that is in mariage." (III.1–3)

Unlike fragile heroines who rarely express their hope that ardent lovers might enter their beds, Alisoun of Bath proclaims genuine appetites in a refreshingly real, personal style very different from anything yet heard in the *Canterbury Tales*. There is, of course, danger in yielding to this appeal. If characters like Griselda and Emelye seem unrealistic because they hardly ever express their inner passions, might not Alisoun be equally unrealistic since she seems to speak of nothing else? Indeed, the longest debate concerning the Wife—as yet far from adjourning—focuses on degree: Is she realistic enough to be a particularized individual, or so unrealistically exaggerated that she can only be an iconographic symbol? From time to time this discussion has wandered to fields remote from the Wife's haunts, revealing indecision not unlike her own. Walter Clyde Curry, one of the finest early scholars of the Wife of Bath, argued with convincing erudition that her character could be entirely explained by the contradictory influences of the heavens at the moment of her birth, but at the same time rejected such a theory for leaving her little better than a "highly colored dummy."[1] The equally erudite, though oppositely oriented D. W. Robertson, Jr., revealed a similar indecision by basing remarks like the following on contradictory assumptions:

Alisoun of Bath is not a "character" in the modern sense at all, but an elaborate iconographic figure designed to show the manifold implications of an attitude.[2]

To say "Alisoun . . . is not a 'character,'" rather than "Alisoun has no character," implies a discussion of the literary context itself, that Alisoun responds to people and things within the *Canterbury Tales*. But the words "designed to show" suggest her existence in the imagination of her creator and his readers, who are not themselves part of the *Canterbury Tales*. These are two very different Alisouns. The obligations placed on the Alisoun who is "designed to show" something do not preclude the other from possessing a fully developed personality for her fellow characters to perceive. As Curry's earlier studies took him aloft, Robertson's took refuge in the fourteenth century, that is, in what he called "historical criticism," by arguing for the Wife of Bath's relation to material in St. Augustine, Peter Lombard, the *Glossa Ordinaria,* and St. Jerome, which would have been familiar, he claimed, to the fourteenth century.[3]

The studies of Curry and Robertson—great as they are—demonstrate two hazards in working with the Wife of Bath. In order to encompass the magnitude of Chaucer's creation, critics are often eager, first, to have it both ways: in Curry's case to have the preclusive influences of Mars and Venus neatly embodied in a character type, and at the same time to hold out for the uniqueness of this particular individual; in Robertson's to have an example of what the anti-feminist tradition warned against, and to have a woman so unreal as to make that same tradition seem to attack a chimera. Second, critics frequently reach for analogues whose contradictions are somehow said to explain the contradictions in the Wife. Robert A. Pratt, for example, suggested a sequence in which Chaucer is said to have composed the Wife's part of the *Canterbury Tales.*[4] Chaucer's changes in direction, his adjustments of balance and emphasis, and the general evolution of his aesthetic design, sound plausible in Pratt's speculations. But the detailed explanation of this creative odyssey takes the place of an explanation of the Wife, and inevitably suggests that the conflicting aims of a developing process in writing are responsible for disunity in the Wife. Yet Pratt, too, wishes to have it both ways, for he makes the Wife seem a more coherent character than her alleged piecemeal construction might otherwise have produced. Similarly Curry's persuasive explanation of the conflicting influences of the planets quietly passes for an explanation of the Wife's conflicting impulses. And when Robertson denies the Wife's individuality in favor of a moot court of Canon Law, he invites the chilling judgment that the devil made her do it.

Despite the appeal of many of the studies just noted, the most reliable interpretations of the Wife of Bath still come from the subject herself, that is, from the thought processes that might be inferred from what she actually says. As Pearsall has noted, her character takes shape as one of Robert Browning's dramatic monologuists comes to life, as a "nexus of conflict" disclosed in a "totally unforced revelation."[5] In the light of such a method it may be useful to offer here a summary of what will be argued in the following pages.

The *Wife of Bath's Prologue and Tale* can be blocked out as neatly as the acts and scenes of a stage play. The first part of the Prologue (III.1–162), an appeal to authority, professes a traditional theory of sex and marriage derived from Scripture, "wexe and multiplye; / That gentil text kan I wel understonde" (III.28–29). Following an interesting exchange with the Pardoner (III.163–92), the second part (III.193–452) describes the experience of her first three marriages as well as her response to that experience. During this section she seems unaware that her manipulative practices in these three marriages, as she describes them, contradict the theory she enthusiastically proclaimed earlier. The last part of her Prologue (III.453–828), recalling her fourth and fifth marriages, brings her bifurcated nature into clearer focus by disclosing the hidden yearning that has probably been her only lifelong desire: not to live according to the theory of sex and marriage she articulated at first, nor to behave as the sovereign shrew she described thereafter, but simply to love and be loved in return.

For there are two Weavers from Bath pointing toward Canterbury. One we may call the "Wife," who claims publicly that throughout her five marriages she has always had power over her husbands and led a supremely satisfactory life. The other we may call "Alisoun," whose unguarded remarks let slip the sad, private woman who wants to love her husband but cannot make him love her. Fluctuating like nature itself, she struggles to harmonize the competitive, worldly values of the public Wife with the laudable, interior values of the private Alisoun.[6] Unfortunately, she applies the Wife's methods to reach Alisoun's goals, not only losing her objective but guaranteeing that loss. Finally, her Arthurian *Tale* (III.857–1264) exposes the anguished reality her boisterous public personality has been trying to conceal. The two centers of interest in the *Tale,* the knight-rapist and the old hag, confront each other as the symbolic representatives, respectively, of the Wife's public and private selves, here unprotected by the elaborate facades that shielded them in the *Prologue.* To unmask the public posture of a woman who delighted in always gaining control of her husbands, the *Tale* creates the image of a knight-rapist who gains that control through physical force. Similarly, it replaces the raucous sounds of a life she claims is filled with love and affection with the desperate echoes of a lonely old hag reduced to trapping a husband through moral force. But the *Tale* also differs from the *Prologue* by managing to reconcile these competing standards. Whereas the woman herself still fluctuates between the Wife's worldly pose that boasts success and Alisoun's private reality that still longs for it, the unlikely couple she creates in her *Tale* at length seem to reconcile their differences in a marriage apparently based on mutual love and respect. Like a phase transition in nature, hag and knight miraculously reach the loving state that the Wife of Bath herself has perhaps never known.

THE PUBLIC FACADE

Alisoun's first sentence does not actually claim a division between "experience" and "auctoritee," but implies instead that these two sources of knowledge reinforce each other. Nevertheless, by positioning the inductive and deductive dialectic at opposite ends of the first line, the sentence foreshadows the internal division of the Wife herself. Although she mentions experience first, suggesting her eagerness to share it, an interesting chain of associations leads her elsewhere. To claim experience requires a foundation, but to base that experience on a foundation of five successive marriages calls for self-defense, in view of clerkish opinions that successive marriages were unlawful. Thus she postpones the subject of her experience until she first legitimizes it, turning to authorities, not on the "wo that is in mariage" that she originally promised, but on the legality of five marriages.[7] This characteristic of altering her direction under the pressure of an audience's imagined reaction shows up again and again in the Wife's discourse.

She introduces her authorities for successive marriages by first alluding to one of St. Jerome's arguments against them:[8]

"But me was toold, certeyn, nat longe agoon is,
That sith that Crist ne wente nevere but onis
To weddyng, in the Cane of Galilee,
That by the same ensample taughte he me
That I ne sholde wedded be but ones." (III.9–13)

If this is a literal, rather than symbolic argument, it disintegrates in its own absurdity. By paraphrasing a ridiculous argument from a typical antifeminist tract, the Wife undercuts the tradition while also introducing important evidence for the legitimacy of marriage. Because of Christ's presence at Cana and the foreshadowing miracle He performed there, the exemplum as a whole emphasizes the sacramental nature of the ceremony, despite its misinterpretation by Jerome to prohibit successive marriages.

If this rhetorical refutation of Jerome has been missed, a logical refutation follows in a second exegetical argument that misconstrues the biblical account of Christ and the Samaritan woman (John 4:6ff.) in the same way Jerome misconstrued the story of the marriage feast at Cana:[9]

> "Herkne eek, lo, which a sharp word for the nones,
> Biside a welle, Jhesus, God and man,
> Spak in repreeve of the Samaritan:
> 'Thou hast yhad fyve housbondes,' quod he,
> 'And that ilke man that now hath thee
> Is noght thyn housbonde,' thus seyde he certeyn.
> What that he mente therby, I kan nat seyn;
> But that I axe, why that the fifthe man
> Was noon housbonde to the Samaritan?
> How manye myghte she have in mariage?" (III.14–23)

Like the exemplum of the marriage feast at Cana, this story of Christ and the Samaritan woman stresses the difference between a sanctified union and an illegitimate one, but is misunderstood by the Wife to focus on the correct number of spouses one may successively have: five, if one merely misinterprets the scriptural text; four, if one both misreads and misinterprets it as St. Jerome and the Wife do.[10]

If we wish to focus exclusively on the character of the Wife of Bath, we are faced with two possible interpretations, that she deliberately misconstrues the story to direct attention to Jerome's misconstruction, or that she naïvely misinterprets it. Resolving the matter may not be crucial, since her more important point is to remind her listeners that Christ's exact words unmistakably identify the same number of husbands she herself has had: "Thou hast yhad fyve housbondes." Having thus disingenuously (or perhaps unwittingly) rebutted the arguments *against* successive marriages, the Wife can now shrewdly appeal to other Old and New Testament exempla that argue *for* them.

But if we are also seeking Chaucer's unifying principle for this long stretch of tales introduced by the Wife's performance, we should not overlook the theme clearly laid before us in these opening lines: that different characters often take different meanings from the same language. The scriptural account of the woman at the well has a central point plain for all to understand, one would think. Yet the response to the passage, first by Jerome whom the Wife of Bath is paraphrasing, and then by the Wife herself, emphasizes a meaning so different from what the text implies that it distorts the passage. The phenomenon also occurs—in fact does so more often—in a character's manipulation of his or her own language. Of course, most of Chaucer's characters at one time or another use language that conceals their private thoughts, as any randomly chosen speech by Pandarus or Criseyde will confirm. But the tales that the Wife's performance initiates do more than employ this theme incidentally. They elevate the relationship between language and meaning to an organizing principle.

One widely held belief about language assumes a direct correspondence between objects and the words that signify those objects—between "referent" and "symbol," to use technical terms. We feel that when people speak to each other (apart from when they intend to speak playfully), they enter into an implied contract that their words will truthfully convey their thoughts. However, only very few verbal communications remain on a literal level, while most speech rests on convention somewhere between literal truth and complete falsehood. The more serious the subject or occasion the more likely that the language associated with it will approach literal truth; the less serious the more likely it will drift, not toward falsehood *per se,* but toward an artful relation to truth. But even this assumption may be too simple. Statements that appear to have literal meaning often call for some slight interpretation, because language is always artful to some degree.

The Wife of Bath's performance may be the *locus classicus* of artful language. Though her first lines make her sound like the most accessible of Chaucer's characters, she promises more than she delivers. Take her uncomplicated assertion, "after wyn on Venus moste I thynke" (III.464), which seems to call for only slight interpretation. "Wyn," connoting a session of drinking, and "Venus," symbolizing the lovemaking always associated with that goddess, almost certainly imply that whenever Alisoun was slightly intoxicated she would think about making love. However, we do not know where on the truthful/artful line the Wife of Bath casts this speech (or any other, for that matter), especially since she often speaks most artfully when she is most serious. The remark is placed in some doubt by an earlier, slightly more complicated comment:

"For wynnyng wolde I al his lust endure,
And make me a feyned appetit;
And yet in bacon hadde I nevere delit." (III.416–18)

(The Wife may partly have literal "bacon" in mind here, but for the moment her metaphorical sense interests us.) If "bacon" represents in this line the act of lovemaking, as the ten lines preceding it and the immediate antecedent "lust" (III.416) imply, then her distaste is surprisingly at odds with the wine-Venus connection just quoted. On the other hand, "bacon" may not refer to lovemaking, but to her husbands in general, on the ground that gristly, dried fleshmeat suggests something of her tired old first three husbands. If true, then her metaphor is strangely out of sorts with her immediate context. And if she means the whole concept of marital tranquility, which bacon clearly symbolizes 200 lines earlier (III.217), then we must doubt the implied objective of marital bliss for which she elsewhere says female sovereignty provides the best means. No matter. However elusive or false the line may be literally, it contains clear rhetorical truth, for this entire section of her *Prologue* discusses neither bacon, sex, nor anything of the sort. She is explaining the stratagem of using inducements to elicit desired responses. The specific inducement is unimportant. In other words, we are squarely in the world of rhetorical manipulation, talking about it and demonstrating it at the same time.[11] As she herself says four lines earlier, "With empty hand men may none haukes lure" (III.415). She knows the usefulness of sexual enticement as a means of gaining the sovereignty she claims she has always wanted.

We want to know where this artfulness stops. Since she has already admitted a fondness for rhetorical strategy, we wonder if every professed objective might not be an artful means for obtaining something else. Is sovereignty her final goal, or simply an artful means of achieving something else, as elusive to criticism as it may be to her? And none of the other information she volunteers about herself carries any greater assurance of truth. For example, her claim to have had five husbands, though never doubted, rests exclusively on her own word, yet lacks the corroborating evidence that offspring might provide. I am not suggesting that the claim is a fiction, though a woman of her verve would have little difficulty creating three wealthy husbands as the plausible source of her present financial independence, thus concealing its more pedestrian origin, a lifetime of work as a skillful cloth maker. Fiction or not, her self-report still provides our richest source for discovering the woman she may be trying to conceal.

At best the Wife scores a Pyrrhic victory with her interpretations of Scripture, since her mostly male audience probably believes "the devel made a wyf for to preche" (to adapt the Host at I.3903). Perhaps to prevent that reply she quickly concludes by denigrating the entire practice of interpreting Scripture while celebrating the one clear scriptural text that not even her antagonists can refute or misread:[12]

"Men may devyne and glosen, up and doun,
But wel I woot, expres, withoute lye,
God bad us for to wexe and multiplye;
That gentil text kan I wel understonde." (III.26–29)

The two remaining sections of this opening movement of the Wife's
Prologue—one a fifty-five-line argument unimpeachably placing virginity
in proper perspective (III.59–114), the other a wonderfully logical thirty-
six lines on the function of external genitalia (III.115–50)—follow the
same pattern of concluding with noble dedications to life and love:

"I wol bistowe the flour of al myn age
In the actes and in fruyt of mariage." (III.113–14)

"In wyfhod I wol use myn instrument
As frely as my Makere hath it sent." (III.149–50)

Since she has been justifying the use of sex organs by arguing the necessity
and legitimacy of procreation, these lines on the use of her instrument
also imply the procreation that comes with it. Thus, each of the three
arguments that open her Prologue proclaims the laudatory ambition to
impart life. The ultimate conclusion—perhaps also final refutation of
Jerome—could not be stated more persuasively: marriage and especially
sex are good because they lead to procreation.

Before returning to her first order of business, her experience in marriage, the Wife shows again how her rhetoric and her sense of audience
lead her from one subject to another. In the midst of a convincing statement of resolve she surprisingly converts that noble dedication into a
shrewish battle for sovereignty:

"If I be daungerous, God yeve me sorwe!
Myn housbonde shal it have bothe eve and morwe,
Whan that hym list come forth and paye his dette.
An housbonde I wol have—I wol nat lette—
Which shal be bothe my dettour and my thral,
And have his tribulacion withal
Upon his flessh, whil that I am his wyf.
I have the power durynge al my lyf
Upon his propre body, and noght he.
Right thus the Apostel tolde it unto me,
And bad oure housbondes for to love us weel.
Al this sentence me liketh every deel." (III.151–62)

The first two lines (III.151–52) merely enforce the point she has been
making all along. However, the third line, containing the powerful image

of a debtor and particularizing the ambiguous "it" of the previous line, is a familiar circumlocution for marital sex. Similarly, the next line, "An housbonde I wol have—I wol nat lette—" flows naturally from arguments she advanced above, but again prompts her to define the particular activity that makes a husband pertinent to her point—that is, sexual companionship. That activity again calls for the familiar circumlocution, this time expanded to both "dettour and . . . thral." The remaining seven lines simply surrender to the power of her metaphor, abruptly converting her exegetical methods into a mode of discourse aimed specifically at married laymen.

When Alisoun finally enters the vast sea of her prior experience, her subjects may change, but her technique of trimming her discourse to suit some present tack remains unchanged. Let us take as an example one of the first pieces of information we learn about her experience as a married woman, her swift judgment on her five husbands:

> ". . . tho housbondes that I hadde,
> As thre of hem were goode, and two were badde.
> The thre were goode men, and riche, and olde." (III.195–97)

She must have in mind her first three husbands as the good ones, since she clearly says that her fifth was poor and twenty and that her fourth was sexually active, implying his youth. However, when we look for the basis of her evaluation, the remark is difficult to understand. She certainly disparages the lovemaking of her first three husbands (III.198–202), and their companionship, too, if we can judge from the lengthy shouting matches she says she had with them. Conversely, if we look ahead to the two "bad" husbands, to discover her basis for evaluating them, her criteria recede even farther, since her fifth husband would seem to the average sensibility to have been ideal on all counts. If, however, Alisoun intends the early stages of her Prologue to establish a kind of success different from the one she claims later, there may not be as sharp an inconsistency as initially appears. If Alisoun were interested first in establishing her commercial success, her first three husbands would naturally be called "good," since they were quick providers of wealth; if she later wants to claim success in marriage, her last mate would naturally be called "good," since he was a virile, loving husband.

Confirmation that the Wife's language must be interpreted in the light of her tactical objectives, rather than as accurate reflections of her inner thoughts, may be found in the confusing question of her extramarital conduct. It may be, as Donaldson says, that "she is a habitual fornicator and adulterer."[13] Some evidence, though slight, does point in this direction:

(a) Housbondes at chirche dore she hadde fyve,
    Withouten oother compaignye in youthe . . . (I.460–61)

(b) She koude muchel of wandrynge by the weye. (I.467)

(c) ". . . if I have a gossib or a freend,
    Withouten gilt, thou chidest as a feend,
    If that I walke or pleye unto his hous!" (III.243–45)

(d) "I swoor that al my walkynge out by nyghte
    Was for t'espye wenches that he dighte;
    Under that colour hadde I many a myrthe." (III.397–99)

Since none of these lines clearly points to sexual indiscretion, Howard's view may be more accurate: "we may suspect her of being an adulteress, but it is part of Chaucer's game that we cannot come up with any evidence."[14] Indeed, lines I.460–61, above, may even assert Alisoun's innocence as a child. Instead of containing the strained ellipsis "she had five husbands without [counting] other liaisons in her youth," the remark probably omits the verb *to be:* "she had five husbands [but was] without other youthful experience." Elsewhere she implies an entirely traditional attitude to sex:

(e) ". . . I wol nat kepe me chaast in al.
    Whan myn housbonde is fro the world ygon,
    Som Cristen man shal wedde me anon." (III.46–48)

(f) "In wyfhod I wol use myn instrument
    As frely as my Makere hath it sent." (III.149–50)

(g) "And yet of oure apprentice Janekyn,
    For his crispe heer, shynynge as gold so fyn,
    And for he squiereth me bothe up and doun,
    Yet hastow caught a fals suspecioun.
    I wol hym noght, thogh thou were deed tomorwe!" (III.303–7)

(h) ". . . if I wolde selle my *bele chose,*
    I koude walke as fressh as is a rose;
    But I wol kepe it for youre owene tooth." (III.447–49)

Though the evidence for the Wife's promiscuity does not actually contradict the evidence for her conventional morality—the former does not admit fornication or adultery, the latter does not insist on marriage as an irrevocable condition for using her instrument—the evidence as a whole implies incompatible attitudes to sexual morality. If we look at these passages in the context of their intended audiences, however, a consistent pattern emerges. Those passages originally addressed by the Wife to her husbands, and subsequently quoted by her to the pilgrims, that is, passages (c), (g), and (h), contain specific disclaimers of wrongdoing. On the other hand, the passages addressed exclusively to the pilgrims, either by the Wife directly, or by her through the Narrator, that is, passages (a), (b), (d), (e), and (f), all belong in an ambiguous category, alluding to promiscuity as easily as to virtue. For our purposes here it is of no consequence whether the Wife tells the truth to her husbands and equivocates to the pilgrims, or the other way around. What does matter is that her audience, not truth, determines the substance of what she says.

Before examining other contradictions in the second part of the Wife's Prologue, it might be well initially to note some ideas about marriage, as a fourteenth-century Christian would have understood it. Often used as a metaphor to describe the union of Christ and the Church—Christ as the bridegroom, the Church collectively or each Christian individually as the bride—the institution of marriage acquired some of the properties of the metaphor.[15] As Scripture considers Christ the sovereign King over His spouse-subject, the Church, so a Christian husband thought of himself as sovereign over his wife.[16] Never mind that other scriptural evidence disagrees with this implied inequality, a fourteenth-century audience never doubted that God intended the husband to be the senior partner in every marriage.[17]

In addition to this popular notion of a husband's dominance over his wife, respected theologians were generally agreed on the nature and purposes of marriage. Thomas Aquinas states them well in a discussion of the Holy Family and the ideal Christian marriage:

> I answer saying that Marriage or wedlock is said to be true because it attains its perfection. Perfection of anything is twofold, however. The first perfection consists in its very form, from which it receives its species; while the second consists in its operation, through which in some way it attains its end. Now the form of matrimony consists in a certain inseparable union of minds, by which each partner is bound indivisibly to be faithful to the other. And the end of matrimony is the begetting and upbringing of children: the first of which [i.e., begetting] is attained by conjugal intercourse; the second [i.e., upbringing] by the other duties of husband and wife, by which they help one another in rearing their offspring.[18]

In England, Peter the Lombard's *Sententiae,* Book IV, would have been a more familiar authority than Aquinas, but Lombard's aims of marriage— derived from Otto, Bishop of Lucca,[19] Gratian, and ultimately Augustine—differed only in the order presented: "The institution of marriage is twofold. . . . First, that nature might be multiplied, second, that nature might be elevated, and vice suppressed."[20] Of course, many a theologian interpreted Thomas's *fides* and Lombard's "*ut natura exciperetur, et vitium cohiberetur*" as referring solely to the avoidance of adultery, as if the avoidance of evil could ever be a *bonum* in itself. But anyone familiar with marriage, in that age or any other, or anyone who had merely read the *Franklin's Tale*, would have difficulty deciding which is the more preposterous proposition: that mutual love and support are *not* a legitimate benefit of marriage implicit in the concept of *fides;* or that its only *bonum,* other than children, is sexual faithfulness. On the contrary, logic suggests that marital love is a necessary *a priori* condition from which sexual fidelity follows as a consequence; it is doubtful that sexual fidelity by itself would ever lead to marital love. Moreover, if the only legitimate purposes of marriage were reproduction and the avoidance of concupiscence, it is difficult to see why such a marriage would be a frequent metaphor for Christ's relationship with His church. It is reasonable to assume, therefore, that the average fourteenth-century Englishman accepted as the two chief aims of marriage, first, mutual faith and love, and second, the procreation and raising of children. Other purposes of marriage, such as the avoidance of lechery or as the means of rendering the marriage debt, received equal (sometimes excessive) attention but were widely believed to be venially sinful and thus in no way equivalent to the two primary aims. In any case, these lesser aims do not immediately concern us. In the light of this background let us return to the Wife of Bath to notice how the conduct she describes in the second part of her Prologue contradicts both the theory of marriage she stated in the first part and the accepted aims of a Christian marriage.

The Wife's lengthy self-quotation (III.235–378) makes a pathetic joke of one of the legitimate aims of Christian marriage, the comfort and solace each partner should offer to, and derive from, the other as they both work toward salvation. According to her own testimony she accuses one or another husband of visiting a neighboring woman (III.239), plotting with her maid (III.241), incessant complaining about her going out (III.244–45), drunken preaching (III.246–47, 381), distrusting her thrift (III. 308–9), and trying to lock her up (III.317). Scarcely pausing for fresh gulps of air, she energizes this attack with claps of thunder that carry undiminished across 600 years: "goth al to the devel," "Moote thy welked nekke be tobroke," "olde barel-ful of lyes" (III.262, 277, 302). As her earlier patristic mode ridiculed scholastic philosophy, yet made her half a clerk and equally ridiculous, here she defeats her purpose by assaulting the anti-feminist tradition with a force that gives the tradition new validity. Who can doubt that she would never have won a famous local prize for marital happiness:

> "The bacon was nat fet for hem, I trowe,
> That som men han in Essex at Dunmowe."[21] (III.217–18)

Something about this unrelieved blast of heat makes us doubt its sincerity, for the virulence of her attack, scarcely matching the relatively tame injustices she claims her husbands committed against her, sounds more like a show of anger than anger itself.

The other legitimate aim of a Christian marriage, the begetting and raising of children, fares no better. Despite her enthusiastic paean for waxing, multiplying, and the conjugal acts that make them possible, and despite her unabashed statement that she enjoys sex and wants it often, nothing in these claims agrees even remotely with what she describes as her actual sex life in marriage. The woman who emphatically declares that she will use her instrument in marriage as freely as her maker sent it (III.150) apparently charges for her marital lovemaking:

> "How pitously a-nyght I made hem swynke!
> And, by my fey, I tolde of it no stoor.
> They had me yeven hir lond and hir tresoor;
> Me neded nat do lenger diligence
> To wynne hir love, or doon hem reverence." (III.202–6)

And the woman who says she will "bistowe the flour of al myn age / In the actes and in fruyt of mariage" (III.113–14), must be a wilted flower indeed by the time she submits:

> "Namely abedde hadden they meschaunce:
> Ther wolde I chide and do hem no plesaunce;
> I wolde no lenger in the bed abyde,
> If that I felte his arm over my syde,
> Til he had maad his raunson unto me;
> Thanne wolde I suffre hym do his nycetee." (III.407–12)

It is significant that bacon, having symbolized 200 lines earlier one of the rejected aims of Christian marriage, its mutual affection (cf. III.217–18, quoted above), now symbolizes the other, the sexual advances of her husbands for which, she claims, she had to feign an appetite (III.417).

Though the intrusion of the Wife's commercial practices into the intimate life of her marriages does not actually prove she had little regard for the command to wax and multiply, nor that she continually withheld herself from her husbands, the conspicuous absence of any reference to children makes her barrenness a likely possibility. On this subject much is implied by a significant omission at one point in her summary of her husbands' accusations against her:

"Thou liknest eek wommenes love to helle,
To bareyne lond, ther water may nat dwelle.
Thou liknest it also to wilde fyr." (III.371–73)

This accusation against women paraphrases Scripture (Proverbs 30:15–16), yet omits Scripture's fourth image of unfulfillment, the barren womb, which would perhaps have touched her too closely to include.[22]

That four of her husbands—possibly five[23]—have died suggests that she may represent privation in general, including death, more clearly than the lustiness and vitality she is often thought to represent. Some figurative language offers further evidence. Alisoun's deafness, which Chaucer ignores as a tool of humor he could easily have exploited, may have been added for its symbolic force. Most discussions of this malady concentrate only on its cause, a responding cuff on the ear by her fifth husband, but overlook its greater appropriateness to Alisoun's general malaise than, say, a broken nose or missing tooth might have been. In a deaf person sound reaches—indeed penetrates—a normal external organ, while the inner organ's incapacity prevents hearing, or mental conception, from occurring.[24] Perhaps, then, the Wife's deafness symbolically suggests both her sexual barrenness and her unavailing life in general. The strategic concluding lines of her portrait in the *General Prologue* may convey a similar meaning:

Of remedies of love she knew per chaunce,
For she koude of that art the olde daunce. (I.475–76)

Though Ovid's *Remedia Amoris* comes to mind, a medicine to cure a condition, even a love condition, seems an odd allusion for the Wife who would naturally want to make love more ardent. On the other hand, since medicines attack effects, while the system itself either absorbs or eliminates their cause, the pharmacological phrase "remedies of love" perhaps refers to methods by which one cures or prevents unpleasant effects of love. Consistent with other life-denying impulses throughout the Wife's Prologue, these lines too may allude to the denial of life, specifically the deliberate thwarting of conception, and thus account for an otherwise inexplicable silence regarding children by a woman who refers often and lustily to sexual intercourse.[25] With the possible exception of her fifth marriage everything the Wife touches either fails, withers, or dies.

The overwhelming discord in the entire second movement of the Wife's Prologue overshadows any excuse one might make that her first three husbands provoked her to behave thus. According to her own words the Wife of Bath has systematically frustrated the two legitimate aims of Christian marriage as the fourteenth century understood them: she has failed to promote between herself and her husbands the inseparable union of minds that defines the form of Christian marriage; and she has withheld from them the free expression of physical love that might have produced children. As a result, her opening remarks, theorizing that marriage and sex are good because they lead to procreation, must now be replaced by the entirely contradictory description of her actual practice: marriage and especially sex are useful for gaining sovereignty.

What has been said thus far may seem to leave little room to rehabilitate the Wife's reputation. One redeeming argument may be detected in an overlooked feature of the Wife's harangue. Her own attack, occupying only fifteen lines of a total of 144, responds to specific instances of what she claims was her husbands' misconduct or maltreatment.[26] A full ninety-one lines repeat her husbands' charges against her. Their accusations, however, turn out to be vague assaults against women in general, closely following the intemperately anti-feminist *Liber Aureolus de Nuptiis* of Theophrastus and *Epistola adversus Jovinianum* of Jerome.[27] Only two of these accusations bear any connection with the Wife, and these scarcely distinguish her from the rest of mankind: she craves flattery and likes fine clothes. The only serious, specific accusation against her, that she has had an affair with the apprentice Jankyn, is apparently untrue (cf. III.303-7). Yes, the Wife may have tailored this entire section to exonerate herself and blame her husbands. But if she has not, then her Prologue reveals a woman more sinned against than sinning.

Of course, behind every charge that has been leveled against her prowls the nagging thought that her literal words cannot be trusted, or to put it another way, that she intends to create a "feyned appetit" for some tactical advantage. Even her quest for sovereignty and her boast of the pleasure principle are protested too much to be believed. And then, her selective use of Scripture—quoting from St. Paul only what the husband owes the wife, not the reciprocal—sounds too obvious, too artful, too much like a rhetorical game.[28] In fact, her obvious omissions from Scripture, implying her intemperance in arguments that might better proceed in game, may also imply her higher regard for action, where they are taken in earnest. Most important, the strategy she claims to follow would be fruitless in the extreme, if sovereignty has been her real objective. Elsewhere her own words lead us to believe she would have used subtler methods to gain control of her husbands:

"We wommen han, if that I shal nat lye,
In this matere a queynte fantasye:
Wayte what thyng we may nat lightly have,
Therafter wol we crie al day and crave.
Forbede us thyng, and that desiren we;
Preesse on us faste, and thanne wol we fle.
With daunger oute we al oure chaffare;
Greet prees at market maketh deere ware,
And to greet cheep is holde at litel prys:
This knoweth every womman that is wys." (III.515–24)

Since Alisoun describes a campaign far from subtle, we suspect she may have ulterior motives for claiming she constantly fought for sovereignty in marriage, especially since her audience for this claim are fellow pilgrims who can only measure worldly success, not husbands who already know her private failures.

The argument that the Wife of Bath's public personality is largely defined by excessive zeal in pursuing tactical objectives with an immediate audience implies that somewhere in her consciousness she has a strategic objective, an ideal, that she longs to realize. We can never expect a woman like the Wife of Bath to admit to holding such an ideal, but despite her bluster and pride some hints of it come through in the very barrage we have just been discussing, where she describes an attitude she wants her husband to adopt:

"Thou sholdest seye, 'Wyf, go wher thee liste;
Taak youre disport; I wol nat leve no talys.
I knowe yow for a trewe wyf, dame Alys.'" (III.318–20)

There is nothing in these lines of Alisoun's much touted interest in sovereignty. On the contrary, the obviously causal relation between this imagined husband's belief in her faithfulness and his liberal policy toward her suggests a measure of sovereignty on his part, though justly exercised. Equally significant, the sentence about his disbelieving tales, coming as it does in the midst of familiar anti-feminist allegations, obliquely refers to the scurrilous anti-feminist tradition itself. The marriage ideal so tenuously constructed in these three lines approaches more closely at least one of the fourteenth century's acceptable aims for a Christian marriage than anything else we have heard from the Wife thus far.

If three lines uttered in the heat of a quoted debate sound less than a full-voiced account of her private ambition, the next stage of the Wife's Prologue brings fuller detail to her marriage ideal and reveals a surprising degree of poignancy in her life.

THE PRIVATE REALITY

The Wife of Bath's fourth and fifth husbands differ greatly from her first three. The youthful girl whom wealthy older men could entice into marriage, seems in later life to find younger mates in the same way, by offering them the hard-earned wealth she apparently obtained from her former husbands (cf. III.630–31). But the youth and poverty of her last two husbands do not set them apart from the others as much as the different effect they have on her. Her fourth husband dominates her by his indifference, and her fifth shows her what she really is.

The Wife's account of her fourth marriage begins with a professed interest in discussing her fourth husband, but quickly—and with apparent illogic—shifts to herself:

> "My fourthe housbonde was a revelour—
> This is to seyn, he hadde a paramour—
> And I was yong and ful of ragerye,
> Stibourn and strong, and joly as a pye." (III.453–56)

This abrupt transition from husband to self does not permanently shift the subject, for some twenty-five lines later she picks up again the subject of her husband as if she had never dropped it:

> "Now wol I tellen of my fourthe housbonde.
>   I seye, I hadde in herte greet despit
> That he of any oother had delit." (III.480–82)

The intervening stream of consciousness, far from transitioning illogically, flows very naturally from the Wife's memory of her husband's mistress.[29] While retreating from her publicly announced subject, these lines take us into the privacy of a painful inner reverie: "Why did my fourth husband need a mistress, when I was his wife and a better partner in every way?" The comments describing how well she could dance and sing, how much fun she was when flushed with wine, and how hungry and ardent a lover she was on such occasions, are all designed to justify her implicit claim of having been a more desirable partner than her husband's mistress was, and coincidentally to fix blame for her failed marriage entirely on her husband. Instead of achieving their desired effect, her words reveal a pathetic longing for the marriage ideal that has always eluded her. She wants simply to love and be loved in return.

Although we tend to pity the Wife for her missed ideal, we also wonder if her words are not partly an attempt to convince herself. She may well have been the jolly, amorous partner she claims to have been, though it is hard to believe that by her fourth marriage she was as young as her claims imply. And the comfort she takes "That I have had my world as in my tyme" (III.473) makes us wonder when she might have done so, since she began marrying at twelve, has had only brief intervals between her five husbands, and has scarcely had uninterrupted marital joy over the past thirty-odd years.

The painful truth behind this implied comparison with her husband's mistress fades into another melancholy reverie disclosing her present anguish:

> "But age, allas, that al wole envenyme,
> Hath me biraft my beautee and my pith.
> Lat go. Farewel! The devel go therwith!
> The flour is goon; ther is namoore to telle;
> The bren, as I best kan, now moste I selle;
> But yet to be right myrie wol I fonde." (III.474–79)

The personification of Age faintly echoes the Wife's characteristic attempt to remove responsibility from herself. But no weakness of character, however heinous, no falsification of the past, however understandable, can mitigate the suffering inherent in these lines. Two metaphor clusters—beauty/pith, flour/bran—carry meaning far beyond their immediate appeal. The second cluster, "flour" and "bran," might also be called fruit and chaff, for they obviously identify essence and accident. The more difficult first cluster, "beautee" and "pith," seems at first to stand parallel to "flour" and "bran," that is, to divide a human being in the same way— inner essence and outer shell, respectively. But in the Wife's usage both "beautee" and "pith" have disappeared, that is, they both parallel "flour," inner essence. Though beauty resides in the external body only, a reader might be justified in taking it as a metaphor for essence, since beauty implies a finer quality than plainness—flour has greater value than bran. The more complex "pith" serves the same purpose. Both the *OED* and the *Middle English Dictionary* quote this occurrence in the Wife of

Bath's Prologue under the meaning "strength, force, energy, vigor." Surely this is incorrect, for if there is anything the Wife will retain to the very grave—perhaps beyond—it is her ability to battle. In any case, apart from Chaucer's line and two other ambiguous occurrences in *Cursor Mundi* (MS Edin. 22793, MS Fairf. 7090) this meaning does not gain currency until almost a century later. The primary meaning of the word, amply attested both before and after Chaucer, is "(a) the central column of . . . tissue in the . . . branches of . . . plants . . . (b) the flesh of a fruit. . . (c) the interior tissue (of a part of the body)."[30] If the word has this usual force here, especially in association with the Wife's beauty, a richly suggestive meaning suffuses the entire passage. Feminine beauty performs an important service made more noticeable in many of its metaphors. Ripeness, lushness, newness of a pere-jonette tree, and a hundred other gustatory images describing beauty, suggest means by which appetite is stimulated. In the case of pears or "apples leyd in hey or heeth" (I.3262), attractiveness stimulates taste buds which make one want to eat. Or, as the Wife's scholastic models might have said, attractiveness stimulates the accidental appetite by which essential nourishment is accomplished. Designed to stimulate masculine appetites so that the essential business of human love and perpetuation of the species may be fulfilled, a woman's beauty normally accompanies her reproductive years.

Alisoun, we recall, was first married at twelve and shows up on the road to Canterbury some time after forty, or at the approximate ages, respectively, of menarche and menopause in the fourteenth century.[31] Her five marriages, then, have entirely spanned her fruitful years, yet show a significant failure either to achieve love or bear fruit—that is, to realize the two basic purposes of marriage. Now it may be too late; the Wife cannot reverse nature. Faded is the beauty that might have attracted the opposite sex; gone is the "pith" that might have made her marriages fruitful. Indomitable to the end, the Wife does all she can under the circumstances: feigns "to be right myrie" (III.479) to give hope of mutual comfort and solace; and affects an insatiable lustiness to create a presumption of continued fruitfulness.

While still married, Alisoun commanded a wider range of responses. As she explicitly says in recounting the history of her fourth marriage, she made him pay dearly for rejecting her and taking a mistress:

> "But he was quit, by God and by Seint Joce!
> I made hym of the same wode a croce;
> Nat of my body, in no foul manere,
> But certeinly, I made folk swich cheere

That in his owene grece I made hym frye
For angre, and for verray jalousye.
By God, in erthe I was his purgatorie,
For which I hope his soule be in glorie.
For, God it woot, he sat ful ofte and song,
Whan that his shoo ful bitterly hym wrong.
Ther was no wight, save God and he, that wiste,
In many wise, how soore I hym twiste.
He deyde whan I cam fro Jerusalem." (III.483–95)

The reaction itself is not surprising, for the Wife has already testified convincingly to her habit of strong reaction. But the similarity between the conduct she reveals here and her earlier descriptions of shrewish behavior toward other husbands casts suspicion on her long campaign for sovereignty. She may have developed that pose for the same purpose she pursues here, as a plausible explanation for conduct whose real cause, prior rejection, is too painful to admit. From all indications the Wife of Bath preferred to be taken as an indomitable shrew rather than be known for a failure as a woman.

Alisoun's detailed account of her fifth marriage confirms what can only be inferred from her disjointed and intentionally deceptive account of her first four. Though the external circumstances imply that the fifth marriage would repeat the fourth, the Wife's lengthy account of her courtship suggests otherwise. She describes the fifth from their first meeting to their wedding, savoring every detail, including her professed tactic of manipulating with falsehoods, as if she were recalling the love of her life for the delight of a granddaughter who eagerly looked forward to her own betrothal:

"I bar hym on honde he hadde enchanted me—
My dame taughte me that soutiltee—
And eek I seyde I mette of hym al nyght,
He wolde han slayn me as I lay upright,
And al my bed was ful of verray blood;
'But yet I hope that ye shal do me good,
For blood bitokeneth gold, as me was taught.'
And al was fals; I dremed of it right naught." (III.575–82)

". . . me thoughte he hadde a paire
Of legges and of feet so clene and faire
That al myn herte I yaf unto his hoold." (III.597–99)

"What sholde I seye but, at the monthes ende,

This joly clerk, Jankyn, that was so hende,
Hath wedded me with greet solempnytee." (III.627–29)

Recalled after the marriage culminated successfully, these reminis-
cences of courtship, especially the erotic coloring of III.577–81, are re-
counted with pleasure. Though silent about her motives for other marriages, she says she married Jankyn the clerk "for love" (III.526)—it is the
first time Alisoun has used the word thus. He was twenty, she forty, and
she gave him "al the lond and fee / That evere was me yeven therbifoore"
(III.630–31). Initially the marriage showed no greater signs of success
than her earlier attempts, but in at least one significant detail Jankyn behaved toward Alisoun quite differently from the way his immediate predecessor behaved toward her. The fourth husband rejected Alisoun for a
mistress, ignored her rather than cast her aside. Jankyn, on the other hand,
confronts her directly, establishing the contact on which future communication would have to be based. Apparently he disapproved of Alisoun's
long habit of wandering about the town visiting whom she liked. At issue
was the question of the husband's leadership in the family, not only a traditional Christian concept but an ancient custom too, as his "homilies" of
Symplicius Gallus and P. Sempronius Sophus indicate. The Wife considers
the matter far from crucial and virtually ignores it, directing her attention
instead to Jankyn's reading matter—the chief anti-feminist writings from
which he would laughingly quote aloud—and striking back that clerks
cannot speak well of women. Ever the scholastic, she thrusts first with a
witty *sic probo* of authority, arguing that more men write stories than
women do and that, since most of these men are clerks under the sign of
Mercury, Venus's antagonist, "Therfore no womman of no clerk is prey-
sed" (III.706). She thrusts next with the unanswerable logic of experience:

"The clerk, whan he is oold, and may noght do
Of Venus werkes worth his olde sho,
Thanne sit he doun, and writ in his dotage
That wommen kan nat kepe hir mariage!" (III.707–10)

The implicit dangers of *ad hominem* arguments, as the Wife employs
them, eventually undo her. Not only does she partly demonstrate the truth
of Jankyn's charge, but she provokes him to dip deeper into the inex-
haustible Valerius and Jerome for a number of cases of husbands brought
to death by their wives, many of whom were given to lechery.[32] Now this
attack strikes very close to home, for as the argument continues Jankyn
seems to be describing his own wife—a shrewish, four-time widow—with

increasing accuracy. Perhaps the Wife recognizes herself as a potential chapter in Theophrastus's book of women responsible for their husbands' deaths. Yet, if she does, she simultaneously recognizes that these stories have nothing to do with her private self—with Alisoun, who desperately seeks love—but describe instead the countless fabrications of her public image, which was only designed to conceal the yearnings of her private self. Moreover, the frequent occurrence of lechery in these literary allusions signals that Jankyn has fallen for her ruse, that is, has assumed her socializing includes adultery. Both aspects of this prolonged attack bear heavily on the traditional view of Christian marriage. The double point reaches a climactic synthesis in Jankyn's final assault:

> "'Bet is,' quod he, 'hye in the roof abyde,
> Than with an angry wyf doun in the hous;
> They been so wikked and contrarious,
> They haten that hir housbondes loven ay.'
> He seyde, 'A womman cast hir shame away,
> Whan she cast of hir smok'; and forthermo,
> 'A fair womman, but she be chaast also,
> Is lyk a gold ryng in a sowes nose.'" (III.778–85)

These lines pointedly accuse the Wife of a failure of love and a failure of virtue. The striking image of a "gold ryng in a sowes nose" places those failures in the context of marriage, historically solemnized in a ring ceremony, calling attention to its debasement through loss of chastity. To the extent that Jankyn's aphorism applies specifically to the Wife of Bath, he surprisingly calls her "a fair womman," fit for the metaphor of "a gold ring." Hence her moral character alone draws the ugly image of a sow. And yet, to the best of our knowledge, Alisoun's virtue has not been compromised; this last accusation has no basis. Nevertheless, Jankyn's belief in his wife's infidelity lets us know that her whole course of action has backfired. She had given free rein to her gregarious nature—perhaps to make her husband jealous and more ardent, or perhaps because it is just her way—but she had probably also remained faithful to the love she wants him to show her. Even more ironic, line III.781 may imply that he has always loved her, and still does. In other words, her ploy was completely unnecessary. Instead of making Jankyn jealous, it moves him to an angry accusation of infidelity, in turn calling forth Alisoun's most spontaneous and revealing outcry:

> "Who wolde wene, or who wolde suppose,
> The wo that in myn herte was, and pyne?" (III.786–87)

Never one to suffer in silence or without some assuaging reaction, the Wife brings this argument with her fifth husband to a dramatic climax which may be quickly summarized: When Jankyn refuses to stop reading aloud, Alisoun rips out three pages (grown from one page in line 635 to three in line 790, perhaps as an indication of increasing intensity in her telling) and knocks him backward into the fire; Jankyn recovers to strike Alisoun the blow that partially deafens her, but realizing its severity kneels down to apologize; when he is close enough, Alisoun strikes him back; at length they make up. The felt energy of this fistfight conceals the extraordinary literary complexity of a scene in which symbols and the attitudes they inspire disclose the even more powerful forces that have led to the fight. Alisoun's initial move of ripping three pages from Jankyn's antifeminist book accomplishes the immediate end of depriving him of his text and thus forcing him to stop reading. That she attacks *him* as well as his book, emphasizes her anger at his willingness to draw a parallel between herself and some hideous concept of woman. If it is true that the private Alisoun wants to love and be loved, the anti-feminists—Theophrastus, Jerome, and now her fifth husband—have wrongly accepted a gross exaggeration of Woman as an accurate description of the Wife herself. But, to be sure, the Wife's self-portrait partly corroborates what they have said. Her admission that Jankyn's reading caused her pain (III.787) indicates that she too realizes how closely her public personality reflects the perception these writers have had of Woman, and how ugly that personality is. Alisoun's gesture, then, objectifies her now familiar ambivalence. By ripping three pages from her husband's text she both silences the unjust misogynists from whom she has suffered much and commits a self-annihilating act, destroying that part of herself that they accurately describe.[33]

The remainder of the fight has prominent, symbolic overtones for both Jankyn and Alisoun. The clerk's violent reaction to the damaging of his book and to his unexpected trip to the fire satisfies his immediate anger, but displays a clear change of character as well. From what might have been a fiery death, he springs up again, no longer to pace and read like the "authorities" to whom he has always deferred, but with an "experience"-born passion to meet his wife with a deafening cuff on the ear. As for Alisoun, deafness makes explicit an internal condition from which she has long suffered. When this battle with Jankyn takes place a lifetime of habits has made her as unlikely to become a forthcoming spouse as her age prevents her from becoming a literal mother. Her sudden, irreversible deafness—albeit in only one ear—becomes, then, an external symbol of her inability to develop a fruitful human relationship.

As with everything else she has done, Alisoun responds ambivalently to her husband's blow. She certainly wants to get him close enough for a matching blow, but she may also be expressing a desire for affection:

> "'O! hastow slayn me, false theef?' I seyde,
> 'And for my land thus hastow mordred me?
> Er I be deed, yet wol I kisse thee.'" (III.800–2)

With equal suddenness Jankyn converts the passion of anger into the passion of love. His regret at having lost his self-control, as well as her words of affection, inspire his own loving response:

> "'Deere suster Alisoun,
> As help me God, I shal thee nevere smyte!
> That I have doon, it is thyself to wyte.
> Foryeve it me, and that I thee biseke!'" (III.804–7)

It has been a long battle, but the end is in sight.

Eager to convince her fellow pilgrims that her overall philosophy of sovereignty in marriage has finally prevailed, the Wife attributes the eventual success of her fifth marriage to her acquisition of control. The facts do not bear her out. Sovereignty gained from a gratuitous gift—the only way to describe Jankyn's offer at the end of their fist fight—differs greatly from sovereignty gained in a deliberate quest or a calculated barter. Though Alisoun had bribed and browbeaten her former husbands into surrendering sovereignty to her, none of those marriages was marked with noticeable happiness. At the beginning of her fifth marriage, and without being asked, Alisoun gave her young husband complete control over everything she owned. Again, the marriage was not markedly blissful. Only when Jankyn responded with his own selfless gesture at the end of a long battle, offering Alisoun complete control over her own activities and over their affairs, does the marriage begin to succeed:

> "'Myn owene trewe wyf,
> Do as thee lust the terme of al thy lyf;
> Keep thyn honour, and keep eek myn estaat'—
> After that day we hadden never debaat." (III.819–22)

Jankyn's offer to let her keep her own honor accomplishes something of the marriage ideal to which Alisoun alluded much earlier (III.318–20), not because it grants sovereignty, but because it establishes a basis of trust and confidence. Despite the Wife's emphasis on the sovereignty she gained, which serves well her public personality's need to appear triumphant, the final words of her Prologue leave us with a picture, not of "maistrie" but of mutual accord—perhaps even love:

"God helpe me so, I was to hym as kynde
As any wyf from Denmark unto Ynde,
And also trewe, and so was he to me." (III.823–25)

THE TALE

As the Wife began her Prologue praising experience and denigrating authority, she begins her Tale by extolling the imaginative experience of the land of "fayerye . . . manye hundred yeres ago" (III.859–63) and ridiculing the authorities of the disenchanted present. Longing for her private conception of the Arthurian world—ruled by women, refreshed by knights, and quickened by incubi—she vaguely blames her own age for many of her unnamed torments. The great differences between these two worlds cannot, however, obscure the underlying parallel between the Wife's fourteenth-century Prologue and her Tale of Arthurian Britain.

The Tale's knight-rapist bears striking similarities to the Wife of Bath in more than his inclination to violence. Though his crime is more overtly physical than any Martian act of the Wife, his abusive treatment in forcing mechanical sex on another reflects the Wife's professed indifference to her husbands, as she too employs sexual stratagems to gain sovereignty over them. And yet, her description of that practice agrees neither with the interest in sex that she professes elsewhere, nor with her profound hurt at her fourth husband's sexual rejection. Hence, the knight of her Tale reflects only the false image Alisoun has cultivated as a lustful wanton bent on sovereignty. The knight is further associated with the Wife's public pretense when he begins to collect suggestions of what women most desire. The entire catalogue—wealth, honor, clothes, sex, several husbands, flattery, freedom (III.919–48)—has been claimed at one time or another by the Wife herself. Yet these too are false ideals. Perhaps most clearly of all, we recognize the knight's role in objectifying the Wife's public self when he protests strenuously against marrying his ugly deliverer:

"Allas and weylawey!
I woot right wel that swich was my biheste.
For Goddes love, as chees a newe requeste!
Taak al my good and lat my body go. . . .
Thou art so loothly, and so oold also,
And therto comen of so lough a kynde,
That litel wonder is thogh I walwe and wynde." (III.1058–61,
1100–2)

While his plea to "lat my body go" would impress at least one deflowered virgin with its bitter irony, his specific charges against the hag summarize popular attitudes to marriage: in choosing a partner men usually seek youth, beauty, and fortune.[34] These, we recall, are the very attributes Alisoun claims for herself, though for at least two of her marriages she was not young, for at least three she was not wealthy, and for all five she came from low rank and may have been plain—to judge from her buck-teeth (*gat-tothed* prob. <OE *gat-toped,*, goat-toothed)[35] and absence of testimonials to her beauty. It is reasonable to assume, therefore, that one or more of these popular attitudes plagued the Wife of Bath throughout her life.

In the old hag may be found other, equally obvious parallels with the Wife of Bath. Both women turn all their energies to promoting marriage; they are adept at scholastic argument; and score their greatest victories through boudoir rhetoric. The parallels become stronger when the hag is compared with the Alisoun who approaches a fifth marriage. Both women make initial overtures to their men out of a spirit of love, the Wife granting Jankyn complete control over everything she owns, and the hag giving the secret that will save the knight's life. After the Wife's marriage to this fifth husband she apparently ignored marital decorum and pro-ceeded to argue her right to do so, thus precipitating the fight discussed above. So too in the Tale, when the hag finally succeeds in making the knight marry her, she overlooks the unconventionality of their match and consistently ignores her husband's point of view by arguing that inherent worth vastly surpasses the accidental details that probably moved him to rape a maiden. Because her reasoning, though unanswerable, almost com-pletely misses the point, it provides insight to her own helpless position rather than a persuasive rejoinder. Her arguments—that gentility should descend from Christ and accrue to those who perform gentle deeds, that wealth brings more burdens than benefits, and that age is to be honored— have no effect on her husband, as even she must know on some profound level, for as the Tale unfolds *she* capitulates to *his* sense of values, not he to hers.

The knight and the hag have, then, a complicated relationship to the Wife of Bath. They represent, respectively, the Wife's public and private character traits, stripped of the elaborate pretenses that surround them in the Prologue. While the knight subscribes to the crass ethics of a fallen world, objectifying the successful, selfish image that the Wife herself has tried to project, the hag embraces the Wife's private ethical standards, which she has largely tried to conceal. The knight makes explicit society's rejection of women like Alisoun on a host of human battlegrounds: sex, sovereignty, looks, age, wealth; the hag reveals the physical characteris-tics that explain that rejection and the profound suffering that it has brought to Alisoun. To state the point another way, the knight-rapist represents the Wife's public self, which wants to triumph by the world's system of values, including youth, beauty, a lofty birth, and sexual sovereignty. The old woman represents Alisoun's private self, which *really is* old, ugly, and of low estate, but which wants to replace the world's values with others of more durable worth.

The chief difference between the Wife and her surrogates, that is, between the Prologue and Tale, is no more than the difference between concealment and exposure, pretense and revelation. The Tale does not cloak the knight in the elaborate justifications that protect the Wife, nor hide the hag beneath pounds of headgear and layers of clothing. Whereas the Wife's self-righteous arguments and claims of worldly success conceal the egoism of her public personality, the knight stands before us nakedly acquisitive, incapable of recognizing the rights of the young woman he violated, unwilling to honor an obligation solemnly promised, and intolerant of his deliverer's appearance, age, and humble origins. And whereas the Wife's claims of joviality and lustfulness conceal the damage to her interior self caused by a world that cares little for her virtues, the hag stands before us pathetically calling in a debt of marriage and debating with her husband for his love.

To narrow the enormous ethical distance between hag and knight requires a twofold effort. The old woman must partly grant the validity of the knight's sense of values, and he must be made to acknowledge hers. The method by which this is achieved follows the pattern of reciprocity evident in Alisoun's fifth marriage, with appropriate differences. After extending the overture that saved the knight's life, the old woman has waited long for a reciprocating gesture, as Alisoun waited—less patiently—for Jankyn to return her love. At length, in a second overture, she lets him choose whether he wants her young and fair but possibly unfaithful, or old and plain but faithful, prefacing this choice with words that let him know how clearly she understands him:

> "syn I knowe youre delit,
> I shal fulfille youre worldly appetit.
>   "Chese now," quod she, "oon of thise thynges tweye:
> To han me foul and old til that I deye,
> And be to yow a trewe, humble wyf,
> And nevere yow displese in al my lyf,
> Or elles ye wol han me yong and fair,
> And take youre aventure of the repair
> That shal be to youre hous by cause of me,

Or in som oother place, may wel be.
Now chese yourselven, wheither that yow liketh." (III.1217–27)

While these words offer a choice between the hag's sense of values and the knight's, they also capture rival aspects of the woman who tells their story. The public Wife argues long and hard to convince her husbands and her fellow pilgrims of the rightness of her position and that she is a flirtatious beauty whose spice has not yet run out. The reality, however, discredits this pose. Her logic collapses under the weight of her own contradictions; and the facts of her life point to an aging, overdressed, bucktoothed fighter of doubtful attractiveness to the opposite sex. Bereft of her boisterous counterattacks for sex and sovereignty, and stripped of the public disguise designed to make her look attractive, the private Alisoun of secret longing and desperation shines through clearly in the ugly figure of the old hag. The preclusive choices offered to the knight represent the real Alisoun competing with the fake. When the errant knight accepted the old woman's first gratuitous offer earlier in the Tale, he bound himself to a contract as enforceable as the contract that ideally governs marriage, though the old woman did not emphasize the point at that time. This second gratuitous offer, despite posing a dilemma, merely sustains the conditions of that earlier contract, not only because it grants the knight the right to choose, but also because it implies the equality of her values and his. By giving youthful beauty equal weight with fidelity in the choices she offers him, the hag admits that the knight's sense of values, however inferior to her own, cannot be denied. Neither his habit of judging the world in sensual terms, nor her own habit of judging it through the intellect, can stand alone. As a result, the endgame of this argument in the Tale differs significantly from the final blows that conclude the Prologue. Whereas the Wife's unconventional behavior fetched intemperate instruction from Jankyn, in turn provoking the simmering Wife to a final glorious charge, the hag's reasoned rebuttals to difficult arguments aimed at her person produce no heat, no dramatic crescendo of ripped book and boxed ear, but instead lead to a subtler, more tender dénouement, eventually achieving the same harmony that battle alone had wrought for the Wife and Jankyn. The Tale makes explicit, therefore, what Alisoun's fifth marriage could only test in combat: that a human relationship will succeed as the parties to the relationship respect each other and honor the reciprocal agreement on which it is based.

However unlikely a prospect the knight may seem to be, the old woman's final gambit achieves its desired effect. For instead of leaping at the sensuous choice we have come to expect of the knight, a sudden pang of generosity awakens his first awareness of her ethical standards. Perhaps out of fatigue from listening to her lectures, or perhaps out of genuine enlightenment, he invites her to make the decision, and thus stumbles into the principle of mutual accord on which all successful contracts, including marriages, must rest:

> "My lady and my love, and wyf so deere,
> I put me in youre wise governance;
> Cheseth youreself which may be moost plesance
> And moost honour to yow and me also." (III.1230–33)

The Wife of Bath would have us believe that these lines demonstrate the triumph of sovereignty, since she interrupts the flow of her Tale to let the hag gloat out of character:

> "Thanne have I gete of yow maistrie," quod she,
> "Syn I may chese and governe as me lest?"
> "Ye, certes, wyf," quod he, "I holde it best." (III.1236–38)

But the knight's words demonstrate nothing of the sort. Like Jankyn's words to Alisoun (III.819–21), these do not allow unbridled freedom; they merely grant the privilege of choosing a means to bring about their greatest mutual happiness and honor. At no time in the Tale does the hag imply she desires sovereignty, not even when she gives the knight his winning answer, which she designed merely to suit the public discussions at court and win a pardon for a lusty young knight, not to profess an ideal she holds for wives. Regardless of how Alisoun may interpret her own Tale, the hag's actions uphold the truth of a desire that has motivated every word and deed in her careful plan, and that may yet provide the deepest insight into Alisoun of Bath:

> "I nolde for al the metal, ne for oore
> That under erthe is grave or lith above,
> But if thy wyf I were, and eek thy love." (III.1064–66)

Though she said these words much earlier, when claiming her half of the contract that saved the knight's life, they are equally pertinent at the end of the Tale. The valuable metals in these lines are not metaphors, or even preclusive alternatives to "wife" and "love." Rather, she says she would care nothing for things of material value unless she were the knight's wife and love. Inherent value makes material value possible. In returning to the old woman the right to make her own choice, the knight addresses her "My lady and my love, and wyf so deere" (III.1230), thus acknowledging the private values she has been trying to advance. As in Alisoun's own marriage to Jankyn, where a reciprocating pattern of largess eventually controls the gestures that husband and wife make to each other, here the woman swears to be both beautiful and true, adding that if she fails in her promise to be beautiful complete sovereignty will be his, "Dooth with my lyf and deth right as yow lest" (III.1248). An equation is drawn between fidelity and physical beauty. Just as important, both of these qualities stand in opposition to sovereignty. As with the precious metals noted above, which were contrasted to love, here the virtue of fidelity and the beauty that it confers stand in implied contrast to the arbitrary value conveyed by similes of worldly rank. By the end of the Tale the old woman's ambitions for a marriage based on love have been realized, and the knight's quest for an exciting young mate has also ended successfully:

> And whan the knyght saugh verraily al this,
> That she so fair was, and so yong therto,
> For joye he hente hire in his armes two.
> His herte bathed in a bath of blisse.
> A thousand tyme a-rewe he gan hire kisse,
> And she obeyed hym in every thyng
> That myghte doon hym plesance or likyng. (III.1250–56)

The confrontation of opposites in the *Wife of Bath's Tale* has re-created the dilemma of Alisoun's own life. She knows that the ideals that lie hidden in the deepest reaches of her heart constitute an inherent beauty that outshines the beauty of the world. But she also knows that the world in which she is forced to live values neither her nor her ideals. The mortal stuff of which she is made cannot find cheer in unrequited private ideals, or long remain aloof to the world's attractions. In consequence of restlessly searching for contradictory goals, her efforts to convert the world to her own ideals of marital love and harmony are overwhelmed by stronger efforts to prove she has triumphed according to standards prized by the world. Thus it is that Alisoun's Tale re-creates an image of the world as it ought to be. Only the miraculous fertility of the Wife's imagination can turn the *foulest wight* that man may devise into a damsel young and fair. In the reconstructions of romance, the public utterances of the wife, here projected into the knight, cease conflicting with her deepest desires as seen in the old hag. And the lady herself cannot be kept ugly by the judgments of men—the clear implication of line III.999—but becomes as fresh and true as the thoughts in her heart. Finally, the system of values long held by the world, and evident in the pale character of the knight, responds to the interior beauty of the hag-Wife by reshaping itself in her image. The perfect union of husband and wife takes place at last, signaling the internal peace for which the pilgrim who gave them existence has always yearned.

In one crucial respect the old lady in the *Wife of Bath's Tale* shares a telling limitation with the Wife of Bath. They both discuss marriage as if it had little to do with human emotion. Although the frustrations of marriage caused Alisoun deep emotional pain, she nonetheless stresses its contractual arrangements. She argues vociferously against the traditional understanding of that contract and seeks to replace it with an equally rigid contract of her own devising. The old lady in the Tale, despite commendable generosity, tricks the knight into honoring a contract of marriage. Few in any age need to be told that love does not grow from contracts, but from some elusive stimulus in the emotions. The private Alisoun may secretly recognize this process. Whereas the knight in her Tale had complained of the hag's ugliness, age, and low degree (III.1100–1); and whereas the hag shrewdly recognizes that ugliness and age perhaps amount to a tautology, while "low degree" implies the absence of wealth and the gentility wealth is often assumed to confer (III.1106–16); the Wife as storyteller emends only the ugliness of her surrogate in the Tale—that feature alone which might genuinely stimulate the knight's masculine emotions.

Art often presents a brilliant alternative to life, but it never provides a substitute. By the end of the *Wife of Bath's Tale* we realize, sadly, that the magic of Alisoun's Arthurian world has not disguised its fantasy. The restoration of the hag's youthful beauty, the enlightenment of her tinsel knight, and the incredible claim that the two lived happily ever after occur only in a fairy tale. As for the Wife of Bath, who lives not in a fairy world but in the very real and very cruel world of the fourteenth century, she must still wander wearily by the way, slouching toward some Canterbury that may never take shape on her horizon.

9

꧁

Two Witty Glosses

Friar's Tale and *Summoner's Tale*

An initial tribute must be made to Chaucer's skill in setting at the right level the continuing battle between two of the most mean-spirited adversaries in all of Chaucer, the Friar and the Summoner. Though capable of innuendo and subtlety when on the attack—of seizing on a *stalke* in their enemy's eye while ignorant of the *balke* in their own—these two competitors much prefer a literary version of broadsword and mace. The Friar creates in his tale a *somonour*[1] who acts with all the naked greed and hardhearted tenacity that often characterized summoners in Chaucer's day, only to be answered by the Summoner's creation of a *frere* who relies first on strained textual interpretations and later, in frustration, on tenacious greed, in the manner of many a late-fourteenth-century friar. Crude overkill notwithstanding, both performances are also rich in irony, as when words and actions originally occurring innocently or in rhetorical excess are later recalled for having foreshadowed literal events. An example from each tale will suffice to illustrate the technique.

Early in the *Friar's Tale* the word "forsake" in the yeoman's casual remark that he will "holde compaignye with [the *somonour*] / Til it be so that thou forsake me" (III.1521–22) seems to carry only the physical sense of parting company on this present journey. But the *somonour*'s denial (III.1523–34) draws so lavishly on hyperbole as to force attention on the possible metaphysical sense of renunciation. His boldfaced Falstaffian lie, "I am a yeman" (III.1524), just after his companion has accurately named him a "somonour" (III.1474) and himself a "feend" (III.1448), is followed by an exaggerated protestation of brotherhood. As a result, what earlier seemed to be a conversational hyperbole ironically predicted what will literally occur at the end of the tale, that the *somonour* will never renounce Satan:

"Nay," quod this somonour, "that shal nat bityde!
I am a yeman, knowen is ful wyde;
My trouthe wol I holde, as in this cas.
For though thou were the devel Sathanas,
My trouthe wol I holde to my brother,
As I am sworn, and ech of us til oother,
For to be trewe brother in this cas." (III.1523–29)

A similar echoing of language occurs throughout the *Summoner's Tale*.
The freeloading *frere*, having explained to his hostess that he wishes "To
grope tendrely [her husband's] conscience" (III.1817), though his unwavering interest is Thomas' money, proceeds to denigrate the prayers of
opulent clerics with the aural "Lo, 'buf!' they seye, '*cor meum eructavit!*'"
(III.1934), in contrast to the prayers of his own brethren, which "Up
springeth into th'eir . . . to Goddes eres two" (III.1939–41).[2] Later the
word "grope" recurs bawdily in a reader's mind as the *frere* greedily
thrusts to Thomas's "tuwel," while the onomatopoeic ridicule of his competitors' prayers echoes in the flatulent thrust with which Thomas en-
riches the *frere*'s hand. With more greed than forgiveness, more scolding
about anger than tenderness for conscience, the *frere*'s sermon is as windy
as Thomas's "buf," a mere "ferthyng" (III.1967) that "Up springeth into
th'eir."

Apart from the similar uses of irony within each tale, verbal echoes link
both together. Where the earlier tale speaks of bailiffs, albeit somewhat
misleadingly, the later tale's *frere* describes his occupation with the same
metaphor: "I walke and fisshe Cristen mennes soules / To yelden Jhesu
Crist his propre rente" (III.1820–21). The devil who figures so prominently
in the *Friar's Tale* is balanced by the Summoner's bawdy anecdote in the
Prologue to his Tale about friars' normal habitation in hell (III.1675–99)
and by a late claim that Thomas must be "certeyn a demonyak" (III.2240).
In both tales the central characters prove incapable of distinguishing between the physical world and the world of spirit. Compare the *somonour's*
interest in the devil's physical shape, as well as his assumption that the devil
would be interested in physically hauling off a hay cart and its horse, with
the *frere*'s argument that Matthew's beatitude "Blessed be they that povere
in spirit been" (III.1923; Matthew 5.3) specifically refers to friars because
friars lack material possessions.

Especially in their relation to the Wife of Bath, however, are these two
tales most instructive, for they function as companion footnotes to her
performance, clarifying what her overpowering presence has perhaps concealed. We might understand the full significance of these "footnotes" by

examining how each tale follows the same basic structure, containing seven sections that parallel each other so closely as to suggest Chaucer was following a formula:

1. An *ad hominem* prologue advancing the continuing battle between the Friar and the Summoner (Fr. III.1265–1300; Su. III.1665–1708).

2. A general description by the teller of each tale showing how his central character—an image of his adversary—usually goes about his crooked craft (Fr. III.1301–31; Su. III.1709–60).

3. A sudden interruption by each teller's antagonist, who is then swiftly silenced by the Host (Fr. III.1332–37; Su. III.1761–64).

4. A resumption of section (2) above (Fr. III.1338–78; Su. III.1765–1917).

5. A lengthy moral/theological conversation between the central character and another character, confirming the earlier description of the central character's venal methods (Fr. III.1379–1536; Su. III.1918–2120).

6. Central Action, Part I, establishing certain terms and conditions which will influence what follows (Fr. III.1537–70; Su. III.2121–55).

7. Central Action, Part II, wherein the main character is undone by his own excesses according to terms established in (6) above (Fr. III.1571–1644; Su. III.2162–2294).

THE FRIAR'S TALE

The greatest single impasse to understanding the *Friar's Tale* arises when its yeoman-devil enters the scene. He is nowhere in sight at the beginning of the tale, when we hear general remarks about the *somonour's* business liaisons, his thievery, and his nose for lechers. But when we learn the predatory details of his current outing, presto! the yeoman appears instantly:

> And so bifel that ones on a day
> This somnour, evere waityng on his pray,
> Rood for to somne an old wydwe, a ribibe,
> Feynynge a cause, for he wolde brybe.
> And happed that he saugh bifore hym ryde
> A gay yeman, under a forest syde. (III.1375–80)

The suddenness of this appearance, in the next line following the *somonour*'s expressed intention to extort money, suggests a causal relationship: the sinfulness of the errand brings the devil on stage. (This is, of course, not his first sinful outing, to judge from his earlier description [III.1321–72], but it is the first we see and thus serves as a truncated representation of what he has long been doing and what he has now become.) A short time later the *somonour* brags of his extortions, admits he has no conscience, and—worst of all—refuses to seek forgiveness while cursing all confessors (III.1434–42). Only now does the yeoman disclose his identity, as if the *somonour*'s own words convert the man by degrees from yeoman to devil, as indeed they do:

> In this meene while
> This yeman gan a litel for to smyle.
> "Brother," quod he, "wiltow that I thee telle?
> I am a feend; my dwellyng is in helle,
> And heere I ryde aboute my purchasyng,
> To wite wher men wol yeve me any thyng." (III.1445–50)

Despite his being a "feend" (III.1448) and therefore implying incarnate evil,[3] his sudden appearance, behavior, and entire significance emanate from the *somonour* himself. Let us be clear about this point. We should not think of the yeoman-devil as an antagonist of the *somonour,* locked with him in mortal combat for his immortal soul. Rather, from one perspective we might look upon him as a choric figure on the margins of the scene. Instead of influencing the action in any way, his words articulate the contract God makes with every soul:

> Et qui bona egerunt, ibunt in vitam eternam;
> Qui vero mala, in ignem eternum.[4]

The *somonour*'s contract, then, is not with the yeoman-devil; it is with God, for Whom the yeoman-devil is a valid spokesman on this occasion.

Nor is it accurate to say that the yeoman-devil objectifies his traveling companion's sin, that he represents evil allegorically. On the contrary, from another perspective he is a spiritual *memento mori*, a reminder that sinful conduct brings consequences as inevitable as the consequences arising from physical laws. Far from duplicitly cloaking himself in fleshly delight, the yeoman-devil eschews artifice, revealing himself after only a few minutes as an instrument of God's will:

> "For somtyme we been Goddes instrumentz
> And meenes to doon his comandementz,

Whan that hym list, upon his creatures,
In divers art and in diverse figures.
Withouten hym we have no myght, certayn,
If that hym list to stonden ther-agayn.
. . . and al is for the beste.
Whan he withstandeth oure temptacioun,
It is a cause of his savacioun." (III.1483–88, 1496–98)

As we see, the yeoman-devil is a complicated literary trope. In addition to being a kind of representative of God by clarifying the meaning of His promise—that to merit damnation an evil act must be accompanied by an avowed intention to commit the act—the yeoman-devil is also an allegory of the fallen soul that the *somonour* has become, an allegory that takes shape by slow degrees during the course of the tale.

Despite the unambiguous—though complex—significance of the devil's presence, the *somonour* remains oblivious to its pertinence for himself. Neither recoiling from the presence of this devil nor wondering at the devil's interest in himself, the *somonour* tries to engage him in dialogue, thus taking another step toward converting his new companion from yeoman to fiend. Like Faustus trying pathetically to make an intellectual quest more important than the progress of his soul, the *somonour* cannot conceal his obsession with the physical dimensions of the demonic world. He wants to know if devils have real shapes, and what those shapes may be. The devil rises (perhaps stoops) to the subject, but at the same time reveals in a flash his power to see through the physical world to the *somonour*'s essence, specifically to know that he *is* a *somonour* (III.1474).

Although the yeoman-devil is partly a reflection of the *somonour,* these two companions are noticeably different from one another in the very different attitudes they have to language. The *somonour* apparently assumes that, by listening carefully to his knowledgeable companion-teacher, he will acquire an intellectual understanding of hell, yet fails to grasp the clear meaning of the yeoman-devil's literal words, that he will become an expert by actually residing in hell: "Thou shalt herafterward, my brother deere, / Come there thee nedeth nat of me to leere" (III.1515–16). And when speaking rather than listening, the *somonour* distorts truth to dupe his gulls, while insisting that others keep to the literal meaning of their words. His first exchange with his new traveling companion attempts to deceive on two counts: by claiming that the widow rightfully owes him money, when in fact she has committed no offense, and by pretending that her money will be forwarded to his superior, although it will probably stay in his own pocket (III.1390–91). His second speech similarly attempts to deceive when he conceals his true profession by calling himself a bailiff: "He dorste nat, for verray filthe and shame / Seye that he was a somonour, for the name" (III.1393–94). The devil, on the other hand, holds a directly opposite attitude to language. He knows that men often speak deceivingly and thus shapes his own words to convey absolute truth, taking care that his literal words match his actual thoughts. His yeoman's dress, green jacket, bow, and arrows all suggest what is undoubtedly true, that he serves another, a lord whose prey he guards. Nor does his claim to be a bailiff (III.1396) mislead. He does indeed make collections for a superior.

These different attitudes to language receive clearest exposure in the first part of the tale's central action, when the two traveling companions come upon a man struggling with a loaded cart mired in a ditch, a scene that follows directly after the devil's explanation of his profession. Though the carter literally curses his cart and horse, "The feend . . . yow fecche, body and bones, / . . . The devel have al, bothe hors and cart and hey!" (III.1544, 1547), these formulaic curses have little to do with the carter's intention. Nonetheless, the *somonour* knows a loophole when he sees one, especially when it concerns the physical world to which his vision is limited. On the authority of the carter's literal words he advises the devil to seize the cart and horse, as he would do if he were in the devil's shoes. The devil declines, explaining the immediate point of this brief thirty-line scene as soon as the horse pulls the cart out of the ditch: because "It is nat his entente . . . The carl spak oo thing, but he thoghte another" (III.1556, 68).

Not only does the *somonour* reveal in this scene his view of language as a tool for exploitation, he also fails to see that he could learn a good lesson from the horse, who actually reveals the moral core of the tale. By persevering at its assigned task and overcoming its limitations, this horse demonstrates how salvation may be achieved. The high praise it earns from its master would be meaningless hyperbole, if the words did not also allude to the actual reward the *somonour* will miss at the end of the *Tale* for want of a willingness to repent:

> "Heyt! Now," quod he, "ther Jhesu Crist yow blesse,
> And al his handwerk, bothe moore and lesse!
> That was wel twight, myn owene lyard boy.
> I pray God save thee, and Seinte Loy!
> Now is my cart out of the slow, pardee!" (III.1561–65)

If the *somonour's* failure to repent is at the moral core of the tale, his attitude to language is at its literary core, for this scene with the carter makes clear that Robert B. Burlin's reference to "the old tag, *intentio judicat hominem,"* tells only half the story.[5] To leave the *Summoner's Tale* there, hanging in *judicat*'s eternal balance, may be all well and good for the theological issue involved, but it ignores the poetic context, the connection with the seven tales from the Wife's to the Franklin's. The focus of that wider context is not intention alone, but the further question of whether literal language in any given speech agrees with, or contradicts, the actual intention lying behind that literal language.

The question of literal language versus intent occurs again in the specific speeches of the second part of the tale's central action. But, again, we must be careful to understand which particular language and which intention trigger the devil's collection of the *somonour*'s "Body and soule" (III.1640), for several declarations come in quick succession in the scene. First, the *somonour*'s attempt to extort twelve pence from the old widow, though "of hire knowe I no vice" (III.1578), brings no response from the devil. Nor does his subsequent rejection of the widow's plea for mercy: "Nay thanne . . . the foule feend me fecche / If I th'excuse, though thou shul be spilt!" (III.1610–11). Like the carter's earlier curse, the remark is clearly hyperbolic and in any case unlikely ever to apply, since the *somonour* has no intention of desisting in his attempted extortion. After all, he is at this moment showing off. But at the end of the scene a quick exchange between the widow and the devil brings the action to a head. The widow's own hyperbole, "Unto the devel blak and rough of hewe / Yeve I thy body and my panne also" (III.1622–23), prompts the devil to inquire into her actual intention. She then amends her words, pulling them back from hyperbole to actual intent: "The devel . . . so fecche hym er he deye, / And panne and al, but he wol hym repente!" (III.1628–29). The taunt is too much for the *somonour* to resist: "Nay, olde stot, that is nat myn entente . . . for to repente me" (III.1630–31).[6] Now, and only now, does the devil claim his prey—not at the *somonour*'s mere wrongdoing, nor at the widow's wish that he go to the devil, but only when the *somonour* insists he has no intention of repenting.

In view of its central character's inability to appreciate either the significance of his language or the consequences of his actions, the *Friar's Tale* makes an obvious comment on the preceding performance of the Wife of Bath. Though the old *ribibe*'s widowhood might make the Friar's audience think of the much widowed Wife of Bath, whose echoes are perhaps still ringing in their ears, the contrast between these two is far more striking than the similarity. The Wife takes enormous liberties with language, deliberately speaking untruths, often to fetch material gain, constantly berating her husbands, hinting that she has been unfaithful, and delighting in the belief that her Canterbury companions accept her as a sexually liberated, triumphant woman. And she also maintains the opposite, that she has not fought back with her "body, in no foul manere" (III.485). In fact, the liberated braggadocio may be untrue; or the protests of innocence may be false; indeed, *all* her claims may well be false. The widow in the *Friar's Tale* is a very different woman. When the *somonour* falsely accuses her of having cuckolded her husband, she replies swiftly and clearly. And we believe her:

> "Thou lixt!" quod she, "by my savacioun,
> Ne was I nevere er now, wydwe ne wyf,
> Somoned unto youre court in al my lyf;
> Ne nevere I nas but of my body trewe!" (III.1618–21)

And she apparently respects language as a medium that should communicate the truth, to judge from the way she quickly amends her intemperate explosion with words that sound like the judicious speeches of the yeoman/devil himself. The net effect of the confrontation between the lying, scheming *somonour* and the truthful widow is to create a tableau of the two aspects of the Wife of Bath's character: the public "Wife" who coerces her husbands in order to achieve material goods, and the private "Alisoun" who claims to have remained faithful to her husbands but has nonetheless had to suffer their false accusations. Although the Wife was moderately effective in masking the tension between these two halves of herself, the confrontation between the extorting *somonour* and the wronged widow objectifies that tension with great power.

THE SUMMONER'S TALE

If the *Friar's Tale* explores the fundamental agreement between God and Man, where God will never renege nor mistake someone's ill-considered language for actual intention, while Man often does both, the *Summoner's Tale* depicts business as it is usually conducted between two human beings, where both parties have learned the ways of a fallen world.

A self-interested *frere* visiting a home where he has often been welcome finds his host Thomas "Syk . . . Bedrede upon a couche lowe" (III.1768–69). Despite this obvious condition, the *frere* offers not the slightest sympathy, mentioning instead how often and well he has eaten here in the past, while chasing a cat from what must be the most comfortable seat in the house, cats being cats. We suspect that he has only thought to visit Thomas's home because earlier in the day he noticed Thomas's attractive wife at Mass (cf. III.1797). In fact, he asks for her shortly after arriving and, upon her appearance, embraces her suggestively (III.1802–5). Then, despite a claim of self-denial, he hypocritically orders a grand meal with the sophistication of an experienced epicure (III.1838–43).

This preoccupation with fleshly concerns moves Thomas to ask where the *frere* has been these last two weeks, for it was just two weeks ago that Thomas and his wife lost a son (III.1852–53) and could perhaps have used some comforting. Again, the compassion we might have expected when the *frere* learns of this recent death—no doubt for the first time—is missing from the transparent lie claiming that he and his confreres had a vision of the boy ascending to heavenly bliss. Yet even this fabrication trails off into a boastful comparison of the greater efficacy of the prayers of his house than those of "burell folk" (III.1874).

Later in his groping conversation, the *frere* turns each of his host's remarks—whenever Thomas can squeeze one in—into an opportunity to focus on his own needs rather than on his host's. When Thomas interjects that he has spent on a variety of friars "Ful many a pound; yet fare I never the bet" (III.1951), the *frere* has no interest in offering the theological answer that grace does not come in measurable ways, but instead chastises Thomas for giving money to other friars instead of to a perfect recipient, himself. He unwittingly undercuts his argument with metonymy, as he uses the word *leche* instead of *phisicien* when asking the rhetorical question, "Why would someone who has a perfect leech seek medical attention elsewhere?" Given the least chance, the *frere* would bleed Thomas white. Finally, when Thomas declines confession, having confessed to his parish priest earlier in the day (III.2095), the *frere* drops his last hour's pretense of moral concern in favor of the naked appeal—"Yif me thanne of thy gold, to make oure cloystre" (III.2099)—in turn triggering Thomas' creative insult.

If we compare the next major section in the *Summoner's Tale* (that is, the insult itself) with its counterpart in the preceding *Friar's Tale,* we recognize that Thomas and the *frere* stand in relation to each other very differently from the way the *feend* and the *somonour* relate to each other. Whereas the *feend* and the *somonour* are markedly dissimilar regarding their use of language (the *feend* using it truthfully, the *somonour* duplicitly), Thomas and the *frere* have an almost identical interest in using language to mislead the other. No less than the *frere,* who thinly conceals his quest for gold behind a long-winded pretense of concern for Thomas's soul, Thomas too intends to mislead the *frere* into believing a pouch of mattress money will shortly be his. Hence, the agreement to which they swear is understood differently by the two parties. Thomas knows very well it has nothing to do with gold; the *frere* thinks it does. In the previous *Friar's Tale* no flawed agreement regarding cart, hay, and horse is entered into, because the *feend* understands very well that the carter's literal curse and his actual intention are two very different things. And he will only take what is freely intended. But here in the *Summoner's Tale*, where both parties conceal their actual intention, a handshake seals what is in effect a flawed agreement:

> "Now wel," quod he, "and somwhat shal I yive
> Unto youre hooly covent whil I lyve;
> And in thyn hand thou shalt it have anon,
> On this condicion, and oother noon,
> That thou departe it so, my deere brother,
> That every frere have also muche as oother.
> This shaltou swere on thy professioun,
> Withouten fraude or cavillacioun."
> "I swere it," quod this frere, "by my feith!"
> And therwithal his hand in his he leith,
> "Lo, heer my feith; in me shal be no lak." (III.2129–39)

When Thomas's thunderous fart propels the *frere* like a "wood leoun" (III.2152) to the lord of that village, it is more than a redress of blasphemy the *frere* seeks. His ire wants vengeance. Though claiming that the blasphemy done to his house (III.2183) upsets him more than the insult to himself, the *frere* leaves little doubt whether the once-noted blasphemy or the thrice-repeated "odious meschief" sends him into his tooth-grinding rage.[7]

But let us not lose the point of the tale while we delight in the humorous image of an outraged *frere* who seeks vengeance after preaching at length that an honest Christian should purge all traces of ire from his heart. The need to avenge an insult addresses only the *frere*'s immediate emotional desire. Still pending is a legal obligation arising from the literal words of a solemn handshake agreement between Thomas and the *frere*. Thomas has now performed his part of the literal bargain: "Swich thyng as is in my possessioun . . . that may I yeve, . . . And in thyn hand thou shalt it have anon" (III.2124–31). But the *frere* has yet to perform his: "On this condicion . . . That thou departe it so . . . That every frere have also muche as oother" (III.2132–34). Consequently the lord of the village focuses on the literal contract, specifically on Thomas's cleverness in diabolically setting an impossible task for the *frere*. The *frere*, on the other hand, focuses on Thomas's outrageous conduct, which in his opinion should be assigned by the lord the punishment it deserves. But, of course, the *frere*'s enraged quest for vengeance does not arise from the literal words of that contract, which he may have had no intention of honoring, but from the greedy intention that drove him to enter the agreement in the first place.

The tale's concluding hilarity provides a final irony. As with the former tale, where the frivolous, and hence ignored promise of a cursing carter is followed by a more serious agreement to which the *somonour* is held literally accountable, so here in the *Summoner's Tale* a deliberately misleading agreement is followed by another whose terms are strictly observed. Perhaps for the first time in his professional life the *frere* is forced to consider the literal significance of language, unvarnished by the glossing explications he assumes simple folk like Thomas need, "Nat al after the text of hooly writ" (III.1790). An ingenious squire, not missing a chance to strike an agreement of his own—a "gowne-clooth" for his effort—gains literary immortality for wagon wheels everywhere by offering a crude arse-metrical solution to the nearly impossible half of the *frere*'s earlier agreement.

The poetic justice of the *Summoner's Tale* has clear significance for the Wife of Bath and for all the tales that comprise what might better be called "the Contract Group" than "the Marriage Group." A formula emerges for the smooth operation of all social intercourse: use language with care, saying what you mean and meaning what you say. Especially when used obliquely, words can have consequences their speakers never intend, rising to artistry or descending to falsehood. We shall see how the next fragment explores both uses of language in stories that have long impressed readers as more important than the two witty glosses we have just discussed.

❧

Two Kinds of Agreement

Before God and Before Man

CLERK'S TALE AND MERCHANT'S TALE

The previous chapter's discussion of language and intention noted that the *Friar's Tale* and the *Summoner's Tale* each focuses on an agreement or a contract. In the former tale the two parties to the agreement are mismatched, one honoring both the literal words of the contract and its intention, the other attempting to manipulate both language and intention. In the latter tale the two parties are evenly matched in as far as they both use language misleadingly in an attempt to deceive the other party. The two tales of Fragment IV make exactly the same points as those of the Friar and the Summoner, in exactly the same order, employing narratives that seem more weighty, less a joke. Taking his cue from the *Friar's Tale,* the Clerk highlights the different attitudes Griselda and Walter have to their word, the former never speaking falsely nor reneging on a vow, while the latter does both, despite good intentions at the outset. The second tale, told by the Merchant, echoes the *Summoner's Tale* by focusing on the agreements made by two manipulators, January and May, both of whom use language for ulterior purposes.

There is, however, one significant way in which the two tales of Fragment IV differ from their precursors in Fragment III. Whereas the Friar and the Summoner are in complete control of their tales, perhaps because those tales are relatively unambitious, the tales of Fragment IV resemble the *Wife of Bath's Prologue and Tale* by featuring tale-tellers who have only tenuous control of their material. Perhaps A. C. Spearing is correct that the Clerk resists the tale he has chosen to tell.[1] Or perhaps the Clerk does not understand the revisions Chaucer made in Petrarch's version.

Whatever the case, some of his comments run counter to the main thrust of his tale. Loss of control is even more noticeable with the Merchant, who, while intending to tell one kind of tale, unwittingly tells another when January grows beyond his pilgrim creator. In this respect the tales of Fragment IV are intermediate steps in the poem's progress toward Fragment V, where the Squire and the Franklin are beyond their depth.

THE CLERK'S TALE

The Clerk's tale of Griselda has rested uneasily in the prickly wrappings of literary criticism. Depending on our critical approach, we find something very wrong either in the *Tale,* or in its meaning, or in its telling. If we read the *Tale* socially, with the critics of an earlier era, we try to explain Griselda's monstrous silence in the face of intolerable suffering.[2] If we read it symbolically, with D. W. Robertson, Jr., we try to justify God's relentless testing of Griselda, as if she were another Job.[3] If we read it dramatically, with A. C. Spearing, we try to appreciate the Clerk's struggle with material he finds unacceptable.[4] In other words, we make the *Tale* succeed at the expense of Chaucer, whom we tacitly blame for these shortcomings.[5]

A common assumption underlies these responses. The readers who puzzle over a docile Griselda in the face of cruel torment disbelieve that a normal human being would behave as Griselda does. Those who are discomforted by Griselda's repeated trials disbelieve God would behave in literature as Walter does. And those who would find literary art in the Clerk's struggle with his material assume that he would agree either with the former or the latter, probably with both. Notice that the implicit assumptions—Walter equals God, Griselda equals human being—arise from some reasoning like the following: "God is to man as King is to people as husband is to wife" (Cramer 1990, p. 492). But it is *we* who apply this analogy to the story of Griselda and Walter, for Chaucer's text does not. On the contrary, it offers abundant evidence of analogy between the metaphysical relationship between God and Man and the social relationship between human beings, where the relationship in both instances is based on virtue, not rank. That is, God is to Man as Perfection is to Imperfection. In the light of this unassailable analogy, an equation leaps off the page: God is to Man, as Griselda is to Walter.

This interpretation may be difficult to reconcile with the current critical discussion, now free of earlier claims that the tale allegorizes God testing a Job-like subject. More recently we have heard that it represents "the problems of sexual politics and gendered poetics."[6] But the critical problem need not be stated in such polemical terms, when the interpretive task is actually more fundamental. For the tale simultaneously obeys the rules of two genres, which lead to contradictory conclusions. On the one hand, the tale pursues a traditional account of how a certain lord, whose absolute power over his subjects could give him a well-born wife, instead chooses for his bride a humble yet virtuous young girl. On the other, it is an allegory of the relationship between God and Man, not in the usual way, with the husband representing God while the wife takes the role of frail humanity, but the reverse, where the wife represents God's earthly manifestation, Christ, and the husband plays the fickle, inconstant, devious human being. This allegorical level of meaning implies the wife's absolute authority over her husband, a direct contradiction of the tale's other genre where the husband is thought to have absolute authority over his wife. The contradiction is only apparent, since temporal lords exert authority only over the physical world; divine authority, though potentially unlimited, yields temporal authority to mankind's free will while choosing to reign over only the spiritual world.

The *Clerk's Tale* associates Griselda with God in both human and divine form, that is, with Christ. While any virtuous life inevitably shares features of the life of Christ, Chaucer seems to have made the analogy stronger. He places less emphasis on the similarity of Griselda's virtues to the virtues of Christ than on a few key details, and a few reactions of others to her, which make us see in Griselda's relation to Walter a faint allegory of Christ's relation to every human being. Viewed thus, the critical discomfort noted above completely disappears. If patient submission to cruel torment seems inexplicable in a normal human being, no one faults Christ for turning His other cheek. And if that cruelty comes doubtfully from God, we have grown to expect it from His creatures. To demonstrate this thesis requires some attention, first to the immediate context of the *Tale,* and then to Chaucer's subtle revision of his source.

Discussions of the Clerk's place in the dramatic context of the *Canterbury Tales* have been dominated by suggestions that he wishes to respond to the Wife of Bath. Perhaps he does. But an even more immediate context with Harry Bailly may share equally in determining the kind of tale the Clerk tells. The Host's specific request, "Telle us som myrie tale" (IV.9), receives two remarks noticeably short on mirth, a biting remark about having to obey his governor-of-the-moment, and a lugubrious observation about the grim reaper. Hardly merry. But if these words do not entirely comply with the host's call for a certain style, they actually do respond by setting the theme for the tale about to be told. The remark about governing foreshadows the story of how Walter's governance is eventually ruled by Griselda's servitude, while the reference to the death of Petrarch, from whom Chaucer adapted the Griselda legend, introduces a subtler dimension.[7] The Clerk's two flat statements that Petrarch is now dead (IV.29, 38) enclose a pair of oblique allusions to life beyond death. The first, referring to Petrarch's work, tells us that the laureate poet once "Enlumyned al Ytaille of poetrie" (IV.33), implying that despite death he still lives on, specifically in the Tale we are about to hear. The second, referring to his soul, actually starts to emphasize a termination, when a metaphor draws attention to the opposite. Death does not permit us to dwell here, the Clerk says (without clarifying just where death does permit us to dwell), adding what may be a borrowing from Bede's story of the conversion of Edwin, that death grants life no more than "a twynklyng of an ye" (IV.37).[8] The force of the reference brings to mind not the cessation of all, but the brevity of life compared with what goes on before and after the twinkling of that eye.

Against this brief background of life under a governor and in the shadow of death, the Clerk sketches the Marquis Walter, an admirable man with only a few faults:

> I blame hym thus: that he considered noght
> In tyme comynge what myghte hym bityde,
> But on his lust present was al his thoght,
> As for to hauke and hunte on every syde.
> Wel ny alle othere cures leet he slyde. (IV.78–82)

Walter may give due consideration to one of the Clerk's motifs, governing well, but he disregards his obligation to prepare for death, until a trusted spokesman of the people urges on him the idea of marriage, stressing the short term of life and the inevitability of death. Two stanzas emphasizing that we know neither the day nor the hour (IV.116–26) again remind us of Bede's *Conversion of Edwin,* where a close advisor notes that life flees as swiftly as a sparrow through a hall; we know nothing of whence it came or whither it goes. Only after this little homily has made its point does Walter's adviser add what seems to be an afterthought, his concern for regal succession (IV.136–39). The advisor is reminding Walter of a twofold obligation, to prepare himself for death and to provide a successor for the kingdom. We can readily understand that marriage would meet part of Walter's obligation, the begetting of an heir. But how could marriage prepare Walter himself? The answer is found, not in the institution of marriage by itself, but in the nature of the bride, for in Chaucer's adaptation of Petrarch's story several distinct allusions convert the arrival of Griselda into an image of the coming of Christ.

Petrarch understood his own version of Griselda's story (to quote Severs's summary) as "an example for all human beings to follow under the afflictions with which God may see fit to try our human frailty" (p. 13). The Latin author implies that his Walter represents the deity testing his human subject Griselda, and that by remaining obedient Griselda stands as a shining example for other human beings to emulate. That Chaucer had an opposite design for his *Clerk's Tale*, despite using Petrarch as his primary source, seems clear even in his earliest descriptions of Griselda. Where Petrarch dismisses Griselda's poverty with the cliché that the grace of heaven sometimes visits the shacks of the poor ("pauperum tuguria non numquam gratia celestis invisit" [II.3–4]), Chaucer adjusts the line with what Robinson calls an allusion to the Nativity, thereby making Griselda analogous to God's very offspring, instead of a mere gift from heaven:

> But hye God somtyme senden kan
> His grace into a litel oxes stalle. (IV.206–7)

Twice more he associates Griselda with an ox's stall (IV.291, 398), without parallel either in Petrarch or in the anonymous French text that Chaucer may also have used.

After Griselda becomes Walter's bride, her ability to promote the common profit and to appease discord, rancor, and heaviness suggested to Petrarch a familiar formula about her saintliness, that everyone said the woman had been sent from heaven for the public's well being: ". . . omnes ad salutem publicam demissam celo feminam predicarent" (II.96–97). Again Chaucer emends Petrarch's sentence, converting Griselda from merely a heavenly creature into a figure of Christ, a savior of the people:

> So wise and rype wordes hadde she,
> And juggementz of so greet equitee,
> That she from hevene sent was, as men wende,
> *Peple to save and every wrong t'amende.* (IV.438–41, emphasis added)

Later in the story another detail reinforces Chaucer's design—again without parallel in either Petrarch or the French version. As Walter's emissary explains to Griselda that he must take her young daughter, Chaucer adds:

Grisildis moot al suffre and al consente,
And as a lamb she sitteth meke and stille,
And leet this crueel sergeant doon his wille. (IV.537–39)

Not only does the simile of a lamb draw upon the most frequent symbol
of Christ,[9] but the image of a "crueel sergeant" as agent in an expected
execution, while that lamb remains "meke and stille" throughout, bears
strong parallels to the crucifixion of Christ.

A similar reference occurs after Griselda's next ordeal: the removal of
her son. Petrarch remarks that Walter might have suspected her of hard-
ness of heart, if he had not known her for the most loving of mothers
("nisi eam noscet amantissimam filiorum" [IV.40–41]). Chaucer elevates
her from comparison with other mothers to the level of perfection associated only with God:

> if that he
> Ne hadde soothly knowen therbifoore
> *That parfitly hir children loved she,*
> He wolde have wend that of som subtiltee,
> And of malice, or for crueel corage,
> That she hadde suffred this with sad visage. (IV.688–93, emphasis
> added)

If Griselda's humble birth in a stable, her description as a savior and a
lamb, as well as her perfect love, all suggest parallels with Christ, her
career as Walter's wife also follows a pattern similar to Christ's life on
earth. But here a distinction must be made between Christ's humanity,
which traveled through several stages—humble exemplar of virtue and
love, exalted hope of the people, tested and tormented victim, outcast
rejected and executed by temporal rulers, and finally a resurrected God/
Man—and His divinity, which remained constant throughout, making
possible the triumph over fleshly death, which proved His Godhead. In
the *Clerk's Tale* too there is a clear distinction between Griselda's changing circumstances and her absolute constancy. Chosen by Walter "for he
saugh that under low degree / Was ofte vertu hid" (IV.425–26), and accepted by the people because "evere vertuous was she" (IV.407), she becomes their chief hope for peace and common profit (IV.428–41). Later,
despite torments and rejection, her humble acceptance of her treatment
provides the very means of demonstrating her undiminished fidelity and
of restoring her to her position as Walter's spouse.

I have been arguing that Chaucer's adjustments of Petrarch's text accomplish the unusual feat—especially so for the fourteenth century—of depicting Griselda as a figure of Christ. Normally a woman like Griselda would be ideally suited to represent the Church, following St. Paul's famous passage in Ephesians 5:23-25, where Christ is analogous to the husband and the Church analogous to the husband's spouse.[10] In the *Clerk's Tale,* however, Chaucer departs interestingly from tradition to show the union of human and divine in the more accurate image of a single person rather than in the merely analogous relationship of two. While his figurative language associates Griselda with Christ's divinity, he discards nothing of her humanity. He retains her girlish awe in the presence of her country's Marquis; he preserves her affection for her father, husband, and children; he has her express a disinclination to suffer death (IV.364); and he even repeats her anxiety later in the *Tale* when she is on the point of being turned out of the palace unclothed as a spectacle before her former subjects. While these human emotions would have been inappropriate for the divinity *per se,* they provide a key element in the representation of Christ, whose essential characteristic is the simultaneous possession of divinity and humanity. As a finite woman Griselda takes part in the workaday chores of her world, feels joy and sorrow, loves her husband by whom she has children. As an embodiment of divine perfection, she subordinates these human activities and emotions to loftier virtues displayed to an infinite degree.

While the marriage of Griselda and Walter reflects a failed relationship between Christ and man, respectively, in which she loves her husband enough to die gladly for him and he responds by tormenting her and "killing" her children, the presence of those children and their relationship to Griselda show us what the mutual love of God and man can become at its ideal. Griselda's love for her children, and theirs for her, call forth an echo of Christ's obligation to the Father, and Man's to God: "this nyght shaltow dyen for my sake" (IV.560; cf. Matthew 10:39, 16:25). In fact, the children only appear to die. Their restoration several years later reminds us, first, of Christ's Resurrection, and then, of the promise of triumph over death that every faithful Christian receives. As flesh of her flesh, they partly signify Griselda's role as a figure of Christ, loosely standing for Christ's human form, which appeared to die but was later restored to life. As children of Griselda, the son and daughter resemble faithful Christians who symbolically follow Christ's path in finding their life through losing it.

Griselda embodies the medieval Christian's perception of the great irony of the Incarnation, the deliberate absence of all the symbols and demonstrations of worldly power. The Redemption called for Christ will-

ingly to submit Himself to temporal authority, to become subject to creatures who owe their very existence to Him. Every medieval Christian had
the exclusive power to determine his relationship with his Creator by deciding whether or not to accept the grace offered to him. When he did, he
approached the Christlike model that Griselda represents. When he did
not, he resembled Walter in one of his particularly cruel moments. Hence,
by presenting a temporal ruler as the spouse and governor of a physically
humble yet spiritually perfect wife, the *Clerk's Tale* represents precisely
the task facing the medieval Christian who would earn salvation. Christ,
so accessible, so obviously in command of the right way, nevertheless re-
poses temporal authority entirely in man, who turns easily from that right
way in order to satisfy human appetites he thinks more important. In
Walter's case, simple curiosity to learn the extent of Griselda's human
virtues prevents him from recognizing their divine proportions.

The *Clerk's Tale* expands this fascinating paradox of sovereignty and
service to universal significance. Though Walter attempted to govern his
world with standards of temporal worth—finery, beauty, passion, cruelty—Griselda's virtues of patience, constancy, and fortitude ultimately
govern him. Even in the role of serving girl near the end of the *Tale,* she
determines its outcome by remaining steadfast. As Walter once said, justifying a false claim of obedience to his subjects, and ironically ignoring a
larger significance:

> "But now knowe I in verray soothfastnesse
> That in greet lordshipe, if I wel avyse,
> Ther is greet servitute in sondry wyse." (IV.796–98)

And yet the *Clerk's Tale,* though evoking sympathy for Griselda and
her children, chooses neither for its central subject. It highlights Walter, as
the only figure who changes in the course of the tale, in particular regarding his treatment of his spouse. We recall his initial indifference to the idea
of a spouse, reluctantly agreeing only after his people urge him to marry
and insisting that his wife be taken on his own terms and arrayed as the
world reckons beauty:

> this mayde bright of hewe
> Fro foot to heed they clothed han al newe.
>   Hir heris han they kembd, that lay untressed
> Ful rudely, and with hir fyngres smale
> A corone on hire heed they han ydressed,
> And sette hire ful of nowches grete and smale.
> Of hire array what sholde I make a tale?

Unnethe the peple hir knew for hire fairnesse
Whan she translated was in swich richesse. (IV.377–85)

The word "translated" provides a rich irony.[11] Though Chaucer often
uses the word in its restrictive modern sense, it can also signify a change
to a higher state of being. Here it calls attention to the irrelevance of the
worldly array Walter prescribes for a bride already translated by her virtue. That the people have difficulty recognizing her suggests the importance they ascribe to superficial appearances, even when considering
worth not of a superficial sort. In any case, Griselda's new array and
fancy hairdo say less about her than about the material dimensions that
alone measure Walter's world.

Nothing makes clearer the enormous difference between Griselda and
Walter than their different attitudes to language. For Griselda's part, her
word is absolute. At her wedding she makes an unambiguous promise
that she vows never to break:

"I swere that nevere willyngly,
In werk ne thoght, I nyl yow disobeye,
For to be deed, though me were looth to deye" (IV.362–64)

Later, at the sad hour when she believes her son will follow her daughter
in death, she confirms her vow with words alluding to the Redemption:

"But now I woot youre lust, and what ye wolde,
Al youre plesance ferme and stable I holde;
For wiste I that my deeth wolde do yow ese,
Right gladly wolde I dyen, yow to plese." (IV.662–65)

Walter has an entirely different attitude to language. Despite his promise to cherish and honor his wife, which we assume he must have made on
a scale similar to the fourteenth century's Christian marriage contract in
the *Sarum Manual*, Walter later treats his wife outrageously.[12] Marriage
vows notwithstanding, we hear nothing from him to match the promise
he exacts from her, perhaps because this tale concerns the larger questions
of *trouthe* and *steadfastnesse*, rather than the narrower one of marriage.
Nevertheless, even if we overlook his presumed marriage vows, there is
still ample evidence that Walter thinks nothing of speaking deliberate
falsehoods as a tool for manipulation. His promise to Griselda's father—

"If that thou vouche sauf, what so bityde,
Thy doghter wol I take, er that I wende,
As for my wyf, *unto hir lyves ende*" (IV.306–8, emphasis added)

—hardly squares with his later declaration to her that he is about to take another wife and that the Pope has given consent:

"I may nat doon as every plowman may.
My peple me constreyneth for to take
Another wyf, and crien day by day;
And eek the pope, rancour for to slake,
Consenteth it—that dar it undertake." (IV.799–803)

Three falsehoods in one speech: Walter's subjects are not at all displeased with Griselda, but vent their displeasure on him for his cruelty (IV.729–32); the Pope has not even been petitioned—no permission was granted by these counterfeit bulls (IV.743–49); and Walter has no intention of taking a new wife. One might add that the reference to "every plowman," though intended by Walter as a reference to his duty to produce noble progeny, implies another falsehood. Rank confers no exemption from morality; a marquis, no less than a plowman, must honor his word.

Walter's habit of using false language to manipulate others is especially active during his cruel campaign to test his wife's fidelity to her vow of obedience. Petrarch saw in this campaign what most Chaucerians see in it, "the paradigmatic Christian 'preved' by God."[13] But what might be argued for Petrarch's version cannot apply to Chaucer's. Whereas Petrarch makes no comment beyond the simple statement that Walter wished to test his wife, the Clerk's editorial comment makes it impossible to see Walter as a representative of God:

But as for me, I seye that yvele it sit
To assaye a wyf whan that it is no nede,
And putten hire in angwyssh and in drede. (IV.460–62)

More important, words like "test" and "trial" seem entirely inappropriate for Chaucer's Walter, who does not in fact *test* Griselda at all; he *tempts* her, "O nedelees was she *tempted* in assay" (IV.621, emphasis added). The word *tempt* (and its related forms, *tempted, temptatioun,* and *tempter*) has unambiguous meaning in Chaucer. It occurs seventeen times in the *Parson's Tale* where sin is the explicit subject; three times of a devil in the *Friar's Tale,* and again of a devil in the *Man of Law's Tale;* and once in the *Tale of Melibee* to explain the relation between sin and temptation.[14] Thus, even before examining *tempt* in the *Clerk's Tale,* we have good reason to suspect it connotes something evil here too. Since seven of its eight occurrences in the *Clerk's Tale* are either straightforward additions or substitutions for Petrarch's *experiendi* or *retentandi,* neither of which is exclusively pejorative, we may reasonably infer that the word holds an important key to the *Tale*'s meaning, and that its connotations of wrongdoing probably play an important part in that meaning.[15]

In the light of this strong emphasis on temptation, rather than on simple testing, a brief passage in James seems pertinent: "Let no man say when he is tempted, that he is tempted by God; for God is no tempter to evil, and he himself tempts no one. But everyone is tempted by being drawn away and enticed by his own passion" (James 1:13–14). Indeed, both Petrarch and Chaucer quote part of this very passage—it is the only instance in which both authors agree in their use of tempt: "ipse [i.e., God] neminem temptet" (Pet., VI.75; *CT*, IV.1153). Interestingly, both authors depart from James's text to amplify his meaning:

> But [God] ne tempteth no man that he boghte,
> As seith Seint Jame, if ye his pistel rede;
> *He preeveth folk al day*, it is no drede. (IV.1153–55, emphasis added)

If these additional words apply to anyone in the story, they describe Griselda, for it is she who brings out—"prooves"—Walter's better nature with her own constant fidelity to an absolute vow of obedience that needs no proof itself.

The evidence is overwhelming: in Chaucer's version of Griselda's story, Walter simply cannot represent God testing or tempting man. This is not to say that the tale has no temptation, only that it is not God who does the tempting. The worldly values that almost always describe Walter in Chaucer's *Tale* restrict him to human levels, where temptation too often characterizes the actions of man. Not only does man tempt himself and others, as St. James and many of the Tales of Canterbury make clear; what is worse, he tempts his Maker.

At length Walter mends his ways, converting from cruel tormentor to believing spouse. In view of his past acts, we may be inclined to doubt his sudden conversion, as we are inclined to credit fatigue rather than careful thought for the metamorphosis of a young knight-rapist into a loving husband at the end of the *Wife of Bath's Tale*. Walter may have understood that there are no more punishments to inflict, short of torture and death, although Griselda's gentle rebuke to be kinder to his next wife than he has been to others (read "than to me," line 1039), would hardly compel a steely campaigner like Walter. More likely, he finally understands that at the time of his wedding Griselda made an absolute vow she will never break. For Walter conversion has not been a product of reasoning from within, but a slow experiential progress toward what others had known from the beginning, "That she from hevene sent was, as men wende, / Peple to save and every wrong t'amende" (IV.440–41).

The dramatic context too, which began with the Clerk taking orders from the Host, concludes in a perfect analogue to the *Tale*. The Host had commanded the Clerk to tell something *simple* that all might understand. The Clerk responds that he must naturally obey, since the Host has governance of them all. The *Tale* he tells, however, contradicts both counts. While appearing simple, and to that extent to comply with the Host's request, at its profoundest levels the *Tale*'s inversion of typical medieval expectations proves very difficult to understand, and thus contradicts the Host. At the same time the Clerk makes us wonder who is governing whom. By professing to tell a simple merry tale, and giving instead a sober tale of man's callous treatment of God, the Clerk behaves toward the Host as Griselda behaves toward her husband—like an obedient master, achieving great lordship through great servitude.

The Clerk's admiring glance in the Wife of Bath's direction marks another echo of the *Tale*'s fundamental irony, the acquiescence that ultimately controls. If Alisoun was, indeed, trying to catch the Clerk's eye throughout her performance, his response (IV.1163–72) must be taken as a final, if oblique, rejection. She had reminisced fondly of her fifth husband, a clerk, implying that he was what she prayed all women should have, a husband "meeke, yonge, and fressh abedde" (III.1259). When the pilgrim Clerk, upon finishing his *Tale*, admits the unlikelihood of finding more than two or three Griseldas in a whole town, claiming thus to endorse the Wife and all her sect, his transparent point must cause that anguished woman yet more pain: no man on earth would marry Alisoun, if he could but think of Griselda.

THE MERCHANT'S TALE

Criticism has had as much difficulty with the *Merchant's Tale* as with the *Clerk's Tale*, though of a different kind. The story of January and May neither poses a complicated allegory, nor asks a heroic suspension of disbelief regarding a gentle wife's endurance. And yet its most famous scene, involving two pear-tree lovers and their *dei* from a garden *machina*, seems so bizarre, so like bawdy slapstick, that we overlook the *Tale*'s real significance. Not that the *Tale* receives little attention; it simply gets the wrong kind. We treat it like a fabliau, though it has almost nothing in common with the famous fabliaux of the *Canterbury Tales*: the *Miller's Tale*, the *Reeve's Tale*, and the *Shipman's Tale*. Moreover, standing at the geometric center of the entire poem,[16] and enshrined in the middle fragment of the longest run of tales in the whole Canterbury collection, it deserves to be accorded a more important place in the poem's overall design than it has been given.

If manuscript evidence had not already settled the *Merchant's Tale*'s place in the same fragment with the *Clerk's Tale,* there would nonetheless be little doubt that it belongs there. Both tales describe husbands who resist marriage until extraneous pressures urge it on them. Subsequently they both find that marriage presents more problems—largely of their own making—than anticipated, but eventually seem to work out an arrangement with a hopeful future. Additionally, the tellers of both tales seem somewhat out of touch with their material, the Clerk slightly misunderstanding the story of Griselda and Walter, and the Merchant inadvertently following January and May in directions he should perhaps avoid. What separates the tales is the different preoccupations of these two pilgrim story tellers. The Clerk, as one of the more enthusiastically endorsed pilgrims in the *General Prologue,* prefers

> Twenty bookes, clad in blak or reed,
> Of Aristotle and his philosophie
> Than robes riche, or fithele, or gay sautrie. (I.294–96)

It is not surprising, therefore, that his *Tale* emphasizes the philosophic and theological dimensions of marriage. The Merchant, familiar with commerce, merchandise, and money—all measurable things—highlights the physical aspects of the courtship and marriage. However, to appreciate the subtler ways in which the *Merchant's Tale* relates to its predecessor, to the other five tales in this section (that is, in Fragments III and V), and to the entire poem, we must discuss it on its own terms.

More than any other tale told on the road to Canterbury, the *Merchant's Tale* insists we remain alert to narrative point of view. Though many of the tales feature four levels of narrative depth—the poet's, the Narrator's, the pilgrim tale-teller's, and the several characters within a pilgrim's tale—only the *Merchant's Tale* leaves us in some doubt over whose voice we are listening to.[17] I am not now referring to what Donald R. Howard calls "unimpersonated artistry" (1976, p. 231), where the author puts some of his own constructions into the mouths of characters who could not be expected to invent them. Rather, the tale has a number of speeches susceptible to several interpretations, all well within their speaker's competence, which call for a plausibility test to determine whether any given meaning should be accepted. The foundation of such a test rests on an understanding of the character of the pilgrim who tells the Tale.

The Merchant discloses in his own Prologue a marriage less than happy, a wife less than Griselda, and a speaker too little and too late aware of the extent of his self-revelations. As no reader believes the auto-biographical disclaimer from this veteran of a two-months-old marriage responding to the Host's request for a tale of married life—

> "Gladly," quod he, "but of myn owene soore,
> For soory herte, I telle may namoore" (IV.1243–44)

—so no pilgrim would doubt that the story of aged January and youthful May, whose marriage has grave trouble in its first few months, pinches the Merchant's own foot. To prevent the possible connection his audience may make between his material and himself occupies a good bit of his tale-telling energy.

The description of January with which the tale opens shares, if not precisely the years, at least the marital condition of the Merchant, that he lived "sixty yeer a wyflees man" (IV.1248). Whether he shares other fea-tures, in particular an interest in following "ay his bodily delyt / On wommen, ther as was his appetyt" (IV.1249–50) we cannot say with cer-tainty, though Chaucer does nothing to discourage our speculation. To wit: In describing why the sixty-year-old lecher January would suddenly feel an urge to marry, the Merchant makes two suggestions, both designed to conceal the truth:

> Were it for hoolynesse or for dotage
> I kan nat seye . . . (IV.1253–54)

If *dotage* refers to a mental condition, as the *OED* suggests (q.v., 1.a,b), we may rule out the suggestion immediately. Nowhere does January show signs of senility. He may reason on false premises, express unacceptable opinions, and display extraordinary naïveté regarding women and mar-riage. But he retains his shrewd reasoning to the very end. Similarly, we may discard an alleged attack of holiness. If sin were suddenly abhorrent to January, he need only mend his ways, adopt a celibate life, and sin no more. Marriage would have nothing to do with it. But January somehow sees marriage as an inevitable consequence of his professed resolve to refrain from the sin of lechery. This reasoning could only follow if celi-bacy were unthinkable to him, a requirement he conveniently neglects to mention. We meet January at the unattractive age of sixty, with question-able vigor (see the discussion below), when he must not be as successful a lecher as he once was. If celibacy is indeed an unacceptable condition, he clearly has a problem. The solution that presents itself would seem perfectly logical to his mercantile-thinking Merchant creator. Never mind the holiness or senility that the Merchant misleadingly suggests for January's sudden desire to marry. More likely, he wants to have a young girl under contract, bound to his bedroom as a nurse-concubine for the rest of his days. It is not the thrift of general husbandry he has in mind when he thinks of the beauty of marriage:

> She seith nat ones "nay," whan he seith "ye."
> "Do this," seith he; "Al redy, sire," seith she. (IV.1345–46)

Little wonder the Merchant cannot list contractual lechery with "hoolynesse" and "dotage" as possible explanations for January's sudden impulse to marry. It comes embarrassingly close to his own situation.

That the tale-teller's mercantile process of thought may also be alleged of January is evident in the latter's meditations on marriage, which reveal an attitude to women no different from that of the unreformed womanizer he once was:

> "I wol noon oold wyf han in no manere.
> She shal nat passe twenty yeer, certayn;
> Oold fissh and yong flessh wolde I have fayn.
> Bet is," quod he, "a pyk than a pykerel,
> And bet than old boef is the tendre veel.
> I wol no womman thritty yeer of age;
> It is but bene-straw and greet forage." (IV.1416–22)

As telling as these gustatory metaphors are, January's grammatical subject, "It is but bene-straw" instead of "She is . . . ," ignores his future wife as a person, while bringing her flesh into sharper focus. When he later makes May undress in front of him (IV.1958), we suspect he does not gaze lovingly on his wife, but surveys lasciviously the "tendre veel" he hopes will make his vigor match his lust. January's attitude to his wife immediately before and after his wedding seems no different from his presumed attitude to other women over the past sixty years.

The Merchant's effort to distance himself from his central character on the question of why an old man would suddenly wish to marry is not the only instance of manipulative language in the *Merchant's Tale*. Every character in the tale employs deliberately misleading language. January speaks platitudinously about the sacrament of matrimony (IV.1319ff.) and about his fear that no man may have "parfite blisses two" (IV.1638), though we doubt he cares a hoot about morality or theology.[18] As a newly married man, a travesty of a traditional bridegroom, he speaks to his bride with pathetic sexual bravado (IV.1828–41), his first speech to her in our hearing, though he knows he will have trouble consummating his marriage. Even his final speech to May much later in the tale, when he welcomes her back from her "struggle" in the pear tree, may be manipulative, if he is actually trying to deceive her into believing she has deceived him (as I will argue below). His advisor Placebo, intent only on spouting what he thinks January wants to hear, admits that his whole life has been a fabrication to endorse the wishes of his employer (IV.1478–1518). His other adviser, Justinus, by claiming his words on wives suffice for all womanhood, falsifies the entire gender (IV.1519–65), as anyone just hearing the story of Griselda would know. May too, hardly in need of instruction in the art of dissembling, professes marital fidelity in her first quoted speech to her husband (IV.2188–2206), while simultaneously gesturing her lover up the tree where marital infidelity will occur. We even doubt her later claim to be suffering from the cravings of pregnancy, for truth is an unlikely utterance from a woman so keen to deceive. Whether pregnant or not, May nevertheless uses these words to manipulate her husband into helping her to Damian's embrace. And, of course, her brilliant retort (with Persephone's help) to January's astonished outburst stands as the classic husband-duping, perhaps in all of English literature:

> "me was taught, to heele with youre eyen,
> Was no thyng bet, to make yow to see,
> Than strugle with a man upon a tree.
> God woot, I dide it in ful good entente." (IV.2372–75)

Habitual reliance on the language of deception carries great risk, often gaining tactical advantage at the price of strategic loss. One of January's calculated speeches to May provides a case in point. It occurs immediately after May, following custom, has kept to her room for the first four days of her marriage. On reappearing she hears of the illness of Damian whom her worried husband urges members of his household to visit. January's promise that he and May will pay their respects after dinner (IV.1914) apparently overestimates his energy, for within a dozen lines he instructs May to convey regards for both of them, while he takes a nap. Just before sending May to Damian, however, January describes for his wife some of the squire's valuable assets:

> "He is a gentil squier, by my trouthe!
> If that he deyde, it were harm and routhe.
> He is as wys, discreet, and as secree
> As any man I woot of his degree,

And therto manly, and eek servysable,
And for to been a thrifty man right able." (IV.1907–12)

This is more than general concern for the health of someone in the household. Several of the words in this speech sound like attributes of a successful courtly lover. True enough, "discreet" and "secree" are admirable virtues, especially in a servant, but by implying that some affair must be concealed from view and unspoken in gossip they have always had special pertinence for illicit love. Even more striking, "manly," appearing in the next line, particularly in connection with "servysable," seems oddly out of place describing a squire whose official duties cannot have been physically taxing. Yet "manly" only *connotes* muscular strength, while it actually *denotes* sexual vigor. Let us suspend for the present our interpretation of these lines, until we have a clearer sense of their context. For our understanding of whether they actually do possess the suggestive force I am proposing, or merely describe Damian in generally favorable terms, depends on our "sense of the whole."[19]

It was suggested above that January's plan to gratify his sexual obsession leads him naïvely to the sacrament of matrimony: "'Noon oother lyf,' seyde he, 'is worth a bene, / For wedlok is so esy and so clene, / That in this world it is a paradys'" (IV.1263–65). Irony aside, this grossly mistaken notion of marriage arises naturally from January's mercantile comparison of a wife to "londes, rentes, pasture, or commune, / Or moebles" (IV.1313–14), despite the greater value he assigns to a wife than to these other possessions.[20] Metaphors like "wedlok" (IV.1264, 1347, 1836), "boond/bound" (IV.1226, 1261, 1262, 1285), "snare" (IV.1227), "yok" (IV.1285, 1837), and "knyt" (IV.1391) emphasize physical constraint as the essence of marriage, a condition prohibiting either party, but especially the wife, from exercising freedom. Viewing marriage as a binding contract for services, he entirely overlooks its human dimension, as he salivates over the imagined dedication of the woman he intends legally to bind to his will:

If he be povre, she helpeth hym to swynke;
She kepeth his good, and wasteth never a deel;
Al that hire housbonde lust, hire liketh weel. (IV.1342–44)

The success of January's plan depends on his success with his bride during the early days of his marriage. And there's the rub. Though we eavesdrop on two of January's sexual fantasies—whether this is the Merchant's intentional device to reveal January's character, or an unwitting revelation of his own, we do not know—these thoughts are neutralized by January's evident concern over his ability to consummate his marriage. His worry that May will perhaps be unable to sustain the vigor of his "corage" (IV.1757–61), though shaped as a prayer to conceal its prurience, becomes a joke in view of the "ypocras, clarree, and vernage / Of spices hoote [he takes] t'encreessen his corage" (IV.1807–8) as the moment of truth draws near. And the nearer the moment, the more his fear of inadequacy intrudes upon his fantasy. A statement of frank sexual fact— another pornographic fantasy masked as an apology for a duty he must, alas, perform—dissolves into a transparent bluff trumped by his own disclaimer:

> "Allas! I moot trespace
> To yow, my spouse, and yow greetly offende
> Er tyme come that I wil doun descende.
> But nathelees, considereth this," quod he,
> "Ther nys no werkman, whatsoevere he be,
> That may bothe werke wel and hastily;
> This wol be doon at leyser parfitly." (IV.1828–34)

If these words before the attempted consummation betray his growing apprehension, the event itself proves he had good cause for concern. January cannot consummate his marriage. Though progressing from one grotesque detail to another—a bristly beard and "skyn of houndfyssh" (IV.1825) shaking loosely on the old man's neck (IV.1849)—the repugnant scene is overshadowed by the night's probable failure. Four separate references to fatigue (IV.1857, 1926, 1949, and 1957) hint at the nuptial impotence a later remark confirms: "And thynges whiche that were nat doon abedde, / He in the gardyn parfourned hem and spedde" (IV.2051–52). Before this garden success January occupies an untenable position. Having just married to guarantee the sex that still obsesses him, he finds he cannot perform adequately. Thus his praise for this wise, discreet, secret, manly, serviceable, thrifty, and capable Squire Damian cannot but call attention to the sexual strength that the old man lacks.

These words undoubtedly carry such a potential meaning. But we are unsure if that meaning applies equally to all four of the tale's points of view. The poet certainly knows their full range of meanings and probably chose them for that reason, if we can judge from the way he has Pandarus delicately engineer a number of trysts in *Troilus and Criseyde*. Whether Chaucer-the-Pilgrim does too is unanswerable, and probably of no consequence. The more important question is whether the Merchant and January know.

The Merchant is eager, here as elsewhere, to belittle January, specifically to emphasize his stupidity in misunderstanding the nature of wives, particularly after Theophrastus had been so clear on the subject (cf. IV.1298–1304). But the claim that he shapes the speech at lines IV.1907–12 to ridicule January's sexual weakness, in contrast to Damian's "manly serviceability," fails on two counts. First, Damian's manliness is bludgeoned by his own style, when he lies prostrated in a sick bed, when he cringes fearfully behind a low bush, and especially when he perches ludicrously in a pear tree. Second, and more significant in view of his own difficult, two-month-old marriage (cf. IV.1213–39), the Merchant cannot risk calling attention to January's sexual failures without raising questions about his own. However much a reader may suspect January's sexual failure, and perhaps the Merchant's as well, since the two parallel each other in a number of other ways also, from the Merchant's point of view January's words have nothing to do with impotence. At most they ridicule January by foreshadowing May's later infidelity, not January's present sexual inadequacy.

Finally, let us consider January's perspective. To understand his approximate state of mind during these early days of marriage we might imagine what he would do if the situation were reversed, if he were sexually willing and able, but his bride were not. Very likely he would consider the contract broken and throw her out; no sex, no marriage. Indeed, May might concur, since she later makes a point of saying what ought to happen to her if she were to break the contract by being unfaithful: "put me in a sak, / And in the nexte ryver do me drenche" (IV.2200–1). Termination of marriage, as a remedy for its difficulties, definitely comes to May's mind. And since her own fondness for commercial metaphors suggests that she really is "lyk to [January]" (IV.1329), termination of marriage would probably come to January's mind too.[21] Thus, in the early days of his marriage, when May "preyseth nat his pleyyng worth a bene" (IV.1854), January may be in some fear of losing his wife.[22]

At this point January's mercantile mind might conclude that May would remain if she were sexually content. That she would have to be secretly attended by someone other than himself would scarcely matter to a man whose life-long refusal to scruple over moral technicalities makes it unlikely he would do so now. Moreover, the blow to his pride from compromising his exclusive ownership of May, which might make other medieval men reject such a tawdry scheme, would have little impact on a man whose pride had long since vanished in sixty years of licentious living. More hedonist than egoist, January cares more about copulation than reputation. The plan would amount to playing percentages, as might his own creator, the Merchant: fifty percent of *something* is better than a hundred percent of *nothing*. Like a shrewd owner who wishes to keep a valuable possession in good working order—a horse, say, which must be exercised often to be ready for the master's next ride—January might well wish to plant surreptitiously in May's mind an image of Damian as a "manly," "servysable," and "thrifty" stable hand. An ugly motive indeed, but quite in keeping with his distorted view of a wife as a possession and of marriage as a contract for services.

Instinctively we want to reject this reading. We have no difficulty accepting January's praise for his squire as the Merchant's ironic jest at an old husband too stupid to realize his wife will cuckold him. He simply gives January a speech that unwittingly foreshadows his future, like the dramatic ironies that typically advance the plot of every *fabliau*. But to suggest that the speech is a husband's conscious attempt to plant in his wife's mind, without her realizing he has done so, the crude proposal that she seek sexual solace elsewhere, violates our sense of Chaucer's discretion. His humor includes jealous dotards and panting clerks, cuckolded husbands and boudoir athletes; never the sordid trafficking of one's own spouse.

True enough, though Dorigen in the *Franklin's Tale* would perhaps think differently. But before discarding this astounding possibility, we might note how well it agrees with January's frequent duplicity to gain some tactical advantage. Earlier in the tale he lavishly praised marriage, though he had no interest at all in the sacramental nature of the institution, because it presented the only practical way of securing a partner. Later, in no doubt of his cuckolding in a pear tree, "Ye, algate in it wente! . . . He swyved thee; I saugh it with myne yen" (IV.2376–78), he again utters words he does not believe, in order to avoid a confrontation that might end his marriage: "Now, dame," quod he, "lat al passe out of mynde. / Com doun, my lief, and if I have myssayd, / God helpe me so, as I am yvele apayd" (IV.2390–92). Like these other deceptions, January's praise of his squire may well be another artful speech to advance an ulterior aim. This possibility would make of the tale a more complex piece of literature than the *fabliau* it is usually taken to be, for it sees January's character as more interesting than his story.

January's blindness illustrates well the tale's expansion to something more ambitious than a *fabliau*. Blindness in literature often has symbolic significance. Like Sophocles's Oedipus and Milton's Samson, January lacks inner vision when his eyes are normal. What has escaped notice is whether he acquires insight while blind and, more difficult yet, retains this inner vision. Only two hypotheses receive attention in the early parts of the *Merchant's Tale,* both of which January apparently resists. First, he has apparently been blind to the sacramental nature of marriage, for the platitudes he recites about holy wedlock fail to restrain the lascivious images in which he delights. Even after blindness has set in, one could argue that an isolated reference to theology is overshadowed by more practical concerns:

> "Beth to me trewe, and I wol telle yow why.
> Thre thynges, certes, shal ye wynne therby:
> First, love of Crist, and to yourself honour,
> And al myn heritage, toun and tour." (IV.2169–72)

The other hypothesis is Theophrastan. Despite Justinus's lengthy warning about the inclinations of wives, many of which should have special pertinence for January, this long-in-the-tooth bridegroom rejects them out of hand, relying instead on his "yes man" Placebo to support his intention to marry. Again, the tale later provides abundant evidence of Justinus's prescience, for May does indeed cuckold January. Thus the motif of blindness seems to pose a question like the following: When January's outward eyes are able to see, is he inwardly blind to the sacramental nature of Christian marriage, or to the Theophrastan nature of women?

Certainly it is true that the religious dimension of marriage means no more than hollow ritual to January as he approaches his wedding. But our concern is not merely with January's perception of sacramental truth, as the fourteenth century understood it, but with his understanding of what makes a marriage successful. A proper understanding of marriage as a sacrament may have much to do with salvation, as an abuse of that sacrament may contribute to damnation. But the theological or philosophic understanding of marriage in the abstract has little to do with its earthly success. To assume the opposite is to believe with the Wife of Bath that a miraculous gesture can turn a failed marriage between a hag and a rapist into the blissful union of a faithful, beautiful princess and a chivalrous knight. The neighborhood where January and May live bears little resemblance to the fairyland of Alisoun's imaginings, despite the shadowy presence of Pluto and Proserpine, whose influence on states of mind is very different from the hag's skill at shape-shifting. And January's blindness, as a symbol of the impediment to a happy marriage, has little to do with his failure to understand the sacramental nature of marriage.

The Merchant's simplistic understanding of January's inward blindness undoubtedly includes only the Theophrastan view of women as deceivers. His aphorism, "as good is blynd deceyved be / As to be deceyved whan a man may se" (IV.2109–10), immediately follows a reference to the notes and signs Damian and May exchange under January's blind eyes, and precedes a description of the new key to January's garden, which May presses in warm wax to give to her intending lover. Moreover, the main thrust of his tale, as he probably understands it, upholds a Theophrastan view: May does indeed deceive January. However much this anti-feminist view may appeal to Justinus and the Merchant, it too must be rejected as the plausible thing to which January was blind when his outward eyes could see. Anti-feminism's patent absurdity, to all but the small group of misogynists who wrote its tracts and had never heard of Griselda, leads us to an entirely different understanding of January's blindness.

January's gravest error in the beginning of the tale, having nothing to do with his ignorance of either Theophrastus or the sacramental aspect of matrimony, rests entirely with his blindness to the human dimension of marriage. Much later in the tale a very different January, blindly groping about his garden with his hand on his wife's shoulder, uses nothing even remotely like his earlier metaphors of commerce and feasting. The plush language of the *Song of Songs* expresses what sounds like profound affection for May:

> "Rys up, my wyf, my love, my lady free!
> The turtles voys is herd, my dowve sweete;
> The wynter is goon with alle his reynes weete.
> Com forth now, with thyne eyen columbyn!
> How fairer been thy brestes than is wyn!
> The gardyn is enclosed al aboute;
> Com forth, my white spouse! Out of doute
> Thou hast me wounded in myn herte, O wyf!
> No spot of thee ne knew I al my lyf.
> Com forth, and lat us taken oure disport;
> I chees thee for my wyf and my confort." (IV.2138–48)

We could claim skeptically with the Merchant—"Swiche olde lewed wordes used he" (IV.2149)—that this is yet another gambit, more desperate than the others, to keep his wife. Perhaps so, at least to some extent. Yet personal feelings now seem more prominent than his earlier fixation on the rites marriage would permit him to perform. Note that some of his favorite earlier words—"make," "yok," "bound," "ycoupled"—are missing, replaced by "love," "lady," and "spouse." A new awareness of May as a human being has now been added to his physical attraction for her. January's slow-arriving inward vision may finally have shown him that marriage is neither a contract for services nor admission to a clean and easy terrestrial paradise, as he once supposed, but a relationship fostered by love, until now an absent guest at this feast.

One of the subtle achievements of Chaucer's art is his unwillingness to provide evidence to solve interpretive dilemmas. As we shall never know what precisely motivates Criseyde, how the *House of Fame* would end, or which pilgrim would dine free at the Tabard, so we shall never be certain of January's attitude to May in their garden at the end of the tale. Again, two possibilities seem to present themselves. Either: A duped January sincerely invites May to come down from her tree of ignominy, with the tacit understanding that they will both try to rise above their flaws to make a success of their marriage. Or: January is at it again, trying to manipulate May into remaining with him, as he once manipulated his counselors into advising marriage, his priest into quickly exiting the nuptial chamber, and a new wife into seeking solace with a young squire. The parallel structures of Chaucer's *Canterbury Tales* and Dante's *Commedia,* though unlikely to provide unanswerable proof of either possibility, may nevertheless offer guidance.

The *Merchant's Tale,* standing in the exact center of *Canterbury Tales* at the midpoint of the seven-tale section I have been calling the cybernetic or self-governed group, corresponds to the midpoint of *Purgatorio,* the seventeenth canto containing "the central argument that is basic to the whole moral order, i.e., the general exposition of Love" according to Charles S. Singleton,[23] where the wayfarer Dante experiences a "conversion." The issue continually raised throughout this section "concerns the radical difference . . . between possessing earthly goods and possessing heavenly goods." As Dante pauses at the center of the seven terraces of Purgatory, gazing back on the three he has just left and forward to the three yet to be ascended, he learns "that he must adjust the eyes of his mind to a polarity of difference between cupidity of material things (which means looking down at them) and the charity of Heaven, where possession of spiritual goods increases by sharing." Although the *Merchant's Tale* is not the middle tale in either the Ellesmere or Non-Ellesmere ordering of the seven tales in this section, it nevertheless stands at the very middle of the entire poem. And although these seven tales do not precisely cover the seven deadly sins governing Dante's *Purgatorio,* they touch enough of them for us to suppose that the author once considered having them do so. The parallel between Dante and Chaucer is thus strong enough in these corresponding sections to suggest that Chaucer may have considered January a wayfarer like

Dante, at a moment of conversion, aware at last that the earthy concerns that controlled his earlier life and led to marriage as a strategy to continue pursuing them pale before the prospect of human love. Though very differently talented and placed in very different settings, January and Dante are fellow pilgrims.

When the Merchant had January praise his squire Damian, he had no idea that his own creator, Chaucer, would make January outgrow him. The Merchant had intended to ridicule January for foolishly believing marriage a state of instant bliss, and thus to blame the institution itself for his own failed marriage. But January leaves the Merchant behind, mired in a fabliau, while he actually matures as a direct result of his crass hint that his wife take a lover. May's final words in the Tale, though said of the climactic discovery scene in the pear tree, describe well January's recognition that his earlier attitude to marriage had been gravely mistaken:

"Ful many a man weneth to seen a thyng,
And it is al another than it semeth.
He that mysconceyveth, he mysdemeth." (IV.2408–10)

After he finally realizes his wife's humanity, and his own natural fear that she might become unfaithful (IV.2169), he can hardly show indignation when his newly opened eyes confirm that fear beneath a pear tree. That ugly scene shows him the fruit of his own suggestion rather than the weakness of his wife. Hence, after the shock settles, he responds with the first gesture of genuine love we have seen in the entire tale. He pretends to accept his wife's explanation, in effect forgiving her, apologizes for his own conduct, and entreats her to join him as they face the future together.

The Merchant naturally sees that future differently. In his view January is either an old fool in a *fabliau,* duped by a quick-witted wife, or a calculating bargainer reduced to begging her for kindness. Little difference, when the outcome will be the same. To him, January will probably end up like his garden fairy Pluto, sharing his wife with Damian, a further harvest of his own sowing. That reading cannot be denied. But neither can we deny the higher vision, in which January and May face the future as our first parents did when they were expelled from their garden: certain of their own frailty, disenchanted of the belief that either the formulaic bliss of a sacrament or the delights of the flesh will guarantee a successful marriage. As human beings they face toil and pain, a future in which they must daily woo and win each other anew to work out their own happiness. It is one of the most hopeful moments in Chaucer.

❀

Two Versions of Magic

Squire's Tale and *Franklin's Tale*

Five tales and several hundred lines before Harry Bailly calls upon the Squire to "sey somwhat of love" (V.2), the Wife of Bath determined the kind of tales the Squire and the Franklin would tell when she startled the Canterbury pilgrims with the various forms of coercion she uses to make men docile. In her *Prologue* she described the physical force that gave her superiority over five husbands: verbal assaults, conjugal rights denied, deceptions to promote jealousy, and plain old fisticuffs. She employs a different kind of force in her *Tale* where her hag-surrogate exerts moral compulsion on an Arthurian knight reluctant to become a spouse: reminders that promises must be kept, that accidents of birth, wealth, and age cannot be faults, and that nobility properly comes from gentle deeds, not pedigree. Taken as a whole, then, her performance overwhelmingly advocated one or the other kind of force to make the world conform to her sense of right order.

But Alisoun is also a practical woman. Somewhere deep in her instinctual being she must know that coercion, whether of the physical or moral sort, at best produces a temporary result unless the one being coerced genuinely desires that same result. Forcing a spineless knight-rapist to honor his agreement to marry scarcely tested her mettle. But making him *want* to marry called for skills apparently beyond her grasp. Thus, despite having gambled her whole life on the efficacy of coercion, she hedged her bet in the last hour of her *apologia* by invoking a quite different kind of force: magic, to change her hag into a beautiful young princess capable of stimulating the knight's desire.

The *Squire's Tale* and the *Franklin's Tale,* the final two tales in this central section of the *Canterbury Tales,* pick up this magical thread that flashes at the end of the Wife's otherwise solid fabric of tough combat.

Fanning the futile hope to which nearly everyone turns in desperate times—everyone from Sir Gawain facing the Green Knight to an aging veteran of five marriages facing a lonely future—the Squire and the Franklin center their stories on the naïve magic of fairy tales. As Alisoun's coercion took physical and moral forms, the magic in these two tales also takes, respectively, physical and moral forms. The Squire describes various objects whose magical powers permit their owners to overcome physical limitations, especially those that prevent them from fully understanding the intentions of others. The Franklin celebrates *trouthe* and the Golden Rule whose moral magic induces two schemers to rise to gentle deeds and restores to a seriously tested marriage the happiness and tranquility it once knew.[1]

The addition of these tales in Fragment V completes for the huge center of Chaucer's poem the now familiar design he so often uses elsewhere. Fragment III and Fragment V stand before us as unacceptable extremes, the former for its repulsive force, the latter for its unrealistic magic. Nestled between them, the tales of Fragment IV contain the only practical method of achieving human harmony: a constant working at the give and take of physically limited lives, a continual adjusting between a reality we cannot accept and an ideal beyond our grasp, to produce relationships based on mutual respect and care otherwise known as love.

THE SQUIRE'S TALE

For all his appeal, the Squire is a walking cliché. His leisured pursuits of music and poetry, his flowery clothing, his skill at the social arts, all suggest the gentle pasture of a typical youth. His experience to date, such as it is, has been gained in cavalry campaigns where he hoped to appear more heroic in ladies' eyes, in contrast to his father's career that has mainly been in crusades for presumably noble purposes. ("Noble" here includes both the publicly professed intent of restoring the Holy Land to Christendom and the unstated intent of acquiring wealth.) We have little doubt he is a good lad, to judge from the image of humility and fealty in line I.100, where, like a servant, he carves meat at the table in front of his father. Indeed there is every expectation that in due time the Squire will outgrow the cliché we see before us and become just like his father, equally as much a cliché though of a more thoughtful, mature kind.

Similar to his father in another way, the Squire is unlikely to walk off with a prize for storytelling. After setting the time, place, and characters of his tale (seventy-five lines), he introduces a mysterious knight (thirty-two lines) who explains the powers of four curious gifts he has brought, a steed of brass, a mirror of glass, a ring of gold, and a naked sword, giving about a dozen lines to each, more to the horse (fifty-six lines). Next, the people of the kingdom speculate about these objects in the same order, switching only the ring and the sword, and again giving more attention to the horse (seventy-three lines). All their speculation trails off into a catalogue of phenomena that the science of the day had not yet understood, until the king rises from the banquet and the court occupies itself with dancing, spices and wine (forty-one lines). Finally, the king examines again his steed of brass, learning from its mysterious donor more of its properties (forty-one lines). Whew! Soldiering through his tale as if it were a military instruction book aimed at a dull recruit, the Squire has no sense of pace, no understanding that incidental details need less attention than important ones, and no awareness at all that audience interest is not long sustained by mysterious objects by themselves. It wants action. Yet that is all there is in the 340-odd lines of Part I: a mere setting out of all the paraphernalia to introduce a likely cycle of four tales featuring each of the four objects already presented.

To reverse Dryden on another author, the Squire knows better than he makes, for he acknowledges late into his material what every listener and reader has long been eager to shout:

> The knotte why that every tale is toold,
> If it be taried til that lust be coold
> Of hem that han it after herkned yoore,
> The savour passeth ever lenger the moore,
> For fulsomnesse of his prolixitee;
> And by the same resoun, thynketh me,
> I sholde to the knotte condescende,
> And maken of hir walking soone an ende. (V.401–8)

And just what is this knot now long overdue? Since the Squire turns to his tale of Canacee immediately after bringing up the point about wandering storytelling, the knot must have something to do with her tale. Of course, the question implies a wider reference. That is, what knot does the *Squire's Tale* contribute to the larger design of Fragments III–IV–V and to the *Canterbury Tales*? Ever since the Wife of Bath's opening words in Fragment III, the unvarying subject has been deceptive language, often in matters of the heart, but as a broader category as well. Immediately after the Squire's self-admonishment returns him to the story of Canacee and her golden ring, this story too emphasizes the subject of deceptive language. For the story is not about the golden ring at all, which fades from sight after performing a useful service, but about a sorrowing peregrine falcon who gave her heart to a long-suffering tercelet. Because the tercelet performed "his cerymonyes and obeisaunces, / And [kept] in semblaunt alle his observaunces / That sownen into gentillesse of love" (V.515–17), the falcon little suspected that all this fine conduct was but the insincerity of a hypocrite. When he subsequently gave his love to another, the falcon was thrown into the depths of suffering we observe when Canacee meets her.

The Squire apparently has no other reason for choosing this story than to provide a task for Canacee's recently received golden ring, which enables its possessor to understand the thoughts and dreams of birds and to converse with them in their own language (V.433–37). And he has no other method than to wring from his story every drop of emotion and from his listeners every tear. Chaucer, however, pursues a subtler point. Although Canacee's ability to learn the cause of the falcon's suffering involves only the golden ring, it is clear that the full suite of four magical objects—horse, ring, mirror, and sword—would overcome all the physical limitations that make life and social interaction problematic. The brass steed would overcome spatial limits, permitting one instantly to traverse distances (V.115–30); the mirror would protect one against willful deception (V.132–41); the ring would overcome barriers of language (V.146–55); and the sword would exert total power over the flesh, enabling one to inflict as well as heal wounds (V.156–67). It is significant that these objects do not pertain to the moral realm. Their power remains terrestrial, making their possessor immune to earthly limitation. Singled out for particular attention are the ring and the mirror in combination, which would be especially useful in matters of the heart and for this reason are given to the king's daughter Canacee (V.143–45). If the falcon had had Canacee's ring and mirror she would have understood the tercelet's speech as the hyperbolic language of a lover and recognized his gentility as mere outward show. She would not be in the sad state we find her in:

"[He] semed welle of alle gentillesse;
Al were he ful of treson and falsnesse,
It was so wrapped under humble cheere,
And under hewe of trouthe in swich manere,
Under plesance and under bisy peyne,
That no wight koude han wend he koude feyne,
So depe in greyn he dyed his coloures." (V.505–11)

The ring and mirror could have aided more than the falcon. They would have enabled the *somonour* in the *Friar's Tale* to realize that his companion was awaiting his soul. In the *Summoner's Tale* they would have protected Thomas against the deceptions of the *frere,* the *frere* against those of Thomas. Griselda would have been spared grief for the children she thought dead, Walter spared anxiety over Griselda's faithfulness. The *Merchant's Tale* might not have gotten under way, since January's actual motives for his wedding would have been known from the beginning. If it did, the garden scene would surely have unfolded differently. And if the pilgrims and reading audience of the Wife's lengthy performance had Canacee's ring and mirror, they would recognize Alisoun for the lonely, insecure, unloved prevaricator she really is. The magical properties of these objects direct attention to what has been impeding the progress of all the relationships throughout this lengthy section of the *Canterbury Tales,* that people use language in formulaic ways, scarcely ever saying exactly what they mean or meaning exactly what they say.

However eager the Squire may be to tuck himself into successive stories of a brass horse, a glass mirror, and a naked sword, as if he means to stretch a parody of Froissart into the next century, his creator will not let him. As author, Chaucer needs only the physical magic of the golden ring to make his point. With that contribution now on record, he assigns the Franklin the task of gracefully extricating the young man from the tale that is now, alas, only one-quarter finished.[2]

THE FRANKLIN'S TALE

Finding a way to minimize the Squire's embarrassment comes easily to the Franklin, for he deeply admires the young lad—unfortunately for all the wrong reasons. Occupying a class that received voting privileges by acquiring land, the Franklin can still only dream about the class to which (he assumes) the Squire belongs by birth.[3] As so often happens among those who have risen to positions of financial security, the Franklin confuses the symbols of quality with its essence in both his life and his tale. Consider the important role food plays in his life. His lavish board need not lead us to wonder, with Jill Mann, whether his portrait demonstrates either "estates satire" or "sins satire," but to see him as simply a showoff.[4] While the admiring Narrator sees the Franklin's celebrated hospitality as cause to name him "Seint Julian . . . in his contree" (I.340), others may notice that his table draws attention for its extravagance and variety rather than for the benefit it affords. In the Franklin's eyes a plentiful table demonstrates generosity, a reputation he seeks to cultivate because the aristocracy is especially admired when acting generously. In the eyes of everyone else his ostentation may upstage his generosity.

A similar confusion between essence and its symbols governs his attitude to the pilgrim Squire whose substance he cannot see behind the many
accidents that mark his class. Although the young man's virtues and vices
may be unremarkable (unless bad storytelling be heinous), it would make
little difference; the Franklin would admire him in any case, for several
hints in his conduct reveal a man more alert to cost than value, more
familiar with surface than substance. His merciful interruption of the
Squire, for example, contains a number of comparisons and emphases
that are, like his table, more revealing than their professed intent. Seeming to praise the Squire, he inadvertently undercuts his performances: not
much should be expected from such a young person; the true test of a tale
is the passion with which it is told; his best days are still ahead; and the
best part of the performance is the sound of his speech (V.675–81).

When the Franklin abruptly shifts the subject to his own son, contrasting him to the more polished Squire, his figure of comparison gives us
more of his values than he knows:

> "I have a sone, and by the Trinitee,
> I hadde levere than twenty pound worth lond,
> Though it right now were fallen in myn hond,
> He were a man of swich discrecioun
> As that ye been!" (V.682–86)

Wishing to emphasize how much he wants his son to be like the Squire,
the Franklin reaches for an image of absolute worth, an image he assumes
everyone would place above all else, but which he would reject in favor of
his son's improvement. He selects for his item of comparison a parcel of
land worth twenty pounds, intending his listeners to marvel at the self-
lessness of his parenting. He fails to realize that a comparison with any
item of commerce, especially one of such meager value to anyone but an
acquisitive landholder (the rough equivalent of a modest suburban parcel),[5] reduces his son to a similar value. We wonder if the Franklin has not
perhaps always been more interested in acquiring land than raising his
son. Moving to particulars, he complains that the lad is fond of gambling.
But a double reference to losing money outweighs his single reference to
dice playing, again making us wonder which is more loathsome to the
Franklin, gambling or losing:

> But for to pleye at dees, and to *despende*
> And *lese* al that he hath is his usage. (V.690–91, emphasis added)

And in giving an example of the low-life associations his son should avoid,
the Franklin inadvertently insults his own creator by disparaging the spe-

cific position, "page" (V.692), which Chaucer once held in the household of Elizabeth de Burgh.[6]

Finally, the Franklin rounds out his own portrait with a complicated self-revelation on the subject of rhetoric:

> "But, sires, by cause I am a burel man,
> At my bigynnyng first I yow biseche,
> Have me excused of my rude speche.
> I lerned nevere rethorik, certeyn;
> Thyng that I speke, it moot be bare and pleyn.
> I sleep nevere on the Mount of Pernaso,
> Ne lerned Marcus Tullius Scithero.
> Colours ne knowe I none, withouten drede,
> But swiche colours as growen in the mede,
> Or elles swiche as men dye or peynte.
> Colours of rethoryk been to me queynte;
> My spirit feeleth noght of swich mateere.
> But if yow list, my tale shul ye heere." (V.716–28)

The passage has been justly cited for the irony of its disclaimer, in view of the highly rhetorical tale about to follow. It has at least three other dimensions consistent with the characteristics we have been discussing.[7] First, the Franklin wishes to let his audience know that, despite his disclaimer, he really does know much about the so-called mysteries of rhetoric. In a familiar modesty *topos*, he frankly admits "rude speche" (V.718), perhaps to fetch a rebuttal from someone who remembers his authoritative pronouncement on eloquence in his recent comments on the Squire's performance. When no one rises to the bait, he has to lay out his own credentials by dropping the names of two ancients deeply implicated in rhetoric, settling once for all that he is far from "a burel man" (V.716). Parnassus and Cicero, representing skill, respectively, in producing and understanding literary expression, flatly contradict the "bare and pleyn" (V.720) speech he says he prefers. Second, he intends at the same time to belittle rhetoric and those who pursue the craft. The cute addition of "sleep . . . on the Mount of Pernaso" (V.721), though chiefly designed to disclose his familiarity with The Nine, their Well, and the whole of literary history, also hints at the indolence often attributed to those who meditate the thankless muse. The success of his allusive little joke, warming him to the game, leads to a deeper level of self-satisfied fun at the expense of those who do work within the rhetorical tradition. The fun comes, he thinks, in calling attention to the silly use of "colors" as a metaphor for figures of speech. To make his point, small as it is, he need merely mention the literal meaning of color, as he does by referring to the flowers that "growen in the mede" (V.724). While engaged in this small game of one-upmanship, and overdoing it, a third dimension takes shape in the speech. The cautious afterthought—that literal colors are found in more than flowers, they occur in dyeing and painting too—implies a literal-mindedness that reveals a thinner knowledge of rhetoric than he would have us believe. Instead of being non-rhetorical uses of "color," dyeing and painting are other forms of artifice, methods of embellishment. By failing to realize that these activities have more in common with rhetoric than with flowers, he persuades us that the underlying logic in the metaphor of rhetorical colors remains entirely beyond his grasp.

I have taken some care to look closely at evidence of the Franklin's superficial sensibility in order to make more convincing the connection between his character and the tale he tells. For there are a number of inexplicable turns in his tale that might have been expected to develop differently. The explanation suggested here attributes these inconsistencies to a familiar Chaucerian technique found throughout the *Tales,* most recently in the *Squire's Tale,* the limitations of the pilgrim who tells the tale. But the Franklin differs from the tale-tellers in Fragments III and IV who deliberately conceal truth behind a variety of artifices. Here the Franklin simply does not recognize the difference between the complicated protocols that succeed in a world of high artifice and the simplistic way he represents that world in the lines of a formal tale. Though one can agree with Kittredge that the Franklin "is no cloistered rhetorician, but a ruddy white-bearded vavasour" (1915, p. 210), land-owning nevertheless implies a shrewdness and sophistication that he leaves behind when he enters the world of formal creative literature. The *Franklin's Tale* and the Franklin himself become perfect illustrations of the central point of Fragments III, IV, and V, that truth and its representation are often at odds.

To the many unexplained items that have long made critics wonder about the tale,[8] we might add a few other unremarked instances of the Franklin's literary naïveté. After Dorigen has been so worried about the danger to her husband's return voyage from a certain group of black rocks, devoting an entire twenty-nine-line speech (V.865–93) to their pointlessness, their destruction of man, and their suitability to hell, why is there no further mention of how Arveragus safely avoids these rocks when he returns (V.1087–89)? And does it not seem that the Franklin loses track of his tale? Although he has Aurelius declare his love for Dorigen and has Dorigen rashly promise to return that love in exchange for removing the rocks *while Arveragus is still abroad,* he commences Aurelius's lengthy strategy to make the rocks magically disappear (or seem to disappear) *after Arveragus has returned and the rocks are no longer a threat.* Later the Franklin has to send Arveragus off on a second trip (V.1351, 1460) to provide a suitable time for Aurelius to call in Dorigen's debt and for Dorigen to bewail her dilemma. If the Franklin had given any thought to narrative economy he would have compressed the two trips into one, permitting Aurelius's magician to conceal the rocks during Arveragus's long sojourn. Had he done so, he would have gained the added bonus of making Dorigen seem indebted to Aurelius for her husband's safe return and her moral obligation toward him more credible.

In at least two other instances the Franklin reveals how recently and ill-suited he has come to literature, despite the credentials he so assiduously lays before us in his Prologue. The following lines include an extraordinary lack of control:

> Til that the brighte sonne loste his hewe;
> For th'orisonte hath reft the sonne his lyght—
> This is as muche to seye as it was nyght. (V.1016–18)

The problem is not the flowery excesses of the first two lines, but the abrupt departure from rhetorical convention in the third. Two interpretations are possible. On the one hand the Franklin may simply be patronizing those who dedicate their lives to the discipline of rhetoric, laughing at the unnecessarily elaborate way they are taught to say "at night." On the other, he may be patronizing his audience by offering a painfully obvious explanation for his learned imagery on the assumption that they could not possibly recognize the rhetorical convention he just used. In either case he reminds us of people who explain punch lines, coincidentally disclosing their own too literal minds by assuming that others need the explanation they once needed. Here the Franklin unwittingly implies that at one time he was confounded by the figure he just used.

The second instance departs from narrative convention as startlingly as the previous departs from rhetorical:

> Paraventure an heep of yow, ywis,
> Wol holden hym a lewed man in this
> That he wol putte his wyf in jupartie.
> Herkneth the tale er ye upon hire crie.
> She may have bettre fortune than yow semeth;
> And whan that ye han herd the tale, demeth. (V.1493–98)

With one stroke he destroys a Chaucerian staple, suspense. We have already seen this technique well used in other tales, like the Miller's, Wife of

Bath's, Friar's, Summoner's, Clerk's, and Merchant's; *Troilus and Criseyde* raises audience suspense to a fine art. But here the Franklin's unfamiliarity with the way literature works makes him confuse the intensity of suspense with the discomfort of anxiety. To achieve the smooth simplicity he thinks best characterizes life at its highest ideal, and which he thus wants his audience to feel, he puts their mind at ease by blurting out unsolicited, if not actually that the butler did it, at least that the most sympathetic character did not.

The primacy of surface appearance in the Franklin's life apparently also controls the tale he tells. Its treatment of its three principals, the knight-husband Arveragus, the squire-suitor Aurelius, and the faithful wife Dorigen, gives a strong indication that Chaucer was seeking to emphasize throughout the tale the complex relationship between reality and the symbols that represent it.

Arveragus, it seems, proposes the terms on which his marriage to Dorigen will proceed. It will be a perfect marriage, we are told, in which the husband freely swears never to exert authority over his wife nor ever to oppose her will, but to obey her in everything. He apparently assures his wife he will act toward her in marriage "As any lovere to his lady shal" (V.750). He must have in mind the kind of love depicted in courtly romance, where every act provides an intending lover an opportunity to demonstrate the depth of his love. Since that depth is already abundantly clear to himself, the important word here is "demonstrate," that is to show *others* his dedication. The next two lines disclose the apparent inconsistency that can emerge from such an emphasis:

Save that the name of soveraynetee,
That wolde he have for shame of his degree. (V.751–52)

Despite the laudable terms of his marriage, its essence as it were, Arveragus wishes to give an entirely different image of it to everyone outside the marriage. The inconsistency between the vow of obedience and the name of sovereignty is only apparent, since the force driving both modes is the same, the need to create an impression. What may seem to the Franklin to be a delicately balanced stance, encapsulated in an aphorism more appealing to the eye than the mind, "Servant in love, and lord in mariage" (V.793), might more accurately be described "servant in the eyes of his wife, lord in the eyes of others." Obviously the crucial consideration is how others will view him, while the objective is to present a pleasing image, even if it calls for inconsistent images to please different expectations. The quest for reputation is still motivating him later in the tale, when he

Shoop hym to goon and dwelle a yeer or tweyne
In Engelond . . .
To seke in armes worshipe and honour—
For al his lust he sette in swich labour. (V.809–12)

The activities of Squire Aurelius similarly indicate the tale's emphasis on surface appearance as a characteristic distinct from essence. The conditions playfully laid out for him by Dorigen offer two options, *either* "remoeve alle the rokkes, stoon by stoon, / That they ne lette ship ne boot to goon" (V.993–94) *or* "[make] the coost so clene / Of rokkes that ther nys no stoon ysene" (V.995–96). To become her lover he may choose either the first option, which includes reality, or the second, which concerns only appearance. The subsequent activities of Aurelius leave no doubt that he chooses a strategy consistent with everything else in the tale, the manipulation of appearances rather than stone-by-stone dismantling. He uses the "language of seeming" three separate times in the thirteen lines describing his intention (V.1140, 1146, and 1151) and finally concludes in an unambiguous commitment to the craft of shape-shifting, trickery designed to last a week or two:

For with an apparence a clerk may make,
To mannes sighte, that alle the rokkes blake
Of Britaigne weren yvoyded everichon,
And shippes by the brynke comen and gon,
And in swich forme enduren a wowke or two. (V.1157–61)

Despite choosing only one of the two methods Dorigen offered him to complete his part of the bargain—that is, if any reasonable person would agree that a valid contract is in force—he nevertheless implies, when pointing out that Dorigen must now deliver her half of the bargain, that both methods have been accomplished:

"I have do so as ye comanded me;
And if ye vouche sauf, ye may *go see*.
Dooth as yow list; have youre biheste in mynde,
For, quyk or deed, right there ye shal me fynde.
In yow lith al to do me lyve or deye—
But wel I woot *the rokkes been aweye*." (V.1333–38, emphasis added)

However confident he may be that Dorigen will find no rocks when she looks out to sea, to imply that on that account the rocks are away is less than candid. They are not away. They only appear to be.

Though Dorigen's conduct is certainly quite different from Aurelius's—

she would never willfully manipulate appearances to deceive others, while he is only too eager to do so—her greater sensitivity to outward show makes her prone to accept appearance in place of the reality it often conceals. With regard to her fixation on the black rocks off Brittany's coast, her confusion between symbol and fact leads to inconsistent conclusions. Her first references to these rocks reveal great fear that her husband may dash his vessel on them and be destroyed upon his return voyage (V.857–94). Here the rocks symbolize an impediment to the marriage: while present the marriage is in jeopardy, if absent the marriage is safe. Later, however, after responding to Aurelius's seamy proposal with words that leave no doubt about her faithfulness to her husband,

"Ne shal I nevere been untrewe wyf
In word ne werk, as fer as I have wit;
I wol been his to whom that I am knyt.
Taak this for fynal answere as of me." (V.984–87)

she playfully continues their conversation by implying an entirely different value for the rocks off the coast. Here they become a symbol of the marriage itself, ever solid, ever indestructible:

"Looke what day that endelong Britayne
Ye remoeve alle the rokkes, stoon by stoon,
That they ne lette ship ne boot to goon—
I seye, whan ye han maad the coost so clene
Of rokkes that ther nys no stoon ysene,
Thanne wol I love yow best of any man." (V.992–97)

No reasonable person would see in these lines anything but a firm statement that Dorigen will never become Aurelius's lover. They constitute hyperbole, conveying a sense of degree rather than a subject. Indeed, the literal words seeming to comprise a kind of contract actually shift the subject from Aurelius's proposal—firmly rejected in the previous ten lines—back to Dorigen's anxiety over her husband's safety. Thus the overall effect of using rocks for contradictory symbolic values calls more attention to the symbol than to the subject it is intended to clarify.

We might add a final note regarding this group of rocks. Certainly their presence as a literary device is not unusual. A Breton Lay typically features a prominent symbol involved in some way with a magical occurrence, and perhaps as well uses its symbol in an ambivalent way. But as the *lais* of Marie de France demonstrate, the symbol should suit the thing symbolized. Her symbols for love include vines and birds, living creatures and plants that catch nicely the delicacy and dynamism of a human relationship. In the *Franklin's Tale* these inert, black, forbidding rocks seem entirely out of place as a symbol for marriage. Their inappropriateness directs us, therefore, to the dual objectives of the tale: what the Franklin intends to convey and what his creator Chaucer achieves within that intention. From the tale-teller's perspective the black rocks connote the solid foundation of Arveragus's marriage to Dorigen. From Chaucer's, the idea of impending danger still lingers. That is, the greatest danger to the marriage comes neither from the rocks that might damage a husband's vessel, nor from a neighboring squire intent on adultery, but from the naïve belief that a marriage can resemble a rock, forever fixed in an unchanging stability, impervious to adversity. Like a tide that conceals danger beneath its risen surface, the mere declaration that a marriage is an equal partnership, especially when the outside world is led to believe otherwise, resembles sleight of hand by altering only the surface, never the reality beneath. Living things, like January's *hortus conclusus,* present a more appropriate symbol of marriage because their constant need of nourishment and attention captures the essential dynamism of a human relationship, which calls for both parties attentively to tend each other's needs to ensure strength and harmonious growth. By consciously using black rocks to objectify the danger to her marriage, and then paradoxically using the same rocks to objectify its solidity, Dorigen (actually the Franklin) shows a tendency to let figurative language overpower a subject. Rocks, not marriage, dominate her thought in the early part of the tale; had the subject been the price of *mottelee* in Hainault, she might have used the same rocks to frame her ideas.

Eventually the rocks vanish from view. Though Dorigen had earlier called their presence God's unreasonable work (V.872), now their absence seems to her "agayns the proces of nature" (V.1345). This tendency to use figurative language inconsistently and to lose her point, shows itself again when Dorigen's rash promise to Aurelius returns to haunt her and a new figurative cluster displaces the ominous black rocks. Now an array of literary heroines parades before her mind, women whose dilemmas suggest to her more than a passing similarity to herself:

> Hath ther nat many a noble wyf er this,
> And many a mayde, yslayn hirself, allas,
> Rather than with hir body doon trespas? (V.1364–66)

The phrase "er this" does more than identify her immediate case; it also places her in the company of "many a noble wyf . . . And many a mayde." While there may be little fear that a third phrase, "yslayn hirself," would ever be a serious possibility for a woman like Dorigen (cf. the Franklin's ever-so-slight hint of her self-conscious style, "As doon thise noble wyves whan hem liketh" [V.818]), nevertheless the catalogue of women who now come to her mind—seventy-nine individual women in twenty-two separate stories[9]—offers a delicious company with whom to take refuge. Her figurative language again commands greater attention than the subject it was originally summoned to clarify; tragic women displace black rocks as the new symbol governing her thought. The names at the beginning of the list are perhaps on point, women who preferred suicide to rape (V.1367–1404), but these give way to other women who killed themselves *after* being raped (V.1405–38), who in turn yield to a broader category of generally faithful women.[10] As the broader category eclipses the narrower, Dorigen's recollection becomes increasingly perfunctory. She gives twelve lines to the first story, then eight, seven, and six to the next three. By now she is in her second category of eight stories: Lucresse has four lines; the maidens of Milesie three lines; Habradate's wife five; and the remaining five stories get thirteen lines. Finally, the concluding category of ten stories receives only eighteen lines, with the last three heroines sharing a single sentence. Dorigen has obviously stopped considering the specific crises these women faced and begun searching her memory for simply the names of distressed women in literature. In view of the Franklin's eagerness to demonstrate his knowledge of literature (cf. V.673–81, 709–28, 944–52), Dorigen's shift from her specific crisis to an endless list of analogues, ultimately reflects his literary pretension, a self-indulgence that often favors breadth over depth.

We have seen that Aurelius and Dorigen approach the relationship between reality and its appearance at an uncomplicated level. Both may overlook the former while giving excessive concern to the latter, yet neither is in any doubt about reality itself. In the case of Arveragus, however, the relationship is more complex. His preoccupation with appearances, and especially his attempts to create a desired appearance, actually distort his understanding of reality. The extent of his misconstruction is not as plain in the Tale's early lines where he permits two views of his marriage—equality within the home, masculine sovereignty without—as in its final scenes where a gross distortion of the nature of marriage is the only conclusion we can draw from his response to Dorigen's predicament. Let us look closely at these final scenes.

There is no reason to doubt Dorigen's sincerity when she lists the three horrors to which death is preferable:

> "yet have I levere to lese
> My lif than of my body to have a shame,
> Or knowe myselven fals, or lese my name." (V.1360–62)

Nor has her mind changed when, exhausted from recalling the stories of faithful ladies who chose death before dishonor or who remained faithful to a deceased spouse, she describes for her husband the rash promise she made to Aurelius. With a response that sounds like a parody of some preposterous decision by Marie de Champagne in Andreas Capellanus's *De arte honeste amandi,* her husband tells her to keep her word, that is, "Go and give yourself to Aurelius" (cf. V.1474), followed by a second order, that she never reveal this matter to anyone, upon pain of death (V.1481–86). Never mind that both commands flatly contradict his earlier vow never to oppose her will (his first order disregards her loathing of Aurelius's tawdry intention, and his second includes a threat of death), here we are more concerned with how his commands address Dorigen's dilemma. In particular, will either of his commands assuage her three fears? For the sake of discussion we might grant that his ordering her to keep silent may lessen her fear of losing her name, though this may be doubted, since her second fear, "knowe myselven fals," implies that her own awareness is more important than the opinion of others: silence may keep her falsehood from others; it can never keep it from herself. In any case, her first two fears, shame to her body and knowing herself false, are still very much present. Absolutely nothing in Arveragus's order either mitigates the defilement to her body or alters her knowledge that she will falsify her marriage vow. Apart from its slight benefit to superficial appearance, Arveragus's command has no effect in the realm of reality. That is, Dorigen must still face her physical and moral crisis, *as she sees that crisis.*

And yet, Arveragus apparently thinks he has solved the problem. A clue to why he thinks so may be found in his explanation of his hierarchy of values, lines that reduce him to tears:

> "Ye shul youre trouthe holden, by my fay!
> For God so wisly have mercy upon me,
> I hadde wel levere ystiked for to be
> For verray love which that I to yow have,
> But if ye sholde youre trouthe kepe and save." (V.1474–78)

The first and last lines in this passage say the same thing: keep your word. The intervening three lines, letting us know how important it is to him that she do so, seem to say "So help me God, I would much rather be stabbed for the love I have for you, unless you kept your word." This unusual syntax seems to imply that Arveragus would rather suffer a stab wound than have her break her word.[11] Now this is a most unexpected statement. Instead of naming two alternative threats to Dorigen — living in exile or reneging on a promise, say — and choosing what he considers the lesser evil to her, he mentions himself three times. What does *he* have to do with *her* defilement? Apparently he believes that whatever defilement will arise from Dorigen's keeping her promise to Aurelius will accrue to *him*, not to her. His view of what troubles Dorigen has little in common with her view, which she articulated as three fears, defilement of her body, knowledge of her falsehood, and loss of her name. He apparently sees only two, unauthorized possession of his property, and the public's knowledge of the event. From his point of view granting the right of use, like managing a parcel of land, converts an illegality to a legality, or in terms appropriate to the case at hand, erases defilement. His second command, to keep silent upon pain of death, guards against public knowledge. By responding to Dorigen's crisis as he does, Arveragus effectively reduces her to a piece of property, in the same way the Franklin earlier reduced his son to a possession by granting that the lad is worth more than even a twenty-pound parcel of land.[12]

To Arveragus, as to his Franklin creator, all is for show. When Aurelius releases Dorigen from her "obligation" to him at the end of the Tale, no less than when the clerk subsequently releases Aurelius from his debt of a thousand pounds, the issue is not morality or the restoration of right order. It is a contest over the appearances of gentility: who can be more *fre*. Aurelius, impressed that Arveragus "were levere han shame" (V.1529) than have Dorigen break her *trouthe*, sees himself in competition with Arveragus, lest his *gentillesse* lag behind: "Thus kan a squier doon a gentil dede / As wel as kan a knyght" (V.1543–44). The clerk competes with both men for the same reason:

> "Leeve brother,
> Everich of yow dide gentilly til oother.
> Thou art a squier, and he is a knyght;
> But God forbede, for his blisful myght,
> But if a clerk koude doon a gentil dede
> As wel as any of yow, it is no drede!" (V.1607–12)

Since both of these men relinquish their interest in a physical gain, we might well ask if Arveragus's act should not also be viewed as a gracious gesture for the same reason, the relinquishing of a physical object to which he has exclusive right. To be sure, it is. The language of weighing things in balance, of comparing two items to determine the greater worth, abounds in this section of the Tale, where *levere* ("preferable") occurs six times in

125 lines.[13] If Arveragus cannot see the difference between "the great truth" he denies and "the petty truth" he serves, as Pearsall puts it,[14] might it not also be true that the Franklin sees little difference between Arveragus's largesse in sending his wife to Aurelius and his own in providing a lavish board for all to enjoy?

The Franklin may have thought his Tale would be a persuasive endorsement for the virtue of *gentillesse,* a demonstration that each gentle act begets another. But his Tale undercuts him by misunderstanding *gentillesse* and by naïvely assuming the efficacy of the Golden Rule. Though he lavishly celebrates its trappings, the Franklin fails to grasp the essence of *gentillesse* as completely as the pilgrim Chaucer loses the essence of knighthood and verse beneath their trappings in *The Tale of Sir Thopas.* Except for Dorigen, every character in the *Franklin's Tale* acts on the pleasure principle rather than out of a sense of *gentillesse.* Arveragus derives pleasure from status and reputation. Flouting the vows of marriage, he values the kind of *trouthe* he remembers from romance, a context in which he is pleased to see himself,[15] where knights and ladies pursue premarital or extramarital dalliance, and marriage rarely matters. Aurelius is driven by prospects of an adulterous liaison; the clerk of Orleans by visions of a thousand pounds. Even their alleged gentle acts much admired by the Franklin at the end of the Tale testify more surely to self-interest than to *gentillesse.* Now that anticipated pleasure has vanished before Arveragus's full knowledge, Aurelius's release of Dorigen and the clerk's of Aurelius may have more to do with an attack of conscience than a spur to *gentillesse.*

Finally, the Franklin's naïve belief that the Golden Rule could ever govern society, especially the kind of society he describes in Armorik, runs counter to everything in his Tale and everything in the preceding tales back as far as the Wife's. It has been suggested that Dorigen momentarily forgets the order of things when she gives in to her outbursts about the rocks and about suicide.[16] True enough. But it is also of the order of things that a naïvely simplistic view of the world cannot long survive. Without question in the best of all possible worlds each act of kindness would prompt a kind response. But in the fallen world of the *Canterbury Tales* — perhaps in every society — nothing courts ruin faster that the habit of relying on the kindness of others. Alisoun of Bath's overtures to two of her husbands received rejection in one case, a cuff on the ear in the other. Her first three husbands' overtures to her fetched a tireless harrangue, financial exploitation, and conjugal manipulation. Walter's belated reform at the end of the *Clerk's Tale* (hardly *gentillesse;* rather the minimum conduct expected in every marriage) had nothing to do with Griselda's *gentillesse*—or, for that matter, with Alisoun of Bath's paraphrase of Dante's *gentillesse* (III.1109–30)—and everything to do with his own inability to prove her false. That I may be oversimplifying two highly complex marriages here I do not deny. But that is precisely my point regarding the *Franklin's Tale,* that it is naïve in the extreme. The overwhelming evidence of all seven tales in the great central section of the *Canterbury Tales* testifies to the very opposite of the Franklin's simplistic formula for success. The lone gesture that might support him is the deliberate lie told by January to avoid dissolving his marriage to May. In any case, the response January's kindness evokes from May is yet to be heard; it may be kind, or it may not.

If a central truth about human relationships does arise from the *Franklin's Tale,* and indeed from the 6,300 lines from the beginning of the Wife's performance to the final lines of the Franklin's, it concerns the preeminent importance of language, specifically the moral necessity to express meanings in words that accurately convey those meanings. Had all the characters and tale tellers in these three fragments held such a view, an untold amount of heartache might not have been felt. Perhaps as well, a pilgrimage to Canterbury might not have been needed.

PART III

❀

From Flesh to Spirit

In the whole of the *Canterbury Tales* no threshold has more significance than the transition from Fragment V to Fragment VI, for it marks the conclusion of the first half of the tales and entry to the very different second half. The tales in these two halves are not precise counterparts, as if individual tales in the second half were to respond to specific tales in the first, as some of William Blake's *Songs of Experience* answer specific lyrics in his *Songs of Innocence* and Milton's *Il Penseroso* echoes the cyclic pattern and very metaphors of *L'Allegro*. Nevertheless several themes and situations are represented in both halves of the *Canterbury Tales* where their different treatments give rise to different critical responses. A given action producing a mild or even cursory response in the first half evokes a more troubling, portentous response in the second. To see this point more clearly we might touch briefly two tales that loosely parallel each other, the *Merchant's Tale* from the first half and the *Shipman's Tale* from the second.

Despite the foreboding image of January and May leaving their Edenic garden at the end of the earlier tale, its concluding lines are dominated by implied questions that look backward for logistics: How did May get away with her ruse? Was January duped, or did he deceive May into believing he was duped? Was May speaking truthfully when she implied she was pregnant? Is Cato right about someone of January's age marrying a younger woman? Does Theophrastus describe May accurately? And so forth. The *Shipman's Tale* has a similar man and wife, surviving a similar close call, and facing an equally precarious future. At its end, however, the focus is forward, the inquiry metaphysical: Does the amorous homecoming mood (VII.377–81) of the merchant of Seint-Denys suggest that financial stability makes conjugal love possible, and that the merchant's thousand-franc profit (VII.372) therefore assures future marital bliss? Two famous remarks by the wives in the two tales epitomize the contrast even more clearly. With the help of Persephone May certainly makes the more ingenious response about her "strugle with a man upon a tree" (IV.2374), yet her aim is to wriggle out of a compromised past. In the *Shipman's Tale* the earthy remark of the wife, "score it upon my taille" (VII.416), lays strategy for a hopeful future. Will her husband, we wonder, accept the remark as a coquettish invitation on which he and his wife might build that future? The literarily more complex *Merchant's Tale* tends to linger in laughter; the simpler *Shipman's Tale,* closely reflecting the banal problems of many a marriage, paradoxically leaves us with deeper philosophical questions to contemplate.

We see an equally pronounced difference in corresponding aspects of the Wife of Bath, who dominates the first half of the poem, and the Prioress, who tells her tale in the second half. Each woman uses her tale, perhaps without realizing it, to articulate personal ambitions. Alisoun of Bath discloses her longing to be a storybook princess cherished by her Lochinvar, worldly goals very different from Madam Eglentine's otherworldly longing for martyrdom, sainthood, and the virginal apotheosis she seeks with an intensely passionate piety. While we may suspect that the methods of both women will drive their goals ever beyond reach, the goals themselves are as different from each other as this world is from the next. We can empathize with Alisoun because her ambition lies entirely within our worldly experience. We are confounded by the Prioress, who leads us to uncertain metaphysical terrain. The equation between her tale's physical passion and its pious objective leaves us uncertain either that her equation is wrong or that our objection is. As for the power of passionate piety and the visceral tale expressing it to earn salvation for the teller, we are least certain of all.

The difference between the two halves of the *Canterbury Tales* takes even sharper form in their respective treatments of death. In the first five fragments death is very nearly insignificant, occurring with prominence only in the death of Arcite near the end of the *Knight's Tale.* Yet that death, as we saw in chapter 4, has more to do with allegory than with an occasion for lasting sorrow; it signifies the removal of an impasse to maturity, through which Palamon/Arcite can free himself from the tyrannizing influence of passion. The many deaths in the *Man of Law's Tale* are mere facts remote from the main story, including the death of Alla (II.1144), which gives more reason to rejoice at an ascension than to grieve a death. As the teller himself says "I lete al his storie passen by; / Of Custance is my tale specially" (II.1124–25), a remark equally suited to the Wife of Bath, whose former husbands similarly die off stage and whose knight-rapist benefits from a commuted death sentence. There could have been a death at the end of the *Friar's Tale,* but no one dies there either; the *somonour* who attempts to extort an old widow appears to be summoned alive to hell, without any indication of a death that, ecclesiastically speaking, would have to occur before the devil could claim him (cf. III.1634–41). The only deaths in the *Clerk's Tale* are imaginary, occurring in Griselda's mind. In the second half of the *Canterbury Tales,* however, death is the central event in seven of eleven tales, and a hot-breath threat in an eighth, the *Nun's Priest's Tale.* Death passes over only the *Shipman's Tale,* the *Tale of Sir Thopas,* and the *Canon's Yeoman's Tale.*

The different levels of attention the first and second halves of the poem give to death becomes startlingly clear in a comparison, again, of the Wife of Bath in the first half and the equally talented liar from the second half, the Pardoner. Both pilgrims attempt to compensate for their unhappy lives by reshaping for themselves public personas designed to appear happy. Though both tales undermine this strategy, they do so in very different ways. The Wife's *Tale* denies death by reprieving a knight-rapist's death sentence, by magically restoring an old hag's youth, and by concluding with the delightful yet thoroughly worldly image of young newlyweds — all preposterous wish-fulfillment fantasies that disclose the extent of her anguish. The *Pardoner's Tale* is a *memento mori* in which the haunting voice of an unhappy old man and the silence of three corpses finally place the sad Pardoner himself, silent at last, in the wider context of eternal life. When Alisoun rests from rhetorical battle, her audience is left with questions that might be drawn from their own daily lives: Is her eagerness for battle the cause, or the result, of earlier rejections? And will she ever achieve happiness in love? After the Pardoner falls silent they are metaphysically troubled by his attempt to persuade them that his own system of values, though very different from theirs, is equally valid, perhaps even superior. That his values would overthrow theirs forces them to ponder the moral significance of the performance they have just heard for the performer who has just given it.

Despite the inference one might be tempted to draw from the preceding paragraphs, it would be a serious misunderstanding of the *Canterbury Tales* to conclude that the first half of the poem concerns this world while the second concerns the next. In a sense both halves remain fixed in the familiar world of time and space, though for different ends. The twelve tales in the first five fragments concern the often misguided arrangements people make — or try to make — among themselves to establish a happier, more pleasurable life. The twelve tales in the second half of the poem, not excluding the *Shipman's Tale,* concern people's internal capitulations — their private deliberations — to advance values that will bring them and us to a new order of being. While these values are often moral, and to that extent the foundation on which Christian teaching says salvation is based, they are not about that afterlife nor exclusively aimed at the moral values that lead to salvation. What Glending Olson says of Fragment VIII applies as well to the tales of Fragments VI and VII: "It is the struggle that is emphasized, not the goal of the struggle or the grace that makes it possible" (1982, p. 232). These ten tales focus on the nature and extent of the yearning itself and the idea of "transformation" to which that yearning leads.[1] By rotating, as it were, Dante's vertical axis where *Paradiso* is above and *Inferno* below (Figure 7),

Dante's *Commedia*

Figure 7

to a horizontal plane with the tales of increasing disintegration on the left and those yearning for a new order of being on the right (Figure 8), Chaucer makes available for his pilgrims, all of whom are still in the middle of their own road, a wider range of ideals than Dante's single focus on salvation for subjects who, excepting only himself, are already in the afterlife.

Chaucer's *Canterbury Tales*

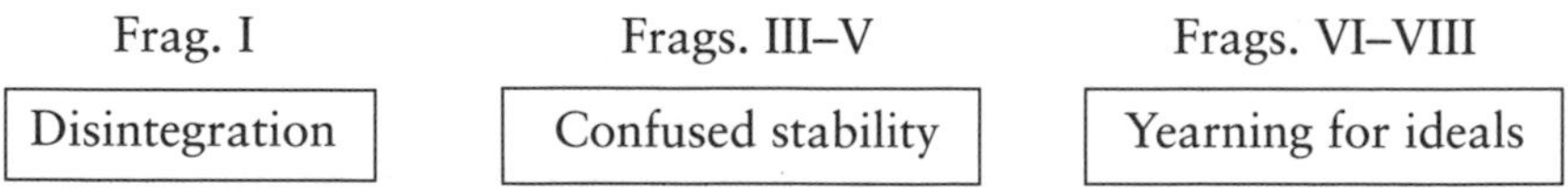

Frag. I	Frags. III–V	Frags. VI–VIII
Disintegration	Confused stability	Yearning for ideals

Figure 8

In the case of some Pilgrims, for example the Prioress and the Second Nun, the ideal sought is probably eternal salvation. But others, too, aim for abstract goals quite different from those preoccupying the pilgrims in the first half of the poem. The Pardoner seeks social acceptance, the Monk respect, the Canon's Yeoman sympathy. The Physician and the Shipman attempt to rearrange society's values, the former elevating sexual purity and a contest of wills above life itself, the latter engineering a scheme to preserve a marriage while also sharing its conjugal wealth. The Nun's Priest tries to gain philosophic understanding. And at the center of this run of tales from the Physician's to the Canon Yeoman's, that is, as the fifth tale-teller in a group of nine, the pilgrim-narrator with two identities applies all the limited talent of one persona toward a suitable contribution to the pilgrimage, while his other persona wittily orchestrates a formal discussion of literary aesthetics throughout the whole of Fragment VII.

Paralleling this distinction in subject matter, the two halves of the poem follow very different structural patterns, linear in the first half, circular in the second. In chapter 7 we noted that Chaucer may have been considering two different methods of ordering the tales of Fragments III, IV, and V, the linear Ellesmere type and the circular Non-Ellesmere. He seems to have preferred the former for the first half of the poem, where tales are connected to each other by some dramatic interaction (like the exchange between the Miller and Reeve), by some literal language of the Host making clear that a continuing scene is unfolding (like the Prologue to the *Miller's Tale*), or by a strong thematic connection suggesting that the subject itself prompts the succeeding tale to follow (like the obvious connection between the performance of the Wife and the *Clerk's Tale*). Thus the tales of Fragment I are primarily connected dramatically; those of Fragments III, IV, and V are chiefly linked thematically. This linear principle creates the sense of an ongoing temporal process, analogous to the central journeying image of the *Man of Law's Tale* and consistent with the pilgrims' linear progress to Canterbury.

The tales in the second half of the poem follow a circular pattern, thus emulating the circularity that dominates the concluding lines of *Paradiso*. Apparently Chaucer was profoundly influenced by the final canto of Dante's *Commedia*, for he adapted much of St. Bernard's prayer for the opening lines of his *Second Nun's Tale*.[2] Bernard's prayer ends with a plea that the Virgin will intercede to dispel every cloud of Dante's mortality that the Supreme Pleasure may be displayed to him:

E io, che mai per mio veder non arsi
più ch'i' fo per lo suo, tutti miei prieghi
ti porgo, e priego che non sieno scarsi,

perché tu ogne nube li disleghi
di sua mortalità co' prieghi tuoi,
sì che 'l sommo piacer li si dispieghi. (*Par.,* 33.28–33)

[And I, who never for my own vision burned more than I do for his,
proffer to thee all my prayers, and pray that they be not scant, that
with thy prayers thou wouldst dispel for him every cloud of his
mortality, so that the Supreme Pleasure may be disclosed to him.]
(Singleton trans.)

The imagery with which Dante concludes the canto responds, in effect,
to Bernard's prayer. Its dominant form, a circle, "the perfect figure . . . an
emblem of perfection,"[3] may have been the chief influence on the circular
design of the entire second half of the *Canterbury Tales*. First Dante describes three separately colored circles that represent the Trinity, "tre giri
/ di tre colori e d'una contenenza" (*Par.,* 33.116–17). Next, these three
apparently merge into one circle ("Quella circulazion," 127) representing
the triune God, which seems to Dante to contain an effigy of himself.
Though his senses focus on the sight, it is as impossible for him to comprehend it with pure thought, as measuring a circle ("lo cerchio," 134) is
impossible to the geometrician, yet both the one and the other inexplicably find what they need. Finally, as he wishes with insufficient ability to
see if his image conforms to the circle ("al cerchio," 138), his wish comes
true like a flash striking his mind, and the love which moves the sun and
the stars in their own circular orbits now makes both his desire and his
will turn like an evenly revolving wheel ("rota," 144):

ma già volgeva il mio disio e 'l *velle,*
sì come rota ch'igualmente è mossa,
    l'amor che move il sole e l'altre stelle. (*Par.,* 33.143–45)

[But already my desire and my will were revolved, like a wheel that
is evenly moved, by the Love which moves the sun and the other
stars.] (Singleton trans.)

In chapter 2 we discussed how the six tales of Fragment VII are arranged in a circular pattern according to their literary form. The circular
movement of this formal pattern echoes a circular theme in each of the
four literary tales in the Fragment. In the *Shipman's Tale*, a hundred francs
travel a horizontal, or exclusively physical circle, from the merchant to
the monk, from the monk to the wife, and from the wife back to the
merchant (in kind). In the Prioress's performance the circle is, as it were,
in a vertical, metaphysical plane. In her *Prologue* God descends from

heaven in the person of Christ, while in her *Tale* a soul returns to heaven as the Christlike little Clergeon. Continuing in this abstract direction, at the end of the *Monk's Tale,* when the constantly downward-turning Wheel of Fortune threatens to bore the company, the Knight reminds us of its upward turn (VII.2767–79), thus completing a philosophic, Boethian circle. And the *Nun's Priest's Tale* completes by its end a circle in the imagination, when its chickens return to the tranquility of a barnyard, and its fox to the wood, after flirting anthropomorphically with philosophy, theology, epic, and death.

The circularity of structural design gains added force from thematic similarities in tales on the same ring. On the first ring the near-disaster that might have befallen the wife in the *Shipman's Tale,* had her dalliance with the visiting monk been discovered, counterpoints the near disaster that might have befallen Chauntecleer in the grip of the fox, had his wit not purchased his freedom. That both escape with a great lesson clearly demonstrated, though probably not learned, must also have been intended as a parallel in the fragment. The yearning for ascension in the Prioress's performance on the fragment's second ring, an obvious response to the downward movement of her clergeon's physical situation and the descent to earth of the Father's Sapience, balances the Knight's call for upward movement from the Monk to respond to the unbroken series of *de casibus* tragedies already heard.

To emphasize the importance of Fragment VII to the second half of the poem, Chaucer has bracketed its six tales with Fragments VI and VIII, mirror images that expand the ring structure to ten tales (see Figure 9).

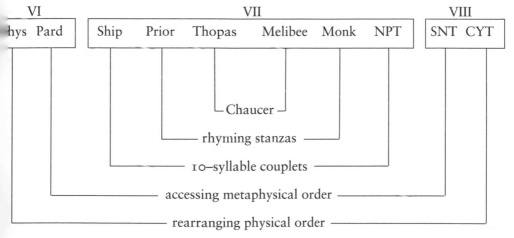

Figure 9

The two tales of Fragment VI constitute an interesting pair of ironies, as both the Physician and the Pardoner tell tales that undermine the aims of their professions. Contrary to the logical expectation that a physician's instinct would naturally celebrate the preservation of physical life, Chaucer's Physician tells a tale of a father who slays his daughter in order to gain the vaguely stated benefit of saving her from the hands of a lecherous judge. And instead of hearing from the Pardoner an account of how charitable giving ensures spiritual life, we witness blasphemous behavior that risks spiritual death in order to search for some ill-defined psychological gain. These ironies give the two tales of Fragment VI a kind of generic unity on one level, while the marked difference between the Physician's physical subject and the Pardoner's spiritual subject keeps them apart on another.

This same pattern of similarity and difference governs the two tales of Fragment VIII, where the mirrored pattern presents them in reverse order. Here an account of spiritual regeneration and apotheosis comes first in the tale of the Second Nun, while the tale of physical enhancement—the constant goal of alchemy—stands second. Both tales stress the "bisyness" and "werk" that their subjects imply, an activity leading to God in the former tale, away from God in the latter. Fire, an important presence in both tales, has no effect on St. Cecilia for she is already purified by her virtue, whereas it brings forth both sweat and discoloration in the yeoman of the second tale. The convert Valerian in the tale of St. Cecilia is linguistically echoed in the alchemist's herb valerian, which is useless as a means of conversion.[4] These similarities and differences duplicate the pattern of similarities and differences in the tales of Fragment VI, producing a design exactly like the discarded ring structure of Fragments III, IV, and V. Here two tales that would rearrange the values of the temporal world (Physician's and Canon's Yeoman's) comprise the outer ring, while two tales of yearning for some spiritual ideal (Pardoner's and Second Nun's) constitute the next ring as the pattern moves inward to the tales of Fragment VII, whose ring structure has the formal and thematic design already noted.

The persona of Chaucer himself stands at the center of the pilgrims in this main run of tales in the second half of the poem, stretching from the Physician to the Canon's Yeoman, not out of a sense of egoism, nor because this one pilgrim is more deserving than any of the others, nor even because the object of his yearning is any more worthy than what others hope to achieve. He is there because, of all the pilgrims whose tales arise from their own lives, Chaucer alone achieves that objective to which he obviously dedicated his life, the creation of poetry. The Prioress may still long for salvation, the Pardoner for acceptance, the Wife for a loving companion. But Chaucer has made his poem. While there may be some justification for believing that poetry pales beside salvation, and ought therefore not be given the prominence implied by the pilgrim Chaucer's central location in the second half of the poem, nevertheless a different argument could suggest with equal justice that Man most closely approximates the Creator when he is himself creating. That his creation may be limited to a fictive world weakens the argument less than we might think.

Fragment VI

The *Physician's Tale,* The Pardoner, His Prologue, and His Tale

THE PHYSICIAN'S TALE

Agreement on any Chaucerian subject would normally evoke a chorus of gratitude, one would think. The nearly unanimous opinion of the *Physician's Tale* is another matter. A consensus has developed that this hobbled entry, by Livy out of Jean de Meun's Reason, has long odds in the tale-telling stakes. Emerson Brown, Jr., admits that the tale "has long been depreciated as a work of art" (1981, p. 129), Anne Middleton that "it would be folly . . . to attempt to reverse [its] 'unjustified' neglect" (1973, p. 9), Jerome Mandel, noting that the tale has not had an enthusiast since Harry Bailly, that "no critic of the poem . . . has almost 'caught a cardynacle' as a result of it" (1976, p. 316), while Donald R. Howard offers a plausible reason for this neglect, "a dramatic example of misguided moralism: [Chaucer] praises virtue in a tale that is morally revolting" (1976, p. 334).

Although responses to these opinions may vary, some disagreeing entirely, no Chaucerian would recommend the tale to an interested student eager to read something matching Chaucer's reputation. That the tale is more troubling than satisfying, more apt to be viewed as history or treatise than as literature, perhaps describes the reaction of the pilgrims too, who are surprisingly silent on the horror they hear. Of course we must be careful to distinguish the Physician from Chaucer, a caution not meant to invoke the catch-all claim that every infelicity is an intended irony and that the tale has deliberately been left confused as a means of revealing the Physician's literary naïveté. Such claims confine themselves to the relation between a tale and its teller, whereas I mean to suggest in this chapter a much wider context. Before moving to this point, we might review a number of inconsistencies that have led to the Tale's current reputation.

Let us start with the unpredictable populace in the tale, silent on one occasion, volatile on another. The citizens of the town are nowhere in evidence when Virginius, alone and helpless, is defeated by corrupt Judge Apius's legal stratagem to abduct his daughter Virginia. Yet later, after Virginius "saves" his daughter by taking her life, "a thousand peple in thraste, / To save the knyght" (VI.260–61) from a sentence of death leveled against him by the same Apius. Where was this support, we want to know, when it could have helped Virginia? Or rather, why did Virginius not think of this potential support when his daughter pathetically asked, "Goode fader, shal I dye? / Is ther no grace, is ther no remedye?" (VI.235–36).

Nor does Virginia seem quite as certain as her father that her life should be ended. In addition to the plea just quoted, that some other remedy be found, she makes what at first seems an irrelevant reference to Jephtha's daughter, a maiden slain by her father who, to prevail in battle, had promised to sacrifice the first creature to emerge from his house on his return. His daughter, alas, was the first to greet him. Virginia sees in this scriptural story (Judges 11:34–39) two comparisons to herself, one explicit, the other implied. If Jephtha's daughter had been granted two months to collect her thoughts before she was to be killed, could not she, Virginia, have some time "to compleyne a litel space" (VI.239). When she adds that her biblical counterpart's only fault was that "she ran hir fader first to see, / To welcome hym with greet solempnitee" (VI.243–44), no reader can fail to infer that Virginia's equal innocence and equal loyalty to her father are rewarded with less gratitude. Perhaps Virginius believes the violent beheading of his daughter will be lessened by the tender compassion with which he carries it out—after a few minutes' delay. More significant, many medieval theologians agreed that Jephtha's vow to God in gratitude for conquering the children of Ammon was thoughtless.[1] It is logical to assume, therefore, that Chaucer's audience, reminded of foolish Jephtha, would realize that Virginius's decision was foolish as well.

Still another surprising inconsistency concerns the Tale's anticipated Christian dimension. Though set in a pre-Christian era, many of its particulars follow a typical saint's life, making it what Helen Cooper calls "a kind of secular hagiography" (1983, p. 155) similar to other Chaucerian tales of courageous women, like Lucretia in the *Legend of Good Women* and especially Griselda in the *Clerk's Tale.* Like the heroine of the *Clerk's Tale,* Virginia is young, virtuous, beautiful, and favored by the most powerful man of her town. The strong similarities between the two admirers in these tales make it difficult to decide which of the two tormentors is the more heinous. Walter's cruel insistence on testing Griselda's loyalty includes apparent death to her two children, divorce, and humiliation, whereas Apius merely conspires at court to secure Virginia as a concubine. That the former has the doubtful legitimacy of a husband's authority over a wife and brings about the death of no one, while Apius has no standing with Virginia yet sets in motion a lecherous scheme that leads to her death, to his own suicide, and to the execution of other conspirators, says nothing about who is more blameworthy in setting his strategy in motion. Nor about which woman is more severely oppressed, Griselda who surrenders her children or Virginia who surrenders her life. Though both are treated with unspeakable cruelty, by a husband in one case, a judge and then a father in the other: neither Griselda nor Virginia disobeys. In other words, like the *Clerk's Tale*, the *Physician's Tale* has everything in place for an expected declaration of the spirit's triumph over the flesh, if not in Christian terms, which would have made it anachronistic, at least in pre-Christian terms consistent with the time of Livy. The Clerk demonstrates that servitude can triumph over sovereignty (IV.114, 797–98), that Griselda's moral gain from refusing to break her vow of obedience to her husband is greater than the physical loss of her children, her status as Walter's wife, and her worldly self-respect. We anticipate that the *Physician's Tale* will make a similar comment epitomizing its implicit point that Virginia's moral gain from avoiding shameful ignomy at the hands of the lecherous Apius is far greater than her physical loss from giving up her life. Surprisingly, we never hear the expected clarification that her gain is spiritual, her loss physical.

On the contrary, unlike the *Clerk's Tale*, great care is taken to place the *Physician's Tale* in the context of natural law, rather than moral or theological law as the Christian Middle Ages understood it. In quick succession at the beginning of the Tale there is (a) a twenty-one-line digression imagining Nature soliloquizing her ability to create a thing of perfection, to which the Host alludes later with the lame explanation that Virginia's beauty caused her death (VI.297), and (b) a thirty-three-line lecture to governesses and parents instructing them not to allow their daughters to become "To soone rype and boold" (VI.68). These passages comprise almost 20 percent of the tale yet are conspicuously free of any spiritual reference, let alone Christian doctrine to which they would have seemed well-suited. The few allusions to God in the tale—chiefly an imagined comment by Nature, "He that is the formere principal / Hath maked me his vicaire general" (VI.19–20), several figures of speech, and an irrelevant moral drawn by the Physician (VI.277–86)—suggest nothing of the glorious reward that awaits Virginia for preferring to sacrifice her life rather than suffer the defilement of sexual slavery.[2] One can accept that a Christian context might have been thought irrelevant, not only on grounds of anachronism, but also because medieval Christianity understood "that unwilling victims of rape remain, morally, virgins" (Emerson Brown 1981, p. 136). But some suggestion of the primacy of spirit over flesh would have been useful in showing that Virginia's death was not entirely gratuitous. There is none.

Perhaps the most glaring inconsistency is also both the easiest to explain and the most difficult to explain away. It concerns Chaucer's craftsmanship. The manuscript evidence leaves no doubt that the *Physician's Tale* belongs in the same fragment as the *Pardoner's Tale.* Now the Prologue and Tale of the Pardoner reveal Chaucer at the height of his powers, whereas the *Physician's Tale* has been held in "relative critical disrepute and even neglect" (Bloch 1991, p. 102). It makes little sense, we want to argue, that Chaucer would link one of his best tales with one of his indifferent tales. And yet, the undoubtedly genuine link joining these two tales makes it clear that Chaucer himself intended the two tales to reside in the same fragment. Making this inconsistency even more puzzling, the *Physician's Tale* is no slavish rendition of a prior author's effort, as many of Chaucer's early works were, but one in which his creative hand is abundantly present. As C. David Benson says, "perhaps most striking in a tale not highly regarded, most of the material and treatment are original" (L. Benson 1987, p. 902). The disparity between Chaucer's apparent satisfaction with the *Physician's Tale* and current critical dissatisfaction with it suggests different sets of expectations. Comments like Howard's, "I find the barebones narrative not comic [as Robert Longsworth suggests] but chilling,"[3] imply that both he and the critic with whom he disagrees expect the tale to stand on its own feet. From Chaucer's perspective, however, the tale's backward glance to the *Franklin's Tale* and forward glance to the *Pardoner's Tale* may well point to a different role entirely. To grasp that role we might first be clear on which character the tale is really about.

With all due respect to Anne Middleton (1973) who argues that Chaucer "shifts the narrative emphasis and ethical interest toward the virgin courage of the daughter, away from the other two principal characters and their chief moral attributes: the perversion of justice in Apius and the stern patrician resolve of the wronged father" (p. 10), I must disagree. A tale's narrative center may often be determined by finding the character who seems most to develop or change in some way, as opposed to remaining essentially static throughout. Apius remains unchanged in his single purpose, from the moment he first conceives the corrupt plan to abduct Virginia until his very suicide. Virginia, too, is a constant throughout, her virtue as strong just before her death as in the beginning of the tale. True, she has a momentary pang when she hears of her fate, and makes an ineffective attempt to forestall her death. But this fleeting indication of her feelings achieves the narrative effect of turning our attention to her father, especially in relation to Jephtha and whether the decision of either father (i.e., Jephtha or Viginius) may be justified. We suspect, therefore, that Chaucer is not inviting readers to concentrate on either the unshakably virtuous maiden or the lecherous, one-dimensional judge—he takes them for granted and expects his readers to do so as well—but on the only problematic figure, Virginius, a man apparently torn between his love for his daughter and his loathing of the judge's intention and strategy.

If the tale does indeed feature Virginius at its center, the decision to sacrifice his daughter is his most poignant moment. Whether this decision is justified or not may never be solved, complicated as it is by the shift in Chaucer's source from Livy's focus on the legal corruption of his day to an emphasis on human motivation, as now in the *Physician's Tale*.[4] In either case, if prudence is the issue, discovering whether Virginius is right or wrong may be less important for the present study than recognizing that the motif flows naturally from the imprudent, playful promise by Dorigen in the preceding *Franklin's Tale* that she would become Aurelius's lover if he removed some treacherous rocks. In particular the motive prompting Virginius to solve his daughter's dilemma with the calamitous stroke that removes the daughter herself almost exactly parallels Arveragus's reason in the previous tale for his equally extraordinary response to his wife's dilemma, namely, male pride. After Arveragus decrees that his wife must submit to Aurelius he seems more concerned about the potential damage to his own reputation, if reports of the adultery circulate, than about the consequent defilement of his wife. In the *Physician's Tale*, too, Virginius turns his daughter's dilemma into a contest between himself and the lecherous judge Apius. For the story does not end with Virginia's death, but extends to the triumphant scene where Virginius presents the head of his daughter to her intending abductor. There are echoes here of *House of Fame* where Dido freezes her fame at its zenith, lest she slip into anecdote. By choosing suicide she declares that Aeneas was not just the first in a long line of future lovers, but the single greatest event of her life (*HF,* 345–74). A very large difference separates Virginius's decision to slay his daughter and Dido's to slay herself, yet the motive may be the same. Virginia's death certainly preserves her from sexual defilement, but even more it safeguards her reputation for all time. When Virginius presents Apius with the lifeless head of his daughter, he dramatically demonstrates that no judge, however powerful, will ever bring ignominy upon an extension of himself.

Another connection to the *Franklin's Tale* also forges a link with the following *Pardoner's Tale*. Both Arveragus and Virginius willingly sacrifice what seem to be higher values in order to preserve lesser values. In the *Franklin's Tale* Arveragus sacrifices his solemn marriage vow by ordering his wife to follow the vague, highly questionable courtly ideal that one's literal words must be honored, however rashly they were uttered. In the *Physician's Tale* (set in classical Rome, let us keep in mind, when society would not yet have acquired a "theology of virginity"[5]) Virginius sacrifices his daughter's life in order to avoid having her pass into the control of a lecherous judge. And in the *Pardoner's Tale,* to be discussed presently, both the rioters in the tale and their Pardoner-creator pursue lesser ideals while sacrificing greater. Distracted by thoughts of wealth, the rioters lose their physical and spiritual lives. The Pardoner, too, places his spiritual life in grave danger for the trivial gain of approval.

These valid links between the last tale in Fragment V and the first tale in Fragment VI imply that the two tales of Fragment VI, which Chaucer apparently intended to appear together, the *Physician's* and *Pardoner's Tales,* would be bound by equally strong or stronger links. Their closely related central motifs have nearly identical patterns, differing mainly in that the former is confined to temporal matters, physical life and death, while the latter deals exclusively with the subtler, less accessible questions of spiritual life and death. Since the brief (286 lines) *Physician's Tale* unfolds in a straightforward way, sounding almost like a précis from which qualifiers and moral dilemmas have been excised, it seems to act as an instruction booklet, on how to read the lengthier (682 lines) *Pardoner's Tale,* whose design is less easily grasped precisely because its deep exploration of the forces that motivate its teller obscure its horrific parallels with its predecessor. Read by itself, the *Physician's Tale* invites a reader to concentrate on the poignant plight of Virginia (as Middleton does), to weigh her threatened doom at the hands of Apius against her costly sacrifice at the hands of her father. Similarly, the *Pardoner's Tale,* by itself, encourages one to study the rhetorical techniques and personal motivation of its teller. Read together, both tales make us recognize the enormity of what is sacrificed compared to the lesser significance of what is sought.

THE PARDONER'S TALE

The Pardoner has been in the back of readers' minds ever since the early lines of the Wife's Prologue, when he interrupted her to make a few points of his own. It is a familiar Chaucerian technique, a hint that the cloth maker who "passed hem of Ypres and of Gaunt" (I.448) and the craftsman who surpassed other pardoners "fro Berwyk into Ware" (I.692) should perhaps be compared. The hint is often overlooked, as critical preoccupation with the Pardoner's sexual makeup obscures his close similarity to the Wife.[6] Nevertheless, these two pilgrims precisely reflect each other, while their Prologues and Tales closely follow a single pattern.[7] As characters they whirl about in the same "neurotic circle,"[8] privately yearning to belong to a community whose standards will always exclude them, yet publicly pursuing courses that make acceptance impossible. As performers they emerge in stages, like crinkly vellum slowly revealing ancient palimpsests, as their darker realities take faint shape beneath masks of professional success and personal joy.

The Pardoner's entire performance follows a deliberate strategy. By carefully adopting the antithetical roles of conventional sinner, and man of God, he hopes to be judged on his ability to manipulate appearances. As Alisoun's hour on stage dashes her hopes, the Pardoner's performance peels back his several fictions to disclose the anguished reality they had been designed to conceal. Beneath his Prologue's unrepentant sinner and his claim to enjoy delicious excess, lies the Tale's joyless old man condemned to a life bereft of pleasure. Beneath its equally skillful pulpit impersonator who offers eternal life, lie the Tale's three revelers intending to slay Death but actually performing Death's office. As one would expect in this more portentous half of the *Canterbury Tales,* the old man and the three rioters who reveal the Pardoner's hidden reality are more foreboding surrogates than the old hag and knight-rapist who reveal the Wife's. Yet the pattern remains the same. As the Pardoner turns his attention from *Prologue* to *Tale* he slowly reveals a deeper text that proclaims that his bold exchange of accident for substance has been mere bravura. Like the Wife, whose failure to sustain human love makes her obsessed with the forms of physical affection, the Pardoner's failure to imagine divine love makes him obsessed with death. The "joyless old man" in him yearns for death to free him from the prison of his life; the "reveler in blasphemy" in him trembles at the thought of what that death will bring.

Conscious Aims: The Prologue

At once enormously intriguing, yet extremely difficult to grasp, the *Prologue* to the *Pardoner's Tale* has become a frustrating paradox. Together with the Narrator's remarks in the General Prologue (I.669–714), it seems to hold the key to understanding the "noble ecclesiaste's" entire performance. But the idiosyncrasies of both these informants may do more to confound that understanding than assist it. The wide-eyed credulity of the Narrator does little to illuminate his shadowy fellow pilgrim, while the Pardoner's own calculated sleight of hand almost entirely conceals the motives that lie beneath his gratuitous confession of fraudulence.

The Narrator's reliability depends on whether or not he exceeds his limitations. When reporting information gained by his senses he may be trusted completely; anything else he says must be closely scrutinized. For example, his description of the Pardoner's "heer as yelow as wex" (I.675) may be accepted without hesitation because he bases it on visual evidence. But his further comment about the Pardoner's income is uncertain:

Upon a day he gat hym moore moneye
Than that the person gat in monthes tweye. (I.703–4)

How does the Narrator acquire this knowledge? To credit him with intermittent omniscience would hint of circular reasoning: we accept the remark because it fits our sense of the Pardoner's abilities, while the remark itself contributes to that sense. On the other hand, if the Narrator simply heard the Pardoner brag about his income, the remark belongs in the same category as the comment about his hair. The latter reports what his eyes had seen, the former what his ears had heard. We can trust the Narrator's accuracy, but not the Pardoner's. Other evidence must be sought to substantiate or contradict the Narrator's accurate report.

Even less credence should be given to our only other witness, the Pardoner himself, who, though a font of information, can neither be verified nor contradicted. To be sure, we may discredit some of his claims, like the assertion that his "male" contains what was once Our Lady's veil (I.694–95), not because the Narrator implies his own disbelief by calling it a pillowcase, but because our own good sense makes us doubt that such a veil would have remained intact for 1,300 years, or found its way into the Pardoner's blasphemous life if it had. Other claims, though impossible to disprove, may be doubted. The sly insinuation that he is a young man (III.187) scarcely accords with his thinning hair (I.679). Still other claims have been widely accepted, yet rest on extraordinarily slim evidence. Hardly anyone doubts the Pardoner's avarice, though the only evidence for it comes from his own frequent insistence.

As the Pardoner warms to his own Prologue he discloses an important secret of his profession: that the bulls and seals authorizing him to preach need only perfunctory attention—

"First I pronounce whennes that I come,
And thanne my bulles shewe I, alle and some.
Oure lige lordes seel on my patente,
That shewe I first, my body to warente,
That no man be so boold, ne preest ne clerk,
Me to destourbe of Cristes hooly werk." (VI.335–40)

—for his real legitimacy is conferred by rhetoric:

"'Goode men,' I seye, 'taak of my wordes keep;
If that this boon be wasshe in any welle,
If cow, or calf, or sheep, or oxe swelle
That any worm hath ete, or worm ystonge,
Taak water of that welle and wassh his tonge,
And it is hool anon. . . .
    "'Heere is a miteyn eek, that ye may se.
He that his hand wol putte in this mitayn,
He shal have multipliyng of his grayn. . . .'" (VI.352–57, 372–74)

A bull with the Pope's seal may be impressive, but it is nothing compared
to a bone that enables water to cure cattle and a mitten that doubles a
crop. With awe thus aroused, the Pardoner turns passive enthusiasm into
a willingness to act by claiming that sinners "shal have no power ne no
grace / To offren to my relikes in this place" (VI.383–84). The innocent
will contribute out of just pride; the guilty in order to protest innocence.

This opening movement of the Pardoner's Prologue actually contributes to two scenes. First, it forms part of the scene enacted on the road to
Canterbury where a large group of pilgrims are both players and audience. And it also implies—and lavishly quotes from—another scene that
has often taken place, we assume, between this Pardoner and one of his
typical congregations. While giving the former group a detailed description of his preaching strategy, he makes a convincing case for his ability to
manipulate the latter:

"Lordynges," quod he, "in chirches whan I preche,
I peyne me to han an hauteyn speche,
And rynge it out as round as gooth a belle,
For I kan al by rote that I telle." (VI.329–32)

The great satisfaction he takes from the bell-like quality of his voice totally eclipses his interest in his memorized sermon. Both the message and
the congregation are nearly forgotten as the control he exercises over his
emotive powers completely absorbs him. He imagines that the joy he takes
in his ability to articulate with body and voice will bring equal joy to his

congregation. In short, the Pardoner is an accomplished actor who, as A. C. Spearing has noted, takes greater pleasure in the role itself than in the responsibilities that go with it (1965, pp. 8–9). He stretches his neck,

> "And est and west upon the peple I bekke,
> As dooth a dowve sittynge on a berne.
> Myne handes and my tonge goon so yerne
> That it is joye to se my bisynesse." (VI.396–99)

The Pardoner knows that the pilgrims could have two very different reactions to him. They could be perfunctorily moved by his persuasive sermon, much as they are at the end of the *Man of Law's Tale,* the *Clerk's Tale,* the *Physician's Tale,* and even the *Tale of Melibee,* or they could have an aesthetic reaction to him as a performer. As one who relishes his acting ability, the Pardoner cannot let his material upstage his performance. To understand how he encourages the aesthetic response he much prefers, we might look at a useful observation made 500 years later by John Ruskin:

> Whenever anything looks like what it is not, the resemblance being so great as *nearly* to deceive, we feel a kind of pleasurable surprise, an agreeable excitement of mind. . . . Whenever we perceive this in something produced by art, that is to say, whenever the work is seen to resemble something which we know it is not, we receive what I call an idea of imitation. . . . Now two things are requisite to our complete and more pleasurable perception of this: first, that the resemblance be so perfect as to amount to a deception; secondly, that there be some means of proving at the same moment that it *is* a deception.[9]

To promote an aesthetic reaction the Pardoner creates the first requisite (in Ruskin's terms) by telling his pilgrim audience that he earns his living by acting the part of a holy man of God on his pulpit-stage, a claim he amply demonstrates in his Tale. As he more than willingly discloses in the first half of his Prologue (VI.329–99), he portrays a legitimate Pardoner who ostensibly believes what he preaches, furthers the word of God, and saves souls. The success of that role is hard to dispute. Not only do we have the Narrator's assumption that the Pardoner was an accomplished preacher (I.692–93), as well as the man's own testimony (VI.389–90), but we can actually judge for ourselves later, when we read the text (VI.463–968) that deceives us into thinking we "hear" a preacher. Moreover, we have hard evidence that his performance on the road to Canterbury, despite its admission of fraud, is a religiously moving event, for some observers argue that the good work of the Pardoner's sermon mitigates his guilt.[10] And listen to the famous reaction of one—hardly "lewed"—observer, commenting on and paraphrasing lines 916–18:

> Then, suddenly, unexpectedly, without an instant's warning, [the Pardoner's] cynicism falls away, and he utters the solemn words: "May Christ, the physician of our souls, grant you His pardon, for that is better than mine! I will not deceive you, though I get my living by fraud!" . . . The Pardoner has not always been an assassin of souls. He is a renegade, perhaps, from some holy order. Once he preached for Christ's sake; and now, under the spell of the wonderful story he has told and of recollections that stir within him, he suffers a very paroxysm of agonized sincerity. (Kittredge 1915, pp. 216–17)

When critics well apprised of the Pardoner's fraud mistake their own paroxysm for a trance in the Pardoner, we need hardly wonder at his effectiveness as a performer.

Merely declaring that for him the profession of pardoner is essentially a performance will not, by itself, fetch the response he wants. He must also meet Ruskin's second requisite, that is, have in place, even before he begins to preach, the "proof" that his performance in the pulpit is an enormous deception. He must make his audience presume that his "real self" is a man of profound corruption who enacts the devil's will. To this end he devotes the second movement of his Prologue in what becomes an even more convincing performance, and a greater deception, than the one he creates in the pulpit.

In the sixty-three lines that comprise the second half of the Pardoner's Prologue (VI.400–62) forty-four explicitly refer to his sinfulness. In six separate statements he insists he is an avaricious man who preaches only for profit.[11] We may wonder if these are truthful confessions, or if they simply protest too much (as the Wife of Bath does on another intimate subject), but there is no doubt that in advertising his corruption he speaks with unmatched persuasiveness. The opinion of an earlier generation was unanimous. Kittredge called him "the most abandoned character among the Canterbury Pilgrims" (1915, p. 211); Malone claimed that "by the time he has finished his prolog we know him through and through. . . . The Pardoner belong[s] to a category . . . of wicked vicious clerics. . . . For [him] there is no excuse, no saving grace" (1951, pp. 179, 185). More recent critics have been equally persuaded by the Pardoner's insistence on his own evil, such that Spearing's comment, "the Pardoner . . . fixes them with his 'glaring eyen' and draws them into his own evil" (1965, p. 23) could as easily refer to modern readers as to the Canterbury pilgrims.

That such critical conviction rests on no more reliable evidence than the Pardoner's own words is less astonishing than it would seem. We are so accustomed to the human tendency to conceal misdeeds that when someone deliberately reveals a fault, especially a particularly grievous one, we believe him without question. Hence, a natural guard against hoodwinking lowers when we listen to the Pardoner. Actually, if the Pardoner's ploy were taken out of the moral sphere we would recognize it immediately as a familiar disclaimer of formal training or painstaking effort, permitting people to make their achievements appear natural and thus more remarkable. Sprezzatura, no less transparent in the sixteenth century than in the fourteenth (or the twentieth), has gone unnoticed in the Pardoner because of the direction in which he leads his audience. A courtier, ancient or modern, affects styles in order to imply an inherent reality; the Pardoner affects an inner reality in order to call attention to his range of styles.

The moral sphere in which the Pardoner chooses to demonstrate his own artifice presents enormous difficulties, especially to the Pardoner. The problem lies less in preaching an effective sermon than in convincing his audience of his own immorality. It is not enough merely to claim fraud and moral turpitude; he must prove it, and do so according to what his audience considers immorality to be. In short, he must demonstrate his fondness for their sins. He selects lechery and avarice because he knows that the pilgrims, mindful of their own attractions to these sins, can well understand another's surrender to them. Yet lechery and avarice may well be the only sins for which the Pardoner feels not the least attraction.

Although the Pardoner has most often been called simply a eunuch, the earliest and still most helpful scholar of the question, W. C. Curry (1926), distinguished two kinds of eunuch, the *eunuchus qui castratus est* and the *eunuchus ex nativitate,* concluding that the Pardoner belongs in the latter category (pp. 59–62). Curry overlooked what may be the most important reason for Chaucer's electing to make the Pardoner a *eunuchus ex nativitate.* According to Rasis, whom Curry quotes, such a eunuch, whether born *sine testiculis* or *parvissimos habens eunuchus apparet,* would reach mature age without passing through puberty, in contrast to a *castratus* who is unnaturally prevented from reaching puberty or maimed afterward. Modern medicine calls such a person a cryptorchid eunuch, one whose testicles never matured. Despite Curry's later remark about the Pardoner's efforts "to arouse an atrophied desire," a cryptorchid eunuch suffers from arrested sexual development and can never have had a desire in the first place, much less an atrophied desire, which would be more appropriate to a castratus.[12]

Some of the pilgrims (for example, Physician, Clerk, Man of Law, and so forth) may have been familiar with the medieval physiognomies and treatises on which modern research attempts to establish the Pardoner's condition. Yet the Narrator, perhaps the least knowledgeable of them all, may speak for the intuition of all when he offers a tentative opinion: "I trowe he were a geldyng or a mare" (I.691). To convince the pilgrims of his lechery, then, the Pardoner must first overcome their suspicion that he could not experience normal masculine desire. His conscious aping of avant garde dress (I.682), and his artful linking of himself with young lovers eager to learn of the Wife's craft (III.187), promote the idea of his youthfulness and thus associate him with passion. Similarly, his boast of "a joly wenche in every toun" (VI.453), along with his earlier banter with the Wife of Bath on the subject of marriage, are designed to create the impression of healthy masculinity. By claiming he planned to marry (III.166), he implies a normal sexual appetite; by further declaring that he will break those plans (III.168), he underscores his normalcy by suggesting he is less insistent on his sexual vigor than we would expect him to be if he wished merely to perpetuate the fiction of his virility. And by subordinating this entire subject to an ostensible attack on the Wife's shrewish nature he succeeds in diverting attention from his specific plan while carefully insinuating it in each pilgrim's mind.

The Pardoner's celebrated friendship with the Summoner provides another means of convincing the pilgrims of his capacity for lechery. Much has been made of the libidinous duet of the high-voiced, putative "mare" and the excessively masculine Summoner who "bar to hym a stif burdoun" (I.673), literally a strong stick or staff. But neither this nor any other evidence suggests that the Pardoner travels with the Summoner as a homosexual partner. He rather hopes that some of his companion's reflected masculinity will land on him. Since the Summoner is readily associated with two of the metaphoric meanings of "stif burdoun," erect phallus and thunderous base, we infer that the Pardoner's care to ring out his sermon in "hauteyn speche" is a calculated attempt to imply his own vocal and sexual energy. Such, then, is the Pardoner's elaborate plan to publicize his virility, not for its own sake, but to establish the basis on which his claims to lechery must rest.[13]

No apparent condition makes avarice as unlikely a possibility for the Pardoner as lechery is. Nor can we point to convincing evidence in support of his supposed avarice. He may well be a kind of photographic negative of the Merchant. But whereas few have been fooled by the avaricious Merchant in beaver hat and costly shoes, whose "Sownynge alwey th'encrees of his wynnyng" (I.275) does much to convince us of a decrease, almost everyone has taken at face value the Pardoner's continued insistence on his avarice. With so persuasive a service to offer, he may indeed have collected a hundred marks a year for some time, and may even be far wealthier than the Merchant pretends to be. Our question, however, concerns not his wealth but his self-proclaimed avarice. Nothing in his appearance suggests the satisfaction that the Merchant so obviously derives from costly possessions. More significant, there is no indication that the pleasure he takes in money rivals the pleasure he gets from his histrionic skills. Alas, we hear constantly of the purpose for which he preaches, and only once—rather coldly—of the results:

> "By this gaude have I wonne, yeer by yeer,
> An hundred mark sith I was pardoner." (VI.389–90)

On the implicit evidence of the *General Prologue* and his own Prologue the Pardoner cares little for either lechery or avarice. His explicit references to his profession imply that he cares equally little for piety or formal theology. On the contrary, the Pardoner seems committed only to displaying his technical virtuosity as a performer. Deprived by an unfortunate medical condition of a normal physical life predicated on sensual attraction, and unable to conceive a spiritual life that depends on analogies with physical attraction, the Pardoner has sought to create a new reality out of his consummate ability to manipulate appearances. His creation of the appearances of moral abandonment renders all the more dazzling his ability to manipulate the completely contradictory appearances of a professional man of God.

Unconscious Failure: The Tale

The "moral thyng" to which the Pardoner says he will turn following his extraordinary Prologue must await completion of a further apparent digression. The short homilies on gluttony, gambling, and swearing are a useful hook for rendering his audience attentive by affording them an opportunity to experience sin vicariously, and an apt overture to a story about accomplished drinkers, gamblers, and swearers. They have an even greater appropriateness for the Pardoner himself, not because he too is a drinker, gambler, and swearer, for at worst he sins only mildly at these, but because they embody the Pardoner's major error of confusing accident and substance.

He begins these introductory homilies with a significant general condemnation of a company of young folk who

> daunce and pleyen at dees bothe day and nyght,
> And eten also and drynken over hir myght,
> Thurgh which they doon the devel sacrifise
> Withinne that develes temple in cursed wise
> By superfluytee abhomynable.
> Hir othes been so grete and so dampnable
> That it is grisly for to heere hem swere. (VI.467–73)

A spurious etymology, encouraged by Isidore of Seville and reflected in
Chaucer's spelling, traced "abhomynable" to *ab homine* and assumed that
the word meant a departure from what is characteristically human.[14] One
who cultivates the habits described in these lines retains, of course, the appearance of human nature, but contradicts that nature by his actions. Hence
the appropriateness for the Pardoner, who masquerades as a man both dis-
solute and moral, when in essence he is neither saint, sinner, nor even a fully
functioning man. Each of the sins described in the Pardoner's three introductory homilies implies a similar confusion between substance and accident. The first homily on "glotonye," or more specifically a formidable
example of pulpit pyrotechnics on its subheading "dronkenesse," includes
scriptural examples of drunkenness, a comment from Seneca, and an emotive apostrophe compressing its underlying logic:

> O glotonye, ful of cursednesse!
> O cause first of oure confusioun!
> O original of oure dampnacioun,
> Til Crist hadde boght us with his blood agayn! (VI.498–501)

Skillful substitutions remind us of the variations of oral poetry. Enlarging
a particular act of drunkenness to the wider category of gluttony, he expands to a notion of mental confusion, then to moral confusion—that is,
original sin—and finally to an image of Christ's Redemption. The logic is
absurd, of course, regardless of how many in the fourteenth century may
have believed it. No matter. The slim connections are sufficient for the
Pardoner's purpose: "Corrupt was al this world for glotonye" (VI.504).

A second series of tenuous connections gives him another titillating
lead to follow:

> O, wiste a man how manye maladyes
> Folwen of excesse and of glotonyes,

He wolde been the moore mesurable
Of his diete, sittynge at his table. (VI.513–16)

"Sittynge at his table" reminds him of the taste of food, which in turn
prompts him to remark how hard men work for a glutton's good meat.
And meat recalls another scriptural passage which he distorts as deftly as
he distorted the account of the first fall:

"Mete unto wombe, and wombe eek unto mete,
Shal God destroyen bothe," as Paulus seith. (VI.522–23)

The passage in Paul (I Corinthians 6:13) clearly means that everything
has an appropriate purpose. Just as "Render unto Caesar the things that
are Caesar's" implies the appropriateness of money to Caesar, so Paul's
"Food for the belly and the belly for food" implies that food is intended
to be eaten and that the belly is the appropriate place for it. That God will
destroy both merely affirms the temporal nature of material things, not
that God will punish those who eat. The Pardoner, however, seizes a more
exciting meaning. "Mete unto wombe" emphasizes, he implies, the diges-
tive system, beginning with food and ending with excretion. Merely mentioning the process disgusts him and makes him note, as he returns to the
subject of drink from which the last twenty-five lines have been a useful
digression, how much

fouler is the dede,
Whan man so drynketh of the white and rede
That of his throte he maketh his pryvee
Thurgh thilke cursed superfluitee. (VI.525–28)

Notwithstanding the great success of a rhetoric unified by mood and
aimed at the lightning swift exposure of one interesting image after another so as to create the appearance rather than essence of logical connections, the homily nevertheless makes a telling point whose significance
may have escaped the one person for whom it is most appropriate. The
brief mention of Lot and his daughters with which the Pardoner began his
short first homily—and which incidentally constitutes one of the few instances of his scriptural accuracy—emphasizes the effect of wine on wit:

Lo, how that dronken Looth, unkyndely,
Lay by his doghtres two, unwityngly;
So dronk he was, he nyste what he wroghte. (VI.485–87)

Three times in as many lines the Pardoner stresses Lot's unnatural loss of
that faculty peculiar to man alone, his ability to know. Seneca's analogy
makes the point explicit:

He seith he kan no difference fynde
Bitwix a man that is out of his mynde
And a man which that is dronkelewe,
But that woodnesse, yfallen in a shrewe,
Persevereth lenger than doth dronkenesse. (VI.493–97)

If rationality alone distinguishes man, then a drunk, no less than a madman whom the drunk temporarily resembles, presents to the world the mere appearance of a human nature but nothing of its essence. Like the cooks who turn "substaunce into accident" (VI.539), the drunk "Is deed, whil that he lyveth" (VI.548).

In his second homily the Pardoner claims briefly that gaming begets all vices (VI.591 ff.), but quickly limiting his attack to gamblers in high places he strikes the same note we heard in his lines on drunkenness. A nation chooses a governor—at least in theory—for his wisdom, because each of his decisions, being based on reason, has a greater probability of promoting justice than does a decision based on chance. On the authority of Stilboun of Lacedaemon and the King of the Parthians, whose opinions he recounts, the Pardoner implies that governors who gamble will base their judgments on chance rather than on reason. By failing to practice the essence of good decision-making such men affect only the appearances of their high office.

Similarly, in his third homily the Pardoner asserts that "Gret sweryng is a thyng abhominable" (VI.631). The gist of his quotation from Jeremias 4:2 allows that an oath may be taken if the matter is serious and if one's statement is true. But the Pardoner's various examples of swearing, doubtless enunciated with visceral delight, proceed from trifling causes like gambling (VI.656) or from those that are downright false (VI.657). In such cases the form of the oath suggests a degree of profundity and truth which does not exist. Once again, perhaps without being aware of it, the Pardoner has chosen a sin that precisely characterizes his own paradox: an elaborately contrived exterior surrounding emptiness within.

At length arriving at the Tale itself, a surprisingly obvious yet brilliantly profound story, the Pardoner delights, he says, that the avarice against which he preaches feeds the same vice in himself:

Radix malorum est Cupiditas.
Thus kan I preche agayn that same vice
Which that I use, and that is avarice. (VI.426–28)

But this is mere pretense, to encourage his listeners to believe him a typical sinner, little different from themselves, lest they see him for what he is.

For the Pardoner's doubly fraudulent appearance as make-believe sinner and make-believe preacher bears a much more intricate relationship to his Tale than he knows. Both centers of interest in the Tale, the old man and the three rioters, engage in a frantic but frustrating search for Death. Like Tithonus, beloved of Aurora, the old man must walk the earth forever, but remain forever deprived of the physical joys "of happy men that have the power to die."[15] It is not his immortality he loathes but the loss of his youth, a memory he locates unmistakably in the senses:

"Lo how I vanysshe, flessh, and blood, and skyn!
Allas, whan shul my bones been at reste?
Mooder, with yow wolde I chaunge my cheste
That in my chambre longe tyme hath be,
Ye, for an heyre clowt to wrappe me!" (VI.732–36)

For this old man, death betokens no commencement. Nor would a medieval audience assume it to bring eternal bliss to this poor sufferer, for he has given no indication that he has earned it. Rather, death would merely signify the old man's release from suffering.

The three rioters hold an opposite view. From their first appearance in the Tale they understand death to mean privation, as it means in these words from a young boy identifying a body on its way to the grave:

"He was, pardee, an old felawe of youres,
And sodeynly he was yslayn to-nyght,
Fordronke, as he sat on his bench upright.
Ther cam a privee theef men clepeth Deeth,
That in this contree al the peple sleeth." (VI.672–76)

Although nothing in the lad's or in the rioters' words implies greater consciousness of the "hereafter" than in the old man's, a medieval mind would nevertheless have assumed death to bring punishment upon these three, perhaps eternally. Moreover, they unwittingly use language traditionally associated with the triune God whose victory over death was made manifest in Christ's passion and resurrection:

"Herkneth, felawes, we thre been al ones;
Lat ech of us holde up his hand til oother,
And ech of us bicomen otheres brother,
And we wol sleen this false traytour Deeth.
He shal be slayn, he that so manye sleeth." (VI.696–700)

Whereas the old man's expressions invite us to think of him in relation to this world, the rioters' remarks suggest the next. In contrast to the old man who longs for death to release him from the terrible restriction of his life, the three young men fear death because of the great restriction it will bring. The old man's thoughts remain fixed in a joyless present from which he cannot escape; the young rioters are obsessed with a dreadful future which they too cannot escape.

The macabre dance in which old man and revelers hunt for Death is enclosed by a frame that makes its own emptiness more apparent. The first half of the frame, the unsolicited advice offered by a young boy, leaves no doubt that in the face of death's inevitability readiness is all:

"And, maister, er ye come in [Death's] presence,
Me thynketh that it were necessarie
For to be war of swich an adversarie.
Beth redy for to meete hym everemoore;
Thus taughte me my dame; I sey namoore." (VI.680–84)

The moral sphere to which the boy refers contrasts sharply with the physical orientation of both the old man and the rioters. Ironically, the young boy offers the one piece of advice that could be of use to the three men, if they really wanted to slay death, for the simple truth he learned at a woman's knee, especially if the woman were Mother Church, pre-supposes something for which readiness provides a benefit, in short, life after death.

The concluding half of the frame, a profound counterpart to the boy's beautifully simplistic injunction, takes the form of a blasphemous parody of a religious consummation—both Christ's Crucifixion and man's symbolic participation in it. Reminiscent of the centurions who gambled for Christ's outer wrappings because they were unaware of his essential na-ture, the rioters forget their potentially laudable search for Death as they draw lots to set in motion the plot that will end their lives. The concentra-tion of prominent Christian symbols at the death scene makes this three-some intimate participants in an archetypal action that stretches from man's first fall to the consummation of the world. At the end of a "croked wey" (VI.761)—hardly other than a reminder of the straight way of the Lord—stands a tree that carries subliminal associations with the symbolic alternatives of good and evil: the Tree of Life and the Tree of the Knowl-edge of Good and Evil. Beneath its branches two of the revelers re-create a scene in Gethsemane by plotting a betrayal for a heap of coins. Mean-while, the youngest of the three purchases bread and wine at a nearby village. The point of these symbols is not to call attention to the similarity between this scene and events in the life of Christ, but to emphasize the difference between them (Spearing 1965, pp. 41–45). For example, the scene in which the youngest rioter poisons the wine includes several accidental details that appear to emulate Christ's performance at the marriage feast of Cana, while in essence they reverse Christ's first public miracle. Christ miraculously changed water into wine; this young man perversely turns wine into poison. Every other detail that seems to allude to Scripture similarly subverts scriptural meaning. Rather than recognize the Tree of Life in which the rioters would have found an alternative to death, they choose to make it a Tree of the Fruit of the Knowledge of Good and Evil. Instead of characterizing the Trinity they resemble ("we thre been al ones" [VI.696]), they become an anti-Trinity. Despite a boisterous insistence that they will slay Death, the three surrender to him. The dagger thrust in the youngest reveler's side mocks the piercing of Christ's side in the final hour on Golgotha. When the remaining two follow him in death, rendering futile every act that has blasphemed Christian truth, the quiet beneath the tree and the still untouched gold reign in dumb triumph over the consummation of all, like that moment before Resurrection when chaos might have come again, or like that unknown hour when some in the fourteenth century believed it would.

If the manner of the three rioters' death makes their blasphemy clear, the Tale as a whole exposes the Pardoner. We noted above in what ways the Pardoner has been fraudulent. While advertising to the world that in private life he is an avaricious lecher, he carelessly lets escape several hints that make us suspect he is neither avaricious nor a lecher. Similarly, in his professional life he presents a convincing image of a man of God, but undermines that image by his frank admission of role-playing and by his insistence on his own moral corruption. In the old man and the three rioters of his Tale the Pardoner offers us, without his realizing it, vivid portraits respectively of his private and professional lives stripped of the elaborate pretense he has created for each. Like the old man, the Pardoner finds himself committed to life in a temporal world where pain and torment are relieved, at least in design, by certain attractions and pleasures of the senses. Unable to experience these pleasures—due to advanced age in his surrogate, and to a quirk of nature in himself—the Pardoner thus falls heir to the pain of a joyless existence. The misery that the old man does not shrink from describing exposes for us the Pardoner's probable reality, a horrible physical life, unsuccessfully concealed beneath fabrications of avarice and lechery. On the other hand, the three rioters place his reality in the context of eternity by providing a gloss on his professional life. While in the pulpit the Pardoner gives the faithful, in exchange for money, a promise of remission of punishment due to sin. Drawing on their belief in the infinite grace of Christ's redemption, symbolized in the miracle of bread and wine, he professes to slay the eternal death that might otherwise await his congregation. Like the three rioters who seek to slay Death as a help to others, but who merely annihilate themselves, the Pardoner's abuse of his ecclesiastical function may shape his own eternal reward.

The conscious intention of the Pardoner's elaborately conceived Prologue had been twofold. He wished, first, to conceal the emptiness of his life, and second, to lay the groundwork on which he could build a new reality for himself in the freely acknowledged artistic manipulation of his own external appearances. The Tale was to be a demonstration of that new reality—a consummate performance in which a thoroughly immoral man could convincingly persuade others that he was a man of God to whom they should give money to ensure their own salvation. Despite the brilliance of his conception and the technical excellence of his performance, he fails in the most telling way imaginable—in his own mind—by exposing his inability to embrace that reality. The portraits of an old man who frustratingly seeks release from the painful nothingness of his own life, and of three rioters who desperately and futilely hope to defer their accounting in the next, cry out to us with the incomparable ghastliness of the Pardoner's two lives—one lost, the other powerless to be saved—that his effort to replace that nothingness with stylistic brilliance has failed: he is obsessed with death and its consequence for him.

Public Rejection: The Epilogue

No single Chaucerian scene has proved as perplexing as the Epilogue to the *Pardoner's Tale* with its appeal for contributions and its angry response from the Host. Why would the Pardoner ask for money when his detailed confession has already demonstrated that the money will never be used for a charitable purpose and that the pardons and relics purchased with it are utterly meaningless? The argument presented here—that the Pardoner cares little for the actual money he could collect—makes the Epilogue even more difficult to understand, for it removes a plausible explanation for the attempted sale. Other explanations, almost unanimously assuming the Pardoner's inconsistency, argue that he is simply carried away with himself, or drunk, or a masochist, or some other version of irrational conduct. Yet the Pardoner's flawless lucidity up to this point renders any argument based on his irrationality highly suspect. More to the point, no explanation of the Pardoner's supposed irrationality has yet offered a satisfactory explanation of how that conduct accords with the aesthetic unity of his entire performance. Despite the plausibility of any explanation of an individual scene, a higher test of its validity must be its appropriateness to scenes other than the one it explains.

In order to understand how this complex scene is integrated with everything else in the Pardoner's performance we must return briefly to the theater for an important distinction between *impersonating* and *acting*. Each of these two art forms relies simultaneously on both the audience's world and some other milieu present on stage to achieve Ruskin's two fictions, noted above. Depending on which art form is used, the two contexts are manipulated differently. The impersonator copies the voice and mannerisms of some readily recognized figure from the audience's frame of reference to make it appear that his subject has materialized before them. It is, of course, only an apparent, or partial resemblance, for his own identity as celebrated entertainer provides the proof that the impersonation is a fiction. He temporarily abandons his own world in order to enter the audience's by taking on the appearance of someone they know.

For his entire performance our "noble ecclesiaste" has been impersonating both a typical sinner and a typical preacher, neither of which comes to him naturally. Despite this double impersonation, he attempts to make his audience accept the former as his true nature and only the latter as an impersonation. The success of his method depends on the careful distinction he maintains between the two theaters in which he displays his skill. He constructs his world of lechery and avarice, a world abundantly familiar to his pilgrim audience, in the present time of the pilgrimage to Canterbury. He confines his Godly context, in which he impersonates an equally familiar pardoner, to another time and another place, continually recalled in flashback quotation of himself. Having convinced his listeners of the avarice and lechery of his private life, he can then demonstrate his ability to impersonate a pardoner normally found in theirs.

Acting, on the other hand, reverses this direction. The performer creates an internally coherent reality whose sheer presence forces the audience to abandon their frame of reference and join his. For the performer acting presents a far greater challenge than impersonating because it requires the gradual fading of the distinction between the newly created world of the performer and the world of the audience. In the Epilogue to his Tale the Pardoner attempts to destroy that distinction and make the pilgrims enter his world.

As the story of the three rioters comes to a swift and fitting close, the Pardoner initiates his daring Epilogue with an equally fitting rhetorical flourish summarizing every major theme in the Tale and containing an unconscious self-indictment as well (VI.895–903). Nevertheless, since the purpose for which he usually preaches has not yet been realized, he spends a few more lines persuading his audience that his service can protect them from the fate of the three revelers from Flanders:

> Now, goode men, God foryeve yow youre trespas,
> And ware yow fro the synne of avarice!
> Myn hooly pardoun may yow alle warice,
> So that ye offre nobles or sterlynges,
> Or elles silver broches, spoones, rynges. (VI.904–8)

There is no doubt that the "goode men" he addresses here are not the pilgrims riding with him to Canterbury, but the members of a typical congregation which he usually addresses from a pulpit. An earlier address to this imaginary group (VI.573) has prepared us for this second address. But the most convincing evidence that these lines are still part of the Pardoner's lengthy quotation of himself may be found in the line that signals the end of the performance: "—And lo, sires, thus I preche" (VI.915). Everything before this line obviously belongs to the context in which he pretends to be a servant of God collecting alms for God's holy work; everything after it to the context in which he has been pleased to admit his fraudulence, his lechery, and his avarice. And yet, his actual words seem suddenly out of place:

> And Jhesu Crist, that is oure soules leche,
> So graunte yow his pardoun to receyve,
> For that is best; I wol yow nat deceyve. (VI.916–18)

Although this kind of remark properly belongs to "pulpit time," the Pardoner has undoubtedly returned to "pilgrimage time." By shifting back and forth between pulpit and pilgrimage with dazzling speed and abruptness, he brings the two extremes of his total performance as close together as possible in a dizzying display—now of saint, now of sinner—of his best material. His next line, referring to the now complete Tale, and his subsequent remarks, specifically mentioning his fellow pilgrims, emphasize the context we naturally associate with his sinful image. But the words themselves form a logical conclusion to one of his sermons, like the one we just heard him direct to an imaginary church congregation:

> But, sires, o word forgat I in my tale:
> I have relikes and pardoun in my male,
> As faire as any man in Engelond,

Whiche were me yeven by the popes hond.
If any of yow wole, of devocion,
Offren and han myn absolucion,
Com forth anon, and kneleth heere adoun,
And mekely receyveth my pardoun;
Or elles taketh pardoun as ye wende,
Al newe and fressh at every miles ende,
So that ye offren, alwey newe and newe,
Nobles or pens, whiche that be goode and trewe. (VI.919–30)

With amazing virtuosity the Pardoner has fused the two contexts in which he has been alternately performing. By dissolving the distinction between them, he attempts to join his two antithetical realities in a single time scheme that brings pulpit to roadside, pilgrim to parish. Like a performer taking a curtain call—one who played a witch in *Macbeth,* say—who enters in her own person to make an audience wonder who she was in the play, and then slowly assumes the deformities of the crone she impersonated, to the thunderous appreciation of the audience, the Pardoner takes his curtain call by merging the two roles he has been playing. In addition, he furnishes his audience with an opportunity to reward him for his magnificent performance. The money for which he literally asks probably symbolizes a kind of applause for the Pardoner, less important in itself than in what it signifies about his success in manipulating his audience.

Abnormally hungry for that applause, the Pardoner risks debasing his art by demanding its value of the one pilgrim who may be least sensitive to *ars gratia artis:*

I rede that oure Hoost heere shal bigynne,
For he is moost envoluped in synne.
Com forth, sire Hoost, and offre first anon,
And thou shalt kisse the relikes everychon,
Ye, for a grote! Unbokele anon thy purs. (VI.941–45)

However playfully we might want to take these words, the Host understands them as an obscene challenge demanding a response in kind. He does not shrink from responding. With unrivaled finality he lets the Pardoner know what he thinks of his version of piety by claiming it will invite Christ's curse (VI.946), and he passes rude judgment on his sensuality by implying his testicles are no more than relics, or vestiges of manhood (VI.951–55). Disparaging him in the only two areas in which he professed competence, the Host thus reduces the Pardoner to inept silence. Suddenly deprived of an act, he has no lines to speak.

The Pardoner's artistry might have earned genuine applause had he lived only in a world of art, or not in the fourteenth century. Like his creator, who commands a variety of contradictory styles—Knight's and Miller's, Wife's and Parson's—the Pardoner is entitled to an audience's praise. But by the end of his performance, when he looks for symbolic praise in the purchase of his wares, we realize the enormous difference between relics and souvenirs. As no mere manipulation of style can turn a pillow case into the Virgin's veil, so no manipulation of roles can relieve an immortal soul of its eternal obligations. The physical condition from which we assume he has suffered, however psychologically debilitating and however undeserved, can never justify the Pardoner's blasphemy. His efforts to gain approval as a surrogate for his physiological essence have turned his own moral responsibility into the material of art. In the process of doing so he has sacrificed his moral essence. All that remains is the pathetic shell of a creature with absolutely no interior.

The Host's condemnation, though considerably weakened by its angry tone, may strike us as a fitting judgment for the Pardoner, restoring moral orderliness to the pilgrimage. But this view fails to recognize the limitations implicit in the Host's role as spokesman for society's dominant opinions. The Pardoner was attempting to capitulate with his deprived physical condition and in that sense, unlike the old man of his Tale, to rise above it. In the face of so daring and vain an attempt, the Host lacks the imagination to encompass the Pardoner's aesthetic vision. Though the Pardoner's tempting of fate may risk eternity, the Host's condemnation reveals a failure of imagination by insisting a work of art follow his rules.

While the Pardoner's preoccupation with death in his Tale convinces us that even in his own mind his attempt to replace morality with art has not succeeded, this later failure to make art prevail in the eyes of the world is equally painful because it brings with it the rude and final condemnation of society. The Pardoner has wasted enormous talents on a brilliant gambit against an adversary whose limited imagination cannot recognize the game. As the Knight restores order and the pilgrimage resumes its progress, the Pardoner rides to Canterbury a figure of utter tragedy—tormented by the self-destructiveness of his game, humiliated by his opponent's unwillingness to play, and painfully aware that, as a being totally lacking in essence, he is not playing a game at all. He has just lost a misguided fight for life.

14

Fragment VII

The Craft of Letters

If modern criticism of Chaucer, especially of his *Book of the Duchess* and Fragments III, IV, and V of the *Canterbury Tales,* began with George Lyman Kittredge (1915); and *Troilus and Criseyde* criticism began with Kittredge (1915) and C. S. Lewis (1936); and Chaucerian textual studies with Manly and Rickert (1940); modern criticism of Fragment VII began with Alan Gaylord (1967). His seminal *PMLA* article takes brave exception to Robinson's belief that the fragment has no "principle of arrangement save that of contrast or variety" (1957, p. 11) and even disagrees with Larry Benson's more recent, softer phrasing that the fragment lacks "any very clear unifying theme" (1987, p. 910). With convincing argument Gaylord declares that beneath the storytelling gamesmanship, the inadvertent character revelation, and the sheer delight provided by the variety of literary entertainment, there lies a serious attempt to identify the craft of literature as a sustained subject of discussion.

Though initially slow to gain critical acceptance, Gaylord's general claim has by now been vigorously pursued. Trouble is, apart from recognizing that Chaucer represents his literary perceptions through antitheses, particularly as demonstrated by the Pilgrim Chaucer's opposing tales *Thopas* and *Melibee,* no two critics agree on what these literary perceptions might be. In addition, the direction taken by many of these critics, including Gaylord, privileges the *craft of the critic*—the purposes, effects, genres, poetic roles, and actual achievement which the poet's creation testifies to—over the *craft of the poet*—that is, over "the very struggle to get the tale told properly and with understanding and appreciation" (1967, p. 226). At the beginning of his essay Gaylord seems to have in mind the poet as a wright, struggling with his craft, laboring to make his lines just, his finials suitable, yet also to construct an edifice with strength of thought. As the essay develops, however, the poet-craftsman's perspective on the *making* of poetry recedes in favor of the scholar-critic's practice of *judging* poetry. The *sentence* and *solaas* of Gaylord's analysis turns out to be the ubiquitous "teach" and "delight" of every *ars poetica* from antiquity to the present: the purposes for which one writes, not the principles that govern its execution. This is not to suggest that an author's purposes have no influence on the way he shapes his work. But they belong more to what might be called preliminary considerations, when he is deciding to commit himself to the task before him, and less to the actual making of the poem.[1]

At the outset of this discussion of Fragment VII let me acknowledge that I agree with those who claim that the two tales told by Chaucer the Pilgrim hold the key to understanding both the organization and the meaning of this section of tales. They provide the key, however, as a *reductio* does, by driving its point to caricature, where so much is exaggerated that the point made of the normal world may be missed among so much else that is distended. The ring structure of the fragment may illustrate the point. Most literary ring structures are like a flattened mountain viewed from above where the summit, now at the center of concentric rings, represents the epitome, the apex, the highest ideal that the outer rings had once served to uphold. Fragment VII is such a design, provided we understand the great difference between theory and practice. The scaling of the mountain (that is, progress to the center of the rings) brings us to a higher understanding of the ingredients of literary art by grotesquely separating those ingredients from each other and producing, as a result, a nadir of the art itself, what Emerson Brown, Jr., calls tales "of low intrinsic quality" (1990, p. 51). As the least skillful tales in the fragment, *Thopas* and *Melibee* dramatize well a central point about literature's need to balance its ingredients in a coherent whole. Of course, this central point is overwhelmed by an even more obvious rule, "Poets shouldn't write bad poetry." At the opposite extreme, that is, at the outer ring of the fragment's design, the *Shipman's Tale* and the *Nun's Priest's Tale* present an opposite paradox. They are literarily the most accomplished tales in the fragment (discounting, of course, the Canterbury context, which turns a sow's ear called *Thopas* into a silk purse of Chaucerian satire and irony), although as instruction manuals on the nature of literary art, they are probably the least accessible. For these reasons I propose to discuss at some length one of the tales on the middle ring, where the modest craftsmanship and achievement are obvious enough not to be missed, yet neither so grotesque as to be a caricature nor so fine as to be concealed. Both the *Prioress's Tale* and the *Monk's Tale* err by placing too much emphasis on form, the Prioress herself appropriating what she believes is the truest form of piety while missing its essence, the Monk flogging to death what he takes to be the form of tragedy while overlooking entirely the essence of good literature.

Is there another reason for my turning first to the medial ring? Yes, of course. As an eager guide, bursting to describe some new locale, chooses a particular beauty that contains some mark of the whole, I shall discuss in detail the more interesting of the two tales on the medial ring, the *Prioress's Tale*, where the dichotomized ingredients of literature are more easily grasped than in the tales of the Narrator.

THE PRIORESS AND HER TALE

The Prioress and her Tale have the best of two worlds: their immense appeal invites scrutiny, yet leaves few openings. Small wonder commentary on the woman herself makes chiefly negative observations. Her femininity is not really worldly, we hear; but then her vocation may not be genuine. Though "nat undergrowe," she is not really a peasant; but then, she is not particularly gentle, save to dogs and mice. Her Tale inspires a similar response. It does not much alter its source. Nor is it especially anti-Semitic. But neither is it a typical devotional tale. And so on and on. We find it easier to say what the Prioress and her Tale are not, than what they are. Take the most celebrated single comment on Madam Eglentine, the brilliant remark by Lowes discussing the famous *Amor vincit omnia*: "Which of the two loves does 'amor' mean to the Prioress? I do not know, but I think she thought she meant love celestial" (1919, p. 66). Without our knowing it, Lowes—or perhaps the Prioress—suspends us between heaven and earth. Despite the attraction she holds for us, which must not be underestimated, we know we shall not find her in a sphere close to the ninth; despite her limitations, we know she is not one of Chaucer's great sinners. We are tempted to surrender, with Lowes, to the impossibility of ever knowing who or what the Prioress is.

On the other hand, several of the preceding chapters may help our understanding, for in creating the Prioress Chaucer follows the same pattern of oppositions he uses elsewhere. Especially for the characters of the Knight, the Wife of Bath, and the Pardoner is the pattern most useful. That the Prioress's brief, "perfect" performance traces a pattern already laid down has escaped critical notice because Madame Eglentine is very different from these other pilgrims. Though quite as complex as the Wife and the Pardoner, and perhaps a good deal more complex than the Knight, her motives are entirely different from theirs, while her self-awareness may be lower. Not that she is ignorant of her rhetorical power, for no one has a more artfully controlled style than she, but she is surely unaware that the viscerally/spiritually divided woman of her literal language countervenes the image of hushed, elegant piety she thinks she is presenting.[2] Nevertheless, the only structural difference between her performance, taken as a whole, and the patterns we have already observed is in her manner of self-projection. Whereas Chaucer has the Knight, the Wife, and the Pardoner cast their ambivalent selves into two different figures in their tales, who then attempt with varying success to reconcile their differences, he has the Prioress project both halves of her divided self into a single figure, the young clergeon, who then endures a series of events that permit her symbolically to harmonize the unreconciled impulses that govern her own life. We might summarize briefly the broad outlines of this strategy.

As a classic case of ambivalence, the Prioress presents two images to the world, one a nun who would be as perfect, and as perfectly pious, as is humanly possible for a woman of her capacity, the other a highly self-conscious woman who reduces her male companions to superlatives, as Donaldson wittily puts it (1975, p. 884). Nothing wrong so far; it is nowhere written that on taking the veil a nun must cease to be a woman. A problem does arise, however, when we try to imagine each of these impulses brought to a logical conclusion: on the one hand a virginal saint, on the other a conjugally mature woman and mother. For to judge from her hour on stage, she lacks the means to encompass either of these forms, grasping neither the intellectual basis of her vocation and its inevitable sacrifices nor the impossibility of fulfilling her womanly inclinations within the calling of a nun. Thus, unable to achieve her dual goal in reality, she attempts it symbolically on the road to Canterbury. From her Prologue it appears that she yearns to retrace the Incarnation, to rarefy her flesh out of existence, in order to become the pure spirit to which she aspires; and from her Tale that she seeks complete visceral indulgence through surrogate martyrdom. Her strategy—whether she is aware of it or not—metaphorically enacts the same method Christ chose to accomplish the Incarnation, Crucifixion, and Resurrection. That is, metaphors of fleshly consummation continually intrude into her speech, coordinated in such a way as to enable her to achieve symbolically in her performance both the feminine and spiritual ambitions she cannot achieve in life. As with the Wife of Bath and the Pardoner before her, however, the Prioress's performance reveals more than she knows. Despite exuding the style of a chatelaine, perhaps cultivated in all innocence, she compromises her gentility in the violence of her tale. And though everything about her gives the appearance of piety, that dimension too is seriously qualified by the unthinking devotion her tale endorses.[3] By projecting herself into a seven-year-old clergeon, having the boy murdered, and then "fecche[d]" (VII.667) to heaven, the Prioress achieves through her surrogate a three-part goal. She frees herself from intellectual responsibility for her life, attains full consummation of her flesh, and returns to God with her virginal beauty intact. The following discussion attempts to demonstrate the individual points of this summary and to suggest that, finally, the Prioress's quest remains unfulfilled.

Until recently the Prioress used to divide her critics into the opposing camps that Alan Gaylord calls "soft" and "hard" judges of both her and her Tale (1962, p. 614). For some, the mild satire of her portrait discloses another Holy Innocent whose Tale expresses a pious impulse equally naïve. For others, her Tale is vicious, her "tendre herte" a mere surface wound.[4] That the evidence supporting one position contradicts the other suggests that neither can be a final judgment. If, however, we take them as intermediate steps in a critical approach, they share much in common. The sympathetic reader does not deny the disturbing ferocity of the Tale, but claims simply that the Prioress does not recognize its horror.[5] The harsh reader emphasizes the horror and concludes that a woman in the Prioress's position ought to know how unchristian it really is. Both views, therefore, invite us to examine the Prioress's ability to understand her life and its context. The same conclusion emerges when we consider her much discussed courtliness. No one doubts the presence of this dimension, but everyone wonders to what extent she understands the implications of her courtly conduct.

We also wonder whether she understands her Tale. Although the young clergeon martyred for his faith has long been thought an extension of the Prioress, we cannot be certain the Prioress shares that understanding. Even the widely accepted suggestion that she intends to honor the Virgin's power of intercession seems less certain when we compare the Tale with its analogues. Elsewhere the young clergeon springs back to life at the end of the story, whereas in the *Prioress's Tale* the removal of a grain ends both his life and his song.[6] If the Prioress intends to recreate one of the Virgin's great miracles, why does she diminish that miracle? Similarly, we might wonder if she is aware of the many parallels between her words and the liturgy.[7] If we are trying to bring together the two opposed views that critics have of the Prioress, the crucial questions would seem to be these: To what extent does the Prioress understand herself? And does her Tale symbolically explain her to us, if not to herself?

A Dual Nature

Though Chaucer delicately shapes a full portrait of the Prioress, we more often admire the woman inside the nun than the nun inside the woman. If we delight in her refined manners, her perfect cleanliness, her ability to melt males medieval and modern, critics often see that delight in the woman as reason to censure the nun. The details the Narrator so much admires furrow our brows. While he finds pleasure in the innocence of her mild oath "by Seinte Loy" (I.120), in her effort "to countrefete cheere / Of court" (I.139–40), to speak French diligently, and entune the divine service meticulously, we feel that because these details fail to meet *our* expectations for a nun, she must be wanting in piety. We wonder, does she pray to this saint, as other girls did, because he was thought to send visions of future husbands?[8] Is she not lost in a sea of royal gestures and nasal sounds, mistaking as life's essence the style that surrounds it? And the more closely we study the portrait, the more perplexing its details become.

Look, for example, at the famous description of the Prioress's table manners:

> At mete wel ytaught was she with alle;
> She leet no morsel from hir lippes falle,
> Ne wette hir fyngres in hir sauce depe;
> Wel koude she carie a morsel and wel kepe
> That no drope ne fille upon hire brest.
> In curteisie was set ful muchel hir lest.
> Hir over-lippe wyped she so clene
> That in hir coppe ther was no ferthyng sene
> Of grece, whan she dronken hadde hir draughte.
> Ful semely after hir mete she raughte. (I.127–36)

We are not surprised that so delicate a dinner companion "Ne wette hir fyngres in hir sauce depe." But we wonder if *depe* might not be an adverb, giving the quite different meaning that she did not wet her fingers deeply in the sauce—perhaps she stopped short of her rings. Even more curious, the last line (I.136), apparently claiming that the Prioress did not have an indelicate reach, may have another equally plausible meaning to provide the subtle undercut on which her portrait so relies for its success. *After* may have temporal as well as spatial force, and *mete* can mean either foodstuff or the span of a meal, as in line I.127. Hence the phrase *after hir mete* means either "for her food" or "after her meal." The crucial verb *raughte,* instead of resolving the dilemma, deepens it by signifying either the past tense of *rechen* (to reach for) or, more likely in view of its appearance at the end of the meal, a derivative of OE *hrǽctan* (to belch).[9] In the former, table manners seem too important; in the latter, they die on a terminal burp.

Similarly the Prioress's tender care for her hounds (I.146–49) argues the gentleness of her nature, but raises questions about her perspective. We overlook her indulgence in pets and baubles—after all, it is another of those "peccadillos which have a certain charm," as Howard says (1976, p. 98).[10] But we are startled at the kind of food she feeds her animals. Since Avicenna's *Treatise on the Canon of Medicine* recommends soft meats and bread softened with milk as ideal foods for weaning infants (Gruner 1970, pp. 370–71), we wonder if maternal longing has not perhaps prompted the Prioress's affection for her pets.

Finally, we may look at the most famous ambiguity in the entire portrait, a brooch in the Prioress's possession displaying "a crowned A, / And after *Amor vincit omnia*" (I.161–62). Most of the discussion of this motto centers on the double meaning of *Amor,* divinely inspired love or sensual love, and on the latter's ironic association with a rosary.[11] With equally appropriate ambiguity, however, the motto's implicit meaning contradicts its explicit metaphor *vincit* (conquers). A sublime spiritual condition rests disturbingly in a violent physical act, evoking a sense of the Prioress's character as clearly as anything else in her portrait, and foreshadowing the ambivalence of much to come. It is useful to keep in mind an additional irony, that the words come from a monologue about frenzied love, Virgil's *Tenth Eclogue: "omnia vincit Amor: et nos cedamus Amori"* (line 69).

It is these subtle—but unmistakable—ambiguities that have divided our responses to the Prioress into "soft" and "hard." We look at the word *vincit,* uncertain whether we should take it as the relatively neutral "overcomes" or with the full force of "conquers," and wonder whether these incompatible meanings reflect the two irreconcilable halves of the Prioress's divided self. Surely this is wrong. For the ambiguity resides not in the Prioress, nor in the language used of and by her, but in the combination of the two.[12] Chaucerians usually consider language—whether Chaucer's, the Narrator's, or the Prioress's—as something distinct from Madam Eglentine, or at best as a kind of instrument continually pointing to what she *is*. The argument advanced here departs from that practice by suggesting that language nourishes her performance, that through its power she attempts to *become* by the end of her tale something she was not at its beginning.

Madam Eglentine's performance has two dimensions, one a prayer and story expressing conventional piety, the other a complex network of figurative language that often seems at variance with piety. Though her metaphors and allusions show a strong fleshly bias and often explicit carnality, especially by being so arranged as to consume the very dimension in which they exist, this second dimension expresses piety as intensely in its allusive way as the account of a martyred clergeon does in a literal way. As this literal story progresses according to conventional chronology, the figurative language shaping that story reverses time and growth, beginning with imaginative notations of mature men and regressing to the moment when flesh comes into being. Since time is reversed, that moment reverses, turning flesh into spirit at precisely the instant when the literal story martyrs a young clergeon. Both dimensions progress toward a spiritual destiny, though in entirely different ways. By examining closely the tension between, and eventual fusion of the literal story the Prioress tells and the figurative language in which it exists, we realize that she becomes in her Prologue and Tale what she could never be in life.

A Metaphysical Prologue

In due time Madam Eglentine's private thoughts reach public expression, and the piety we doubted takes as striking a form as her wimpled face. We do not "see" this piety until her Prologue, where she conveys her meaning in two simultaneous, yet wholly different ways—one through literal expression, the other through what I call the metaconscious.[13] Her intentional expressions of piety contain nothing unusual for a medieval nun paraphrasing that portion of the canonical hours that she sang daily (Boyd 1967, pp. 33–34, 67–68), but her metaphors arise from a different kind of awareness. In literature generally, figurative language reinforces a meaning already clear, or at least taking shape in a work's immediate text. The Wife of Bath's spurs and the Reeve's slender leg and rusty blade do not surprise us, since other evidence shows the martial character of the one and the niggardliness of the other. Wildflowers, fresh fruit, and unbroken colt accord well with the abundant freshness and spontaneity of Alisoun of Oxford. Even when used ironically, figurative language bears a close, though inverse, relation to an immediate text. We see the forceful Harry Bailly, explicitly in control of his life, implicitly controlled by his wife. The Pardoner boasts of wantonness and promiscuity, while figurative language points to the opposite. By contrast, Madam Eglentine's affecting images do not reinforce the "conscience and tendre herte" others see in her; nor do her violent images contradict them. Almost completely unrelated to literal meaning, these formulas and clichés, whether sentimental or violent, reflect her metaconscious preoccupation, not a trait of character.[14]

As early as the pious opening stanza her metaphors take on a life of their own that seems to have nothing to do with piety:

> O Lord, oure Lord, thy name how merveillous
> Is in this large world ysprad—quod she—
> For noght oonly thy laude precious
> Parfourned is by men of dignitee,
> But by the mouth of children thy bountee
> Parfourned is, for on the brest soukynge
> Somtyme shewen they thyn heriynge. (VII.453–59)

She begins with the simple paradox of the eighth psalm: lofty praise comes not only from the mighty, but from humble children too. However, the phrase "by the mouth of children" influences the thought to develop very differently. Presumably intended as a simple image of helpless innocence, in contrast with "men of dignitee," the phrase becomes more arresting when "mouth" is gratuitously put to breast. The notion of helplessness, toward which the stanza seemed to be moving, disappears behind the more complicated figure of an infant sucking, made more complex in the Prioress's image than in the psalm's simple *lactantium*. And the curious qualifier "somtyme" even suggests that praise depends on some aspect of the sucking, not on the innocence. In addition, the stanza inverts time in a fascinating way. When the Lord's praise is "Parfourned . . . by men of dignitee" in the middle of the stanza, an image of oral praise comes to mind. Thus when "the mouth of children" similarly "parfourned" the Lord's bounty in the next two lines, an oral prayer comes to mind here too, implying children old enough to learn and recite such a prayer. The stanza's conclusion surprises us by reducing those imagined children to suckling infants. In effect, the stanza reverses the process of natural growth, beginning with mature men, pausing at a suggested image of praying children, and concluding with suckling infants.

Both of these motifs—maternal intimacy and inverted time—reach greater force in the second stanza, where literal meaning again yields to metaphor

> Wherfore in laude, as I best kan or may,
> Of thee and of the white lylye flour
> Which that the bar, and is a mayde alway,
> To telle a storie I wol do my labour. (VII.460–63)

While stating a simple, explicit intention to praise God and his Blessed Mother, the Prioress chooses figurative qualifiers that implicitly compare herself to the Virgin. As the white lily flower bore Christ, so the Prioress "wol do [her] labour" to tell a story.[15] Childbirth equals literary creation; infant equals story. Here again, Mary's glory in bearing the Son of God is syntactically followed, and hence eclipsed, by her remaining a maiden. Her achievement seems to come, not from the divinity of her Son, but from avoiding the fleshly defilement normally associated with conception.[16] Time retreats even farther in this second stanza, as its central images, bearing and laboring, take us back to gestation. Indeed, since the phrase *to bear a child* means primarily "to give birth,"[17] these two references themselves reverse normal sequence. Labor precedes birth in nature; here the Prioress's metaphors allude to birth before alluding to labor.

The Prologue now reaches its most forceful and complex stanza, where the combined motifs of intimate fleshly activity and regressing time arrive at a still earlier stage, the central paradox of Christianity, the metaphysical conception through which the Spirit became flesh:

> O mooder Mayde, O mayde Mooder free!
> O bussh unbrent, brennynge in Moyses sighte,
> That ravyshedest doun fro the Deitee,
> Thurgh thyn humblesse, the Goost that in th'alighte,
> Of whos vertu, whan he thyn herte lighte,
> Conceyved was the Fadres sapience,
> Help me to telle it in thy reverence! (VII.467–73)

The reminder of divine presence in physical form, symbolized by the burning but unconsumed bushes in Exodus 3:2 and Acts 7:30, would incline a fourteenth-century audience to see in the burning bush of the present context an image of the unborn Christ child in the womb of the Virgin. But the syntactic parallel between "mooder Mayde" and "bussh unbrent, brennynge in Moyses sighte" creates a different emphasis. In the first line a woman is both a mother and a maiden; in the second a bush is both burning and unconsumed. Since both ideas are paradoxes *in nature,* the two lines seem related to each other semantically as well as syntactically. The bush clearly symbolizes Christ's mother Mary, its flame refers to her motherhood, and the still intact state of the bush to her maidenhood. The Prioress calls attention, then, not merely to the physical presence of God in a mortal woman, but more particularly to the paradox of virgin birth.[18] Thus, the language of this third stanza has a more profound effect than simply an influence on style, as it has in the first two stanzas. Here fleshly metaphors not only enrich meaning, they take it over. A simple, pious request occupies the main syntax: "O mooder Mayde . . . help me to telle it [that is, the "storie" of line 463] in thy reverence." Nevertheless, this straightforward meaning has been driven to the outer margins of the stanza by the tortured syntax of the intervening relative clause, which literally has Mary ravishing the Holy Spirit, while the action itself works the other way. Despite Mary's active verb "ravyshedest," the masculine principle of the Holy Spirit (*vertu* <L.*virtus*, cognate with L.*vir*, man) becomes the actual instrument of conception: "Of whos vertu . . . Conceyved was the Fadres sapience." The physical dimension of the act ("the Goost that in th'alighte") as well as the metaphysical ("whan he thyn herte lighte") have the Holy Spirit as agent and Mary the object acted upon.[19] The entire stanza gives a mutual active/passive role to both Mary and the Holy Spirit, while it also converts flame into light. Literal language re-creates the most significant feature of the Incarnation, a spiritual union so intense it springs to life in the flesh of Christ, while metaphoric language works the other way, continuing to reverse time, from the physical act of alighting in the Virgin, which represents her fleshly reality, to the light that symbolizes the Holy Ghost's spiritual power.

This inverse parallel of literal and metaphoric expression harmonizes in a stunning way the two discordant sounds of the Prioress's dual nature. One praises God and his Blessed Mother, the other resounds with the visceral strains of human nature, especially its femininity. Innocent impulses by themselves, they will ultimately clash. Religious life culminates in formal orders and a virginal apotheosis; femininity leads to physical consummation and motherhood. Although Mary achieved both states, Madam Eglentine cannot. Chaucer shows both impulses strongly occupying the Prioress's mind, though in different ways. Her literal language reveals her conscious thoughts of piety, while her fleshly metaphors suggest her metaconscious preoccupation with her physical nature. By having the Prioress indulge these intrusions, yet confine them to metaphor, Chaucer permits her both to luxuriate in the subject and sublimate it at the same time. The technique reaches its richest development when Chaucer resolves the incompatibility within its own terms, by using the very material of fleshly consummation to deny flesh's existence. To do this he combines the motif of the Incarnation that has increasingly taken form in the Prioress's metaphors, and the motif of regressing time as these metaphors are presented in reverse sequence. The Incarnation, we recall, initiates the central religious paradigm, not only for the fourteenth century, but for all Christianity. By reversing time, Chaucer enables the Prioress to reverse the steps of the Incarnation in her own Prologue. Whereas God originated the process from His eternal state in spirit to become flesh in Christ, the Prioress begins in the flesh. She must diminish, deny, rarify out of existence, the flesh in which she originated to become the pure spirit to which she aspires.

This sequence of images that reverses normal time was foreshadowed in the *General Prologue*, when we saw how fastidiously the Prioress eats her meals, as if delicate table manners might somehow minimize her corporeal presence. We noticed, too, her fondness for little creatures—the smaller the better—admirable to her because growth has not lessened their worth. Here, in the Prologue to her Tale, the motif recurs in the sequence of images that reverse the normal process of growth, enabling the Prioress to create a path from flesh back to spirit. As she literally petitions the Lord and His mother Mary, the metaphors of her first three stanzas take us from adulthood to youth, to infancy, to childbirth, to labor, and to conception. By the end of her third stanza the Prioress's imagery has brought us to the very threshold of the spiritual world. Accordingly her next stanza lists abstractions—the Virgin's "bountee . . . magnificence . . . vertu . . . humylitee"—qualities remote from the world of men where no tongue can describe them (VII.474–75). The word "vertu" by itself captures this movement in tableau. Having conveyed only the physical half of its wide range of meanings in the previous stanza, here "vertu" (VII.475) has no connection with the physical world. Within four lines the word has expanded metaphysically from flesh to spirit, as a few lines earlier the syllable "light" expanded from a gentle physical verb to a profound miracle of theology.

When contact with the tangible world has been metaphorically broken, the Prioress can at last insinuate herself, in the final stanza of her Prologue, into the very process we have been describing. The weak power of intellection she professes to have (VII.481), and the infant simile she chooses for herself (VII.484), move her backward in time, away from man's imperfect world of futile adult knowledge, toward Mary's virtuous world of childlike spiritual perfection. Innocence frees her from the dead "weighte" (VII.483) of knowing, declaring, and expressing, making her as apt for the light of Mary's guidance as humility made Mary apt for the Holy Spirit's enlightenment.

By the end of the Prologue three strains have emerged. First, the Prioress asserts that the spiritual energy of God and the Virgin can be transmitted as the ability to tell a tale in their honor. Second, she petitions for that spiritual energy. Finally, through metaphor she expresses the fervent belief that salvation is the reward for intensely passionate faith, rather than for an intellectual understanding of theology.

THE TALE

Like its Prologue, the Prioress's disarmingly simple story of a young boy murdered for his faith conveys more meaning in its figurative language than in its plot. Indeed, as a development of the Prologue, the Tale bears a close relation to the five stanzas that precede it. By honoring the Virgin, the Tale confirms the Prologue's claim that spiritual power resides in the Virgin, and demonstrates that the help sought there was actually granted. In other words, the Tale makes concrete what the Prologue stated abstractly. The same relationship also appears in more specific details. Where the Prologue's first stanza includes general metaphors, like "men of dignitee" and "children . . . on the brest soukynge," the opening stanzas of the Tale make those metaphors specific, converting "men of dignitee" into a "lord" of a particular country in Asia, and suckling infants into St. Nicholas who, according to legend, caught the religious spirit so young that he fasted at the breast.[20] The two parts of the Prioress's performance are related, then, not merely as general is related to specific, or abstract to concrete, but more significantly as metaphor to reality. The Prologue had used figurative language to clarify a metaphysical truth; the Tale uses literal language in a concrete story to achieve the same metaphysical truth.

Many of these thematic parallels occur at corresponding places in the two halves of the Prioress's performance. As the parallel columns below indicate, the little clergeon's effort to learn the *Alma redemptoris mater* and sing it in praise of the Virgin, while corresponding thematically to the Prioress's effort to tell a tale for the same reason, corresponds structurally as well. The widow's inability to locate her son parallels, both thematically and structurally, the Prologue's claim that no tongue can express Mary's attributes. Each of these is immediately followed by a statement about guidance: the Prologue claims that the Virgin often guides us to her son; the Tale concretely shows us the widow being guided to *her* son. And so on.

PROLOGUE	TALE
An assertion of God's and the Virgin's power; a petition for the ability to tell a tale in their honor.	The assertion demonstrated, the petition granted.
Stanza 1 (453–459)	Stanzas 1–4 (488–515)
The Lord is praised not just great men,	In a Christian city in Asia a Jewry is sustained by the leader of that city;

PROLOGUE	TALE
but by babes sucking at the breast.	but the Virgin is praised by a little clergeon, reminiscent of St. Nicholas who fasted at the breast.
Stanza 2 (460–466)	**Stanzas 5–10 (516–557)**
In praise of God and his Blessed Mother, the Prioress will labor to tell a story.	In praise of the Blessed Mother the clergeon struggles to learn, and finally sing the *Alma redemptoris mater.*
Stanza 3 (467–473)	**Stanzas 11–14 (558–585)**
In contradiction of the laws of nature (like fire that does not consume),	Hated by forces contradictory to God (i.e., Satan and the Jews),
Mary ravishes the Holy Spirit, who metaphysically embraces her,	the clergeon's throat is cut and he is then cast in a privy place,
but preserves her virginity.	but he will join the virgins of the Apocalypse.
Stanza 4 (474–480)	**Stanzas 15–20 (586–627)**
No tongue may express in any branch of learning the bounty and magnificenc of Mary.	Through normal reason and inquiry, the clergeon's widowed mother cannot learn the location of her martyred son.
Often the Virgin grants us the light to find her son.	Jesus places an idea in the mother's thought, directing her to her son, whose continued singing testifies to God's miraculous power through the intercession of his mother Mary.

PROLOGUE	TALE
Stanza 5 (481–487)	Stanzas 21–28 (628–683)
	The murderers are punished.
	The abbot cannot understand how the boy miraculously sings despite his cut throat.
The Prioress's "konnyng" is too weak to declare Mary's great worth.	The clergeon's "konnyng" and power are not his own,
Therefore, she begs Mary to guide her song so that her childlike expressions will be correct.	but have come from his simple love of Mary.
	The abbot removes from the boy's tongue a grain placed there earlier by the Virgin; the boy dies (his soul ascends), and the abbot and convent fall back in awe.
	Stanza 29 (684–690)
	Envoi to Hugh of Lincoln, Martyr.

An important inference may be drawn from this relationship. While the oft-heard claim is true that the Prioress projects herself into her Tale, the process also works the other way around. The entire Tale, like a gloss to clarify a text, partly creates her (Leicester 1980, pp. 217–18). There is, however, a difference. Whereas her self-projection into her Tale takes form in obvious ways, the reverse process, in which her language defines herself, occurs only in the subtler details of texture and metaphor. The complicated relationship between the Prioress and the clergeon provides an example. The young boy's dedication to Mary, his habit of singing a song in her honor, and his innocence, are all obvious details of plot that coincide with features of the Prioress. She too displays a deep dedication to Mary, calls her Marian Tale a "song" (VII.487), and remains celibate. She even gives the clergeon the very colors of her green and coral beads (I.158–59), symbolizing his chastity and martyrdom:

This gemme of chastite, this emeraude,
And eek of martirdom the ruby bright. (VII.609–10)

Where the Tale turns back to define the Prioress, however, is in its subtle elaboration of the boy's innocence, particularized here as his virginity. Notice that the Prologue's reference to Mary's virginity (VII.467) corresponds structurally to the Tale's statement that the clergeon will join the virgins in heaven (VII.579ff.). Now this is a most unusual detail, especially since the boy's virginity receives its highest praise immediately after his martyrdom, as if the faith that cost him his life were a lesser achievement than the virginity that survived his ordeal. We may doubt that the seven-year-old clergeon's struggle to preserve his virginity was especially difficult, but the excessive attention the Prioress gives it makes us see *her* instead of him, and turns the green of her beads into a badge of chastity.

Allusions to the clergeon's intellectual innocence have a similar effect. In the Prologue a moving image of an infant conveyed the Prioress's humility topos, a professed inability to sing the Virgin's praise, "But as a child of twelf month oold, or lesse" (VII.484). As this simile lowers the Prioress's own age, so in her Tale she lowers the age of the clergeon in her sources from ten years to seven, the threshold of the age of reason,[21] producing in the boy an innocence parallel to her own. But at the same time another cluster of details excuses the clergeon for failing to understand his devotional song and even seems to link his virtue with his freedom from book-learning. Unfamiliar with Latin, he must learn the song from an older boy who knows only that it "Was maked of our blisful Lady free" (VII.532).[22] To do so he ignores his assigned lessons in the Primer:

"Though that I for my prymer shal be shent
And shal be beten thries in an houre,
I wol it konne Oure Lady for to honoure!" (VII.541–43)

These man-made obstacles would test the clergeon's will to praise the Virgin. The beatings, if they materialized, would measure that devotion—the more painful the one, the more perfect the other—while those who would give them, not unlike a grammarian drilling Latin forms, would stand in opposition to his perfect act of praise. The Prioress's view of herself certainly determines the boy's role as the Virgin's innocent devotee. But her description of his threatened life, and her implied approval of his shirking his lessons, ultimately reflect back on her. We wonder about her own ability to understand herself and her vocation, and if she does not perhaps perceive impious forces whose torments test her own devotion and give meaning to the red in her coral beads.[23]

A similar complexity surrounds the Prioress's relationship to the clergeon's mother. The maternal instinct—already insinuated in the Prioress's treatment of her dogs, in her references to children at the breast, and to an infant who can scarcely speak—intensifies in "This newe Rachel" (VII.627), isolated and heightened by widowhood. Like the Prioress, the widow relies "evere on Cristes mooder meeke and kynde" (VII.597), and raises her son accordingly:

> Thus hath this wydwe hir litel sone ytaught
> Oure blisful Lady, Cristes mooder deere,
> To worshipe ay, and he forgat it naught. (VII.509–11)

The juxtaposition of the widow and her son with "Cristes mooder" reinforces the suggested parallels between Christ and the son, Mary and the widow. Yet maternal instincts never rise to maternal feelings, as the Prioress fails to comprehend either the horror or the meaning of her own story. Rich in sentiment, her vocabulary remains sentimental, less suited to understanding than to sententiousness. Whatever "moodres pitee" (VII.593) the Prioress instinctively possesses rests in the pathetic figure of the widow, while genuine feeling is suppressed beneath a heavily formulaic exaltation of the Virgin. Even when the widow finally does locate her son, the Prioress passes over the emotional scene we might easily imagine, for the metaphors of religion:

> O grete God, that parfournest thy laude
> By mouth of innocentz, lo, heere thy myght!
> This gemme of chastite, this emeraude,
> And eek of martirdom the ruby bright,
> Ther he with throte ykorven lay upright,
> He *Alma redemptoris* gan to synge. (VII.607–12)

As we can see, the widowed mother becomes a complex symbol of the Prioress. In her relation to her clergeon son she represents the Prioress's maternal impulse; by herself she conveys the Prioress's religious impulse.

Criticism often sees these apparent inconsistencies as evidence of a fleshly nature ill at ease in a religious vocation. They may be nothing of the sort. As the visceral metaphors of the Prologue only seemed to undercut the Prioress's devotional sentiment, but were in fact images of meta-physical union, so too her Tale makes a sustained effort to integrate the spiritual and the earthly. We have already noticed some of the images in which the physical and the spiritual worlds merge in the Prioress's imagi-nation, for example the piety of the young clergeon, which makes

> Seint Nicholas stant evere in my presence,
> For he so yong to Crist dide reverence. (VII.514–15)

The image of St. Nicholas fasting at the breast, noted above, yokes together the physical impulse and the spiritual. Helplessness makes the future saint depend on his mother for physical sustenance, while his simultaneous per-ception of the spiritual order enables him partly to reject fleshly comfort. When the clergeon risks a beating to learn his pious song, that beating signifies the depth of his devotion, and is thus more eagerly sought than schoolwork. Essential to the Prioress's method is the suffering that the spiri-tual nature enables the physical to sublimate. The spirit and the flesh con-verge, devotion and physical suffering become interchangeable, making a schoolboy more moving in the throes of discipline, as in the Prologue dogs were more loveable when abused, a mouse more affecting when caught. We shall see that a pious young boy, too, becomes more beautifully triumphant when martyred for his faith.

No motif in the Prioress's performance captures the relationship of flesh and spirit quite as appropriately as song, for it belongs to both. Though physical in origin and perceived by the senses, song has no sub-stance and is aesthetic in form. Moreover, song is everywhere. The Prior-ess paraphrases a song for her Prologue, uses the word "song" to describe her Tale, and begins that story with specific references to oral praise. Song motivates her main character, antagonizes his murderers, and provides the chief evidence of Mary's miraculous power.

If the very nature of song suits the Tale's central conflation of flesh and spirit, Chaucer's specific handling makes it even more so, as the linguistic pattern of the following lines demonstrates:

> This litel child, as he cam to and fro,
> Ful murily than wolde he synge and crie
> O *Alma redemptoris* everemo.
> The swetnesse his herte perced so
> Of Cristes mooder that, to hire to preye,
> He kan nat stynte of syngyng by the weye. (VII.552–57)

The stanza's structure makes the clergeon seem to initiate the action, since song appears first and last. But semantically the Virgin starts the cycle.

Her sweetness pierces the boy, causing him to sing a song, which then returns to the Virgin as praise. This mutual active/passive relationship between the clergeon and Christ's mother parallels the relationship between the Holy Spirit and the Virgin described earlier. In the Prologue the Virgin's humility ravishes the Holy Spirit into using his "vertu" to conceive the Father's wisdom. In the Tale's suggestive metaphors the boy's devotion causes the Virgin's sweetness to pierce his heart and beget his song.

The stanza achieves its metaphysical point through a calculated use of ambiguous language. We assume that "swetenesse" must describe the song, since that is the only suitable referent so far.[24] Only after a conspicuously suspended syntax do we learn that the word actually refers to "Cristes mooder." Our lingering expectation momentarily merges the anticipated referent "song" with the actual syntactic referent "Cristes mooder." Song and Virgin fleetingly become one, before the stanza unambiguously returns to the act of singing. Similarly "perced," often occurring as a metaphor connected with sound, and thus helping to advance the misleading implication that line 555 refers to song, also contributes to the Tale's most profound motif by giving to an abstract quality, Mary's sweetness, the power of a concrete act, initially as metaphor but ultimately as the energy sustaining the boy's song. Moreover, despite its association with the gentle Virgin, "perced" precisely suits the Prioress's habit of using images of fleshly restriction or suffering to turn flesh toward spirit. At length we recognize the analogy to Christ: spiritual energy pierces the boy, inspiring a fleshly act, which takes the form of song and thus returns to spirit.

However beautiful the image of a boy singing, and however devout the hymn, a song remains symbolic, whereas the "Prioress's Tale" presses relentlessly toward a real sacrifice. Before proceeding to that central event, the clergeon's martyrdom, it might be well to recall the significance of the two themes we have been discussing. First, the Prioress's network of metaphors, in both her Prologue and her Tale, concentrates on the point where the physical and spiritual worlds touch each other. But that point itself does not remain static. Rather, the temporal sequence of these metaphors, as we have already seen in the Prologue and will shortly see in the Tale, describes a movement from physical to spiritual. Second, the Prioress subtly insinuates herself as part of the subject of her performance. In her Prologue she calls obvious attention to the challenge she faces as a story teller. And in her Tale she consistently gives her material the kind of emphasis that reflects back on her. Now these features, interesting by themselves, have an extraordinary effect when they occur together. Arranged around the translation of corporeal things into spiritual, and directed back upon itself, the Prioress's performance tries to become a self-redemptive act.

Christianity has always looked upon the Redemption as an expression of divine love for humanity. With no loss of divinity, God assumed humanity as Jesus Christ, and thus inherited the frailties and limitations of a human being. The spirit became flesh. The Virgin cooperated in this miracle by being the perfect vessel through whom the event was accomplished, as the central stanza in the Prioress's Prologue reminds us (VII.467–73). The Prioress attempts the same fusion of flesh and spirit in her performance on the Canterbury pilgrimage. But since she begins with the inferior half of the metaphysical union—with mere flesh in the form of a little boy—she must reverse the process. Flesh must become spirit. If a conventional birth afforded a convenient process for the Incarnation, the Prioress must symbolically reverse birth in the stanzas describing the boy's death, in order to spiritualize the hero of her Tale. While the violent martyrdom of the clergeon, his concealment in a privy, and his later recovery, bear a close parallel to the Crucifixion, Entombment, and Resurrection of Christ, it is well to keep in mind that the Crucifixion/Resurrection is closely related to the Incarnation. As the two points at which God enters and leaves the human world, they deal with the same subject, though in reverse direction, as death reverses birth, as tomb opposes womb. The description of the clergeon's martyrdom forges an imagistic link with the central stanza of the Prologue, where the Incarnation is the literal subject.

Whenever we read the death scene in the *Prioress's Tale*, we are struck by its apparently misplaced emphases. Everything seems wrong. Though the central event would seem to be the murder, that act is rhetorically reduced to one undistinguished fact in a series of four:

> This cursed Jew hym hente, and heeld hym faste,
> And kitte his throte, and in a pit hym caste. (VII.570–71)

The mortal action receives less attention than the privy where the murderer discards the body; the privy, less than the acts that normally occur there; and those acts appear to bring greater dishonor to the Jews than the murder they commission:

> I seye that in a wardrobe they hym threwe
> Where as thise Jewes purgen hire entraille.
> O cursed folk of Herodes al newe,
> What may youre yvel entente yow availle? (VII.572–75)

We are further surprised that the Prioress says nothing of what could easily have been a very gruesome scene. The closest she comes is to use blood as a metaphor in VII.578, seven lines after the fact. If this blood comes from the murder, it is curiously misplaced. Lastly, the rejoicing at the clergeon's virginity puzzles us, since a seven-year-old boy should have little difficulty preserving it. Nevertheless, the Prioress treats it as a superb triumph, as if his murder would normally have implied his loss of virginity, and that his remaining a virgin is as striking a paradox as Mary's virginal motherhood highlighted in the corresponding section of the Prologue.

The difference between our natural expectations and the scene actually described implies an organization of details according to some plan other than the events of the literal scene. That other plan becomes clearer in the pattern underlying five important details in these stanzas: (1) the clergeon's throat is cut; (2) he is stuffed in a privy; (3) blood cries out on the deed; (4) he preserves his virginity; (5) he will eternally sing in the company of the virgins of Revelation. Each of these details implies a particular kind of violation or denial, in a series consistent with regressing time. A cut throat, especially in the case of the little clergeon, denies song. A body stuffed in a privy hole, suggesting a reversal of birth, denies life. Blood symbolizes a denial of flesh, since it can only be produced through some destruction of the flesh. Virginity implies a denial of the conventional sexual embrace. And finally, eternal life with the redeemed denies the world of time and space by affirming the world of spirit described by John. The middle item in this series, blood, surrounded as it is by two strong sexual images, may have sexual connotations too, as it does for the Wife of Bath (cf. III.579). If blood symbolizes a general destruction of flesh, its appearance in a cluster of specific sexual images denies the conception of flesh. These five details, then, deny in order song, life, conception, sexual embrace, and the extended world. It is evident, therefore, that these central stanzas, paralleling the Prologue where the physical process of the Incarnation was presented in reverse sequence, similarly take us from the world of flesh back to the world of spirit. Here, the Prioress has depicted the death of the clergeon in the same sexual overtones, and the same reversed time, in which her Prologue described the Incarnation. That sequence denies all fleshly acts by reversing the process through which physical existence takes form. As in the Prologue, here the Prioress's literal language describes the ultimate consummation of the flesh, while figuratively she reverses the acts of a sexual consummation to deny the begetting and very existence of flesh. Little wonder she considers the clergeon's virginity miraculous. Whereas the divine word achieved fleshly existence through the Virgin's denial of the flesh, the clergeon reaches his spiritual destiny through the fullest possible consummation of the flesh. The Prologue's "ravishing" brought the Christ-child into the world; the Tale's murder chases another innocent out of it (VII.566).

Chaucer's design for the *Prioress's Tale* lacks but a final event to complete its translation of flesh to spirit. That event, the ascension of the clergeon's soul, has been carefully integrated with the major motifs and images developing throughout the Tale. One of these images—the mouth and associated parts—acquires significance from its relation to the throat and the long passage through the trunk of the body. Alleys have been implicitly and explicitly present all along. The street through the Jewish quarter provides a twice-daily passage for the clergeon, as his song passes simultaneously through his throat. A different alley, connected to the main street, has another prominent role in the Tale. Attention has also been called to the orifices at the ends of alleys. The lips wiped clean, the mouths of babes, the implied birth canal, the opening in a wasps nest, the hole in the privy, the clergeon's mouth, as well as the street "free and open at eyther ende" (VII.494), all call attention to the activity associated with the alleys they terminate. It appears that from the Prioress's point of view downward movement calls for disapproval because it produces corporeal things. Food stains, excrement, perhaps blood too, are all associated with downward movement. Even the "litel scole of Cristen folk" is described as "Doun at the ferther ende" (VII.495–96). Upward movement deserves praise because it produces incorporeal things, like song and spirit. The direction of movement, as much as the locale, gives meaning to the Tale's conclusion.

To prepare for that conclusion, the final events of the Tale subtly place the formal church, represented by the abbot, and the martyred boy in opposition to each other. The abbot's question reveals an imagination that cannot transcend physical laws nor recognize a miracle: "Tel me what is thy cause for to synge, / Sith that thy throte is kut to my semynge?" (VII.647–48). The Church seems even more limited when the clergeon's instructive answer connects the abbot with bookish knowledge, in contrast to his own sense of the divine will:

> "My throte is kut unto my nekke boon,"
> Seyde this child, "and as by wey of kynde
> I sholde have dyed, ye, longe tyme agon.
> But Jesu Crist, as ye in bookes fynde,
> Wil that his glorie laste and be in mynde,
> And for the worship of his Mooder deere
> Yet may I synge O *Alma* loude and cleere." (VII.649–55)

The clergeon's words add to a growing list of antitheses—the limitless freedom of the Blessed Virgin, of song, and of passionate devotion, on the one hand, and the strictures of *kynde,* of excrement, and of bookish rules on the other. Nevertheless, the abbot did not ask the boy's motive in singing; he wanted to know how it was physically possible. That the clergeon does not explain, tempts us to associate his miraculous song with the grain placed on his tongue. But this cannot be. The grain was placed on his tongue *after* he began to sing, and will keep him from being summoned to heaven, unless it is removed. The grain, then, is not associated with freedom, but with strictures of *kynde.* Once again, a comparison of Prologue and Tale confirms the significance of the grain. In order that the "Fadres sapience" could be conceived, the "Goost" actually came to rest in the Virgin (VII.470) to enlighten her heart. Normally the Holy Spirit's "vertu" would transmit conventional seed to complete the explicitly carnal metaphor of the surrounding lines. But the Prologue never mentions seed. Indeed the whole point of virgin birth is conception without fleshly seed. The stanza's metaphysical union elevates metaphor to reality; the Holy Spirit becomes the mystic seed, or "Goost," which turns the Word into flesh. The grain, or seed, placed on the tongue of the martyred clergeon—unique in Chaucer's handling, incidentally[25]—serves an opposite purpose from the presence of the Holy Spirit in the Blessed Virgin. The Tale has been striving for a condition so rarefied that seed, and the carnal dimension to which it belongs, will be rejected as impure, completing the real sacrifice in which the parallel between the clergeon and Christ will culminate. When the abbot removes the grain from the boy's tongue, significantly in another upward lifting movement, he completes the final step in reversing fleshly conception and restoring the clergeon to pure spirit:

> This hooly monk, this abbot, . . .
> His tonge out caughte, and took awey the greyn,
> And he yaf up the goost ful softely. (VII.670–72)

These lines contain another linguistic tableau of the Tale's major theme. When one line "took awey," and the very next line "yaf up," we naturally assume that the two lines describe the same action, and the direct objects of the two verbs refer to the same thing. The abbot took away what the clergeon gave up. Yet the objects are not the same. At least, not quite. The abbot takes away a literal seed; the clergeon yields up his soul. Nevertheless, the causal connection between the two lines is so obvious, and the linguistic parallel so close, that "greyn" seems to translate into "goost," flesh becomes spirit, in the same instant it is taken away. Only once before has the Prioress used the word "goost," to name the Holy Spirit just *before* Christ's conception in the Virgin. At the end of her Tale she uses it again, just *after* the last link connecting the clergeon with the natural world has been removed, freeing him to proceed beyond the world of flesh into the realm of spirit.

The abbot's reaction, following his removal of the grain, amounts to a vindication of the young boy's vision of the world and the intensity of his feeling for the Virgin. Seeing the miracle at last, the abbot and his tears fall downward, perhaps from shame that his "ybounde" world prevents him from being part of it:

> And whan this abbot hadde this wonder seyn,
> His salte teeris trikled doun as reyn,
> And gruf he fil al plat upon the grounde,
> And stille he lay as he had ben ybounde. (VII.673–76)

As clearly as the clergeon's widowed mother exemplified the humble sufferer recompensed by Christ's direct communication to her (VII.603–6), so the clergeon has convincingly demonstrated by the end of the Tale a direct communication between himself and God, through the Virgin Mary. There is little doubt among the witnesses to the scene, among the Prioress's pilgrim audience, and among Chaucer's fourteenth-century audience, that the martyred clergeon's soul has been assumed into heaven.

But the Prioress remains, despite doing everything in her limited power to achieve rhetorically for herself what she achieved literally for her young hero. The crossed purposes of her secular and religious impulses paradoxically reach symbolic fruition in her Tale. In creating the young boy as an innocent so like herself, and then describing his martyrdom with the particular physical details she chooses, she attains the fullest possible visceral consummation toward which her secular impulse led her. In the removal of a seed, and the placement of the boy among the undefiled of *Revelation,* she comes as close as possible to attaining the virginal apotheosis toward which her religious calling summoned her. Finally, she makes her point more immediate by completing a process that began with her first public words. The subject of her Prologue, as distinct from its metaphors, lay entirely outside human experience. When she turns her Prologue's theoretical matter into the historical reality of her Tale, and then abruptly shifts the scene from Asia (VII.488) to Lincoln (see L. Benson 1987, note to VII.684), she brings the possibility of apotheosis tantalizingly close. The widely believed parallel story of Hugh of Lincoln, a local martyr of the previous century, gains credibility for her entire performance, especially with the one who most eagerly yearns for it to be true—the Prioress herself.

Before telling her tale Madam Eglentine prayed for guidance merely to recount a popular miracle in reverence of the Virgin (VII.473). Yet her actual presentation projects into the little clergeon her own physical sensitivity and spiritual inclination. As a surrogate for her maternal instincts and a repository of her own virginal devotion to the Blessed Mother, the clergeon symbolizes both the flesh and the spirit. The miracle permitting him to continue singing after his throat has been cut responds to a deep yearning in the Prioress for the miracle that will enable her spiritual and physical lives to flourish harmoniously and fully. Here too, as with other pilgrims, the tale eventually undoes its teller. By casting herself as a seven year old the Prioress virtually proclaims her unwillingness, or inability, to approach her vocation as an intellectually mature adult. By disclosing her passionate yearnings to experience virginal motherhood she advances herself to the rank reserved only for the Mother of God. And finally, by offering a new mode of worship, in which her passionate sense of truth replaces conventional understanding and is miraculously exulted before a humbly prostrate church, she inadvertently reveals a failure to practice the humility her Prologue advanced. As with the Wife of Bath and the Pardoner, the miracle needed to integrate the Prioress's divided self is yet to occur.

Matere and Forme

Nothing of the melting fondness we heard earlier from the Host survives in his response to the *Prioress's Tale* and the sober reaction it draws from the pilgrims. The fawning reaction we had reason to expect gives way to the skills of a master of ceremonies who knows he must liven up the proceedings. Thus it is that Harry inadvertently opens the discussion of literary art that will increase in detail and length over the remainder of the fragment and identify with growing clarity the rubric lying at the heart of this run of tales. Calling for something mirthful (VII.706), and attempting to lead the way by bantering with the next tale-teller, the Host directs attention to the Pilgrim Chaucer. From so *elvyssh,* so small, and so fair-faced a pilgrim Harry can imagine only "Som deyntee thyng" (VII.711). The remark flows naturally from an aesthetic principle about the agreement of form and matter that he perhaps takes for granted, a rule Pandarus put very nicely in another context:

> "hold of thi matere
> The forme alwey, and do that it be lik;
> For if a peyntour wolde peynte a pyk
> With asses feet, and hedde it as an ape,
> It cordeth naught, so were it but a jape." (*T&C,* II.1039–43)

Whatever high hopes the Host has in mind when he asks Chaucer for a tale are soon dashed, for the *Tale of Sir Thopas* is a failure, a brilliant failure. In place of the expected "deyntee thyng"—perhaps one of Marie de France's Breton lays—Chaucer offers an infantile view of knighthood beyond Harry's ability to endure (Patterson 1989, pp. 129–32). Like the preceding tale whose network of metaphors rearranges its allusive fabric in reversed time, Fragment VII as a whole has regressed (see chapter 12). It is not the first time Chaucer has ridiculed his humble poetic beginnings. But whereas the Introduction to the *Man of Law's Tale* patronizes gently and the *Book of the Duchess* lets us to draw our own conclusions about the poetic ineptitude of the Black Knight—who, I still believe, is a persona of Chaucer the struggling, fledgling poet (Condren 1971, 1975)—Fragment VII makes the judgment explicit. Harry objects to *Thopas* exclusively on grounds of its wretched *form*, its "drasty speche," and especially its "drasty rymyng" (VII.923, 30), finally ordering Geoffrey to leave poetry alone. With only prose still available to him, and eager to forestall a future attack, Geoffrey gives a prefatory defense of his next attempt exclusively on grounds of *matter*. Next time don't fault my language, he says in effect, because only the matter matters in my next tale. The illustration with which he underscores this argument has about it the youthful charm of one who makes his point with quivering chin. Indeed, overmakes his point. It takes him twenty-two lines to separate matter from form, ten of which refer explicitly to the evangelists, and in case anyone has missed this authoritative reference he names the four of them. So there. At the poetic nadir of the fragment, then, the link between *Thopas* and *Melibee* calls pointed attention to the two elements that must be present and must remain in balance before any writing can lay claim to literary art: form and matter.

This rubric has particular pertinence for the *Prioress's Tale,* which we have just seen in detail. Though the Prioress's performance has evoked many generations of critical dialogue, it is not the tale by itself that has sustained interest, for her story of a martyred clergeon is simple in its design, spare in its action, and predictable in its aim. On the contrary, we are endlessly fascinated by the Prioress herself, by what we take to be her character, and by the mutually causal influence of her character on her tale and her tale on her character. What constitutes the essential "matter" in both the teller and her tale, we want to know, and how much of both are accidental form? Though we ask these questions in simplistic ways—How could Madame Eglentine be what she appears to be, yet tell the tale she tells?—we remain entirely confused over what it is that she "appears to be." Do the tale she tells and the piety that prompts it constitute her "matter"? Or are they merely her "form," while her "matter" is actually her figurative language and studied elegance? In short, what *we* take to be a huge disparity between matter and form captures most of the interest. The preceding discussion has partly been an attempt to suggest that we may be wrong to see her thus. Not all passion need be impious; not all piety flaccid. Yet without question the Prioress gives her tale more emotive and physiological complexity than we expect from conventional piety. As a result, the piety itself often strikes readers as shallow, unexamined. To claim she is a "pyk with asses feet" would exaggerate, but certainly her piety and the way she expresses it "cordeth naught"; the one seems too little, the other too much.

Geoffrey's second try is classic overcompensation. Where *Thopas* called maximum attention to its form, albeit failing to produce a satisfying one, while overlooking its preposterously childish matter, *Melibee* places all its emphasis on matter, giving neither literary form to its narrative nor moving its philosophy to action. When Melibee announces that he intends "fully / to desherite [his adversaries] of al that evere they han and for to putte hem in exil for evere" (VII.1834–35), it "is a devastating moment," Lee Patterson says, for it suggests "that in fact Prudence's teaching has been largely useless" (1989, p. 157). Far from being a careful deliberation leading to wise action, the tale has been an interminable Boethian dialogue.

Attention is again called to the distinction between matter and form in the link between the *Melibee* and the *Monk's Tale* where the subject makes several different appearances. First, Harry Bailly has missed the main point of *Melibee,* taking it as a demonstration of patient womanhood rather than recalcitrant manhood. Perhaps it is well that his wife Goodelief, a woman with no apparent reluctance to put matter into form, has not heard the tale. If she had, and had grasped better than Harry the futility of Prudence's patience, she might soon be swinging her "grete clobbed staves" at more than Harry's "knaves" (VII.1897–98). In his eager wish that his wife had heard the tale, he incautiously lets us glance briefly at the form his marriage has taken, with a warrior wife constantly berating him for weakness. Regretting that the glimpse implies his own matter, "a milksop, or a coward ape" (VII.1910), he vainly struggles to create for himself an image of a man "perilous with knyf in honde" (VII.1919) whom his wife would do well to restrain, lest he some day slay a neighbor. The attempt to redeem his reputation is ludicrous, sinking him deeper in ridicule with each attempt to recover: that a fierce man like himself cannot overmatch his wife is not inconsistent, he insists, for her arms are huge. He abandons the charade two lines later.

Attention is now directed at the hapless Monk whom the Host eagerly makes the next goat. Assuming with good reason that the external form the Monk presents to the world accurately reflects the man within, Harry attempts to loosen the Monk up with the kind of barroom banter one normally associates with such a man. With mild disparagement intended as praise, Harry sees in the Monk the light duties of a gentle pasture (VII.1933) and what the Narrator saw earlier, the lover of a fat swan (I.206) and the pricker and hunter after the hare (I.191). Of course the Monk seethes, angry that others see him for what he actually is, rather than for what he wants them to believe. Like Harry before him, he over-compensates. The moral tale he hopes will rehabilitate his reputation takes him to unfamiliar terrain, if we may judge from his indecision. The Life of St. Edward comes first to mind, perhaps better remembered for its title than its story, for he drops it immediately in favor of "tragedies . . . Of whiche I have an hundred in my celle" (VII.1971–72). He does not mention a specific text, nor offer a clue to help us guess what he has in mind. But that may well be Chaucer's point. Though the Monk knows he has such reading matter in his possession, he is less certain of its material. It may be one of those collections of homilies newly ordained priests are often given. In any event, Chaucer seems to have in mind the kind of book the Monk long ago resolved not to go mad studying:

> What sholde he studie and make hymselven wood,
> Upon a book in cloystre alwey to poure. (I.184–85)

The Monk's unfamiliarity with his material takes further shape when he feels obliged to orient his listeners to his genre, unwittingly revealing it is he who needs the orientation. Like an instructor who, just the night before, has worked up material culled from the Thrall and Hibbard or Meyer Abrams of his day, the Monk briefly lectures on tragedy while reeking of rote memory and exhausting his knowledge after only nine lines, the first five on matter,

> "Tragedie is to seyn a certeyn storie,
> As olde bookes maken us memorie,
> Of hym that stood in greet prosperitee,
> And is yfallen out of heigh degree
> Into myserie, and endeth wrecchedly" (VII.1973–77)

the next four on form,

> "And they ben versified communely
> Of six feet, which men clepen *exametron*.

In prose eek been endited many oon,
And eek in meetre in many a sondry wyse." (VII.1978–81)

And when he must keep expanding his description of form to include prose as well as more meters than hexameters, the exertion drives him to an embarrassed exit line used by new instructors in every age:

"Lo, this declaryng oghte ynogh suffise." (VII.1982)[26]

It little matters whether the Monk copied his definition of tragedy from one of Chaucer's glosses in Boethius, revised from Trivet (cf. *Boece,* II.Pr.2.70, gloss), inferred it from Boccaccio's *De casibus virorum illustrium,* or learned it elsewhere, since it neither accords with Chaucer's apparent understanding, as implied by his other uses of the concept and word (i.e., *T&C,* V.1786, and the *Nun's Priest's Tale* as a response to the Monk's illustrations of tragedy) nor accurately describes all the stories he is about to tell. Indeed, the disparity between this definition and two others later in the tale (VII.1991–96; 2761–66), as well as its irrelevance for most of the sketches offered, may be one of the points Chaucer expects his readers to notice in this literary fragment.

Up to this point we have been discussing the relationship between form and matter within the tales of Fragment VII and in pilgrims who play prominent roles in the fragment. There are two additional ways in which these concepts figure in the remainder of the fragment: as they affect thought and as they affect a perception of the extended world, in effect change the world. Dame Prudence's insistence that her husband acquire the ability to understand the significance of the attack on his daughter Sophie (VII.1393–1426)[27] prepares us to accept the notion that form and matter, interacting upon each other, can affect thought. Pleading for interpretations (a possible translation of "sentence") based on evidence, she implies that thought can and should be influenced by the precise events one sees and the precise words he hears or reads. She certainly has in mind her husband's response to the aphoristic wisdom she quotes from countless sources ancient and medieval, but her words apply as well to the tale as a whole and to readers' response to names like Prudence and Sophie and to events that strongly point to the tale's allegorical caste. In view of the literary discussion interleaving the fragment, her advice refers as much to the act of literary criticism, as to the response she hopes to elicit from her husband.

The notion also applies to the *Monk's Tale.* No mere coincidence places a definition of tragedy in the tale's Prologue (VII.1973–81), begins the tale itself with another definition (VII.1991–96), and concludes it with still a third (VII.2761–66). To compare the three forms of this definition with their associated texts, as Dame Prudence might have advised, suggests that the Monk adjusts his definition to accommodate his texts, that is, the texts themselves force him to alter his thought. For if we search the Monk's seventeen examples for stories illustrating the essence of tragedy, as implied by the first definition, we find only five. And these are the briefest accounts: Lucifer (one stanza), Adam (one), Pedro King of Castile (two), Pedro King of Cyprus (one), and Bernabò Visconti (one). The remaining twelve certainly include falls from prosperity, but these falls are far from the central interest of the stories. Accordingly, the Monk is forced to recast his definition of tragedy at the end of the story of Croesus:

> Tragediës noon oother maner thyng
> Ne kan in syngyng crie ne biwaille
> But that Fortune alwey wole assaille
> With unwar strook the regnes that been proude;
> For whan men trusteth hire, thanne wol she faille,
> And covere hire brighte face with a clowde. (VII.2761–66)

Here Fortune is credited with intellection, willpower, omniscience, and stealth, while the tragic figure is damned as "proude" in one line yet merely trusting of Fortune in the next. This new definition locates the essence of tragedy in the dynamic between some central figure's self-consciousness and a Fortune able to respond with a moral lesson. And since Fortune, like Anglo-Saxon *wyrd,* is an entirely fictive construct enabling authors to ascribe order to the otherwise inexplicable workings of the human world, this new definition admits of a wide enough range of plot to encompass all seventeen stories.

While there may be tension between Fortune and several of the Monk's central figures, an equally interesting tension occurs between the matter and form of the histories the Monk recites. His Tale seems to have two beginnings. The stories of Lucifer and Adam conform perfectly to his initial definition of tragedy, but the five succeeding stories move away from this definition, as if their teller were resisting the constricting form with which he began. Then, as if forcing discipline upon himself, he begins again with three little vignettes (the two Pedros and Bernabò) that return to the initial definition. The discipline is brief, for he immediately recounts the story of Hugolino, Count of Piza, which has nothing at all to do with any of the three definitions. A close look at the account of Hugolino (VII.2407–62) gives an indication of what pull is being exerted to move the Monk away from his *de casibus* form. At the beginning of the story

Count Hugo is already in prison, that is, his fall has already occurred, as the story concentrates exclusively on the pathos of his young children, starving to death yet begging their father to eat their flesh and so prolong his life. The father's curse against Fortune (VII.2445–46) may appear to link the story with the Monk's evolving theme, but this outburst does not arise naturally from anything in the story nor has any relevance to the main interest, the father's helplessness to lessen his children's painful suffering and his awareness of their love for him. Even Dante, Chaucer's original source and a more profound expositor of the Ugolino story, stresses the irrelevance of justice next to the horror of such cruelty:

> Che se 'l conte Ugolino aveva voce
> d'aver tradita te de le castella,
> non dovei tu i figliuoi porre a tal croce. (*Inf.*, 33.85–87)

[For even if Count Ugolino had repute of having betrayed thee in thy strongholds, thou oughtest not to have set his sons on such a cross.] (Norton trans.)

Pathos and human interest may be at their highest in the story of Ugolino, but this is the dimension that most of the stories share—their focus on unusual details, not their emphasis on a decline in fortune. The story of Sampson emphasizes feats of strength; the story of Hercules, strength and the magical shirt given by Dianira. The interest in the story of Nebuchadnezzar is on his turning into a beast and turning back again repentant. Balthasar's story features mysterious handwriting on the wall and Daniel's ability to interpret it. The longest story in the group, the account of Cenobia, makes only perfunctory reference to her fall compared with the several fascinating details of her life, her masculinity, her military record, her eschewing conjugal relations, unless to beget offspring, and her magnificent array. The dutiful reference to Fortune in the final stanza of her story cannot compete with the details of the story itself.

The same pattern holds for the second half of the *Monk's Tale*. After three accounts underscoring the instability of fortune, its stories turn to different matter: Ugolino's pathos, already noted; Nero's cruelty, the details of his death, and the two who did not hold him in awe; the irony of lofty Holofernes being slain by a woman; the rot and corruption of Anthiocus's living body; the great admiration for Alexander whose glory shines brighter than Fortune can dim, and who in any case was not laid low by chance but by treason; the interesting political details in the story of Caesar; and Croesus's dream interpreted by his daughter. Thus, in the implied debate between form and matter in the *Monk's Tale* matter wins overwhelmingly, not just any matter, but fascinating details capable of commanding attention. The concept of tragic form that the Monk began to teach the group has been eclipsed and forgotten because the mere exposure to story telling has taught him a more important lesson.

Had the Monk world enough and time, he might have learned to tell a passable tale. Fortunately his time is cut short by the Knight. In the exchange that follows this interruption, made ruder by the Host's confidence that the Knight is on his side, we hear yet another lesson on the telling of tales. As the Host's earlier interruption of the Pilgrim Chaucer's tale-telling touched off a discussion of form and matter, this interruption does the same. First the Knight objects to the Monk's matter, faulting not only the uninterrupted heaviness of the Monk's vision, but also the false view he gives of the world by continually noting the downward turn of Fortune's wheel. For every foot of downward turn, the Knight implies, another part of the wheel turns upward. "Swich thyng is gladsom, as it thynketh me, / And of swich thyng were goodly for to telle" (VII.2778–79). Under the protection of so distinguished a detractor, the Host adds a complaint about form to the Knight's objection to matter. Opening with a salvo at the Monk's sudden purple—cruelly perhaps, for Fortune covering her bright face with a cloud (cf. VII.2766) is his first and only experiment with figurative language—the Host quickly moves to a lengthier complaint that his tale's form, less interesting than the tinkling of bridle bells, will lose his audience. Without a form sufficient to hold an audience, any tale would be lost. Harry clarifies the interdependence of form and matter by insisting that a suitable form can enable him—perhaps everyone—to rise to any matter:

> "And wel I woot the substance is in me,
> If any thyng shal wel reported be." (VII.2803–4)

The second, and by far more significant effect that a successful integration of form and matter can have is on the way the world is perceived. To grasp Fragment VII's representation of this effect we must compare two separate sequences in Harry Bailly's role as master of ceremonies: his attitude to the Monk before and after the *Monk's Tale;* and his attitude to the Nun's Priest before and after the *Nun's Priest's Tale.* But first, some prefatory textual remarks.

The first three of these four passages (VII.1924–64; 2767–2807; 2808–20) seem authentic in every respect; the fourth, "The Nun's Priest's Epilogue" (VII.3447–62), has fared less well. As Susan H. Cavanaugh notes, "These lines occur in a group of nine MSS generally taken to be of inferior authority and may have been canceled by Chaucer when he wrote lines 1941–62 of the Monk's Prologue, where the same ideas are repeated" (L. Benson 1987, p. 941). While it is true that nine manuscripts represent only about 16 percent of the Manly-Rickert working group, I cannot agree that these nine should be given low marks. Seven of them are in the Manly-Rickerts "Type *a,* pure" and differ from the Ellesmere only by including this Nun's Priest's Epilogue.[28] The other two are in the Manly-Rickert Anomalous category, one of which (Cx²) is complete except for a missing *Friar's Tale,* and the other (Ch), though adding *Gamelyn* and lacking the *Retraction,* is complete in all other respects. Nevertheless, the editorial question of whether "The Nun's Priest's Epilogue" should, or should not, be included in a critical edition of the *Canterbury Tales* has little bearing on our immediate concern. The lines are unquestionably Chaucer's representation of Harry Bailly's thoughts in Fragment VII, whether his final intention was to address them to the Monk alone, or to both the Monk on one occasion and the Nun's Priest on another.

The Host's invitation to the Monk, as we have already remarked, is full of playful admiration, kidding, warm good humor. That readers may see in it cause to fault the Monk does not alter the convivial expectations of the Host, who looks forward to taking brief part in the Monk's manly world, even if only vicariously through a tale of hunting. In particular the Host notices the Monk's "brawnes," his "myght," and his general fitness for breeding:

> "Haddestow as greet a leeve as thou hast myght
> To parfourne al thy lust in engendrure,
> Thou haddest bigeten ful many a creature." (VII.1946–48)

He perhaps sees in the Monk a striking contrast to his own unfitness for the same activity:

> "Religioun hath take up al the corn
> Of tredyng, and we borel men been shrympes.
> Of fieble trees ther comen wrecched ympes.
> This maketh that oure heires been so sklendre
> And feble that they may nat wel engendre." (VII.1954–58)

If ever a pilgrim had an attentive audience willing to lavish yet more praise, given the least evidence, it is the Monk, perhaps second only to the Prioress. What surprises us is the anger with which this same receptive listener turns against the Monk when the *Monk's Tale* does not live up to expectations. The obvious conclusion cannot be avoided: in the Host's eyes the undistinguished tale itself converted the brawny Monk—a manly potential breeder—into a ludicrous failure who uses precious metaphors and has tinkling bells on his bridle.

Altogether different is the Host's before-and-after attitude to the Nun's Priest. A playful tone accompanies this invitation too, but the admiration is gone. "With rude speche and boold" he orders Sir John "Telle us swich thyng as may oure hertes glade" (VII.2808, 2811), then disparages his nag of a horse with a reverse compliment:

"What thogh thyn hors be bothe foul and lene?
If he wol serve thee, rekke nat a bene.
Looke that thyn herte be murie everemo." (VII.2813–15)

The point is surely not to extol the virtue of a merry heart, but to jibe the Priest for having a pathetic horse. We may speculate that if this priest were of good size, let us say as good a size as the Host earlier claimed the Monk was, we would surely hear about the burden such a man would be on the back of so lean a horse. We hear nothing, suggesting that the Nun's Priest is *not* a man of remarkable size and brawn. Nevertheless, immediately following the Priest's brilliant tale of a cock, a hen, and a fox the Host sings an entirely different tune:

"by my trouthe, if thou were seculer,
Thou woldest ben a trede-foul aright.
For if thou have corage as thou hast myght,
Thee were nede of hennes, as I wene,
Ya, moo than seven tymes seventene.
See, whiche braunes hath this gentil preest,
So gret a nekke, and swich a large breest!" (VII.3450–56)

Has all this brawn appeared suddenly, as if through a miracle? Indeed it has. The Host's different responses to the two tale-tellers has been caused by the different quality of the two tales they tell. The indifferent, even annoying, achievement of the *Monk's Tale* diminishes its pilgrim teller; the miraculous achievement of the *Nun's Priest's Tale* enlarges the Nun's Priest. Art effectively shapes the world.

What then is this tale told by the Nun's Priest, this tale that has—what no literary person has ever believed but dearly wishes were the case—the power to change the world, if only how the world seems?

NUN'S PRIEST'S TALE

The *Nun's Priest's Tale* needs no apologist. The lightest of soufflés, it is at once everything and nothing. It contains within it the political, social, and theological struggles that define much of fourteenth-century culture, yet the central event it portrays—an aborted barnyard skirmish between a fox and a rooster—would occur so swiftly and unremarkably that it would never be noticed, but for its brilliant dilation by the Nun's Priest. Its hero is no one strutting or slinking across its lines and pages, nor any one associated with the fascinating allusions that turn its fifteen seconds of action into 625 lines of sublime text. Nothing of flesh and blood, the hero is vellum and ink, as Talbot Donaldson pointed out a generation ago (1975, pp. 1104–8). The tale's ambivalent nature—nothing but inflated rhetoric at one extreme, and a superb example of creative genius at the other—makes it an ideal representation of human nature and a stunning conclusion to the subject around which Fragment VII has been organized.

Like a fine prism that catches and exposes all the rays that make up humanity, the tale continually represents the extremes of human thought, belief, and action. To change the figure, if nature abhors a vacuum, intellectual nature abhors ignorance, preferring to fill that void with what it knows is false, or an exaggeration, rather than remain silent. A celebrated passage, one among many, illustrates this point with rapier swiftness. It is that moment when Chauntecleer, fatigued from debating the nature and source of dreams and despaired of winning the argument, elects to change the subject with a transparent remark of rank flattery:

> "*In principio,*
> *Mulier est hominis confusio—*
> Madame, the sentence of this Latyn is,
> 'Womman is mannes joye and al his blis.'" (VII.3163–66)

The inflated grace of the lines, the patronizing assumption that a woman could not possibly understand Latin, and the wit of prefacing the lines with the first words of John's Gospel to suggest an immemorial truth the equal of *In principio erat Verbum, et Verbum erat apud Deum, et Deus erat Verbum,* have all long been recognized and appreciated. We take delight as well in the preclusive allusions to heaven and hell. Where *confusio* implies the latter, especially as Dante depicts the essence of *Inferno,* "joye and . . . blis" characterize the former. And it is here that we begin to perceive the full implication of the mistranslation, whether deliberately mistranslated by Chauntecleer or only by Chaucer. Hell and Heaven— antithetical absolutes—as metaphors for Woman inevitably remind us of the preclusive attitudes to women in two of the most numerous genres of the Middle Ages, anti-feminist literature and courtly love literature, one associated with Chauntecleer's Latin, the other with his English mistranslation.[29] Any reasonable person from any age knows that both views are indefensible. Like men, women exist neither at the extreme represented by La Vieille and Duessa, nor at the opposite extreme represented by Griselda and the Virgin. They command a wide range whose center is located at the approximate midpoint between these two extremes. In other words, it is not women who give rise to either of Chauntecleer's aphorisms, but the discourse about women.[30]

This swift little demonstration of opposite views tenaciously held by different camps, and then suddenly rejected by the simple act of ignoring them, "I wol nat han to do of swich mateere; / My tale is of a cok" (VII.3251–52), concludes a much lengthier debate that does exactly the same thing.[31] Discussions of dreams were endlessly fascinating to the Middle Ages, perhaps because both of the two opposing positions advanced in the debating halls held enormous appeal. If dreams were the natural culminations of pre-dreaming conditions (Pertelote's position), and if they were also the deities' effort to communicate the future (Chauntecleer's position), then dreams held a promising key to all of human existence. By conditioning one's day to make a dream on a particular subject highly likely, and then having such a dream in which the future is foretold, the uncertainty of existence vanishes. Perhaps this possibility explains the enormous popularity of dream lore, to judge from the number of surviving manuscripts of Macrobius, Alanus, and others who categorize and discuss dreams. The amount of evidence heaped on the discussion matters not at all in the long run, for within a few lines Chauntecleer turns away from the discussion as easily as he is certain of his mistranslation of Latin.

Still another vexed question, the nature of man's will, takes the same form as the subjects of dreams and women, though in a more extended passage. The Nun's Priest disingenuously claims ignorance of the subject, while dropping hints that he knows the subject very well indeed. The three names he throws out, as if merely to cite a few who *do* have a scholar's familiarity, lay the subject before us in its two opposite extremes and in its medial position. Augustine is associated with free will at one extreme, Bishop Bradwardine with predestination at the other, and Boethius with conditional necessity lying between the two. All the wit of the Narrator's reducing centuries of profitless disputation to twenty lines of summary is magnified when he does it twice. He enacts the positions on free will exactly as he had earlier enacted the positions on the nature of dreams, and with the same result, a cavalier turning away from the subject as if it were irrelevant, as it surely seems to be to the Nun's Priest. The rooster cannot bring himself to believe anything less than that the gods communicate with him (Bradwardine's predestination); the hen that we

choose our own destiny (Augustine's free will) or, as pop psychologists would have it today, "we are what we eat." And when the Nun's Priest "wol nat han to do of swich mateere; / My tale is of a cok" (VII.3251–52), he puts into words what the forewarned Chauntecleer put into action when "he fley doun fro the beem" (VII.3172)—a cock will do what a cock will do (Boethius's conditional necessity).

The transience of the subjects of the *Nun's Priest's Tale,* in contrast to the permanence of the tale itself, may be Chaucer's finest touch. The battle ground of medieval debating halls disappears like a vain bubble burst. The contrasting claims of those who would describe the gentler/harsher sex become a faded echo in a translator's *lapsus linguae.* Even the dynastic struggle between Richard II and Henry Bolingbroke—an allusion that still holds the charm of possibility, despite Susan H. Cavanaugh's claim that "the identification with Bolingbroke is very unlikely, as is the rest of the theory" (L. Benson 1987, p. 939)—has less staying power than the images of Chauntecleer, Pertelote, and Colfox.[32] Above all these, and above all else that every age deems its most important concerns, reigns the tale triumphant, a long leap indeed from the failed efforts of the pilgrim who tried to rhyme about a knight and a giant and who took refuge in treatise. The tale that culminates this long chronicle of Chaucer's poetic maturation leaves us with a complex paradox for Chaucer—not the Chaucer confined to the unrealistic image of a naïve pilgrim, but in the full complexity of the man who is pilgrim, poet, and human being. Among all the pilgrims only Chaucer achieves what he had been yearning to accomplish. Unimportant, elvish, perhaps fit to swell a progress but ransomed for thirteen shillings four pence less than Robert Clinton's horse (Crow and Olson 1966, p. 24), Chaucer is truly eclipsed by only his poetry, which alone survives the turmoil of his time. The Knight and the Clerk still may wish the world were as comprehensible as it appears in their philosophies; the Wife and the Pardoner may still long for the acceptance that love signifies, and that love could be all that they think it is; the Merchant and the Monk may still hope to conceal from the world the men they actually are; the Franklin and the Prioress may still believe that the tales they tell reify their lives. But none of these succeeds. Only Chaucer makes his fictive world real, confers on the transitory models and ideas that inspired him the permanence they could not achieve for themselves. And this artistic achievement, a phase transition in its own right, alone becomes the most effective earthly analogue for the love that all human beings seek, wittingly or otherwise.

A final, poignant paradox yet remains in Fragment VII. The rhetoric that confers permanence on Chaucer's creation will always lack the substance that viewers in any age look for in the events and constructions of their day. It "ys noght but eyr ybroken" (*HF*, 765). Yet despite its seeming triviality, and despite its more frequent application in error than in truth, it must be cherished above all, for on earth poetry alone separates us from the chickens.

❦

Fragments IX and X
Poetic Fruition/Spiritual Apotheosis

Like most Middle English literature, the poems Chaucer wrote before turning to the *Canterbury Tales* usually conclude with a reward. A main character, often a narrator recounting some dreaming or waking adventure, receives a palpable indication that the gods who assist in the completion of poems (or the completion of adventures) have appreciated his effort. The bell sounding "houres twelve" at the end of *Book of the Duchess* (*BD,* 1323) and the entire completed poem—once "so queynt a sweven," now "in ryme" (*BD,* 1330–34)—fulfill a wish for one of his narrators, as a roundel and successful annual meeting of birds in *Parlement of Foules* gratify another. The "tydynges" whirling about in the *Hous of Fame* remunerate the diligent narrator of that poem who has long toiled "Withoute guerdon" (*HF,* 619) in the service of love. In *Troilus and Criseyde* an ascent to the eighth sphere and the wisdom it brings fittingly compensate Troilus for his long, faithful dedication to love.

In the light of so frequent a practice in Chaucer's early poetry, the *Canterbury Tales* may employ a similar motif. Indeed, many an individual tale concludes with some form of reward, or at least a just dessert, as Palamon, Alain and John, the hag and knight-rapist, Dorigen, the little clergeon, Chauntecleer, and others learn to their delight, while Nicholas, the Reeve's miller, the Friar's *somonour,* the Summoner's *frere,* and others learn to their chagrin. Yet, as characters within tales, these are somewhat different from the narrators of the earlier poems who are attempting to get a story told, to acquire a bit of learning, and to understand life and love. A few pilgrims, however, seem almost to be characters within their tales as well as narrators of them, and for these a hoped-for reward energizes the narrative. The Wife of Bath, for example, seems almost to re-create herself in the rejuvenation of her transparent hag-surrogate. Alas, her tale is so manifestly fanciful that the gift of second youth never approaches reality for its teller. The Pardoner and the Prioress, too, weave themselves so thoroughly through every part of their performances that it is fruitless to try to separate the maker from the material, the dancer from the dance. Unfortunately the former will always be a pariah, separated from both the activities and the admiration of society, and the latter cannot achieve salvation for herself through projection into the image of a martyred boy.

The pattern does reassert itself, however, for the overall Narrator of the poem, perhaps the only pilgrim with legitimate expectations of receiving a reward. Somewhat different from Troilus, who is recompensed for faithful service to the *practice* of love, Chaucer's reward will come—if it does—for faithful service to the *craft* of love, with love here understood as authorial affection for the whole of humankind. Both a character in the poem and a teller of his own material, a pilgrim whose ambition and means of achievement are laid open for all to perceive, Geoffrey Chaucer manages to position himself at the verge of success, where no other pilgrim in the poem or character in a tale even comes close.

As the second half of *Canterbury Tales* moves steadily toward its conclusion two carefully crafted patterns emerge, one circular in design and professional in theme, the other linear in design and spiritual in theme. To trace the circular structure of Fragments VI through VIII, with Fragment IX as an attendant gloss, is to recognize Chaucer's own *apologia pro vita sua,* a demonstration and discussion of the profession of poet. To follow the linear structure, beginning with the *Physician's Tale* and extending through the *Retraction,* is to witness a sincere, humble appeal for eternal salvation. What is more, these two patterns merge in Chaucer's daring plan to have the outcome of his appeal for salvation depend on his life as a creator of literature.

The structure of the second half of *Canterbury Tales,* discussed in chapter 12, arranges Fragments VI and VIII in a ring circling Fragment VII. These encircling fragments, each with two tales, are similar in that all four tales attempt to reorder reality, and because each fragment contains a physical tale and a spiritual tale, as shown in Figure 10.

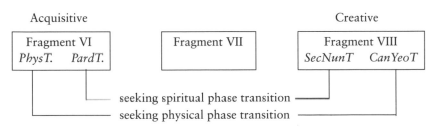

Figure 10

The tale of the Canon's Yeoman, whose alchemical *milieu* exclusively concerns the physical conversion of lead to gold, is linked to the *Physician's Tale* which also remains rooted in the earthly world, as we saw in chapter 13, while the spiritual tale of the Second Nun returns to the spiritual subject of the *Pardoner's Tale*. As to contrast, the acquisitive motives featured in the Physician's and Pardoner's tales lead to destruction, whereas the tales in Fragment VIII attempt to create something new.

Among these four tales only the *Second Nun's Tale,* combining spiritual and creative impulses, ends in success. It would be a mistake, however, to assume with Robert M. Longsworth that success is proved because "the work of the virtuous saint is presumably beneficent, whereas the work of the fraudulent alchemist is malign" (1992, p. 87). It rests more convincingly on a comparison with the other tale in its fragment (CYT) and with the spiritual tale in Fragment VI to which it is linked (PardT). Recalling the subject first introduced by the Man of Law where Christianity was allegorically brought to foreign lands, the story of Saint Cecilia recounts the spiritual expansion of belief from pagan to Christian, whereas the acquisitive impulse in the *Canon's Yeoman's Tale* fails to expand lead to gold. Multiplication in the *Second Nun's Tale* is life-giving, when the faith of Saint Cecilia transforms several contemporaries into saints themselves, whereas the acquisitive impulse in the *Pardoner's Tale* multiplies death, first of "an old felawe . . . yslayn . . . as he sat on his bench upright" (VI.672–73), then of the youngest rioter, and finally of the remaining two.

It may appear paradoxical that four tales seeking phase transitions, two of which are specifically spiritual, should serve as supporting pillars for the six tales of Fragment VII that apparently have nothing to do with altering the existing world or with spirituality. On the contrary, as we saw in the previous chapter, the tales of Fragment VII have everything to do with expansion to a new order and with spirit, provided we recognize that the qualitative difference between, say, *Tale of Sir Thopas* and *Nun's Priest's Tale* is as great as the difference between lead and gold, and provided we understand that the creation of an aesthetic reality is a spiritual act.

That the tightly organized tales of Fragments VI, VII, and VIII include an overtly religious tale in its final fragment should not lead us to conclude that spirituality is its only meaning. The tale that immediately follows the ten tales comprising these three fragments, that is the *Manciple's Tale,* is appended as a typical Chaucerian gloss, as the *Friar's* and *Summoner's Tales* provide instruction on how to respond to the Wife's performance, and as the *Physician's Tale* guides us to an interpretation of the *Pardoner's Tale*. It tells us that the run of tightly organized tales from the *Physician's Tale* to the *Canon's Yeoman's Tale* have an equally important literary significance. Surviving in a fragment unto itself and standing outside the ring structure of the poem's second half, the *Manciple's Tale* is a perfect example of what Talbot Donaldson (in another context) calls Chaucer's habit of making his most telling points while pretending to say something else (1970b, pp. 85–87).

A tableau in the middle of the *Manciple's Tale* specifically directs attention away from the tale's ostensible subject—its concluding moral "keep wel thy tonge," repeated four times in fifty lines (IX.315, 319, 333, 362)—and onto a question of literary decorum. The moment occurs just as the tale notes that Phoebus's wife has a lover:

> And so bifel, whan Phebus was absent,
> His wyf anon hath for hir lemman sent. (IX.203–4)

A literary question suddenly enters the Manciple's mind:

> Hir lemman? Certes, this is a knavyssh speche!
> Foryeveth it me, and that I yow biseche. (IX.205–6)

Thirty lines follow on the justification for making a "word . . . accorde with the dede" (IX.208), when one is describing a lowly deed by a lofty person. The Manciple concludes that nothing separates the immoral acts of two people from different ranks except the words referring to them: one might be a lady, another a wench; one a captain, another an outlaw. But the act is the same. The net effect of this insert is to shift the subject from a particular action within the tale to an author's use of a certain word to describe that action. Having made this question of literary usage abundantly clear, the Manciple then returns to his apparent subject with the sly comment, "I am a man noght textueel" (IX.235).

But Chaucer *is* a textual man. We wonder, therefore, about his strategy in devoting thirty-three lines (IX.205–237), that is twelve percent of the tale, to a discussion of appropriate language. First we hear of Phoebus's jealousy, then of his effort to please his wife, and finally the Manciple's regret that no man may "destreyne a thyng which that nature / Hath natureelly set in a creature" (IX.161–62). Next come three exempla of how nature governs creatures: (1) a bird will prefer the freedom of a cold, rude forest and a diet of worms to a cage of gold with its dainty food; (2) a cat will choose a mouse over tender flesh; and (3) a she-wolf at mating time will lust after "The lewedeste wolf that she may fynde, / Or leest of reputacioun" (IX.184–85). These exempla are immediately followed by the statement that Phoebus's wife did indeed have a lover and that this lover's low station merits the word *lemman*. A reader would be justified in assuming that this animal lore explains by analogy why an amorous woman, *by nature,* will prefer a rogue lover at hand to a noble husband who is absent. Yet this assumption fails to satisfy, for the lengthy section we are discussing has little to do with the tale's main point that great harm is done by not holding one's tongue, a moral clearly directed at a crow who unwisely told Phoebus of his wife's adultery. Phoebus slew his wife, regretted having done so, and punished the crow. The long digression emphasizing the wife's guilt seems irrelevant. What does her guilt have to do with the crow's holding his tongue? If wagging tongues bring great harm, it makes no difference whether the tongue-wagger reports truth or falsehood. The report by itself, not its accuracy, brings about the harm. It is certainly possible that for the sake of irony Chaucer might let his Manciple devote seventy-seven irrelevant lines explaining that the wife's low nature is no different from a bird's, a cat's, or a she-wolf's. But it is unlikely that Chaucer would waste thirty percent of *his* Tale on something that did not serve *his* purpose. That is, these animal digressions and the point about diction may be intended to suggest a different point, albeit obliquely. And the aphorism with which the tale ends may only be the simple, unsatisfactory moral which leads to a more profound meaning.

Despite inserting these digressions on animal behavior between references to the wife's misbehavior, Chaucer's more likely strategy has less to do with the wife's conduct than with the crow's. As a cat cannot pass up a mouse, a crow cannot remain silent. Its nature demands to be heard. And now let us keep in mind whom the crow really represents: tale-tellers, authors, poets. For the digression about animals makes implicitly the same literary subject that the discussion of suitable language makes explicitly. If animals act as they do by nature, then it is assuredly a poet's nature *not to hold his tongue.* The Manciple offers sound advice in the world of affairs, but not in the world of letters.

Only one author has had a continuing presence in *Canterbury Tales,* Chaucer himself, literally in the Man of Law's Prologue and in the *Retraction.* In the *Manciple's Tale* he appears again, obliquely to be sure. As helpless as the crow to choose discretion, the poet Chaucer is compelled to write what his inner and outer eyes see. The *Manciple's Tale,* then, though literally acknowledging the loquacious habits of crows, and disparaging them for it, actually points to the implicit subject of the second half of Chaucer's whole poem, the writer's craft. If it is true that Chaucer modeled several of his characters and situations on historical figures, as Chaucer research used to argue, then the *Manciple's Tale* may also be a witty apology for the *Canterbury Tales,* an explanation for its author's helplessness to avoid writing it.[1]

A linear pattern cuts straight through the circular pattern of the poem's second half. Especially as demonstrated in its most celebrated tales, this linear pattern strongly indicates that a profound appeal for salvation is its objective. For the progression from *Pardoner's Tale* to *Prioress's Tale* to *Nun's Priest's Tale* steadily approaches a canonical understanding of Christianity, leading inexorably to the apotheosis that culminates in the *Retraction.* The Pardoner's account of one man condemned never to die, but to live frustratingly in a world of flesh, and three other men eager to slay a Death that will take them from self-indulgent lives, reveals an obsessive dissatisfaction with the existing order. His careful preparation of his audience to maximize their admiration for his skill and his dramatic self-presentation imply an understanding of divine order entirely different from the beliefs of the fourteenth century, while his tale is the antithesis of vitality. Two tales later the Prioress leaves the conventional understanding of order and salvation securely in place, though she herself inclines to passionate piety while perhaps disapproving devotion that is less intense than hers. And her little clergeon, whose brief life reflects Christ's, lacks the miraculous restoration to life that Christ's Resurrection achieved to demonstrate the truth of His promise. Finally, the *Nun's Priest's Tale* not only accepts the conventional ordering of animal, human, and divine, often wittily exploring man's false understanding of the connections among them, but also celebrates the creative intellect and caps the whole with an unmistakable resurrection motif when Chauntecleer is restored to life, as it were, through a skillful application of wit and wisdom.

A wider view of the poem affords a better perspective on the progression which these three tales highlight. The first half of the *Canterbury Tales* represents increasing chaos in its first movement and stability in its second, accomplishing on a terrestrial plane what Dante's *Inferno* and *Purgatorio* describe on a metaphysical. All the major pilgrims and characters throughout both movements of this first half share a fundamental desire—always vague, unspoken, or overshadowed by a litany of irrelevant desires—to make their life on earth a more agreeable lot. In the second half of the poem, corresponding to Dante's lengthy approach to Paradise, Chaucer isolates and refines this concept of desire, showing it to be more than a wish to rearrange earthly logistics, indeed to be a powerful urge to understand the nature of reality and to bring about a phase transition to a higher order.

Clarifying this yearning, although showing it wrongly directed, Fragment VI opens the poem's second half as if it were a heading for the remaining tales. Virginius and the three rioters, the protagonists respectively of the Physician's physical tale and the Pardoner's spiritual tale, wilfully take a stance superior to the accepted reality of the Middle Ages in order to accomplish their aims. Virginius takes a life to thwart a corrupt judge; the rioters seek to slay death to sustain a wanton life. The protagonists in both tales ultimately fail when their private interests eclipse what might have been laudable aims, Virginius by giving more attention to his triumph over Apius than to saving his daughter, the three rioters by succumbing to greed. The pilgrims who tell these tales also fall short of the mark. The Physician flouts his own profession's respect for life while giving no attention to higher values that might justify the loss of life; the Pardoner fails to persuade either himself or others that the skillful manipulation of appearances may suitably replace eternal truth.

The Seventh, Eighth, and Ninth Fragments interleave with this growing perception of the importance of eternal life the occupation of Chaucer's lifetime. Both subjects have been brought to the surface of the poem in preparation for Fragment X, where they will eventually become one.

FRAGMENT X AND ITS RETRACTION

Chaucer has been specifically mentioned by name several times in this chapter because the poem's relentless drive toward its conclusion compels his presence. It is well recognized that he has a dual identity throughout his great poem, the officious pilgrim who reports everyone's offerings as well as he can, lamely attempting to contribute a tale of his own, and the poet himself whose pure voice is heard in the *General Prologue*'s opening eighteen lines and even more certainly in the *Retraction*. We might add as well a third identity, the Host Harry Bailly. As suggested at the outset of this book, the opposite extremes of Host and Narrator—each unbelievable on his own terms and the diametric opposite of the other—perhaps define the extreme limits within which the poet himself may be found. Like the merger of the Nun's Priest and the poet, both of whom claim that "Al that is writen is writen for oure doctrine" (X.1083; cf. VII.3441–42), Chaucer's three formal identities—Host, Pilgrim, poet—become indistinguishable at the end of the poem, merging in the powerful intellectual currents in Chaucer's life, his professional commitment to creative literature, and his spiritual dedication to Christian salvation.

Before suggesting how each of Chaucer's worldly identities dissolves at the end of the poem, let us acknowledge three ways in which the *Retrac-*

tion has already been well covered in critical discussions, no one of which cancels another.[2] First, the *Retraction* readily responds to the Parson's summons to penance. The Narrator's confession, spoken before a priest, expressing sincere remorse for the sins of a lifetime, metaphorically enumerated as works of his own hand, and atoned for in the lines before us, satisfies all the requirements for the sacrament of Penance.[3] Second, the *Retraction* functions as a palinode, that section at the end of a piece of writing where self-effacing authors, from ancient to post-medieval, revoke what they have written. Usually appearing at the conclusion of a major work, a palinode also gives authors an opportunity to list their other works, as Chaucer does, perhaps to include them in a general revocation or perhaps to place a full bibliography on record.[4] Third, Chaucer's *Retraction* completes the transition from Canterbury pilgrimage to pilgrimage of life. It is this last perception that I should like to explore as the present book draws to its own close.

The poem takes its first step in detaching itself from the pilgrimage, the tale-telling, and from life itself when the Host requests a tale from the Parson. Here the Host's request has a different emphasis from earlier requests of other pilgrims. Instead of simply asking for a lusty tale to requite something just concluded, or a merry one to liven up the proceedings, as has been his custom, the Host expands his words to include his own obligation, as if the scheme for amusement had not been of his own devising but an assignment from elsewhere:

> "Lordynges everichoon,
> Now lakketh us no tales mo than oon.
> Fulfilled is my sentence and my decree;
> I trowe that we han herd of ech degree;
> Almoost fulfild is al myn ordinaunce." (X.15–19)

Although Harry Bailly undoubtedly recites these words, they sound like a comment from the creator of the lone remaining tale, rather than from the one responsible for merely finding its teller. Harry Bailly and Chaucer-the-Poet seem to have become one.

The Parson, too, strikes out in a new direction, perhaps because the "fable" the Host requests, almost as an afterthought, lacks the force of the assignment in the previous line to "knytte up wel a greet mateere" (X.28). He takes the poem a further step from the gaming pilgrimage—perhaps attaching himself to a larger pilgrimage—by eschewing the "draf" of fable, the "rum, ram, ruf" of a northern man, and everything else in verse. The treatise he offers—a formal analysis of the seven deadly sins, called a "penitential,"[5] intended for confessors—takes us to the level of divine law, well above the tales of human action which that law will eventually judge. Then, when the voice we have every reason to assume is the familiar voice of Chaucer-the-Pilgrim begins to confess sins that cannot possibly belong to the pilgrim Narrator, we realize immediately that the voice belongs to Chaucer-the-Poet. Thus a second merger occurs, that of the Narrator and the poet. Yet these are not the only mergers.

There has been some doubt that the *Retraction,* as we have it in twenty-eight manuscripts and all modern editions, should be read as coming entirely from the poet-as-Narrator. Douglas Wurtele argues that the first four lines of the *Retraction* (X.1081–84), along with the final three (X.1090–92), were the original ending of the *Parson's Tale* which otherwise lacks a typical ending.[6] In this case the phrase "litel tretys" (X.1081) would refer to the *Parson's Tale* alone, rather than to the whole of the *Canterbury Tales.* The theory sounds plausible, especially in light of the phrase "preest over alle preestes" (X.1091) which would be particularly appropriate coming from a parson. Nevertheless, lines X.1085–89, impossible from the Parson, must be original lines written for Chaucer's own voice. Hence, if this theory is correct that the *Retraction*'s opening and closing lines originally belonged to the Parson, then the lines referring to Chaucer's works must have been inserted as a way of making the Parson and the poet, too, dissolve into a single entity. The Host, the Narrator, and the last pilgrim tale-teller all lose their identities as pilgrims bound for Canterbury and become one with the author of the poem. Finally, when Chaucer follows the catalogue of his "sins" with a petition for the three conditions which will elevate his confession to a sacrament—"penitence, confessioun and satisfaccioun" (X.1090)—he places himself and the poem at the threshold between this life and the next, a wanderer from the fourteenth century, bound for the New Jerusalem.

How different this confession is from the usual. It begins fairly enough, a penitent declining to take credit for anything pleasing he may have done, when "oure Lord Jhesu Crist" (X.1081) is the one to be thanked, and taking full blame for anything displeasing. But then the penitent veers away from the moral realm where intent is the crucial consideration (cf. *Friar's Tale,* III.1555–68) to settle on the question of ability, where he seems to argue that he is innocent of willful wrongdoing since his will "wolde ful fayn have seyd bettre if I hadde had konnynge" (X.1082). The voice uttering these words—less a confession at this point than an *apologia*—insists that everything he has done has been intended to advance doctrine, as St. Paul urges (Romans 15:4). Even more surprising, the so-called sins he confesses are not at all the kind discussed earlier in the Parson's penitential. The Narrator (or Chaucer-the-Poet, or Chaucer himself, or all three) confesses poems, whereas the *Parson's Tale* enumerated sins of physical action or physical omission, in general the seven deadly sins. As no one has ever been thought a sinner "that may nat stonde a pul" (*PF*, 164), that is, because he lacks physical ability, so it is difficult to imagine anyone has ever been accused of sin because he lacks poetic ability, that his poems are not of higher quality. Quality, however, does not seem to be the issue as much as subject is.

The two categories of writing Chaucer lists in the *Retraction,* works he wishes to revoke and works for which he gives thanks to God, are obviously separated by subject:

> *Works for which forgiveness is sought*
>> translacions and enditynges of worldly vanitees[7]
>> book of Troilus
>> book of Fame
>> book of the XXV. Ladies
>> book of the Duchesse
>> . . . Parlement of Briddes
>> tales of Caunterbury, thilke that sownen into synne
>> book of the Leoun
>> many another book, if they were in my remembrance
>> many a song
>> many a leccherous lay
> *Works for which gratitude is given to Christ and his mother*
>> Boece de Consolacione
>> bookes of legendes of seintes
>> [Books of] omelies
>> [Books of] moralitee
>> Books of] devocioun

With translations on both sides of this ledger, Chaucer's own literary skill cannot be the factor determining whether they should be praised or blamed. A simpler distinction apparently separates them. Those conveying historical or philosophical truth pass; those conveying literary truth, that is fictions, do not.

No one who has read, say, *Troilus and Criseyde* and thought about it in the same breath with *Boece,* which influenced it greatly, can take Chaucer's two categories seriously. Who would argue that the *Nun's Priest's Tale* is more deserving of censure than versions of saints' lives like the *Second Nun's Tale* and the *Man of Law's Tale*? Surely Chaucer is playing yet another game, reminiscent of the irony he achieved when he pretended to tell a tale *in propria persona,* only to serve up a howler. There is a difference. Where *Tale of Sir Thopas* on its own would please no one, least of all Harry the Innkeeper, the *Retraction*'s apology for profane literature might mollify a puritanical strain, even if it flows in the poet himself. For those who have such an attitude to literature, and perhaps for Chaucer's own doubt, the slate is wiped clean.

A more profound reach of Chaucer's art yet remains. Throughout the *Canterbury Tales* one traditional value after another has been held up to close scrutiny by being placed next to some competing value, as if the poem were inviting readers to select one system over the other. Fables are either to be valued or scorned; wives are to emulate either Alisoun of Bath or Griselda; words are either literally binding or subject to intention. Yet the poem always stops short of endorsing any individual tradition or discarding it for a rival. Chaucer's *Retraction* is another instance of this technique. So soon after the completion of the *Parson's Tale,* a pilgrim catching the penitential spirit would have a natural inclination to confess the kind of sins described there. Like other mortals, Chaucer must have had his share of such offenses against divine law. When he confesses morally indifferent poems, however, he sounds on the verge of claiming that the traditional understanding of sin, that is, versions of the seven deadly sins, should be replaced with a loftier understanding. Aesthetic acts, he seems to say, are moral acts themselves which ought to supersede traditional morality. Nothing in the *Retraction* suggests such a proposal. The two standards exist side by side with equal force, joining yet again the two currents that influence Chaucer throughout his whole performance, the traditional morality of the Old Law–New Law, which provides his focus on the persons and actions of the pilgrims, and aesthetic morality, which governs his representation of these pilgrims and their drives.

If a parallel between Chaucer and the Creator leaps off the page at the opening of *Canterbury Tales,* where the world and all that is in it are generated anew, the end of the poem casts this parallel in relief. Confessing poems at a moment when sins should be in mind suggests that the true *imitatio dei* asks more than the avoidance of wrongdoing; it calls for another level of morality, the *quid agas* of scholastic tradition, which points to what one must *do* to gain salvation. To follow in God's image one must also be a Maker. Here the parallel is perhaps strongest. The glory of god is not manifest in the sanctification of individuals who struggle against their appetites—when they make their "plough down sillion shine," as Hopkins would put it—but in the selfless, unlimited love of the Creator for the Created. Chaucer's redemptive plea separates his poem at last from Dante's great *Commedia*. Whereas *Paradiso* brings Dante and his guide to heaven itself, as if exile were over and salvation won, Chaucer remains a suppliant before the gates, humbly and reverently beseeching that the labor of his life—not the work he has produced, but the working he has done—might deserve an eternal home. His appeal rests not in his own sanctity, nor in the beauty of the characters he shapes, who after all are hewn as roughly as we are, but in the devotion, care, and love with which he shapes them.

Appendix

The Chaucer Portrait at the
University of California, Los Angeles

UCLA's English Department, an unlikely place for either a stroke of good fortune or mystery, benefited from both some years ago when it luckily acquired the sober, worried portrait appearing as the frontispiece of this book, and then subsequently discovered what a fascinating artifact it had.

What is known of the story begins in 1959, when Professor Lawrence Clark Powell was on one of his frequent book-buying tours to England on behalf of the undergraduate library that now bears his name. As he wrote in a letter in 1981, "I often went a-buying with the late David Magee, as I recall in my Foreword to his memoirs, Infinite Riches. I believe he was with me the day I bought the Chaucer in the wondrously cluttered basement of Stevens and Browne's Duke Street premises. A pity people die."

Nearly everyone thought the portrait a somewhat amateurish effort, though strikingly similar to the most famous likeness of the poet, the Seddon-Murray Chaucer in the Houghton Library at Harvard. For fifteen years it hung in the English Department's Reading Room, largely unnoticed, until the late distinguished Professor William Matthews, fresh from sleuthing through the Cotswolds, Yorkshire, and Middle English dialects for presumed and authentic Thomas Malorys, and reluctant to lay his tools aside, was curious about the painting's provenance. In particular, he wondered if the hand that painted Chaucer's portrait might also have touched the poet. Intrigued by the crude oak support, he asked Professor Rainer Berger, a specialist in radiocarbon dating, to conduct some tests. To the astonishment of all, Berger's three independent tests all pointed to the year 1400, plus or minus 15, the very year Geoffrey Chaucer died. At least we had a *terminus a quo*. That is, the oak panel came from a tree that had been felled close to the year 1400. Some months after this happy discovery Will Matthews, a lovable cockney of a thousand interests, was summoned to the eighth sphere, where he perhaps smiles down on our attempts to answer questions he raised. A pity people die.[1]

Of three kinds of evidence on which any portrait painting is to be dated—historical, scientific, and stylistic—the historical offers little help. Stevens and Browne could offer nothing of the painting's history. Nevertheless a seal on the back of the oak panel has been identified by the College of Arms as that of the Smythe family, whose genealogy goes back to the late fifteenth century when they held property in and around Lincoln.

The scientific evidence is somewhat more helpful. Apart from the intriguing radiocarbon dating, examinations performed by the Los Angeles County Museum of Art indicate that nothing was painted beneath the portrait, that the ground, a standard lead white, and the pigments were in use continuously between 1400 and 1600. Something further might be said, however, of the color green which, according to the Museum, is composed of iron, magnesium, aluminum, and potassium. Now this is most interesting because after 1500 Terre Verte was always composed of either azurite or (more rarely due to the expense) ground lapis. Though we do not know the composition of Terre Verte before 1500, early-fifteenth-century manuscript illuminations show a very bright, transparent green, suitable for depicting grass, which was composed of metallic substances, usually copper. While it is true that the best contemporary authority, Cennino Cennini (writing during the first quarter of the fifteenth century), does not describe the procedure for making this color, his work chiefly reflects the techniques of northern Italy and thus would not be expected to take notice of a practice among the illuminators of English manuscripts.[2] In any case, the practice apparently died out by the end of the century. It seems, therefore, that the Terre Verte in the UCLA portrait suggests a date earlier than 1500. Additionally, and perhaps more importantly, the portrait's Terre Verte may point to the influence of an illuminator's workshop.

Finally, any attempt to date the portrait must take into account stylistic arguments and common sense. The oak panel itself raises several questions. Such a panel would normally be prepared from wood carefully hewn for the specific purpose of portrait painting and seasoned for several years. By contrast, this hand-hewn panel, deeply dished at the back and containing a large branch grain, is far beneath the quality of most surviving panels. It seems better suited to the tentative strokes of an apprentice than to the skill of an accomplished artist. Yet the panel shows evidence of an atelier working to the exacting standards described by Cennino Cennini. Its two boards are fitted together very carefully and held in place with high quality tape. As with most medieval panels, the glue—a combination of gelatin and gesso—shows no sign of weakening after several centuries. If the same level of care was maintained for the panel's seasoning, if not for its quality, the wood may have had a long career, perhaps as a piece of furniture or a door, before it became scrap wood pressed into the service of art.

The subject, too, gives cause to speculate. If the low quality of the oak panel seems out of place for the shop that used it, the subject of the painting seems equally out of place for the increasingly popular practice of portraiture. Portraits of the recently deceased—the genre is indicated by the date of death in the upper right quarter and a coat of arms with family name in the upper left—were usually commissioned to memorialize the wealthy and the well born. Yet from the perspective of the fourteenth and fifteenth centuries, Chaucer was not widely considered a distinguished figure. He was the descendant of wine merchants, held a few civil service positions, and entertained friends with his pen. Certainly he had a following among the litterati. But such as these have never carried much weight in important circles, either in his time or ours. That Chaucer is its subject at all is the most unusual fact about the portrait.

A final stylistic point should also be noted. The brightness of the portrait, its sharp lines, the greater skill evident in small details—beads, buttons, penner, and attached loop—than in the wide open spaces of the face, hands, and garment, where texture is entirely absent, all imply familiarity with the illuminator's craft. Even the detail of two fingers of the right hand pointing past the penner toward the breast could argue familiarity with the practices of manuscript illumination. In countless manuscript illustrations a clear distinction is always maintained between ordinary personages, even saints, and Christ. Whenever the former are shown gesturing, they always do so with the index finger alone. When Christ is depicted, whether gesturing or not, His index and middle fingers are always joined, pointing outward from the body, and shown separated from the remaining fingers which are curled back. Chaucer's right hand, with its inward-pointing two-finger gesture almost dominating the portrait, may have been intended to symbolize both the creative impulse of the poet and the divine inspiration that resided within. Additionally the painting shows a marked influence from the northern continent, where the specific details of a coat of arms, date of death, name, and emblem indicating the subject's profession, became standard features of this genre. This curious mixture of Dutch composition and English illuminator's skills suggests a craftsman originally trained as a manuscript illuminator now converting himself into a portrait painter to cater to the new fashion. If true, a date around 1490, when manuscript illumination in general was in decline, is even more likely, and two other facts become highly pertinent.

Several other portraits of Chaucer are almost identical to the UCLA Chaucer: same poor-quality support, same location of coat of arms, same folds in garment and headwear, same gesture with the right hand. One, the "Sloane" portrait in the National Portrait Gallery, though similar in all other respects, extends the figure to a full-length portrait, as it appears on the dust jacket of Donald R. Howard's biography of Chaucer. Another, once owned by the Duke of Argyll, was offered at auction by the Lubin Galleries of New York in the late 1980s. Apparently more than one art student took the same class. The second fact explains why Chaucer was so favorite a subject: he was readily available as a model in the miniatures of Hoccleve's *Regement of Princes* (ca. 1411–12). Indeed, two of the manuscripts of the *Regement* have had their Chaucer miniatures cut out, in one case by "summe ffuryous ffoole [with] a barren Brayne," as a sixteenth-century hand reprimands at the bottom of the leaf.[3]

In light of the facts and reasoning just outlined, one might be excused a fanciful speculation perfectly suited to the self-effacing poet. Imagine a handful of student artists poring over a pilfered picture of Chaucer, as they practice an art form different from the one their model revered perhaps more than all other earthly endeavors.

Notes

Chapter 1. The Energy of Creation

1. See Stevens and Cawley (1993, p. 325, line 259).

2. Patterson (1987, p. 53). For a somewhat different view of New Historicism as a critical mode see Pearsall (1986).

3. See Elbow (1975).

4. For the bipolar view that the poem advances one or the other of each of these antitheses, rather than embracing both, see Rogers (1986, p. 14).

5. Howard (1976). Cf. Astell (1996), Frese (1991), Allen and Moritz (1981), Jordan (1967), Lumiansky (1955), Baldwin (1955), and Kittredge (1915).

6. See, e.g., Mâle (1958) and Lewis (1964).

7. While taking aim at a different offense, the Ellesmere editor's grammatical emendations, Pearsall neatly wings with wit the error of substituting a modern predisposition for a medieval: "Ellesmere presents a text, not of what Chaucer wrote, but of what his editorial executors thought he should have written, or would have written if he had known as well as they did what he wished to write" (1985, p. 11).

8. Pearsall (1985, pp. 24–28), responding to Howard (1976), who, quoting Northrop Frye on another subject, calls the poem "unfinished but complete" (p. 1).

9. Donaldson (1970a, p. 193).

10. See Donaldson (1970a, pp. 194–95), and L. Benson (1981, pp. 77–120).

11. N. F. Blake (1985, p. 80).

12. Boltzman (1974), often called the father of entropy, was the first to develop a formula for measuring it. See also Bridgman (1941).

13. On cybernetics see Wiener (1948), who acknowledges a debt to James Clerk Maxwell (1868). Although "cybernetic" has recently been appropriated to describe the sci-fi merger of man and machine (see Porush 1985), here the word conveys Norbert Wiener's original sense, that all systems have innate tendencies to correct themselves.

14. The relation between entropy and cybernetics may be illustrated by the fa-

miliar example of two round-bottomed bowls, one inverted with a marble balanced on top, the other right side up with another marble inside. Perturbing the inverted bowl causes an increasing tendency for the marble to move away from its point of balance, thus illustrating a disorderly tendency. Perturbing the other bowl illustrates a tendency to apply correctives ("cybernetic" is cognate with "govern"), seen in the fluctuations that will ultimately return the marble to its original position. Though the two motions appear to contradict each other, they merely illustrate different perspectives. The marble toppled from the inverted bowl will ultimately come to rest in a broader system. In scientific circles "perturbation" signifies an irregularity in a heavenly body's orbit. Cf. Chaucer's description of "likerous folk" (*PF*, 79–80) who "whirl aboute th'erthe alwey in peyne."

15. See Haken (1984).

16. For the examples in this paragraph—all well known to scientists, if not to literary critics—I am indebted to Haken (1984, p. 44).

17. For a fascinating discussion of information theory's breakthrough in all systems studies, see Campbell (1982, pp. 15–124).

18. Reductionism, as understood by Barbour (1966), is "the attributing of reality exclusively to the smallest constituents of the world, and the tendency to interpret higher levels of organisation in terms of lower levels" (p. 52).

19. Pattee (1970, pp. 117–36).

20. Interest in the relationship between Dante and Chaucer has been exploding of late. See, among others, Boitani (1983), Shoaf (1983), Schless (1984), Taylor (1989), Neuse (1991), and Astell (1996).

21. Boitani (1983, pp. 121–22). Cf. Howard (1976, p. 43).

22. Dante, *Epistola 10* [to Cangrande], sec. 8. On Dante's supposed authorship of the letter to Cangrande, see H. A. Kelly (1989), a response by Robert Hollander (1993), and an exchange between Kelly and Hollander in *Lectura Dantis* (Kelly 1994b and Hollander 1994).

23. For this and subsequent points about chaos, order, and transcendence in the three canticles, see Dickson (1980, pp. 111–16).

24. For a discussion of transcendence in *Paradiso*, see Taylor (1989, pp. 175ff.).

25. Anderson (1980, p. 18). See also Guénon (1951, pp. 51–52).

Chapter 2. The Organization of the *Canterbury Tales*

1. Though unusual in the present context, "mating game" provides a term appropriate for birds and the human beings they allegorize, while also avoiding the possible confusion between love and sex, a concern the *Parlement* does not address.

2. For a learned discussion of how Chaucer's thought, especially in the *Knight's Tale*, is informed by the philosophical and psychological rift represented by Scotus and Ockham, see Roney (1990, pp. 37–38).

3. Emerson Brown (1975, pp. 266 [quoting Charles O. McDonald] and 269). For Chaucer's indebtedness to Ovid, see Fyler (1979).

4. Alanus's description begins in Prose I, line 4, and continues to Meter II, line 23 (Alanus 1908).

5. This and the following quotation are from Donaldson (1970b, p. 153).

6. For Chaucer's general understanding of the theory of the elements, see Curry (1926), Wood (1970), North (1988), and the notes in L. Benson (1987) at I.420, 429–34. For the argument that Chaucer's knowledge of the science of his day came from Vincent of Beauvais, see Aiken (1935, 1936, and 1956). Though Alanus de Insulis does not mention the four elements in his account of creation in *The Complaint of Nature,* he does stress the conjunction of opposites (Prose IV, 330–33; Alanus 1908).

7. On the parallels between these opening lines and the account of Creation in *Genesis,* see Nitzsche (1978), but cf. Hoffman (1954). For the dual account of Creation, see Peterfreund (1986, p. 30).

8. Cf. Dame Nature's comment in Alanus de Insulis's *De planctu Naturae*—to be sure, on a subject different from Chaucer's fair chain of love—that "from [Nature's] universal law man alone exempts himself by a nonconformist withdrawal" (Prose 4; Alanus 1980, p. 131).

9. On ring structure in Ovid, see Otis (1970); in *Beowulf,* see Niles (1979).

10. Pearsall (1985, p. 246).

11. *The Riverside Chaucer* glosses *despendest tyme* (VII.931) "to waste time." However, because the Franklyn's complaint that his son "despende / And lese al that he hath" (V.690–91) may emphasize the act of counting out money as it is spent, the Host's outburst at VII.929–35 may mean "you do nothing more than count syllables." Moreover, the association of *tyme* with the making of poetry, both here and at the end of the *Book of the Duchess* (1331), suggests that "tyme" may also carry a meaning close to "meter."

12. For a generous view of these two tales, see the excellent article by Lee Patterson (1989).

13. Burrow (1971, rpt. 1984).

14. See Manly and Rickert (1940), esp. the charts following II.494, conveniently reprinted in L. Benson (1981, pp. 118–20).

15. Cf. Astell (1996, p. 156). For the claim that this methodology is hopeless, see Rogers (1986, p. 9).

16. Frese (1991, p. 203). Cf. L. Benson (1981, p. 111): "Blocks D, E, and F are, from the standpoint of internal allusions, the most tightly linked of all the Blocks."

17. The argument I am making from the extant manuscripts appeals to what Jean Piaget calls "operational structuralism," where relations among elements are more important than either the parts or the whole. See Piaget (1970, pp. 8–9).

18. Evidence that Chaucer intended Fragment VII to follow immediately after Fragment VI "is almost invariable" (L. Benson 1987, p. 111).

Chapter 3. The First Fragment

1. Howard (1976) concludes his section "The Tales of Civil Conduct" with a convincing discussion of how Fragment I degenerates in social class, setting, or-

der, language, endings, opportunistic lovers, and the disappearance of Chaucer's voice (pp. 245–47). See also Mandel (1992, pp. 130–45).

2. Modern awareness of medieval number composition (or *zahlenkomposition,* to acknowledge the language in which this awareness was most active) perhaps began with Vincent Hopper (1938) and Ernst Curtius (1953, p. 505). See also the essays by R. A. Peck, A. K. Hieatt, and C. S. Singleton in Eckhardt (1980).

Chapter 4. The Imperfect Knight and His Perfect *Tale*

1. See, respectively, Hearnshaw (1928, pp. 25–27), Howard (1976, pp. 94–97), and Jones (1980).

2. Cf. I.72, I.422, and III.1956.

3. Editors usually read "reysed" (I.54) as a neutral word. But see Webb (1947, pp. 289–96).

4. See Frost (1949, pp. 290–304), Schweitzer (1981, pp. 13–45), and Patterson (1991, p. 207).

5. Schmidt (1969, pp. 107–17), and Lloyd (1959, pp. 11–25).

6. On the *Knight's Tale* in the general context of the *Parlement of Fowls,* though not on the point made here, see Burlin (1977, pp. 95–111).

7. Although Roney (1990) comes to different conclusions from those offered here, arguing that Palamon and Arcite represent positions in the scholastic debate between the Will and the Intellect, respectively (p. 57), the semantic evidence she presents in Appendix A (pp. 273–81) supports the similarity of the two knights. See also p. 56, n. 25.

8. Cf. Gayre (1961, p. 24), Wagner (1956, p. 19), and Boutell (1978, p. 108). For a full discussion of the fourteenth century's attitude to chivalric ideals, though for a different purpose from the one argued here, see Patterson (1991, pp. 165–230).

9. The *Prologue* to the *Legend of Good Women* refers to Chaucer's having written "the love of Palamon and Arcite" (F.420, G.408), a probable reference to an early version of the *Knight's Tale.* If, as is generally assumed, *PLGW* was composed immediately after completion of the *Troilus and Criseyde,* a work of the mid-1380s, then the "Palamon and Arcite" had to have preceded that date to be mentioned there. Hence "Palamon and Arcite" must have been composed close to the 1380 date usually assigned to the translation of the *Consolation.*

10. Dedeck-Héry (1952, pp. 170–71).

11. It is interesting to note that neither Palamon nor Arcite complains of injustice at being sentenced to prison for life, but each frequently accuses the other of treason after they become rivals in love. See lines I.1111, 1130, 1142, 1145, 1151, and 1154.

12. Cf. Irving (1995, p. 47).

13. *Inf.,* V.39.

14. The division of a character into component parts follows a familiar medieval expository technique. Cf. *De Nuptiis Philologiae et Mercurii* and the *Debate Be-*

tween the Body and Soul. We could add as well the Black Knight and the Dreamer in the *Book of the Duchess,* as I have elsewhere argued (Condren 1971), and even the allegorical persons of the Trinity.

15. For a discussion of figures in medieval literature that have simultaneous literal and allegorical functions, see Robert W. Frank (1968, pp. 218–22).

16. Schweitzer (1981, p. 29); Neuse (1962, pp. 299–315).

17. Donaldson (1975, pp. 1104–8).

18. For a comprehensive view of gardens in Chaucer, see Howes (1997), especially pp. 87–89, for a discussion of the garden as prison.

19. On the silliness of Palamon and Arcite as young lovers, see Underwood (1959, pp. 455–69), Neuse (1962, pp. 299–315), and Kolve (1984, pp. 139–49).

20. Cf. Muscatine (1964): "Saturn, disorder, nothing more nor less, is the agent of Arcite's death" (p. 190).

21. See Elbow (1975, pp. 79–89).

22. Ian Robinson (1972) argues that Theseus's arrival at this grove constitutes evidence that he represents Destiny (p. 117). But Blake (1973, p. 15) suggests more convincingly that lines I.1661–99 merely affirm Destiny's control over even Theseus's coming and going.

Chapter 5. The Miller, the Reeve, the Cook

1. For the parallels between the *Knight's Tale* and the *Miller's Tale* see, among others, Hieatt (1970, pp. 4–6).

2. It is to the excesses of the "dramatic principle" that Jordan (1967, p. 126) refers here. See Kittredge (1915) for the origin of the dramatic principle and Lumiansky (1955) for its fullest expression. Leicester (1990) may stand for the opposite extreme, which sees characters energized only by the words on a page.

3. The word "boundaries" comes from behavioral psychology. Some personality disorders are marked by a patient's inability to separate his interests from those of others, making him intrude into the spaces, activities, and lives of others. See Bensman (1979) and Hartman (1991).

4. Emelye's acquiescence, both in mid-tale where she agrees to accept the suitor who most wants her and later when she passes silently from Arcite's future to Palamon's, has recently drawn fire in feminist circles, where she is seen as a powerless possession in an insensitive patriarchal society. See in particular the finely written argument by Dinshaw (1989, pp. 106–7). Taken as a whole, however, the *Knight's Tale* is equally matriarchal. Theseus is returning from a land of women when we first meet him; a group of women prevail upon him to march against Thebes (I.898–974); and women later dissuade him from executing Palamon and Arcite battling in the grove (I.748ff.). Indeed all the action in the tale is undertaken in conflict with, at the behest of, or for the sake of Woman.

5. See Condren (1985, pp. 235–39).

6. For the medieval tendency to draw iconographic significance from all things and for these pertinent verses by Alain de Lille, with an accompanying translation

by Frederick Brittin, see Kolve (1984, pp. 59–62): "Omnis mundi creatura / Quasi liber et pictura / Nobis est in speculum; / Nostrae vitae, nostrae mortis, / Nostri status, nostrae sortis / Fidele signaculum" [All creation, like a book or a picture, is a mirror to us—a true figure of our life, our death, our condition, our lot].

Chapter 6. The *Man of Law's Tale*

1. For a discussion of the Host's backward look at the *Reeve's Tale,* see Kolve (1984, pp. 288–89).

2. The strategy of letting Fragment I bring its milieu down to a social and ethical zero in order to prepare for a second beginning is not without precedent in Chaucer. The same technique occurs in *Troilus and Criseyde,* where the principals are portrayed very early as positively antipathetic to love—Troilus because he must save face among his fellows, Criseyde because she has high expectations of Hector's attention. Pandarus thus faces a difficult task in promoting a match because he must overcome a stronger disinclination than might be the case with others more receptive to the idea of love.

3. Kolve (1984, p. 298): "As best I can judge . . . audiences would not have thought the story of Custance a fiction at all: they would have perceived it as history." The next quotation appears on this same page.

4. Kolve (1984, p. 307) reproduces as figure 137 an illustration of the Constance story appearing in a manuscript of Gower's *Confessio amantis.* Though Kolve suggests that Constance is "perhaps giving thanks for safe arrival" and that her gesture in the foreground is not clear, the illustration may be a detailed gloss on the allegory of the spread of Christianity, making one wonder if Gower too was not perhaps as aware of the allegory in Constance's story as Chaucer is in the *Man of Law's Tale.* In the remotest background are stars and easily identified tall objects, navigational aids that mariners—even modern ones lacking electronics—have always used to sail about the globe. In the foreground Constance gazes lovingly on two seedlings, her palms upturned in a gesture encouraging them to rise and flourish. The seedlings perhaps represent the Christian faith, recently planted in a remote land, while the symbols on Constance's dress may refer to the Gospels, the method by which the faith is sown, for the repeated pattern of three or four clustered circles, and in one instance four circles clustered around a larger fifth, reproduces the onion-topped towers by which Eastern Orthodox churches represent the four evangelists positioned around Christ. The three figures standing on the gangplank defy precise identification, as Kolve notes, but their expressions and especially their hands suggest that one ruler has accepted Christianity (the one in the middle, hands joined in prayer, face looking heavenward) and two remain unconvinced (hands extended, palms down, as if to say "no, thank you," and distinctly unwelcoming expressions).

5. There can be little doubt that Chaucer often uses "lamb" as a signal for Christ. In the whole of the *Canterbury Tales,* according to Tatlock and Kennedy (1963), the word, or one of its forms, appears only eleven times. Three clericals

(the Prioress, the Second Nun, and the Parson) account for five occurrences
(VII.581, 584; VIII.199; and twice in X.791). On two occasions it indicates innocent farm animals (I.3704; VI.102). And the four remaining uses refer to Custance
in MLT (II.452, 459, 617) and Griselda in ClT (IV.538).

Chapter 7. Stability and the Language of Agreements

1. Kittredge (1912, pp. 435–67). See also Kittredge (1915, pp. 71, 147) and
Hammond (1908, p. 256).

2. Differing from Ellesmere (El) are: Gg, Ad², Ha³, Tc¹, Hk, Sl¹, En², and Dl.
For this and all other observations in this chapter about the manuscripts of the
Canterbury Tales I rely on Manly and Rickert (1940).

3. The eighteen manuscripts which follow the Non-Ellesmere's ring structure
are: He, Ne, Cx¹, Ha³ (missing only WB), Ln, Py, Nl, Lc, Mg, Ha², Sl¹, En², Bw,
Ry², Ld², Ry¹, Pw, and Mm. Three other manuscripts follow this order very
closely, but either lack FranT (Ra²) or have it in the wrong place (Fl, Il). Another
manuscript Dl, is also close, but it is missing FrT and SuT, and has MLT intervening between MerT and WB. Three other manuscripts (Cp, Sl², and La) would be
either Non-Ellesmere types, if Me were moved to a location between Sq and WB,
or Ellesmere types, if Sq were moved to a location between Me and Fk.

4. The eleven manuscripts that follow the Ellesmere order are: El, Gg (without
links), Dd (missing the Sq-Fk link), En¹, Ds, Cn, Ma, En³, Ad¹, Bo² (missing the
Sq-Fk link), and Ha⁴ (missing lines V.617–1223). As remarked in the previous
note, three other manuscripts (Cp, Sl², and La) would be added to the list of
Ellesmere types if their Sq were moved to a location between the Me and Fk. But,
of course, they would also become Non-Ellesmere types by moving the Merchant
to a location between the Squire and Wife of Bath.

5. Though in some manuscripts Fragment II ends with a small epilogue spoken
by the Host, most modern editors assume Chaucer dropped this section. Similarly,
the Host has a brief epilogue to the *Nun's Priest's Tale* in a few manuscripts. Here
too editors believe Chaucer later moved the lines, in slightly revised form, to the
Monk's Tale (VII.1941–48). If we also follow suit by dropping the epilogues to
Fragments II and VII, then the claim stands: there is no fragment other than Fragment IV that ends with the Host speaking.

6. Christine Ryan Hilary, who prepared the explanatory notes to the Wife of
Bath for *The Riverside Chaucer,* understands "withouten" to mean "not counting," implying the following interpretation for lines I.460–61: that the Wife had
five husbands, not counting other liaisons in her youth. But an equally plausible
reading leads to an opposite conclusion regarding the Wife's sexual experience as
a single woman: she had five husbands but was without other youthful experience.

7. For an approachable study of medieval promises from a legal point of view,
see Arnold (1976, pp. 321–34).

8. Cf. H. A. Kelly (1975, p. 176): "Marriage was made by the consent of the

bride and groom. No other permission, authorization, witness, minister, ceremony, or action was required for the marriage to take effect." The clear implication is that any equivocation would constitute a defect in the "consent of the bride and groom" and therefore that the *sine qua non* for marriage would not be present.

Chapter 8. Two Weavers from Bath

1. Curry (1926, pp. 117–18).
2. Robertson (1962, p. 330).
3. Ibid., pp. 317–31.
4. Robert A. Pratt (1961, pp. 45–77).
5. *The Canterbury Tales,* p. 77.
6. Cf. the "public project" and "reread text" in Leicester (1990, pp. 79–81).
7. By delaying her story until she first establishes her legitimacy, the Wife employs a defensive strategy similar to the Pardoner's, as many have noted. Both pilgrims seek legitimacy first, performance later.
8. On Chaucer's heavy borrowing from Jerome's *Epistola adversus Jovinianum* see, in addition to the notes in L. Benson (1987), Woolcombe (pp. 293–306), Mead (1901, pp. 391ff.), and many others. For a witty discussion of Jerome's outrageous misreading of John 4:6ff., see Donaldson (1977, esp. pp. 5–7).
9. Hanning (1985, pp. 9ff.) includes a thorough discussion of the implications of textual misinterpretation.
10. Had she read the text more closely, the Wife's rhetorical question might have asked why the *sixth* man was not a husband as the first five were. But then she would not have produced the effect she seeks by citing the very number uttered by Christ— "Thou hast yhad fyve housbondes" (III.17)—whose words imply the legitimacy of five, as many husbands as the Wife of Bath herself has had.

The Latin *Vulgate* does not render the distinction between "husband" and "man" as clearly as Chaucer's Middle English, since *vir* may be translated by either. Nevertheless, to appreciate that Christ's allusion to wrongdoing has a different meaning from the one seized by the Wife and St. Jerome see: John 4:16–18, a meaning that the Samaritan woman herself confirms in verse 29.

11. See Kiser (1991, p. 137).
12. For a discussion of the parallel pairs, text/gloss, body/abuse, see the discussion of the Wife of Bath in Dinshaw (1989, pp. 113–31).
13. Donaldson (1985, p. 137).
14. Howard (1976, p. 251).
15. Cf. Peter Lombard, *Sententiae,* IV, xxv, 5–6, and the Middle English poem *Pearl,* lines 409–20.
16. See Ephesians 5:22–24.
17. While equality between husband and wife seems clear, e.g., in 1 Corinthians 7:3–4, its acceptance must have been slight. Speaking in the *De Trinitate* (12, 12) of the relationship of higher reason to lower reason, Augustine resorts to the analogy with a husband's superiority over his wife. And H. A. Kelly (1975, p. 41),

points out, "the woman was considered equal mainly in the matter of sexual intercourse. . . . In most other matters, she was to be subordinate and obedient to her husband." See also the Franklin's remarks (V.751–52). Though a woman like the Wife of Bath would probably not have been literate, for an interesting discussion of how literate women had to teach themselves how to read as women, see Schibanoff (1986, pp. 83–106).

18. St. Thomas Aquinas, *Summa Theologiae* (1969), *tertia pars,* q. 29, a. 2: "Respondeo dicendum quod matrimonium sive conjugium dicitur verum ex hoc quod suam perfectionem attingit. Duplex est autem rei perfectio: prima et secunda. Prima quidem perfectio in ipsa forma rei consistit, ex qua speciem sortitur: secunda vero perfectio consistit in operatione rei, per quam res aliqualiter suum finem attingit. Forma autem matrimonii consistit in quadam indivisibili coniunctione animorum, per quam unus conjugum indivisibiliter alteri fidem servare tenetur. Finis autem matrimonii est proles generanda et educanda: ad quorum primum pervenitur per concubitum conjugalem; ad secundum, per alia opera viri et uxoris, quibus sibi invicem obsequuntur ad prolem nutriendam."

19. According to H. A. Kelly (1975, p. 260n), Bishop Otto of Lucca is wrongly identified in *PL* as Hugh of St. Victor.

20. "Conjugii autem institutio duplex est. . . . Prima, ut natura multiplicaretur; secunda, ut natura exciperetur, et vitium cohiberetur" (*PL*, CXCII, 908). Though the translation of Lombard is my own, I am indebted to the excellent discussion of this subject in Mogan (1970, pp. 123–41). Many commentators, and to a lesser extent Mogan himself, construe Lombard's second *bonum* of marriage to be the slaking of concupiscence. (Mogan [p. 124] discussing Lombard: "As with Augustine, marriage since the Fall . . . is not by precept but by indulgence, 'propter vitandam fornicationem' [*PL*, CXCII, 909].") However, I do not find in Lombard the suggestion that the only kind of *vitium* from which nature is to be lifted (*exciperetur*) is the sin of lechery. He means, I believe, that marriage, through the spouses' support of each other, may elevate them toward a perfection of their nature.

21. "At Dunmow, near Chelmsford in Essex, a flitch [side] of bacon was offered to any married couple who lived a year [and a day] without quarrelling or repenting of their union" (Robinson, note to lines 217–18, in L. Benson 1987).

22. Huppé (1967, p. 120). F. M. Salter (1954, pp. 1–13), has partly anticipated the argument presented here by suggesting that the Wife's bluster, arrogance, and garrulity are designed to conceal her barrenness.

23. The Wife does not make it clear whether her fifth husband is dead or alive at the time of the pilgrimage to Canterbury. Line III.47 implies he is still alive, but lines III.504, 525, and especially 526–27 speak of him in a style normally reserved for the dead.

24. The fourteenth century knew nothing of modern theories of sound waves. Nevertheless, it is clear from the golden eagle's witty discussion of sound in *Hous of Fame* (711–852) that Chaucer associated sound with a movement of energy through the air.

25. On the knowledge of contraception and abortive techniques during the

Middle Ages, see the *Parson's Tale* (X.575–76) and Noonan (1966, pp. 200–30).

26. The Wife's 144-line quotation of herself extends from III.235 to III.378. Fifteen of these lines contain the Wife's accusations against her husbands: III.235–47, 308–9. Ninety-one lines are taken up with her paraphrases of his accusations against her: III.248–61, 263–75, 278–80, 282–83, 285–306, 337–56, and 362–78.

27. See the notes to lines III.235–378 in F. N. Robinson (1957).

28. Cf. III.153, 158–59, and 161 with 1 Corinthians 7:3–4 and Ephesians 5:33.

29. Cf. Donaldson (1985, pp. 137–38), admiring III.453–80 and Mistress Quickly's speech in *King Henry V,* II.iii.9–26: "[they are] passages of unrivaled emotional effectiveness, passages that are as splendid tributes to human vitality as any I know."

30. Kurath and Kuhn (1952–86). See also the *Oxford English Dictionary:* pith, *sb.*

31. According to Hopkins (1964–65, pp. 310–13), menarche occurred between 12 and 14 in the classical period. For the early Middle Ages the most popular gynecological text was evidently *De passionibus mulierum,* attributed to Trottula, who places menarche at fourteen, though mss. vary. Despite this variety of opinion, no authority places menarche earlier than twelve when the Wife of Bath began marrying (III.4). Although there is less information on the date of menopause, the majority of Trottula's manuscripts list fifty, an age which must be close to the Wife's when we meet her. I am indebted for these references to Bullough and Campbell (1980, pp. 317–25, esp. pp. 323–25).

32. Only Xanthippe does not fit this model. But Socrates' celebrated willingness to endure marital travail, as evident in the brilliant retort of III.732, has nearly canonized him as the patron saint of tormented husbands.

33. R. W. Hanning (1985) was one of the first to notice that the Wife's lifelong battle has been with "texts—by Ovid, Walter Map, Jean de Meun, Eustache Deschamps—that perpetuate stereotypes of women as temptresses, gold diggers, whores, and termagants" (p. 18).

34. Specific charges made by the knight and rebutted by the hag are not identical. Knight: *loothly, oold,* and *of so lough a kynde* (III.1100–1). Hag: *foul, oold, poore* (III.1063), and lacking *gentillesse, poverte, eelde* (III.1109–1216).

35. Though F. N. Robinson (1957) glosses *Gat-tothed* (I.468) as "gap-toothed, with teeth set wide apart," there is little evidence in English for alternation between *t* and *p*. The argument rests on either the borrowing of ON *glat* (crevasse) or the expression "gate-toothed." But the former is a strained etymology and the latter never caught on in English. The expression derives more likely from OE *gat* (i.e., goat-toothed). Robinson dismisses this suggestion as an "unlikely etymology," presumably because Old English long *a* normally rose to long *o* in Chaucer's English (cf. *goot* in I.688 and VIII.886). Nevertheless, canonized phrases often retain their original form (cf. NE "goodbye," God be with ye). If "Gat-tothed" is such a term, its meaning would be roughly equivalent to NE "buck-toothed" and be perfectly consistent with Curry's argument (*PMLA* 37:45, noted by Robinson) that the term implies "boldness, falseness, gluttony, and lasciviousness."

Chapter 9. Two Witty Glosses

1. To avoid confusion, references to the pilgrims who tell the tales discussed in this chapter will appear capitalized, in unitalicized form, and in modern spelling, thus: Friar, Summoner. References to the leading characters these pilgrims respectively create will appear in lower case, italicized, and in middle English spelling, thus: *somonour, frere.*

2. On the verbal pyrotechnics of the *Summoner's Tale,* see Beichner (1956, pp. 135–44).

3. Cf. Whittock (1968, p. 133): "The fiend and the summoner become sworn brothers, they are fundamentally alike, but their dedication to wickedness entails a brotherhood of betrayal."

4. "And whoever does good deeds will enter eternal life; but those who do evil will enter eternal fire" (Matthew 25:46; cf. John 5:29).

5. Burlin (1977, pp. 162–64), following Passon (1968, pp. 166–71).

6. Though *repente* can have the force of changing one's mind (*Complaint of Mars,* 17) or of ceasing (*Complaint of Venus,* 56–64), its usual sense is to be sorry for acting wrongly. Of the ninety-three uses of the word and its variants listed in the Tatlock and Kennedy *Concordance* (1963), twenty-two occur in connection with formal sin.

7. The *frere*'s first reaction to the fart is to mention the insult (III.2154) and his promise of vengeance (III.2155). Only after three more references to rage (III.2160, 2161, 2166) and two more to the insult (III.2176, 2179) does the *frere* give his lone reference to blasphemy (III.2183). One more charge of "odious meschief" (III.2190) prepares us for a final promise of vengeance (III.2211). We may doubt that the *frere*'s calling Thomas a "false blasphemour" (III.2213) has religious force, since it occurs in a sentence whose thrust promises to slander Thomas all over town for exacting a solemn promise to perform an impossible task.

Chapter 10. Two Kinds of Agreement

1. Spearing (1972, chap. 4). This chapter does not appear in the first edition, published in 1964.

2. See Bowden (1964, p. 128) and Speirs (1951, p. 152). On the analogy between Griselda and Abraham, whom God ordered to sacrifice his son Isaac, see Muscatine (1964, p. 193) and Whittock (1968, p. 145).

3. See Robertson (1962, p. 376), Howard (1976, p. 259), and Steinmetz (1977, pp. 38–54).

4. Spearing (1972, chap. 4), Salter (1962), and Sledd (1953, pp. 73–82).

5. Cf. Steinmetz (1977): "Patience in adversity is a moral point worth making, though a modern author would make the point more effectively by making it less hyperbolically" (p. 38).

6. Hansen (1992, p. 189). See also Dinshaw (1989, chap. 5).

7. Severs (1972) reprints both Petrarch's text and an anonymous prose French translation of Petrarch, *Le Livre Griseldis* (pp. 254–89). For the view that Chau-

cer knew Boccaccio's version of the story that appears in the *Decameron,* see Farnham (1918, p. 290) and Pratt (1966, p. xvii).

8. It is less likely that the phrase derives from St. Paul, 1 Corinthians 15:52, where it refers to the instantaneous change at the Last Judgment, than from Bede, where it measures the span of life compared to eternity. See Plummer (1896, vol. 13). If this phrase is indeed indebted to Bede, it probably came from the Old English translation of the *Historia Ecclesiastica* rather than from Bede's Latin, for Chaucer's words are closer to the OE, *ac þæt bi an eagan brythm and þæt læsste fæc,* than to the Latin, *sed tamen parvissimo spatio serenitatis ad momentum excurso.*

9. Revelations 14:1–5. Cf. the *Prioress's Tale,* where a martyred clergeon is said to follow "The white Lamb celestial" (VII.581) and to join those "that goon / Biforn this Lamb" (VII.583–84).

10. See also Isaiah 62:5: "the bridegroom shall rejoice over the bride, and thy God shall rejoice over thee"; and Revelations 21:9: "Come, I will show thee the bride, the spouse of the Lamb."

11. See the informative essay by David Wallace (1990) on the political tensions of the fourteenth century in northern Italy.

12. See Collins (1960, pp. 47–48).

13. Dinshaw (1989, p. 146). Cf. Huppé (1967): "what seems intolerable [in the *Clerk's Tale*] is in fact a trial of all men by God." See also Kittredge (1927, p. 196) and Robertson (1962, p. 269).

14. Excluding the occurrences in the *Clerk's Tale* (for which see next note), Tatlock and Kennedy list the following lines for *tempt* and its various forms: B.598, 2610–15; D.1497, 1655, 1661; I.255–60, 330–35, 335–40, 345–50 (thrice), 350–55 (twice), 355–60, 455–60, 710–15, 950–55 (twice), 965–70, 970–75 (twice), 1045–50.

15. Tatlock and Kennedy (1963) list the following occurrences of *tempt* and its various forms in the *Clerk's Tale:* E.452, 458, 620, 621, 707, 735, 786, 1153.

16. The *Canterbury Tales* has 19,314 lines, counting each prose sentence in *Malibee* and the *Parson's Tale* as equivalent to a line of verse, but not counting the small sections that seem to have been marked for excision. If all the tales were numbered consecutively and followed the Ellesmere order, the *Merchant's Tale* would begin at line 9098, with its own line IV.1773 standing at the exact center of the poem.

17. In suggesting four levels of narration, I may be accused of recklessly disregarding "Leicester's Razor." See Leicester (1990): "*narratores non sunt multiplicandi sine absolut[a] necessitate*" (p. 6). While I agree that it is less misleading to account for the author's shifts in perspective by calling them different narrative modes, or stances, rather than different characters all named Chaucer, the narrators I have in mind are of a different sort. Thus, I suggest we not find multiple narrators unless they are actually there.

18. For the view that January does not speak artfully, merely naively, see Laskaya (1995, p. 92).

19. Armstrong (1983): "The classic formulation of the hermeneutic circle holds that we can only comprehend the details of a work by projecting a sense of the whole, just as, conversely, we can only achieve a view of the whole by working through its parts" (p. 341).

20. For January's reduction of May to a commodity, as well as the similar attitude of the age to the institution of marriage, see Aers (1980, pp. 147–52).

21. May's mercantile ethic surfaces the first time we overhear her thoughts, when she decides to take Damian as her lover: ". . . heere I hym assure / To love hym best of any creature, / Though he namoore hadde than his sherte" (IV.1983–85). Her words imply that the ideal lover would be someone like Jay Gatsby with closets upon closets of silk shirts.

22. Despite the greater stability of marriages in the fourteenth century than in the twentieth, efforts to dissolve them during Chaucer's lifetime were not as infrequent or as unlikely to succeed as may be supposed. See Sheehan (1971, pp. 228–63) and Kelly (1975, pp. 169–73), for the evidence from the dioceses, respectively, of Ely and Rochester.

23. Singleton (1965b, p. 1). The next three quotations are from the same article, p. 7.

Chapter 11. Two Versions of Magic

1. Mandel (1992) makes a provocative observation about what I have been calling "physical" and "moral" magic in the two tales of Fragment V. He notes that the magical occurrences in the *Squire's Tale* are concrete, those in the *Franklin's Tale* illusionary, adding: "the concrete generates wonder in the Squire's Tale, and the illusory generates belief in the Franklin's Tale" (p. 96).

2. On the Franklin's deliberate interruption of the *Squire's Tale,* see Peterson (1970).

3. Cf. Burlin (1977): "[The Franklin's] desire to speak a definitive word on 'trouthe' and 'fredom,' as well as marriage, may be taken as part and parcel of the yearning for social acceptability in aristocratic circles" (p. 197).

4. Mann (1973, pp. 152–55).

5. It is notoriously difficult to gain a sense of the value of money in the Middle Ages. Nevertheless, we can approximate the significance of the Franklin's imagined twenty pound's worth of land by relying on Crow and Olson (1966, pp. 533–37): (a) Chaucer's annuities in 1399 totaled £46.13s.8d. (b) Chaucer's successor in Westminster Close paid an annual rent of £3. (c) If Chaucer paid the same rent, he spent about 6.5 percent of his total income on rent. (d) Thus, in 1399 £20 would be equivalent to 43 percent of a comfortable annual income.

6. Cf. Crow and Olson (1966, p. 18): "It might be assumed [that Chaucer] was a page and that he served at least to . . . April 1359."

7. For a *tour de force* on the metaphors of these lines, see Travis (1997, pp. 399–402).

8. See David (1965b), Burlin (1977, pp. 196–207), and others.

9. Though Pearsall (1985) counts "135 ladies" (p. 155), I count only seventy-

nine, assuming two daughters for Phidon and two for Cedasus, though Jerome lists only one for the latter. The specific number is unimportant, when overkill is the whole point.

10. Cf. Baker (1961).

11. Of the sixty-three uses of *liefer* (*lever, levere*) listed in Tatlock and Kennedy (1963), forty-seven are constructed with correlative *than* and explicitly state that two items are compared and which of the two is preferred. Of the remaining sixteen uses all but one (the line in question) leave no doubt about the implied comparison. It seems obvious, therefore, that the line in question also implies the comparison of two items, one of which is preferred. Those items are (a) "that I should be stabbed with a knife" and (b) "that you should break your trouthe." Arveragus prefers (a) over (b).

12. Cf. Crane (1990): "In the tale's closing calculations, [Dorigen] is very like a thousand pounds. Freely sent to Aurelius and freely sent back again, she has become a commodity whose transfer is equivalent, for the clerk at least, to financial sacrifice" (p. 240).

13. The Franklin's general discourse shows an unusually high occurrence of *levere*. Perhaps he always evaluates things in the light of their benefit to him. The construction shows up nine times in 915 lines: V.683, 692, 1360, 1476, 1522, 1529, 1531, 1596, and 1600, the last seven of which occur in the final scenes, compared with twelve occurrences in *T&C,* eight in *Boece,* and eight in *Roman de la rose.* Apart from its use in the *Franklin's Tale,* the construction occurs very rarely in *Canterbury Tales.*

14. Pearsall (1985, p. 151).

15. Cf. Burlin (1977): "There can be no question that [the Franklin] associates the genre [i.e., Breton *lai*] with the kind of aristocratic manner his tale attempts to define and he would be happy to have attributed to himself and his family" (p. 198).

16. Benjamin (1959, pp. 119–24).

Chapter 12. From Flesh to Spirit

1. For "transformation" in Fragment VIII, see Longsworth (1992, pp. 87–96).

2. Lines 36–56 of *Second Nun's Tale* closely follow St. Bernard's prayer in *Paradiso,* 33.1–39. See the notes to L. Benson (1987, p. 943).

3. Grandgent (1972, note to *Par.* 33.144).

4. For an interesting comparison of Fragment VIII with patterns in Dante's *Purgatorio,* see Olson (1981–82).

Chapter 13. Fragment VI

1. Cf. Hoffman (1967, pp. 25–26).

2. Cf. VI.130, 240, 242, 248, 250, 277, 278, 282, and 286.

3. Howard (1976, p. 334n.), responding to Longsworth (1971, pp. 223–33).

4. On Chaucer's different emphasis from Livy's, see Emerson Brown (1981, p. 132).

5. Bloch (1991, p. 105), quoting Brundage (1987, p. 83).

6. A thorough discussion of scholarly opinion may be found in the excellent study by Monica E. McAlpine (1980), who argues that the Narrator's phrase "a geldyng or a mare" (I.691) implies the Pardoner's homosexuality. Of course, he might well project a homosexual nature, as he might project a number of things. But this is to miss the point, as McAlpine's focus on the Pardoner himself misses half his performance, since it almost entirely ignores his *Tale*. It is significant that the excellent points McAlpine makes about the Pardoner's character derive, in my estimation, not from her attempt to demonstrate his homosexuality, but from her sensitive reading of his *Prologue*. That his possible homosexuality does not contradict such a reading, and may even enhance it, misses the point again. Even if the single mocking word "mare" were sufficient to demonstrate homosexuality, though that may be doubted, such a physiological condition would only be ancillary to the larger questions of his character, his relation to his tale, and his place in the whole poem. McAlpine's own study paradoxically demonstrates the irrelevance of the Pardoner's sexual condition, since she offers an insightful discussion of his character without the help of precise medical information.

7. For the view that the Pardoner "is the exact opposite of the Wife of Bath," see Burger (1992, p. 1144). For a comparison of the two pilgrims, see Kernan (1974, pp. 1–25), Patterson (1983, p. 683), and Leicester (1990, pp. 161–66).

8. Howard (1976, p. 355). Cf. Kellogg (1951, pp. 465–81).

9. *Modern Painters,* 2nd ed (1872), part 1, sec. 1, chap. 4, p. 18, cited by Bloomfield (1964).

10. Among others, see Reiss (1963–64).

11. See lines VI.400–404, 424–28, 433, 439–42, 448–51, 459–61.

12. Though practically impossible to document precisely the pardoner's physiological condition, Constantinus Africanus (1962), one of Chaucer's medical authorities, includes as his fourth category of sterile men "those who have neither desire nor potency" ("et allij qui nec appetunt nec virgam erigunt"), a group he links with an effeminate appearance ("si vero frigida fuerit effeminati erunt homines et appetitus deest") (pp. 14–20).

13. Another such hint of lechery may be the still unsatisfactorily explained eating and drinking at an "alestake" (VI.321), for it warns the pilgrims that a ribald tale follows.

14. Pyles and Algeo (1982, pp., 170–71).

15. The quoted line is from Tennyson's *Tithonus,* line 70. For a similar view of the Old Man's joyless existence, see David (1965a). For other interpretations of the Old Man, see Bushness (1931), Hamilton (1939), Owen (1951), and Steadman (1964).

Chapter 14. Fragment VII

1. Other critics of Fragment VII as an *ars poetica* include Green (1980, p. 143), C. David Benson (1983–84, pp. 61–76), Patterson (1989, pp. 117–75), Hill (1991, chaps. 6–8, pp. 95–150 *passim*), and Astell (1992, pp. 269–87), who acknowledges debts to Minnis (1988) and Quain (1945, pp. 215–64).

2. See the useful distinction made by Lanham (1967), between "*homo rhetoricus*" and "*homo seriosus.*"

3. On the simultaneous pious and fleshly dimensions that characterized the cult of the Virgin in the late Middle Ages, see Frank (1979, pp. 346–62).

4. A judicious survey of criticism appears in Ridley (1965). But see also Schoeck (1960, pp. 245–58), Baum (1958, p. 93), Donaldson (1970b, pp. 59–64), and Mann (1973, pp. 128–37).

5. See Despres (1994, pp. 413–27) and Kelly (1969, pp. 362–74).

6. Bryan and Dempster (1941, pp. 447–85).

7. Hamilton (1959), Boyd (1967), and Hawkins (1964, pp. 599–624).

8. Wainwright (1933, pp. 34–37). For a different view, see Frank (1979, pp. 349–50).

9. Though ME derivatives of OE *hræcan* and *hræctan* have not been attested, common sense and the survival of modern English "retch" argue strongly that the words must have existed in Middle English, as the *OED* acknowledges. See Copland (1970, pp. 45–46).

10. It should be noted that, according to H. A. Kelly (1996–97, p. 121), there is no evidence any bishop ever forbade nuns to keep pets.

11. Boyd (1950, pp. 404–16).

12. On the coming together of a text and a reader's imagination, see Iser (1974, p. 54).

13. I use the term "metaconscious" to avoid the heavily Freudian concepts "unconscious" (repressed thoughts) and "subconscious" (not in the conscious mind at a given moment). While Chaucer seems to have been well aware that a preoccupation of the mind can unintentionally intrude into speech unrelated to that preoccupation, it is highly doubtful that he also held Freud's fine distinction. I am grateful to Professor Albert Hutter for this explanation.

14. For the power of language to reveal unintended meanings, see Schroeder (1983, pp. 375–76).

15. Although Chaucer does not use *labour* explicitly to denote the labor of childbirth, he thrice uses *labour* appositively with *travail* (*CYT*, VIII.781; *LGW*, 1509; and *RR*, 4994), and on at least one occasion uses *travaillynge* unquestionably to mean the exertions of childbirth (*KnT*, I.2083–85).

16. On cleanliness and virginity as marks of piety, see Despres (1994, pp. 413, 418–20).

17. See Kurath and Kuhn (1952–86): "*beren*, 10a. To give birth to (a child)." Thus, ca. 1300, *Cursor Mundi* 1051: *the formast barn that sco him bare*, where the dative *him* emphasizes presenting the child to the father, rather than carrying it to term.

18. Cf. Mâle (1958, pp. 146–47), quoting Rabanus Maurus. See also Stevens and Cawley (1993), *Prima Pastorum*, lines 517–31; Chaucer, *LGW*, 1750–51; and *OED, burning*, 1.b. and 2.b.

19. *Ravyshedest* denotes primarily an act of drawing forcibly to some condition (see *OED* 1.c.), as in *CT*, III.1675–76. But as early as 1300 the word connoted a

physical—including sexual—transport: *Cursor Mundi*, 7048; Robert Brunne's *Handling Synne*, 7422; and Chaucer, *Boece*, IV. pr. 5, 23–24, and *T&C*, IV.547–48. For passion attending the Annunciation, cf. Dante's Angel Gabriel in *Paradiso*, 32, 103–5. However, Chaucer is the first, as far as I know, to attribute passion to both the Virgin and the Holy Spirit.

20. See the notes in L. Benson (1987) to lines VII.458, 514.

21. See Thomas Aquinas, *In Sententiae*, 4.27.2.2, and John Burgh, a follower of Thomas, perhaps better known in England, in Emden (1963, p. 107).

22. For a full discussion of the life and duties of fourteenth-century schoolboys, see Carleton F. Brown (1905–6, p. 467–91).

23. For the Prioress's innocence of intellectual understanding and dedication to the sentiment of piety, see Collette (1980, pp. 138–50) and Gaylord (1962, pp. 613–36).

24. On the beauty of the *Alma redemptoris* as a song, see Davidson (1974, pp. 459–66).

25. According to Carleton Brown only the *Prioress's Tale* and three other analogues employ a sacramental object placed in the martyred boy's mouth. One features a lily with a golden inscription, "Alma Redemptoris Mater," another has a precious stone, and the third a white pebble. Of these three only the preposterous lily is contemporaneous with Chaucer, though Carleton Brown doubted he knew it; the other two are from a later date (Bryan and Dempster 1941, pp. 457–58). Professor Brown's suggestion, that Chaucer's version alone among the thirty-three analogues preserves the grain of the lost original, inexplicably overlooks the more logical possibility that the grain placed on the clergeon's tongue was a Chaucerian invention.

26. For informative, detailed discussions of tragedy, see Ruggiers (1973, pp. 89–99) and H. A. Kelly (1993).

27. Cf. Patterson (1989): "In effect, Prudence's task is to teach Melibee how to interpret" (p. 158).

28. These seven are: Dd, En[1], Ds (designated Ds[1] in L. Benson 1987), Cn, Ma, En[3], Ad[1].

29. On the many-faceted significance of Chauntecleer—the name and the creature—see the *tour-de-force* by Travis (1997, pp. 416–27).

30. Cf. Bloch (1991, pp. 65–91).

31. For a very witty, yet highly insightful discussion of the problems caused by language used simultaneously with literal and symbolic force, see Boitani (1995, esp. pp. 26–36).

32. The study that Cavanaugh dismisses, without argument, is by Hotson (1924, pp. 762–81).

Chapter 15. Fragments IX and X

1. Though writing from a different perspective, and reaching different conclusions, Allen (1987) also discusses the pairing of language and profession (or confession) in *ManT*.

2. For a recent, excellent discussion of the *Retraction,* especially in the context of Augustine's *Retractationes* where the word suggests a retracing or recapitulation of prior works, because he would otherwise be unable to recall and emend them (*revocare et emendare*), see McGerr (1998, pp. 131–53).

3. *Catholic Encyclopedia* (1967, vol. 11, pp. 80–81).

4. For the *Retraction* as a generic convention, see Sayce (1971, pp. 230–48).

5. A "penitential" was originally a "tariff book"—that is, a simple listing of specific penances appropriate to certain sins. The *Parson's Tale* is an example of a late penitential which, beginning with that of Alain de Lille, was a general guide for confessors. See *Catholic Encyclopedia* (1967, vol. 11, p. 86).

6. See Wurtele (1980, pp. 335–59).

7. The phrase "my translacions and enditynges of worldly vanitees" should probably not be considered a category distinct from the list that follows, but a general heading to which the items on the list belong.

Appendix: A Chaucer Portrait at the University of California, Los Angeles

1. The findings and opinions of Matthews and Berger are now available in print. See Berger and Matthews (1995).

2. Cennini (1922).

3. Pearsall (1992, p. 289).

Works Cited

All quotations of Chaucer, unless otherwise noted, are taken from *The Riverside Chaucer*, 3rd ed., ed. Larry D. Benson (Boston: Houghton Mifflin, 1987). Abbreviations of works by Chaucer and titles of journals and series conform to the list of abbreviations in this edition, p. 779ff.

Aers, David. 1980. *Chaucer, Langland, and the Creative Imagination*. London: Routledge and Kegan Paul.

———. 1986. *Chaucer*. Harvester New Readings. Atlantic Highlands, N.J.: Humanities Press International.

Aiken, Pauline. 1935. "Vincent of Beauvais and Dame Pertelote's Knowledge of Medicine." *Speculum* 10: 281–87.

———. 1936. "Arcite's Illness and Vincent of Beauvais." *PMLA* 50: 361–69.

———. 1956. "Vincent of Beauvais and the 'Houres' of Chaucer's Physician." *Studies in Philology* 53: 22–24.

Alanus de Insulis. 1908. *The Complaint of Nature*. Trans. Douglas Maxwell Moffat. Yale Studies in English, vol. 36. New York: Henry Holt.

———. 1980. *Plaint of Nature*. Trans. James J. Sheridan. Medieval Sources in Translation, no. 26. Toronto: Pontifical Institute of Medieval Studies.

Albert of Brescia. 1873. *Liber consolationis et consilii*. Ed. Thor Sundby. London: Chaucer Society, 2nd ser., no. 8.

Allen, Judson Boyce, and Theresa Anne Moritz. 1981. *A Distinction of Stories: The Medieval Unity of Chaucer's Fair Chain of Narratives for Canterbury*. Columbus: Ohio State University Press.

Allen, Mark. 1987. "Penitential Sermons, the Manciple, and the End of *The Canterbury Tales*." *SAC* 9: 77–96.

Anderson, William. 1980. *Dante the Maker*. London and Boston: Routledge and Kegan Paul.

Andrew, Malcolm, and Ronald Waldron. 1979. *Pearl: Poems of the Pearl Manuscript*. Berkeley and Los Angeles: University of California Press.

Aquinas, St. Thomas. 1969. *Summa Theologiae. Vol. 51. Our Lady*. Ed. and trans. Thomas R. Heath. London: Blackfriars, in conjunction with Eyre and Spottiswoode.

———. 1882–. *In Sententiae*. In *Opera omnia iussu Leonis XIII P. M. edita*. Rome: Commissio Leonina; Paris: Librairie Philosophique J. Vrin.

Armstrong, Paul B. 1983. "The Conflict of Interpretations and the Limits of Pluralism." *PMLA* 98: 341–52.

Arnold, Morris. 1976. "Fourteenth-Century Promises." *Cambridge Law Journal* 35: 321–34.

Astell, Ann W. 1992. "Chaucer's 'Literature Group' and the Medieval Causes of Books." *ELH* 59: 269–87.

———. 1996. *Chaucer and the Universe of Learning*. Ithaca: Cornell University Press.

Atchity, Kenneth John. 1969. "*Inferno VII:* The Idea of Order." *Italian Quarterly* 12, nos. 47–48 (Winter–Spring): 5–62.

Augustine, St. 1841–64. *De Trinitate. Patrologia Latina,* ed. J.-P. Migne, vol. 42, cols. 819–1098. Paris.

Baker, Donald C. 1961. "A Crux in Chaucer's 'Franklin's Tale': Dorigen's Complaint." *JEGP* 9: 56–64.

Baldwin, Ralph. 1955. *The Unity of the Canterbury Tales*. Anglistica, vol. 5. Copenhagen: Rosenkilde and Bagger.

Barbour, I. G. 1966. *Issues in Science and Religion*. London: S. C. M. Press.

Barthes, Roland. 1972. *Critical Essays*. Trans. Richard Howard. Evanston: Northwestern University Press.

Baum, Paull F. 1958. *Chaucer: A Critical Appraisal*. Durham: Duke University Press.

Beichner, Paul. 1956. "*Non Alleluia Ructare*." *Mediaeval Studies* 18: 135–44.

Benjamin, E. B. 1959. "The Concept of Order in the *Franklin's Tale*." *Philological Quarterly* 38: 119–24.

Bensman, Joseph. 1979. *Between Public and Private: The Lost Boundaries of the Self*. New York: Free Press.

Benson, C. David. 1983–84. "Their Telling Difference: Chaucer the Pilgrim and His Two Contrasting Tales." *Chaucer Review* 18: 61–76.

Benson, Larry D. 1981. "The Order of the *Canterbury Tales*." *Studies in the Age of Chaucer* 3: 77–120.

———, gen. ed. 1987. *The Riverside Chaucer*. Boston: Houghton Mifflin.

Berger, Rainer, and William Matthews. 1995. "The Chaucer Portrait at the University of California, Los Angeles." *PACT* 49: 99–106. Strasbourg: Council of Europe.

Biblia Sacra iuxta Vulgatam Clementinam. 1975. Ed. Weber et al. 2nd rev. ed. Rome: Desclee.

Blake, Kathleen A. 1973. "Order and the Noble Life in Chaucer's Knight's Tale?" *MLQ* 34: 3–19.

Blake, N. F. 1985. *The Textual Tradition of the Canterbury Tales*. London: Edward Arnold.

Bloch, Howard. 1991. *Medieval Misogyny and the Invention of Western Romantic Love*. Chicago: University of Chicago Press.

Blodgett, E. D. 1976. "Chaucerian *Pryvetee* and the Opposition to Time." *Speculum* 51: 477–93.

Bloomfield, Morton. 1964. "Authenticating Realism and the Realism of Chaucer." *Thought* 39: 335–58.

Boccaccio, Giovanni. 1952. *Il Decamerone*. Ed. V. Branca. Firenze: Felice le Morrier.

Boethius [Anicius Manlius Severinus Boethius]. 1969. *The Consolation of Philosophy*. Trans. V. E. Watts. New York: Penguin.

Boitani, Piero. 1983. "What Dante Meant to Chaucer." In *Chaucer and the Italian Trecento*, ed. Piero Boitani. Cambridge: Cambridge University Press.

———. 1995. "'My Tale Is of a Cock' or, The Problems of Literal Interpretation." In *Literature and Religion in the Later Middle Ages: Philological Studies in Honor of Siegfried Wenzel*, eds. Richard G. Newhauser and John A. Alford, pp. 25–42. Binghamton, N.Y.: Medieval and Renaissance Texts and Studies.

Boltzman, Ludwig. 1974. *Theoretical Physics and Philosophical Problems: Selected Writings*. Ed. Brian McGuinness, trans. Paul Foulkes. Dordrecht and Boston: Reidel.

Boutell, Charles. 1978. *Boutell's Heraldry*. Revised by J. P. Brooke-Little. London and New York: F. Warren.

Bowden, Muriel. 1964. *A Reader's Guide to Geoffrey Chaucer*. New York: Farrar, Strauss.

Boyd, Beverly. 1950. "Chaucer's Prioress: Her Green Gauds." *Modern Language Quarterly* 11 (1950): 404–16.

———. 1967. *Chaucer and the Liturgy*. Philadelphia: Dorrance.

Bridgman, Percy Williams. 1941. *The Nature of Thermodynamics*. Cambridge, Mass: Harvard University Press.

Brown, Carleton F. 1905–6. "Chaucer's 'Little Clergeon.'" *Modern Philology* 3: 467–91.

Brown, Emerson, Jr. 1975. "Priapus and the *Parlement of Foulys*." *SP* 72: 258–74.

———. 1981. "What Is Chaucer Doing with the Physician and His Tale?" *PQ* 60: 129–49.

———. 1990. "Fragment VII of Chaucer's *Canterbury Tales* and the 'Mental Climate of the Fourteenth Century.'" In *Traditions and Innovations: Essays on British Literature of the Middle Ages and the Renaissance*, eds. David G. Allen and Robert A. White. Newark: University of Delaware Press.

Brundage, James A. 1987. *Law, Sex, and Christian Society in Medieval Europe*. Chicago: University of Chicago Press.

Bryan, William Frank, and Germaine Dempster, eds. 1941. *Sources and Analogues of Chaucer's Canterbury Tales*. Chicago: University of Chicago Press.

Bullough, Vern, and Cameron Campbell. 1980. "Female Longevity and Diet in the Middle Ages." *Speculum* 55: 317–25.

Burger, Glenn. 1992. "Kissing the Pardoner." *PMLA* 107: 1143–56.

Burlin, Robert B. 1977. *Chaucerian Fiction*. Princeton: Princeton University Press.

Burrow, John A. 1971. "*Sir Thopas*: An Agony in Three Fits." *RES*, n.s. 22: 54–

58. Reprinted in his *Essays on Medieval Literature,* pp. 61–65. Oxford: Clarendon Press, 1984.

Bushness, N. S. 1931. "The Wandering Jew and The Pardoner's Tale." *Studies in Philology* 28: 450–60.

Campbell, Jeremy. 1982. *Grammatical Man: Information, Entropy, Language, and Life.* New York: Simon and Schuster.

Catholic Encyclopedia, The New. 1967. New York: Catholic University of America and McGraw-Hill.

Cawley, A. C., ed. 1958. *Prima Pastorum: The Wakefield Pageants in the Townley Cycle.* Manchester: Manchester University Press.

Cennino Cennini. 1922. *The Book of the Art of Cennino Cennini.* Trans. Christiana J. Herringham. London: Allen and Unwin.

Collette, Carolyn P. 1980. "Sense and Sensibility in the 'Prioress's Tale.'" *Chaucer Review* 15 (Fall): 138–50.

Collins, A. Jeffries, ed. 1960. *Manuale ad usum percelebris ecclesie sarisburiensis [Sarum Manual].* London: Henry Bradshaw Society.

Condren, E. I. 1971. "The Historical Context of the *Book of the Duchess:* A New Hypothesis." *Chaucer Review* 5: 195–212.

———. 1975. "Of Deaths and Duchesses and Scholars Coughing in Ink." *Chaucer Review* 10: 87–95.

———. 1984. "The Clerk's Tale of Man Tempting God." *Criticism* 26: 99–114.

———. 1985. "Transcendent Metaphor or Banal Reality: Three Chaucerian Dilemmas." *Papers on Language and Literature* 21: 233–57.

Constantino l'Africano. 1962. *Il Trattato di fisiologia e igiene sessuale.* Eds. Marco T. Malato and Umberto de Martini. Rome.

Constantinus Africanus. See Constantino l'Africano.

Cooper, Helen. 1983. *The Structure of the Canterbury Tales.* London: Duckworth.

Copland, R. A. 1970. "A Line from Chaucer's Prologue to the *Canterbury Tales.*" *Notes and Queries* (February): 45–46.

Cramer, Patricia. 1990. "Lordship, Bondage, and the Erotic: The Psychological Bases of Chaucer's "Clerk's Tale." *JEGP* 89: 491–511.

Crane, Susan. 1990. "The Franklin as Dorigen." *Chaucer Review* 24: 236–52.

Crow, Martin M., and Clair C. Olson, eds. 1966. *Chaucer Life-Records.* Austin: University of Texas Press.

Curry, Walter Clyde. 1926. *Chaucer and the Medieval Sciences.* Oxford: Oxford University Press.

Curtius, Ernst. 1953. *European Literature and the Latin Middle Ages.* Trans. Willard Trask. New York: Harper and Row.

Dante Alighieri. 1902. *The Divine Comedy of Dante Alighieri.* Rev. ed. Trans. Charles Eliot Norton. Boston: Houghton, Mifflin.

———. 1920. *Dantis Alagherii Epistolae: The Letters of Dante.* Ed. and trans. Paget Toynbee. Oxford: Clarendon Press.

———. 1970. *The Divine Comedy.* Translated with commentary by Charles S. Singleton. Bollingen Series, 80. Princeton, N.J.: Princeton University Press.

———. 1972. *La Divina Commedia*. Ed. C. H. Grandgent, revised by Charles S. Singleton. Cambridge, Mass.: Harvard University Press.

David, Alfred. 1965a. "Criticism and the Old Man in the 'Pardoner's Tale.'" *College English* 27: 39–44.

———. 1965b. "Sentimental Comedy in the Franklin's Tale." *Annuale Medievale* 6: 19–27.

———. 1976. *The Strumpet Muse*. Bloomington and London: Indiana University Press.

Davidson, Audrey. 1974. "*Alma Redemptoris Mater:* The Little Clergeon's Song." *Studies in Medieval Culture* 4: 459–66.

Dedeck-Héry, V. L., ed. 1952. "Boethius' *De Consolatione* by Jean de Meun." *Medieval Studies* 14: 165–275.

Despres, Denise L. 1994. "Cultic Anti-Judaism and Chaucer's Litel Clergeon." *MP* 91: 413–27.

Dickson, Kay. 1980. "Toward Order and Transcendence: Dante's Use of Synaesthesia in the *Divine Comedy*." *Romance Notes* 21: 111–16.

Dinshaw, Carolyn. 1989. *Chaucer's Sexual Poetics*. Madison and London: University of Wisconsin Press.

Donaldson, E. Talbot. 1970a. "The Ordering of the *Canterbury Tales*." In *Medieval Literature and Folklore Studies: Essays in Honor of Francis Lee Utley*, ed. Jerome Mandel and Bruce A. Rosenberg. New Brunswick: Rutgers University Press.

———. 1970b. *Speaking of Chaucer*. London: Athlone Press.

———. 1975. *Chaucer's Poetry: An Anthology for the Modern Reader*. 2nd ed. New York: Ronald Press.

———. 1977. "Designing a Camel; or Generalizing the Middle Ages." *Tennessee Studies in Literature* 22: 1–16.

———. 1985. *The Swan at the Well: Shakespeare Reading Chaucer*. New Haven: Yale University Press.

Eckhardt, Caroline D., ed. 1980. *Essays in the Numerical Criticism of Literature*. Lewisburg: Bucknell University Press.

Elbow, Peter. 1975. *Oppositions in Chaucer*. Middletown: Wesleyan University Press.

Emden, Alfred Brotherston. 1963. *A Biographical Register of the University of Cambridge to 1500*. Cambridge: Cambridge University Press.

———. 1974. *A Biographical Register of the University of Oxford to* A.D. *1500*. Oxford: Clarendon Press.

Farnham, W. E. 1918. "Chaucer's *Clerk's Tale*." *MLN* 33.

Fisher, John H., ed. 1977. *The Complete Poetry and Prose of Geoffrey Chaucer*. New York: Holt, Rinehart and Winston.

Frank, Hardy Long. 1979. "Chaucer's Prioress and the Blessed Virgin." *ChauR* 13: 346–62.

Frank, Joseph. 1991. "Spatial Form in Modern Literature." In *The Idea of Spatial Form*. New Brunswick and London: Rutgers University Press, pp. 5–66. Originally published in slightly different form in *Sewanee Review* 53 (1945).

Frank, Robert W., Jr. 1968. "The Art of Reading Medieval Personification-Allegory." In *Interpretations of Piers Plowman,* ed. Edward Vasta, pp. 217–31. Notre Dame: University of Notre Dame Press.

Frese, Dolores Warwick. 1991. *An Ars Legendi for Chaucer's Canterbury Tales.* Gainesville: University of Florida Press.

Frost, William. 1949. "An Interpretation of Chaucer's 'Knight's Tale.'" *Review of English Studies* 25: 290–304.

Furnivall, Frederick J. 1868. *A Temporary Preface to the Six-Text Edition of Chaucer's Canterbury Tales.* Part 1. London: Chaucer Society, 2nd ser., no. 3.

Fyler, John M. 1979. *Chaucer and Ovid.* New Haven: Yale University Press.

Galen. 1874. *De Placitis Hippocratis et Platonis.* Ed. I. Muller. Leipzig.

Gaylord, Alan T. 1962. "The Unconquered Tale of the Prioress." *Papers of the Michigan Academy of Science Arts and Letters* 47: 613–36.

———. 1967. "*Sentence* and *Solaas* in Fragment VII of the *Canterbury Tales:* Harry Bailly as Horseback Editor." *PMLA* 82: 226–235.

Gayre, Lt.-Col. Robert. 1961. *Heraldic Cadency.* London: Faber and Faber.

Gibson, J. J. 1966. *The Senses Considered as Perceptual Systems.* London: Allen and Unwin.

Gratian. [1879] 1959. *Decretum (Concordia discordantium canonum).* Ed. Emil Friedberg. *Corpus Iuris Canonici,* vol. 1. Graz: Akademische Druck- und Verlagsanstalt.

Green, Richard Firth. 1980. *Poets and Princepleasers: Literature and the English Court in the Late Middle Ages.* Toronto: University of Toronto Press.

Gruner, O. Cameron, ed. and trans. 1970. *A Treatise on the Canon of Medicine of Avicenna.* New York: Augustus M. Kelley.

Guénon, René. 1951. *L'Esoterismo di Dante.* Trans. Corrado Rocco. Rome: Atanòr.

Guillaume de Lorris and Jean de Meun. 1914–24. *Le Roman de la rose.* Ed. Ernest Langlois. 5 vols. SATF. Paris: Firmin-Didot.

Haken, Hermann. 1984. *The Science of Structure: Synergetics.* Trans. Fred Bradley. New York: Van Nostrand Reinhold.

Haller, Robert S., trans. and ed. 1973. "The Letter to Can Grande." In his *Literary Criticism of Dante Alighieri.* Lincoln: University of Nebraska Press.

Hamilton, Marie P. 1939. "Death and Old Age in The Pardoner's Tale." *SP* 36: 571–76.

———. 1959. "Echoes of Childermas in the Tale of the Prioress." In *Chaucer: Modern Essays in Criticism,* ed. Edward Wagenknecht, pp. 88–97. New York: Oxford University Press.

Hammond, Eleanor Prescott. 1908. *Chaucer: A Bibliographical Manual.* New York: Macmillan.

Hanning, R. W. 1985. "Roasting a Friar, Mis-taking a Wife, and Other Acts of Textual Harassment in Chaucer's *Canterbury Tales.*" *SAC* 7: 3–21.

Hansen, Elaine Tuttle. 1992. *Chaucer and the Fictions of Gender.* Berkeley and Los Angeles: University of California Press.

Hartman, Ernest. 1991. *Boundaries in the Mind: A New Psychology of Personality.* New York: Basic Books.

Hawkins, Sherman. 1964. "Chaucer's Prioress and the Sacrifice of Praise." *JEGP* 63: 599–624.

Hayles, N. Katherine. 1984. *The Cosmic Web: Scientific Field Models and Literary Strategies in the Twentieth Century.* Ithaca: Cornell University Press.

———. 1990. *Chaos Bound: Orderly Disorder in Contemporary Literature and Science.* Ithaca: Cornell University Press.

Hearnshaw, F. J. C. 1928. "Chivalry and Its Place in History." In *Chivalry: A Series of Studies to Illustrate Its Historical Significance and Civilizing Influence,* ed. Edgar Prestage. New York: Alfred A. Knopf.

Hieatt, Constance B., ed. 1970. *The Miller's Tale by Geoffrey Chaucer.* New York: Odyssey Press.

Hill, John M. 1991. *Chaucerian Belief: The Poetics of Reverence and Delight.* New Haven and London: Yale University Press.

Hoffman, Arthur W. 1954. "Chaucer's Prologue to Pilgrimage: The Two Voices." *ELH* 21: 1–16.

Hoffman, Richard L. 1967. "Jephthah's Daughter and Chaucer's Virginia." *Chaucer Review* 2: 20–31.

Hollander, Robert. 1993. *Dante's Epistle to Cangrande.* Ann Arbor: University of Michigan Press.

———. 1994. "Reply to H. A. Kelly." *Lectura Dantis* 14–15: 96–110.

Holy Bible, New Catholic Edition Translated from the Latin Vulgate. 1949–50. New York: Catholic Publishing Co.

Hopkins, M. K. 1964–65. "Age of Roman Girls at Marriage." *Population Studies* 18.

Hopper, Vincent. 1938. *Medieval Number Symbolism.* New York: Cooper Square.

Hotson, J. Leslie. 1924. "Colfox versus Chauntecleer." *PMLA* 39: 762–81.

Howard, Donald R. 1976. *The Idea of the Canterbury Tales.* Berkeley and Los Angeles: University of California Press.

Howes, Laura L. 1997. *Chaucer's Gardens and the Language of Convention.* Gainesville: University Press of Florida.

Huppé, B. F. 1967. *A Reading of the Canterbury Tales.* Rev. ed. Buffalo: State University of New York Press.

Irving, Edward B., Jr. 1995. "Heroic Worlds: 'The Knight's Tale' and 'Beowulf.'" In *Literature and Religion in the Later Middle Ages: Philological Studies in Honor of Siegfried Wenzel,* eds. Richard G. Newhauser and John A. Alford, 43–59. Binghamton, N.Y.: Medieval and Renaissance Texts and Studies.

Iser, Wolfgang. 1974. *The Implied Reader: Patterns in Communication from Bunyon to Beckett.* Baltimore: Johns Hopkins University Press.

Jensen, Emily. 1990. "Male Competition as a Unifying Motif in Fragment A of the *Canterbury Tales.*" *ChauR* 24: 320–28.

Jerome, St. 1841–64. *Epistola adversus Jovinianum. Patrologia Latina,* ed. J.-P. Migne, vol. 23, cols. 211ff.

Jones, Terry. 1980. *Chaucer's Knight: The Portrait of a Medieval Mercenary.* London: Weidenfeld and Nicolson.

Jordan, Robert M. 1967. *Chaucer and the Shape of Creation.* Cambridge, Mass: Harvard University Press.

Kaske, R. E. 1959. "An Aube in the *Reeve's Tale*." ELH 26: 295–310.

Kellogg, Alfred. 1951. "An Augustinian Interpretation of Chaucer's Pardoner." *Speculum* 26: 465–81.

Kelly, Edward H. 1969. "By Mouth of Innocents: The Prioress Vindicated." *PLL* 5: 362–74.

Kelly, H. A. 1975. *Love and Marriage in the Age of Chaucer*. Ithaca: Cornell University Press.

———. 1989. *Tragedy and Comedy from Dante to Pseudo-Dante*. Berkeley: University of California Press.

———. 1993. *Ideas and Forms of Tragedy from Aristotle to the Middle Ages*. Cambridge: Cambridge University Press.

———. 1994a. "Cangrande and the Ortho-Dantists." *Lectura Dantis* 14–15: 61–95.

———. 1994b. "Reply to Robert Hollander." *Lectura Dantis* 14–15: 111–15.

———. 1996–97. "A Neo-Revisionist Look at Chaucer's Nuns." *ChauR* 31, no. 2: 115–32.

Kernan, Anne. 1974. "The Archwife and the Eunuch." *ELH* 41: 1–25.

Kiser, Lisa J. 1991. *Truth and Textuality in Chaucer's Poetry*. Hanover: University Press of New England.

Kittredge, George Lyman. 1912. "Chaucer's Discussion of Marriage." *MP* 9: 435–67.

———. [1915.] 1927. *Chaucer and His Poetry: Lectures Delivered in 1914 on the Percy Turnbull Memorial Foundation in The Johns Hopkins University*. Cambridge, Mass.: Harvard University Press.

Kolve, V. A. 1984. *Chaucer and the Imagery of Narrative*. Stanford: Stanford University Press.

Kurath, Hans, and Sherman M. Kuhn, eds. 1952–86. *Middle English Dictionary*. Ann Arbor: University of Michigan Press.

Langland, William. 1888. *The Vision of William Concerning Piers The Plowman*. Ed. Walter W. Skeat. Oxford: Oxford University Press.

Lanham, R. A. 1967. "Games, Play, and High Seriousness in Chaucer's Poetry." *English Studies* 48: 1–24.

Laskaya, Anne. 1995. *Chaucer's Approach to Gender in the Canterbury Tales*. Cambridge: D. S. Brewer.

Legg, J. W., ed. 1916. *Missale Sarum*. Oxford: Oxford University Press.

Leicester, H. Marshall, Jr. 1980. "The Art of Impersonation: A General Prologue to the *Canterbury Tales*." *PMLA* 95: 213–24.

———. 1990. *The Disenchanted Self: Representing the Subject in the Canterbury Tales*. Berkeley: University of California Press.

Lewis, C. S. 1936. *The Allegory of Love*. Oxford: Oxford University Press.

———. 1964. *The Discarded Image: An Introduction to Medieval and Renaissance Literature*. Cambridge: Cambridge University Press.

Lloyd, Michael. 1959. "A Defense of Arcite." *English Miscellany* 10: 11–25.

Longsworth, Robert M. 1971. "The Doctor's Dilemma: A Comic View of the Physician's Tale." *Criticism* 13: 223–33.

————. 1992. "Privileged Knowledge: St. Cecilia and the Alchemist in the *Canterbury Tales*." *Chaucer Review* 27: 87–96.

Lowes, John Livingston. 1919. *Convention and Revolt in Poetry*. Boston and New York: Houghton Mifflin.

Lumiansky, R. M. 1955. *Of Sondry Folk: The Dramatic Principle in the Canterbury Tales*. Austin: University of Texas Press.

Mâle, Emile. 1958. *The Gothic Image: Religious Art in France in the Thirteenth Century*. Trans. Dora Nussey. New York: Harper Torchbooks.

Malone, Kemp. 1951. *Chapters on Chaucer*. Baltimore: Johns Hopkins University Press.

Mandel, Jerome. 1976. "Governance in the *Physician's Tale*." *Chaucer Review* 10: 316–25.

————. 1992. *Geoffrey Chaucer: Building the Fragments of the Canterbury Tales*. London and Toronto: Associated University Presses.

Manly, John Matthews, and Edith M. Rickert, eds. 1940. *The Text of the Canterbury Tales, Studied on the Basis of all Known Manuscripts*. 8 vols. Chicago: University of Chicago Press.

Mann, Jill. 1973. *Chaucer and Medieval Estates Satire: The Literature of Social Classes and the General Prologue to the Canterbury Tales*. Cambridge: Cambridge University Press.

Martianus Capella. 1977. *The Marriage of Philology and Mercury*. Ed. and trans. William H. Stahl and Richard Johnson, with E. L. Burge. New York: Columbia University Press.

Matthews, William. See Berger, Rainer, and William Matthews.

Maxwell, James Clerk. 1868. "On Governors." *Proceedings of the Royal Society of London* 16: 270–83.

McAlpine, Monica E. 1980. "The Pardoner's Homosexuality and How It Matters." *PMLA* 95: 8–22.

McGerr, Rosemarie P. 1998. *Chaucer's Open Books*. Gainesville: University Press of Florida.

Mead, W. E. 1901. "The Prologue of the Wife of Bath's Tale." *PMLA* 16: 388–404.

Metz, Rene. 1967. "Recherches sur la condition de la femme selon Gratien." *Studia Gratiana* 12: 377–96.

Middleton, Anne. 1973. "The *Physician's Tale* and Love's Martyrs: 'Ensamples mo than ten' as a Method in the *Canterbury Tales*." *Chaucer Review* 8: 9–32.

Migne, J.-P., ed. 1841–64. *Patrologiae Cursus Completus*, Series Latina. Paris.

Miller, Thomas, ed. 1890–91, 1898. *The Old English Version of Bede's Ecclesiastical History of the English People*. EETS, orig. ser. London: N. Trubner.

Minnis, A. J. 1988. *Medieval Theory of Authorship: Scholastic Literary Attitudes in the Later Middle Ages*. 2nd ed. Philadelphia: University of Pennsylvania Press.

Mogan, Joseph J., Jr. 1970. "Chaucer and the *Bona Matrimonii*." *Chaucer Review* 4: 123–41.

Muscatine, Charles. 1964. *Chaucer and the French Tradition*. Berkeley and Los Angeles: University of California Press.

Neuse, Richard. 1962. "The Knight: The First Mover in Chaucer's Human Comedy." *University of Toronto Quarterly* 31: 299–315.

———. 1991. *Chaucer's Dante*. Berkeley and Los Angeles: University of California Press.

Niles, John D. 1979. "Ring Composition and the Structure of *Beowulf*." *PMLA* 94: 924–35.

Nitzsche, J. C. 1978. "Creation in Genesis and Nature in Chaucer's *General Prologue* 1–18." *PLL* 14: 459–64.

Noonan, John T. 1966. *Contraception: A History of Its Treatment by the Catholic Theologians and Canonists*. Cambridge, Mass.: Harvard University Press.

North, J. D. 1988. *Chaucer's Universe*. Oxford: Clarendon Press.

Norton, Charles Eliot. See Dante 1902.

O'Brien, D. 1969. *Empedocles' Cosmic Cycle*. Cambridge: Cambridge University Press.

Olson, Glending. 1981–82. "Chaucer, Dante, and the Structure of Fragment VIII (G) of the *Canterbury Tales*." *ChauR* 16: 222–36.

Otis, Brooks. 1970. *Ovid as an Epic Poet*. 2nd ed. Cambridge: Cambridge University Press.

Ovid. 1985. *Ovid in Six Volumes*. Vol. 2: *The Art of Love and Other Poems*. Ed. and trans. J. H. Mozley. 2nd ed., rev. G. P. Goold. Loeb Classical Library, vol. 232, pp. 77–233. Cambridge, Mass. Harvard University Press.

Owen, W. J. B. 1951. "The Old Man in The Pardoner's Tale." *Review of English Studies,* n.s. 2: 49–55.

Passon, Richard H. 1968. "'Entente' in Chaucer's *Friar's Tale*." *Chaucer Review* 2: 166–71.

Patrologia Latina. See Migne, J.-P.

Pattee, H. H. 1970. "The Problem of Biological Hierarchy." In *Towards a Theoretical Biology: Three Drafts,* ed. C. H. Waddington, 117–36. Edinburgh.

Patterson, Lee. 1983. "'For the Wyves Love of Bathe': Feminine Rhetoric and Poetic Resolution in the *Roman de la Rose* and the *Canterbury Tales*." *Speculum* 58: 656–95.

———. 1989. "'What man artow?': Authorial Self-Definition in *The Tale of Sir Thopas* and *The Tale of Melibee*." *Studies in the Age of Chaucer* 11: 117–75.

———. 1991. *Chaucer and the Subject of History*. Madison: University of Wisconsin Press.

———, ed. 1987. *Negotiating the Past*. Madison: University of Wisconsin Press.

Pearsall, Derek. 1985. *The Canterbury Tales*. London: Allen and Unwin.

———. 1986. "Chaucer's Poetry and Its Modern Commentators: The Necessity of History." In *Medieval Literature: Criticism, Ideology and History,* ed. David Aers, pp. 123–47. New York: St. Martin's Press.

———. 1987. "Versions of Comedy in Chaucer's *Canterbury Tales*." In *Chaucer's Frame Tales: The Physical and the Metaphysical,* ed. Joerg O. Fichte, pp. 35–49. Cambridge: D. S. Brewer.

———. 1992. *The Life of Geoffrey Chaucer*. Oxford: Blackwell.

Peter Lombard. 1977–81. *Sententiae in IV libris distinctae*. 3rd ed., ed. Patres

Colegii S. Bonaventurae. Editiones Colegii. Quaracchi: S. Bonaventurae ad Claras Aquas.

Peterfreund, Stuart. 1986. "The Re-emergence of Energy in the Discourse of Literature and Science." In *Science and the Imagination,* ed. G. S. Rousseau. Special issue of *Annals of Scholarship: Masterstudies of the Humanities and Social Sciences* 4: 22–53.

Peterson, Joyce E. 1970. "The Finished Fragment: A Reassessment of the *Squire's Tale.*" *Chaucer Review* 5: 62–74.

Piaget, Arthur, ed. 1941. *Oton de Grandson: Sa vie et ses poésies, Mémoires et Documents Publiés par la Societé d'Histoire de la Suisse Romande.* 3rd ser. Lausanne: Libraire Payot.

Piaget, Jean. 1970. *Structuralism.* Trans. and ed. Chaninah Maschler. New York: Harper and Row.

Plummer, Charles, ed. 1896. *Venerabilis Baedae Opera Historica.* Oxford: Clarendon Press.

Porush, David. 1985. *The Soft Machine: Cybernetic Fiction.* New York: Methuen.

Poulet, Georges. 1959. "Reponse de." *Les Lettres nouvelles* 7, n.s. 17 (24 June): 10–13.

Pratt, Robert A. 1961. "The Development of the Wife of Bath." In *Studies in Medieval Literature in Honor of A. C. Baugh,* ed. MacEdward Leach, 45–77. Philadelphia: University of Pennsylvania Press.

———, ed. 1966. *The Tales of Canterbury.* Boston: Houghton Mifflin.

Pyles, Thomas, and John Algeo. 1982. *The Origins and Development of the English Language.* 3rd ed. New York: Harcourt Brace Jovanovich.

Quain, Edward A., S.J. 1945. "The Medieval *Accessus Ad Auctores.*" *Traditio* 3: 215–64.

Reiss, Edmund. 1963–64. "The Final Irony of the Pardoner's Tale." *College English* 25: 260–66.

Ricoeur, Paul. 1974. *The Conflict of Interpretations.* Ed. Don Ihde. Evanston: Northwestern University Press.

Ridley, Florence H. 1965. *The Prioress and the Critics.* Berkeley: University of California Press.

Robertson, D. W., Jr. 1962. *A Preface to Chaucer.* Princeton: Princeton University Press.

Robinson, F. N., ed. 1957. *The Works of Geoffrey Chaucer.* 2nd ed. Cambridge, Mass.: Houghton Mifflin.

Robinson, Ian. 1972. *Chaucer and the English Tradition.* Cambridge: Cambridge University Press.

Rogers, William E. 1986. *Upon the Ways: The Structure of the Canterbury Tales.* English Literary Studies Monograph Series, no. 36. Victoria, B.C.: University of Victoria Press.

Roney, Lois. 1990. *Chaucer's Knight's Tale and Theories of Scholastic Philosophy.* Gainesville: University Press of Florida.

Ruggiers, Paul G. 1973. "Towards a Theory of Tragedy in Chaucer." *Chaucer Review* 8: 89–99.

Ruskin, John. 1986. *Modern Painters,* vol. 1 of *The Works of John Ruskin.* 2nd ed. New York: John Wiley and Sons.

Ryan, Granger, and Helmut Ripperger, trans. 1941. *Golden Legend.* London and New York: Longmans, Green.

Salter, Elizabeth. 1962. *Chaucer: The Knight's Tale and the Clerk's Tale.* London: Edward Arnold.

Salter, F. M. 1954. "The Tragic Figure of the Wife of Bath." *Transactions of the Royal Society of Canada* 48: 1–13.

Sayce, Olive. 1971. "Chaucer's 'Retractions': The Conclusion of the *Canterbury Tales* and Its Place in Literary Tradition." *Medium Ævum* 40: 230–48.

Schibanoff, Susan. 1986. "Taking the Gold out of Egypt: The Art of Reading as a Woman." In *Gender and Reading: Essays on Readers, Texts, and Contexts,* ed. Elizabeth Flynn and Patrocino Schweickart, pp. 83–106. Baltimore and London: Johns Hopkins University Press.

Schless, Howard H. 1984. *Chaucer and Dante: A Revaluation.* Norman, Okla.: Pilgrim Books.

Schmidt, A. V. C. 1969. "The Tragedy of Arcite: A Reconsideration of the *Knight's Tale.*" *Essays in Criticism* 19: 107–17.

Schoeck, R. J. 1960. "Chaucer's Prioress: Mercy and Tender Heart." In *Chaucer Criticism: The Canterbury Tales,* eds. R. J. Schoeck and Jerome Taylor, 245–58. Notre Dame: University of Notre Dame Press.

Scholes, Robert. 1974. *Structuralism in Literature.* New Haven: Yale University Press.

Schroeder, Peter R. 1983. "Hidden Depths: Dialogue and Characterization in Chaucer and Malory." *PMLA* 98: 375–76.

Schweitzer, Edward C. 1981. "Fate and Freedom in *The Knight's Tale.*" *Studies in the Age of Chaucer* 3: 13–45.

Severs, J. Burke. 1972. *The Literary Relationships of Chaucer's Clerkes Tale.* Yale Studies in English, vol. 96. New York: Archon Books.

Sheehan, Fr. Michael M. 1971. "The Formation and Stability of Marriage in Fourteenth-Century England: Evidence of an Ely Register." *Medieval Studies* 33: 228–63.

Shoaf, R. A. 1983. *Dante, Chaucer, and the Currency of the Word: Money, Images, and Reference in Late Medieval Poetry.* Norman, Okla.: Pilgrim Books.

Singleton, Charles S. 1954. *Dante's Commedia: Elements of Structure.* Baltimore and London: Johns Hopkins University Press.

———. 1965a. "In Exitu Israel de Aegypto." In *Dante: A Collection of Critical Essays,* ed. John Freccero. Englewood Cliffs, N.J.: Prentice-Hall.

———. 1965b. "The Poet's Number at the Center." *MLN* 80: 1–10.

Sledd, James. 1953–54. "The *Clerk's Tale:* The Monsters and the Critics." *Modern Philology* 51: 73–82.

Spearing, A. C. 1972. *Criticism and Medieval Poetry.* 2nd ed. Cambridge: Edward Arnold.

———, ed. 1965. *The Pardoner's Prologue and Tale.* Cambridge: Cambridge University Press.

Speirs, John. 1951. *Chaucer the Maker*. London: Faber and Faber.

Spenser, Edmund. 1981. *Faerie Queene*. Ed. Thomas P. Roche, Jr., with the assistance of C. Patrick O'Donnell, Jr. New Haven and London: Yale University Press.

Steadman, John M. 1964. "Old Age and Contemptus Mundi in The Pardoner's Tale." *Medium Ævum* 33: 121–30.

Steinmetz, David C. 1977. "Late Medieval Nominalism and the *Clerk's Tale*." *Chaucer Review* 12: 38–54.

Stevens, Martin, and A. C. Cawley. 1993. *The Second Shepherds' Play*. In *The Norton Anthology of English Literature*, 6th ed., vol. 1. New York: W. W. Norton.

Stokoe, William C., Jr. 1951–52. "Structure and Intention in the First Fragment of the *Canterbury Tales*." *UTQ* 21: 120–27.

Szittya, Penn R. 1975. "The Green Yeoman as Loathly Lady: The Friar's Parody of the Wife of Bath's Tale." *PMLA* 90: 386–94.

Tanner, J. M. 1962. *Growth at Adolescence*. Oxford: Blackwell Scientific Publications.

Tatlock, John S. P., and Arthur G. Kennedy. 1963. *A Concordance to the Complete Works of Geoffrey Chaucer*. Gloucester, Mass: Peter Smith.

Taylor, Karla. 1989. *Chaucer Reads "The Divine Comedy."* Stanford: Stanford University Press.

Thorpe, W. H. 1974. "Reductionism in Biology." In *Studies in the Philosophy of Biology*, eds. Francisco Jose Ayala and Theodosius Dobzhansky. Berkeley and Los Angeles: University of California Press.

Tompkins, Jane P., ed. 1980. *Reader-Response Criticism: From Formalism to Post-Structuralism*. Baltimore: Johns Hopkins University Press.

Travis, Peter W. 1997. "Chaucer's Heliotropes and the Poetics of Metaphor." *Speculum* 72: 399–427.

Underwood, Dale. 1959. "The First of *The Canterbury Tales*." *ELH* 26: 455–69.

Vincent of Beauvais. [1624] 1964–65. *Speculum Majus*. Facsimile, *Speculum Quadruplex; sive Speculum Maius*. Graz: Academische Druck- und Verlagsanstalt.

Virgil. P. 1972. *Vergili Maronis Opera*. Corrected edition. Ed. Roger A. B. Mynors. Oxford Classical Texts. Oxford: Oxford University Press.

Wagner, Anthony Richard. 1956. *Heralds and Heraldry in the Middle Ages*. 2nd ed. Oxford: Oxford University Press.

Wainwright, Benjamin B. 1933. "Chaucer's Prioress Again: An Interpretive Note." *MLN* 48: 34–37.

Wallace, David. 1990. "'Whan She Translated Was': A Chaucerian Critique of the Petrarchan Academy." In *Literary Practice and Social Change in Britain, 1380–1530*, ed. Lee Patterson, pp. 156–215. Berkeley: University of California Press.

Walsh, P. G., ed. 1982. *Andreas Capellanus on Love*. London: Duckworth.

Webb, Henry J. 1947. "A Reinterpretation of Chaucer's Theseus." *Review of English Studies* 23: 289–96.

Whittock, Trevor. 1968. *A Reading of the Canterbury Tales.* Cambridge: Cambridge University Press.

Wiener, Norbert. 1948. *Cybernetics, or Control and Communication in the Animal and the Machine.* Cambridge, Mass.: MIT Press.

Williams, Raymond. 1977. *Marxism and Literature.* Oxford: Oxford University Press.

Wood, Chauncey. 1970. *Chaucer and the Country of the Stars: Poetic Uses of Astrological Imagery.* Princeton: Princeton University Press.

Woods, William F. 1994. "Private and Public Space in the *Miller's Tale.*" *Chaucer Review* 29: 166–78.

Woolcombe, W. W. [N.d.] "The Sources of the Wife of Bath's Prologue." In *Essays on Chaucer,* part 3, 2nd ser., no. 16, pp. 293–306. London: The Chaucer Society.

Wurtele, Douglas. 1980. "The Penitence of Geoffrey Chaucer." *Viator* 11: 335–59.

Index

Edward I. Condren is professor of English at the University of California, Los Angeles. He has served as a regular book reviewer for the *Los Angeles Times*.